A Persistent Prejudice:

How Antisemitic Tropes and Double Standards Infect the Anti-Israel Movement

Jeremy Havardi

A Persistent Prejudice:

How Antisemitic Tropes and Double Standards Infect the Anti-Israel Movement

Jeremy Havardi

Academica Press
Washington~London

Library of Congress Cataloging-in-Publication Data

Names: Havardi, Jeremy (author)
Title: *A Persistent Prejudice:How Antisemitic Tropes and Double Standards Infect the Anti-Israel Movement* | Havardi, Jeremy.
Description: Washington : Academica Press, 2022. | Includes references.
Identifiers: LCCN 2022935215 | ISBN 9781680537802 (hardcover) | 9781680537826 (paperback) | 9781680537819 (e-book)

'There exists a subterranean world where pathological fantasies disguised as ideas are churned out by crooks and half-educated fanatics for the benefit of the ignorant and superstitious.'

– **Norman Cohn**

Contents

Preface

Growing up in the tolerant atmosphere of modern Britain , I experienced very little antisemitism, either overt or otherwise. It was a life in which being a Jew and expressing a Jewish identity generally carried few risks, even on those occasions where prejudice did rear its ugly head. Extremists from both the far left and the far right were fringe forces of little consequence who posed only a marginal threat to the country's wellbeing. There was scarcely any feeling that the liberal, democratic order that had sustained Jews for centuries was about to be undermined.

That said, I do remember a number of slights and comments that seemed to be quite clearly antisemitic. One classics teacher, noting the level of Jewish resistance under the Romans, made a comment that 'the Jews were always revolting.' At best, he was oblivious to the double meaning, at worst he intended a wounding insult for comic effect. Some classmates made jokes about the Nazi Holocaust while others found the kippah (the Jewish skullcap) an object of ridicule. Later in the sixth form, one Muslim student from Saudi Arabia asked me if Israel should even exist, a reflection of the hateful anti-Zionism that was (and remains) deeply embedded in Saudi society.

During university studies, I found myself in conversation with a Welsh businessman who duly informed me that it was impossible to get a potential client, one 'Mr Goldstein,' to buy his product on account of the fact that the customer was Jewish. When there was an outpouring of grief among Anglo Jewry following the assassination of Yitzhak Rabin, one of my earliest employers questioned me politely about the extent of this 'misplaced loyalty' among my co-religionists. The trope of divided loyalty has long been a staple of British antisemitism. I have often been asked if I am 'British or Jewish,' a question that one might charitably put down more to ignorance than hostility.

In another job, a co-worker, having expressed his contempt for modern authoritarian politics, promptly informed me of his admiration for Hitler, his indifference to the Holocaust and his boundless admiration for the medical 'achievements' of Joseph Goebbels. This gave one of my earliest realizations that antisemitism was both historically illiterate and wholly illogical. While teaching, I overheard a remark that Jewish students were always 'trouble' and that their relative absence from the school was no bad thing.

While I sat on the train in London on FA Cup Final day in 2006, I listened to a group of drunken Chelsea fans amuse themselves with songs that abused the memory of Jews at Belsen, reflecting their hatred of Spurs, a club with a sizeable Jewish following. I also heard rival fans of Spurs hiss at matches, in an attempt to simulate the sound of the gas chambers, and offer abusive references to Jews that would not be out of place in a neo-Nazi gathering. Undoubtedly, this reflected the pathological venom felt by football fans towards their arch rivals as well as old fashioned antisemitism. Even a well-educated, deeply philosemitic friend once told me that Jews such as me 'didn't gamble,' a comment both factually inaccurate and one saturated in stereotype. I have experienced online abuse too, such as a Facebook comment suggesting that, as a Jew, I must have a large nose and an even larger gas bill. The online world can be a truly nasty one.

None of these experiences were particularly scarring or frightening. They cannot be compared to the horrific experience of many Jews on the continent or in the Middle East, a place where being a victim of antisemitism can literally be a death sentence. But they do show the extent to which negative views of Jews remain embedded in the cultural landscape, ready to erupt at a moment's notice in a variety of circumstances.

Barnet Litvinoff, in his magisterial survey of antisemitism *The Burning Bush*, said that there were times in history when Jews had been known to 'discover antisemitism where probably none was intended.'[1] Of course, some Jews can perceive a racist slight where none was intended, as indeed can members of all minorities. The accusation of racism is a serious one but it doesn't always mean that the accused are guilty. On the one hand, it is essential to listen to the stories of marginalized minority groups, both because their voices have so often been drowned out by the louder and frequently more bigoted voices of dominant groups but also because they teach us about the effects of racism on a community. But on the other, perceptions of racism can be flawed, involving the imputation of prejudice to others which is unwarranted by the facts. The prejudices of dominant groups, whether felt consciously or not, are merely one of several factors to explain the structural problem of why certain minority groups fail to make headway in society.

In the case of antisemitism, a more objective approach is needed, one which understands the legacy of racism through the stereotypes, tropes and motifs it has cemented and the ways in which these have been reproduced, wilfully or otherwise, in the narratives and iconography of the anti-Israel movement. The book identifies the key tropes of antisemitism from the last two millennia, explaining in detail how they developed and how they have shaped perceptions of Jews through the ages. It is my contention that all these tropes, motifs and canards of antisemitism have saturated the discourse and actions of the anti-Israel movement today, both in the west and especially in the Middle East. In addition, antisemitism has historically involved Jewish communities being subjected to adverse treatment and double standards within society. Again, this book shows how the modern-day nation state of the Jews, together with its supporters, has been subjected to similarly frightening levels of adverse treatment by its detractors.

---

[1] Barnet Litvinoff, *The Burning Bush* (London: Collins, 1988), 10.

I owe a debt of gratitude to a number of people. Over many years, I have taken part in panel events, attended conferences and listened to prominent historians, scholars and public policy figures on the subject of antisemitism, anti-Israel hatred and human rights. They include Lord John Mann, Dave Rich of the UK based Community Security Trust, David Hirsh, Dore Gold, Israel's former Ambassador to the UN, Dan Mariaschin, B'nai B'rith international CEO, David Matas, senior legal counsel for B'nai B'rith Canada, historian Richard Landes, Manfred Gerstenfeld, Lord Carey, the former Archbishop of Canterbury, the lawyer Anthony Julius, Professor Yehuda Bauer, doyen of Holocaust scholars, the famed historian of modernity Sir Martin Gilbert and many others. I have also enjoyed a long conversation with Niklas Frank, son of the notorious war criminal Hans Frank, and veteran of anti-racism efforts. I have benefited from detailed feedback given by Alan Johnson, senior researcher at BICOM, Professor Brad Blitz, Professor of International Politics and Policy at University College London, Rashad Ali from the Institute of Strategic Dialogue and a number of other academics. Their advice has been invaluable but any mistakes are solely the author's responsibility. I would like to lastly thank my wife Ilana for her forbearance while I have worked hard to finish this script.

Introduction

Antisemitism in the world today

More than seventy-five years after the liberation of the death camps, the menacing shadow of antisemitism lurks over much of the civilized world. Conspiracy theories about the role of the Jew in modern life continue to proliferate, both in the real world and in the murky online world that has become a captive home for millions. The archetypal figure of the Jew remains an obsession for many, a convenient scapegoat for all of society's failings, indeed the primary cause of those ills. As one esteemed writer of modern antisemitism has put it: 'Like some malignant virus, it always lies dormant, ready to wake. Like other viruses, it may be, at various times, more or less virulent, more or less lethal.'[1]

The British Labour party, once a bastion of social democratic values and opposition to racism, was found guilty of 'unlawful acts of harassment and discrimination' (against Jews) by the Equality and Human Rights Commission in 2020. This followed a four year period, since the election of hard left leader Jeremy Corbyn, in which many hundreds of incidents of antisemitism were reported. These included outright Holocaust denial, the propagation of conspiracy theories about the Rothschild dynasty, memes alleging that the UK government was controlled by Jews and Israel, the linkage of Zionists with Nazis and virulently racist attacks on individual members of Parliament, largely because of their opposition to antisemitism. Corbyn, a long term member of the party's radical wing, had become an enabler of this type of hate, given his frequent association with antisemites (Hezbollah, Hamas, Raed Salah, Stephen Sizer and others) and his deafening silence in the face of Jew hatred. On the surface, what is so shocking is how a party of the centre left, a mainstream party committed to tacking all forms of prejudice, could ever become embroiled in a racism scandal. This was a point made forcefully to the author by the Chef de Cabinet of the UN Human Rights Council in 2019.

Though antisemitism is not institutional within the modern Conservative party, one can certainly find instances of such prejudice in recent years. Many remember Harold Macmillan's snide remark that Mrs Thatcher's Cabinet consisted more of 'more Estonians than Etonians,' a form of Establishment prejudice that would have resonated with certain members of the upper classes.

---

[1] Eliot A Cohen, "Socially Acceptable Antisemitism," *The Atlantic*, March 6, 2019.

In 2013, the former MP Patrick Mercer, in a secret recording, revealed that he had met an Israeli soldier on a recent trip to the country. Mr Mercer said that when he was told she was a soldier, he responded: 'You don't look like a soldier to me. You look like a bloody Jew.'[2] As well as making a pejorative reference to the soldier as a Jew, the remark was offensive because it traded on the stereotype of Jews as cowards, not capable or willing to fight for their country.

In 2004, a Conservative politician said that the trouble with the party was that it was 'run by Michael Howard, Maurice Saachti and Oliver Letwin and none of them really knows what it is to be English.'[3] This clearly invoked the age old antisemitic stereotype about Jews possessing a foreign mindset and mentality. Then there were the remarks that were alleged to have been made by Sir Nicholas Soames, grandson of Winston Churchill, to Sir Philip Green in 2004.[4] One can also find examples of this obsessive hatred among supporters of Britain's other parties, including moderate ones.

Turning towards Europe, the continent which witnessed the annihilation of two thirds of its Jewish population between 1939 and 1945, there has been a clear resurgence of open antisemitism in the first two decades of the twenty first century. More than a century after the Dreyfus affair, France continues to be rocked by violent assaults on its Jewish population. In the space of a few months, a French cemetery was vandalized with dozens of tomb stones defaced, Nazi swastikas were painted on Jewish shops and several shots were fired at a synagogue.'. Shortly before, the government protests led by the *Gillets Jaunes* (the yellow vests) witnessed an outpouring of hatred towards French Jewish philosopher Alain Finkelkraut. He was called a 'dirty Zionist' and told that 'France belongs to us,' naturally implying that he was an alien in his own country. The *Gillets Jaunes*, though not an antisemitic movement per se, was infiltrated by extremist voices and their conspiratorial narratives. Such incessant attacks, with these few being only select examples, have been roundly condemned by much of the political establishment. President Macron has warned that antisemitism is 'spreading like poison' and with a reported 74% spike in antisemitic attacks in one year, there are few that would disagree with this viewpoint.[5] France, home to Europe's largest Jewish population, has been rocked by a series of violent antisemitic attacks.[6] Twenty-three year old Ilan Halimi, the child of a Moroccan immigrant, was kidnapped by a group called the Gang of Barbarians because they assumed he was rich. Over a period of days, he was

---

[2] Claire Newell and Holly Watt, "Cash for Questions: Patrick Mercer no stranger to controversy," *The Telegraph*, April 29, 2014.

[3] Simon Hoggart, "A Tory victory – it's a six in 1,800 chance," *The Guardian*, October 9, 2014.

[4] Nicholas Pyke, "Soames accused of race jibe at Green," *The Independent*, July 18, 2004.

[5] Angelique Chrisafis, "Thousands take to streets of France after antisemitic attacks," *The Guardian*, Feburary 19, 2019.

[6] Angelique Chrisafis, "Spreading like poison: flurry of antisemitic acts alarms France," *The Guardian*, February 12, 2019·.

tortured horrifically and found naked and handcuffed near railroad tracks south of Paris. His body was covered in cigarette burns and acid while the young man had also been stabbed. Yet what followed was even more horrific when an investigative magistrate declared: 'There isn't a single element allowing us to attach this murder to an antisemitic purpose or an antisemitic act.' Worse, when retired French doctor Sarah Halimi was murdered by her Muslim neighbour, Kobili Traore, in 2017, there was a refusal for months to acknowledge that this was an antisemitic crime. Later, the French courts declared that Halimi was not criminally responsible for his actions due to his having consumed cannabis. Sammy Ghozlan, a former policeman who is now running the Bureau for Vigilance against antisemitism, said: 'I no longer have full confidence that antisemitic hate crimes in France are handled properly.'[7]

According to a report by the Kantor Centre on global antisemitism: 'Jews do not experience anywhere [else] in the EU as much hostility on the streets as they do in Belgium.'[8] With verbal abuse, Holocaust denial and violence facing Belgium's Jews, the latter including an attack on the Jewish Museum in 2017 that killed four people, many Jews feel unsafe. The papers are not safe from outright prejudice. The novelist Dimitri Verhulst, in an opinion column for *De Morgen* said: 'Being Jewish is not a religion. No religion makes you grow such a nose.' In an attempt to defame Jewish character, he went on to say: 'Because God has His favorites and they have their privileges, Palestinians were driven out of their homes in 1948 to make place for God's favorites.'[9] Shockingly, his paper defended the writer for expressing support for Palestinians living under Israeli rule.

In another example of brazen anti-Jewish hate, a Carnival float in the streets of Aalst featured vile caricatures of ultra-orthodox Jews, showing the hook-nosed figures reaching out for money.[10] There was outspoken condemnation from Daniel Schwammenthal from the American Jewish Committee: 'It's shocking beyond belief that within living memory of the Holocaust a Carnival parade in Europe would peddle such vile antisemitism.' A spokesman for UNESCO, which sponsors the Carnival, also condemned the float, saying: 'The satirical spirit of the Aalst carnival and freedom of expression cannot serve as a screen for such manifestations of hatred.' Yet Aalst's mayor defended the float while the Jews who complained were attacked for not accepting a display that was designed to demean and attack them.[11] In 2013, another float featured Nazi officers, appearing

---

[7] Harry Zieve Cohen, "What's Behind the Resurgnence in French Antisemitism,"*Mosaic*, July 1, 2019.

[8] Jennifer Rankin, "Nazi rhetoric and Holocaust denial: Belgium's alarming rise in antisemitism," *The Guardian*, May 9, 2019.

[9] Cnann Liphshiz, "Jews have ugly noses, Belgian journalist writes in column attacking Israel," The *Times of Israel*, August 3, 2019.

[10] Milan Schreuer, "Jewish Caricatures at Belgian Carnival Set Off Charges of Antisemitism," *The Guardian*, March 8, 2019.

[11] Flora Cassen, "'Stop Whining About Your Holocaust Already': What Happens When Europe's Jews Call Out antisemitism," *Haaretz*, March 15, 2019.

to carry canisters of gas, parading next to a train, an apparent allusion to those which were used in the war to transport Jews to their deaths.

Central Europe too has witnessed some frightening examples of antisemitic rhetoric. In Germany, a new and virulent form of antisemitism has been mouthed by the populist, anti-immigration *Alternative für Deutschland* AFD party. The party made its electoral breakthrough in 2017 by gaining 12.6% of the popular vote, ensuring that it could no longer be considered a fringe group. The party has adopted a pro-Israel position at the national level, not out of any Zionist conviction but in order to dissociate itself from damaging accusations of National Socialism. The AFD rejects the politics of remembrance which necessitates commemorating the victims of the Holocaust and teaching Nazi crimes in school. Instead, the AFD has championed national pride and a shift towards remembering other periods of German history, particularly during the nineteenth century. They call for students to stop visiting Holocaust memorial sites and instead, visit places of importance in German history. There have also been expressions of pure antisemitic prejudice from AFD members.

In Italy, the national football culture has a serious racism problem. As one writer puts it: 'Antisemitism is deeply ingrained in the country's soccer culture.' Many fans of Lazio, especially its Ultras, have disgraced the game with blatant examples of antisemitism and anti-black racism. In a notorious match from 1998, these Ultras unfurled a flag with the words: 'Auschwitz Is Your Country; the Ovens Are Your Homes.' Today, a more common banner is: 'Adolfo Presente,' 'Adolf is still with us.' Such antisemitic hatred can also be found among supporters of other clubs, including Inter Milan, Juventus and other clubs. Italian football is not unique in this respect and similar examples of sporting related prejudice can be found elsewhere in Europe. But it is perhaps the very worst example.[12]

In some respects, the problems are more grave in eastern Europe. Recent attempts by the Polish government to introduce a Holocaust law that would have outlawed and criminalized any reference to complicity in the Holocaust by the Polish nation or state were accompanied by disturbing antisemitic threats. Nationalist demonstrations in support of the government were frequently accompanied by racist language. At a demonstration in New York to oppose a proposed US law to monitor Poland's restitution efforts for Holocaust survivors, demonstrators held placards that denounced 'the Holocaust industry' and a witness reported further antisemitic taunting.[13] The law itself reflected a nationalist attempt to portray Poland as a victim of the Nazi occupation, downplaying the significant role played by antisemitic perpetrators and an indigenous culture of anti-Jewish hatred. Rightly, the government has sought to outlaw any talk of 'Polish death camps' (they were constructed by non-Poles on occupied soil). At the same time, they have played down the idea that Poles conspired with the Germans to kill Jews.

---

[12] Davide Lerner, "Lazio's Anne Frank's 'insult' is Hardly Shocking. Italian Soccer is Viciously Antisemitic to Its Core," *Haaretz*, October 25, 2017.

[13] JC Reporter, "Protestors carry antisemitic signs at anti-Holocaust law demonstration in New York," *Jewish Chronicle*, April 2, 2019.

But while 7,177 Poles (as of 2021) are rewarded with the title of 'Righteous among the Gentiles,' according to Yad Vashem, many thousands also collaborated with the Germans to attack and kill Polish Jews. This reflected the deep animosity that many Poles felt for their Jewish neighbours in the years preceding the war.

In Hungary, the nationalist government of Victor Orban, despite its warm relationship with Israel, has traded in the kind of conspiratorial antisemitism that would not have been out of place in the *Protocols of the Elders of Zion*. The Hungarian business magazine *Figyelő*, a publication with close links to the government, recently printed a cover with the head of András Heisler, head of the Federation of Hungarian Jewish Communities. Paper money was floating around Heisler's head, with one bill protruding from his forehead. With understandable anger, the Federation described the image as 'incitement' and said it revived 'centuries-old stereotypes against our community' depicting 'Jews as money-grubbers.' That Orban, 'the self-styled defender of Christian Europe,'[14] refused to condemn the image was not surprising. The Prime Minister had issued dog whistles to the nationalist right on previous occasions. He praised Miklos Horthy, the Hungarian leader who deported hundreds of thousands of Hungarian Jews to their deaths in WWII, and other antisemitic politicians, including the pro-Nazi Bálint Hóman (1885-1951). Then in a speech delivered in March 2018, Orban issued a speech lacerated with antisemitic undertones:

> We are fighting an enemy that is different from us. Not open, but hiding; not straightforward but crafty; not honest but base; not national but international; does not believe in working but speculates with money; does not have its own homeland but feels it owns the whole world.[15]

Defenders of Orban say he was referring to figures such as George Soros. Now of course it is possible to construct a non-antisemitic criticism of Soros just as for any other Jewish figure. And it is legitimate for political leaders to attack an NGO that is felt to be undermining the interests of their countries. But what is crucial is the language used. Orban's speech, using the vernacular of the *Protocols*, was a dogwhistle (or a foghorn) to antisemitic nationalists, a signal that he was on their side.

Naturally, the hatred that starts with the Jews does not end there. In a meeting with a Hungarian minister in 2019, the author also took issue with the harsh anti-Islamic rhetoric that was being issued by the government, suggesting that one had to differentiate between extremists and more moderate Muslims. He was told that such differentiation was not possible and that Hungary would continue to resist 'the Muslim invasion of Europe.'[16]

---

[14] Ira Forman, "Victor Orban is Exploiting Antisemitism," *The Atlantic*, December 14, 2018.
[15] Shaun Walker, "George Soros: Orban turns to familiar scapegoat as Hungary rows with EU," *The Guardian*, December 5, 2020.
[16] Interview with a senior government official in the Hungarian embassy in London, February 2019.

Outright Holocaust denial and distortion also exists in pockets of European society. In Eastern Europe, attempts have been made to rehabilitate the reputation of wartime nationalists who fought for independence in WWII yet also played a role in exterminating Jews. Among them are Josef Tiso, the wartime Slovakian leader who deported thousands of Jews to their deaths, Stephan Bandera, a leading Ukrainian nationalist responsible for killing thousands of Jews during the war and Jonas Noreika, a Nazi collaborator who had a significant role in the Lithuanian Holocaust. These figures committed atrocities against Jewish civilians and the attempts to whitewash them are thus stained with Holocaust denial and antisemitic prejudice.

Of course, this is all qualitative data and some will dispute whether all the examples just cited suggest a draconian problem with European antisemitism. Quantitative data must buttress any argument that the Continent has a serious issue with Jew hate. A 2018 survey on discrimination and hate crime against Jews in the EU by the European Union Agency for Fundamental Rights, found that on the Continent 'Antisemitism pervades the public sphere, reproducing and engraining negative stereotypes about Jews.' It went on to say: 'Simply being Jewish increases people's likelihood of being faced with a sustained stream of abuse expressed in different forms, wherever they go, whatever they read and with whomever they engage.' [17] When asked in the survey if antisemitism had increased in the previous five years, an astonishing 89% of respondents (out of over 16,000) said that it had. In recent years, the EU has taken concerns about antisemitism seriously. It has established an EU high level group to combat racism, xenophobia and intolerance, one which has gone on to produce various forms of policy guidance.

Turning to the United States, one finds the familiar echoes of antisemitic prejudice in recent political discourse. White nationalists have frequently attacked Jewish journalists and commentators who have dared to criticize President Trump. Many have received deaths threats and been subjected to vile abuse on Twitter and other platforms. The editor of *Atlantic* magazine, Jeffrey Goldberg, who has been inundated by attacks, said he was receiving one hundred messages a day from online neo-Nazis. He summed up their basic theme: '(I) should be gassed and my family should be put in the ovens.' [18] Another Jewish journalist, Julia Ioffe, was trolled by fascistic websites and 'subjected to an outpouring of antisemitic venom and threats, some so vile that they left her concerned for her physical wellbeing.' Among the images that she received was one which had her head photoshopped onto that of an emaciated concentration camp victim whose body was on top of a pile of other victims.[19]

---

[17] "Experiences and perceptions of antisemitism – Second survey on discrimination and hate crime against Jews in the EU," *European Union Agency for Fundamental Rights*, December 10, 2018.

[18] Deborah Lipstadt, *Antisemitism Here and Now* (London: Scribe, 2019), 39.

[19] ibid. p. 47

While President Trump never explicitly endorsed white nationalists or their dark overtones of antisemitism, he scarcely distanced himself from them, knowing that they were a valuable part of his support base. The President was asked what message he had for the people sending these hateful messages and replied: 'I don't have a message to the fans. A woman wrote an article that's inaccurate.' On another occasion, Trump refused to condemn the endorsement of Holocaust denier David Duke, a former Grand Wizard of the Ku Klux Klan, claiming that he knew nothing about Duke or the KKK. He also retweeted messages from extreme nationalist websites, including Britain First, and issued campaign messaging which was understood to be antisemitic by white nationalists. The toxic combination of rampant gun ownership and neo-Nazi white supremacism has produced acts of murderous violence, most recently in the Pittsburgh synagogue where eleven people were killed. According to the FBI, Jews have been the victims of most religion-based hate crimes in the US.

The notion that Jews exercise a malign level of 'control' over hapless western governments finds resonance elsewhere. At a pro-Palestinian rally in Lenasia, South Africa's Deputy Foreign Affairs minister, Fatima Hajaig, said Jews 'control [America], no matter which government comes into power, whether Republican or Democrat, whether Barack Obama or George Bush.' She added: 'Control of America, just like the control of most Western countries, is in the hands of Jewish money, and if Jewish money controls their country then you cannot expect anything.' While such expressions of hate are the preserve of extremists, one can find more respected figures tapping into such prejudice. Thus, the South African civil rights leader and Nobel Laureate Desmond Tutu, in an excoriating critique of Israeli policies towards the Palestinians, wrote the following in 2002: 'People are scared in this country (the US), to say wrong is wrong because the Jewish lobby is powerful – very powerful.'

But even these egregious examples do not represent the very worst strains of antisemitism. When one examines the recent discourse against Jews found among the news commentariat in the Arab and Islamic world, it is obvious just how far this visceral hatred stretches. Arab newspapers, such as the PA's *Al-Hayat Al-Jadida*, accuse Jews of genocide and controlling major governments. A 2007 cartoon in Egyptian paper *Al-Gomhouriyya* depicted Jews as a snake encircling Uncle Sam while *Al-Ahram* in the same year compared Jews to Christ killers.[20] In 2010, an Oman paper printed a cartoon showing an Israeli soldier attacking a person on the Gaza flotilla using a Menorah (Jewish symbol) as a weapon. A Saudi paper in 2010 showed a Star of David with bones from a skeleton and the Israeli flag containing a swastika. Examples like these could be multiplied indefinitely, reflecting the level of support that they receive from the wider society. The epicentre of hatred towards the Jewish people today lies primarily among the peoples who live in Arab and Islamic societies, most of whom reside

---

[20] Cartoon, *Al-Ahram*, May 12, 2007

in the Middle East but which also include sections of the populace in countries such as Pakistan, Indonesia and Malaysia.

The cases outlined here are but a brief sample of the intense volume of antisemitic incidents seen around the world in the last quarter of a century. That antisemitic expression has vastly increased during the last two decades is supported by research carried out by the respected Kantor Centre for the Study of Contemporary European Jewry. According to its chart of major violent incidents carried out against Jews between 1989 and 2020, there were 78 attacks in 1989 and the number of serious incidents has only increased since, with 167 reported in 1992, 311 in 2003, 593 in 2007 and 766 in 2014. Since then, there has been a drop with 456 reported in 2019. Even though the figures show a significant reduction from 2014 onwards, the lowest recent figure (in 2019) is still nearly six times higher than 30 years ago. Jews also suffer the majority of religiously inspired hate crimes, according to data in a number of countries. A study of religious based hate crimes in the US in 2019 showed that anti-Jewish ones made up 63% of the total (compared to 12% which were anti-Islamic) and that pattern remains largely true for the preceding 25 years.[21] In Canada, Jews make up 1% of the population and yet make up 17% of police-reported hate crime, as well as being the religious group most targeted for this type of crime.[22] According to Roger Cukierman, president of CRIF, 40% of violent hate crimes target Jews.[23] Elsewhere, recent figures on antisemitism are alarming. In the UK, the Community Security Trust reported a total of 1,668 antisemitic incidents in 2020, with more than 100 in eleven of twelve months of the year. The CST admitted that 'the actual amount of antisemitic content that is generated and disseminated on online platforms is much larger.'[24] In 2018, the European Union Fundamental Rights Agency conducted a survey on hate crime, discrimination and antisemitism in the European Union, dubbed 'the biggest survey of Jewish people ever conducted worldwide.' The survey, which covered 12 EU Member States and reached almost 16,500 Jews, found that 'antisemitism (pervaded) the public sphere, reproducing and engraining negative stereotypes about Jews' and that 'simply being Jewish increases people's likelihood of being faced with a sustained stream of abuse expressed in different forms, wherever they go, whatever they read and with whomever they engage.' In total, nine in 10 (89 %) respondents felt that antisemitism had increased in their country in the five years before the survey

---

[21] Jewish Virtual Library. "Antisemitism in the United States: Statistics on Religious Hate Crimes (1996-2020)." https://www.jewishvirtuallibrary.org/statistics-on-religious-hate-crimes.

[22] "Jews victims of more hate crimes than any religious group in Canada," *The Jerusalem Post*, March 30, 2021.

[23] Julie Wiener, "French Jewish leader: it's not so pleasant living there as Jews," *The Jerusalem Post*, May 14, 2014.

[24] CST Antisemitic Incidents Report 2020, *CST*, February 11, 2021.

and 85% considered it to be a serious problem.[25] Of course, this data itself dramatically underplays the true scale of the problem, in part because there will be antisemitic incidents that are downplayed by the authorities and regarded as crimes without a hate component. More importantly, there will always be victims who do not report attacks, perhaps for fear of the repercussions. As one survey has made clear: 'The inadequate recording of hate crime incidents, including those of an antisemitic nature, coupled with victims' hesitance to report incidents to the authorities, contributes to the gross under-reporting of the extent, nature and characteristics of the antisemitic incidents that occur in the EU.'[26]

Bierkeller v Bistro: A great deal of the antisemitism just mentioned is relatively easy to spot and appears all too familiar to those who have studied and experienced this form of racism. When it comes dressed in Nazi or fascist regalia, with symbols of swastikas and skulls, when it appears in the form of violent assaults on Jews, attacks on Jewish communal property or outright Holocaust denial, the manifestations of the world's oldest hatred are unmistakeable. They are representative of what is often called 'bierkeller' antisemitism, the type that simmers with crude, racist prejudice and overt bigotry. It is the antisemitism that most criminal justice systems are set up to oppose and which almost all mainstream western politicians will readily condemn. But antisemitism can also be more subtle and hidden, couched in language and imagery that is familiar to racists (and their victims) but elusive to others. This type of prejudice uses codes and cyphers, as well as more nuanced phrasing, to evade detection. It uses language that need not refer to the Jew directly and is often framed in conspiratorial terms, disguising the identity of those it attacks. For example, antisemites are known to have attacked 'cosmopolitans,' 'aliens' and 'globalists,' as well as people on the 'East Coast,' rather than refer directly to Jews. In addition, 'Zionist' is substituted for Jew in much hateful and discriminatory discourse. This is 'bistro'[27] antisemitism, a form of middle-class prejudice promulgated, not just by far-right nativists or xenophobic ideologues, but by those who are considered progressive, liberal and humanitarian. It is the cry of racism from those who consider themselves anti-racists and who are convinced of their own moral rectitude. These 'anti antisemites' cry in despair and rage when their bigotry is called out. They cannot even conceive how such a charge is possible, given the strength of their own conviction that 'they do not have a racist bone in their body.' This book deals mainly, but not entirely, with bistro antisemitism and focuses, less on marginal and extreme actors in society than on more respectable opinion formers such as journalists, cartoonists, politicians, trade unionists, preachers and academics.

---

[25] "Experiences and perceptions of antisemitism/Second survey on discrimination and hate crime against Jews in the EU," *European Union Agency for Fundamental Rights,* December 10, 2018.
[26] "Antisemitism: Overview of data available in the European Union 2008-2018," *European Agency for Fundamental Rights,* November 2019, 5.
[27] The distinction has been made by American journalist Ben Cohen.

A common factor in much of today's bistro antisemitism, one which makes antisemitic discourse more 'respectable' and less taboo, is opposition to the state of Israel. There is a prevailing climate of opinion today, to be found among university elites and student organizations, left wing political parties and much of the media that can best be described as Israelophobic. Israel is frequently demonized and vilified in public discourse. The state has been accused of genocide, war crimes and ethnic cleansing, likened to Nazi Germany, accused of organ harvesting and condemned for child killing. It is frequently depicted as the cause of all the turmoil that takes place in the Middle East, the progenitor of its wars and conflicts as well as the reason for the lack of progress in the Arab world.[28] Opposition to a Jewish state has ignited the global hysteria around Jews, giving renewed oxygen to the army of conspiracy theorists who look to blame them for all the ills of the world. It is a central contention of this book that we are witnessing an explosion of antisemitism within the anti-Israel movement.

Yet at the same time, it is one of the most disputed forms of racism in existence. How often do liberal progressives tell Jews that their complaints about antisemitism are no more than a right-wing smear designed to unsettle humanitarian and progressive causes? How often is antisemitism dismissed as a bad faith accusation by Jews who are desperate to silence critics of Israel? How often is Arab antisemitism disputed on the grounds that Arabs are semites too? How regularly do antisemites hide behind the fact that they have Jewish friends or partners or that Jews are not a race, just a religion?

This book will pierce through the veil of denial, both by showing that those who choose to demean and demonize Israel reproduce the worst tropes and imagery associated with historic antisemitism, and that they are subjecting the Jewish state to egregious double standards. Not all those who engage in such demonological discourse or adverse treatment do so with the conscious desire to defame Jews and Jewish organizations. But antisemitism can be produced by effect and not just by intent. What follows from this is that we are not seeing what is often referred to as a 'new antisemitism.' It is old fashioned antisemitism which has mutated to fit new 'political' circumstances.

The book will be structured in five main chapters. Chapter 1 offers two definitions of antisemitism, the first a brief one from the author and the second, that of IHRA, the International Holocaust Remembrance Alliance. It will also examine a number of key points about modern antisemitism and also identify (and deconstruct) numerous key forms of antisemitism denial. Chapter 2 examines the core tropes of historic antisemitism, including the charges of deicide, devilishness, dual loyalty, avarice, the blood libel, racial contamination and the conspiracy of global control. Each will be spelt out with a full explanation of the charge and the ways in which it has been manifested over the ages. What will become clear is

---

[28] Conversations between the author and the Jordanian Ambassadors of both the UK and the UNHRC in Geneva have revealed how far reaching such conspiratorial views really stretch.

that these tropes are usually not confined to one age or geographic region but have found expression in multiple environments and eras. Chapter 3 examines the various ways in which Jews have been subjected to double standards and adverse treatment in the various Gentile societies where they have resided. This includes the denial of their right to life, laws regulating their domicile, dress and religious freedom and restrictions on their right to education and employment. The next two chapters examine how these themes have played out, and continue to play out, in the demonological discourse on Israel. Chapter 4 details the ways in which the tropes identified earlier have resurfaced in hostile attacks on the Jewish state. Examples abound in Western and Middle East discourse in which Israel is treated as a deicidal, treacherous, poisonous and devilish state or depicted as the progenitor of a sinister conspiracy to control the Gentile world. In each case, there is an unmistakeable thematic affinity between the language and imagery used to attack Israel and that used historically against the Jews. Chapter 5 shows the ways in which Israel is subjected to demeaning double standards and unfair treatment by the international community and by international institutions, principally the UN. While the motivation for such treatment need not be antisemitic, the effect of such treatment is to hold the Jewish state, and its supporters, to a unique standard, and is accordingly antisemitic. It is tantamount to creating a hostile environment for Jews as a whole.

This book offers a discursive analysis of global antisemitism, examining (primarily) the language and iconography that is used to denigrate and demonize both Jews and Israelis. However, this should not be taken to imply that antisemitism can be understood devoid of the context in which it occurs, one where Jews are reduced to a mere abstraction. Antisemitism, on the one hand, is not a proportionate or rational response to the bad behaviour of Jews and it would represent an egregious form of victim blaming to suggest otherwise. But on the other, antisemitism ebbs and flows with changes in society and has usually, though not always, been a response, albeit highly irrational, cynical and twisted, to the presence of Jews and Jewish influence in society. A full socio-economic and political explanation of why antisemitism has arisen at different times and in different places is only hinted at in the book and requires a much fuller analysis elsewhere.

Chapter One

Defining antisemitism – and antisemitism denial

Prejudice is a burden that confuses the past, threatens the future and renders the present inaccessible.

Maya Angelou

Antisemitism consists of a spectrum of irrational attitudes towards Jews, such as hatred, fear, suspicion and resentment, which rely upon stereotyped images that are embedded in myth, popular culture and folklore, and which often manifest themselves in discrimination, double standards and violence against Jews, Jewish institutions or the Jewish state. At its heart is a conspiratorial mindset that pictures Jews as fundamentally different and inferior to non-Jews. According to this mindset, they are seen as a nefarious and malign collective whose *raison d'etre* is to immiserate the lives of Gentiles through tricksy, artful and deceitful behaviour. They have been depicted as a dishonest, cunning, calculating, greedy and manipulative people, the progenitor of sinister plots that harm non-Jews and advance Jewish interests in a cynical and calculated fashion. They have been seen as fundamentally devious and malign, undermining society from within through cunning behaviour and lies. For antisemites through history, Jews are akin to 'the Devil's agents on earth' and 'a preternaturally powerful elite that enslaves and destroys humankind.'[1] Antisemitism is an obsessive form of hatred, one which is 'unified, simple, monochromatic' because 'there is one and only one source of the trouble and one and only one solution for it.'[2]

It has never been hatred for its own sake and is much more than a mere harmful ideology. With its noxious blend of conspiracy theory and base prejudice, antisemitic ideology has historically segued into murderous rage against Jewish communities, culminating in the demonic industrialized slaughter of six million Jews in the Second World War. Antisemitism has bequeathed to the world a series of sinister terms: ethnic cleansing, pogrom, genocide and Holocaust among them.[3]

---

[1] John-Paul Pagano, "Blood Libel: The Conspiracy Theory That Jews Are 'Anti-Human,'" *National Review*, September 23, 2019.

[2] Adam Garfinkle, *Jewcentricity: Why the Jews are Praised, Blamed, and Used to Explain Just About Everything* (New Jersey: John Wiley & Sons, 2009), 54.

[3] This was a point made powerfully by former UK Chief Rabbi, Lord Jonathan Sacks.

For that reason, French philosopher Jean Paul Sartre labelled it a 'criminal passion.'[4] Much modern antisemitism is eliminationist at its core, seeing the destruction of the Jews as a central historic mission which will purify society of its ills, redeem mankind and create a utopia on earth. Such 'redemptive' hatred lies at the heart of Nazi antisemitism and the ideology of Islamist jihad.

In essence, antisemitism is a fundamentally irrational form of prejudice, both because it makes claims about the Jews that lack any credence when tested against facts, evidence, reason or logic but also because the qualities attributed to the Jews by antisemites are mutually incompatible. A number of further points are in order:

Antisemitism and the chimerical Jew: Antisemitism is not about how one reacts to individual Jews. When Isaiah Berlin said that antisemitism was 'disliking Jews more than is necessary,' what he meant was that one could quite reasonably find individual Jews disagreeable, based on a personal negative experience. If, however, over and above that, one disliked them *because* they were Jewish or one attributed their negative traits to their Jewishness, one would be straying into prejudice. There are indeed some disagreeable Jews whose misdeeds and crimes have become a topic of major public discussion. Three examples from recent years include the Hollywood mogul Harvey Weinstein, who was convicted of sexual assault and sent to prison for 23 years, the disgraced financier Bernie Madoff and the American investment billionaire Jeffrey Epstein who was found guilty of procuring an underage girl for prostitution and who died in prison in 2019. For the crimes they committed, these individuals have been understandably vilified in the public imagination. But to argue that the reason they are so disagreeable is because they are Jewish, to argue that their flaws are a characteristic cultural fault possessed by all Jews, is to make a transparently antisemitic argument. After all, those disagreeable traits are held by non-Jews too who commit a vastly larger number of the crimes in question.[5] It should be noted that the crime rate among Jews is low and proportionately lower than for non-Jews, with the exception of certain white-collar offences.[6] It also follows from this that the oft used expression about bad Jews, that they give the rest of the tribe 'a bad name,' is deeply misguided. Individual bad Jews are no more representative of their community than are bad Christians, Muslims or black people. It is antisemites who give Jews 'a bad name' by singling out high profile Jewish wrongdoers for opprobrium while disregarding the same negative behaviour in other groups. They

---

[4] Naturally, this feature is not unique to anti-Jewish racism. Those who attack minorities are usually animated by hatred, fear and contempt of 'the other' with racist violence rarely emerging from a vacuum. Modern antisemitism is unique in its ambitions, given that its worst progenitors have sought to destroy the entire Jewish people. They have acted as if the 'curse' of the Jews cannot be lifted while even some remain alive.

[5] Lipstadt, *Antisemitism*, 14.

[6] For a full discussion, read: Amir, Menachem, "Criminality among Jews: An Overview." *Issues in Criminology* 6, no. 2 (1971): 1–39.

do this because they have bought into and helped promulgate age old stereotypes that apply selectively to Jews, thus confirming their prejudices.

That is why antisemitism is said to involve hostility towards a 'constructed' Jew, a phantom and ultimately chimerical figure, a mythic other as opposed to a representation of real Jewish people. Deriving from centuries of archetypes, tropes, stereotypes and folkloric images, 'the Jew' occupies a central role in the demonic imagination as the bearer of bad news for mankind, a sinner against civilization, a threat to humanity whose sinister and rogue machinations must be tackled comprehensively by society. This mythic Jew is impervious to rational analysis and to facts about real Jews. Such a view helps explain why antisemitic attitudes continue to exist in countries where there are no or very few Jews, such as Pakistan, Jordan and Egypt. Among populations prone to conspiracy theories and irrationally hostile attitudes towards the West, it is only natural that vicious antisemitic myths seem to find such a receptive ear. Robert Wistrich was right to say that, in the imagination of antisemites, the Jew was 'a demonic abstraction more real than any of its individual components.'[7]

That antisemitism is not about the real-world behaviour of Jews and is instead about the enduring influence of racist tropes, canards and perspectives is something that can be discerned by examining opinion polls among modern Europeans. For decades, the Anti-Defamation League in the US has carried out exhaustive surveys of opinion among representative samples of populations in dozens of countries around the world, in which respondents are asked whether they believe a series of clearly racist notions about Jews. The statements that they are asked to evaluate relate to some of the principal antisemitic stereotypes and canards of the modern world. They include the following:

Jews are more loyal to Israel than to the countries they live in
Jews have too much power in international financial markets
Jews have too much control over global affairs
Jews have too much control over the global media
Jews are responsible for most of the world's wars
Jews have too much power in the business world

The ADL has found that large majorities in Arab and Muslim countries (75%) agree that these statements are probably true, despite the fact that hardly any Jews reside in them. Indeed, the only countries in the Arab and Muslim world with a substantial Jewish population are Morocco, Iran and Turkey. But this same phenomenon is largely true in Europe where many countries' populations harbour deeply held antisemitic beliefs despite the fact that they have been largely denuded of their once large Jewish populations. In Austria, where Jews form no more than one tenth of one percent of the population, an astonishing one third of respondents believe that Jews have too much control of global affairs and 30%

---

[7] Robert Wistrich, *A Lethal Obsession: Antisemitism from Antiquity to the Global Jihad* (New York: Random House, 2010), 19.

that they have too much control over the global media. In Germany, where Jews are 1 in seven hundred of the population, these figures are nearly identical with a further 33% of respondents believing that Jews are hated because of the way that they behave. In Portugal, an astonishing 43% believe that Jews are too powerful in international markets and 45% believe that Jews have too much power in the business world, this despite the fact that there are believed to be less than 1000 Jews in a population of over 10 million. Jews form a miniscule fraction of the population of most European countries, yet significant sections of the population have bought into truly fantastical notions of Jewish power and control. They have convinced themselves that there is a Jewish bogeyman who somehow controls the levers of power and has a dominant influence over the commanding heights of the economy. It is the stuff of fantasy and makes no sense unless one accepts that antisemitism, like a superstition, lingers deep in a nation's collective psyche and bursts forth at moments of deep social and economic crisis.

Social v ideological Antisemitism: Antisemitism is also not a homogeneous phenomenon. What that means is that there is a continuum along which antisemitism is typically found and expressed with some manifestations more serious than others. A great deal of antisemitism consists of the lazy, casual expression of stereotypes embedded in western culture. These stereotypes are many and varied (indeed they are often contradictory) and include many of the following: the Jew as cowardly and unpatriotic, the Jew as stingy and avaricious, the Jew as insular, clannish and un-neighbourly, the Jew as good with money, the Jew as obsessed with Israel or the Holocaust. One need not hate Jews to believe in at least one of these viewpoints. Indeed, this can also be true of those who are well disposed to Jews generally and who admire their qualities and intellect. How often might a Jew have heard that he must be 'good with money' or be 'a good negotiator' or that because he is careful with money, he is unlikely to be a gambler? One might call this social antisemitism.

At the other end of the continuum, antisemites cleave to a series of prejudices which serve as an ideological tool for understanding the world. The Jew occupies a diabolical place in their imagination as a source of real harm to the world and as the progenitor of evil. These people are unlikely to embrace anti-Jewish hatred in a casual or occasional manner. Antisemitism is more like a *Weltanschauung*, a superstition, a 'grand unified theory of everything' [8] and an all-embracing philosophy of life that makes sense of the world and its evils. As historian Peter Hayes says, it is 'a kind of superstition.' In this worldview, Jews are assigned a unique role in causing the prevalent ills that plague any given society. In early Christendom, they were responsible for deicide. In the Middle Ages, they were the cause of plagues and natural disasters that befell entire societies. For the Communists, they were the prime movers behind capitalist greed and, for extreme nationalists, they epitomised the problem of racial contamination. Finally, modern progressives see in the Jewish nation state a powerful symbol of colonialism and

---

[8] Bari Weiss, *How to Fight Antisemitism* (London: Allen Lane, 2020), 32.

racism. In the antisemitic imagination, the Jew occupies prime position as the cause of any society's most noxious ills. We might term this ideological antisemitism. Hardcore, ideological antisemitism admits of no nuance because it is wholly impervious to fact, evidence and logic.

Irrationality of Antisemitism: Antisemitism is a fundamentally irrational conception, attributing to the Jew all manner of contradictory attributes that fail the test of basic coherence. If Jews are philanthropic, it is because they are simply too rich and greedy but if not, they are stingy. If they are aspirational, it is because they seek to dominate society but if not, they are a burden on society. If they are weak, that is bad because they are cowardly and go like sheep to the slaughter, but if too strong, they are oppressors. If Jews refuse to assimilate, it is because they feel superior to others but if they do, they are too cosmopolitan and contaminate society through infiltration. For the antisemite, a Jew cannot act from pure motives. Any good Jewish deed can and should be interpreted negatively, and be seen as a contrivance designed to hide his true nature, one which has an ominous, malevolent or deceitful quality. With the Jew, in other words, what you see is not what you get. It is for this reason that any reminder about how Jews have contributed to the betterment of mankind will make no impression on the hardened antisemite. While for those well-disposed, such information is a spur to acknowledge and even copy the Jews' belief in achievement, innovation and scholarship, for the antisemite it is a glaring reminder of their own failure and underachievement. Nonetheless, as Kenneth L Marcus says, antisemitism 'is a way in which people make sense of the world, even if their conceptions are often distorted or nonsensical.'[9]

Antisemitism can harm non-Jews: It is also important to remember that antisemitism can harm non-Jews too, even if they are not the intended victims or targets of prejudice. A classic example can be found in the 1947 film *Gentleman's Agreement*, starring Gregory Peck. In the film, Peck plays a widowed journalist (Philip Green) who is asked to write a feature on antisemitism. To make his account more authentic, he poses as a Jew (Phil Greenberg) and experiences at first hand some examples of prejudice. His mother falls ill and a local doctor advises him to avoid a specialist with a Jewish name in case he is overcharged. A hotel manager refuses to allow Greenberg to register because he is a Jew while the janitor of his block is shocked that there is a Jewish name on the mailbox. Phil's girlfriend, Kathy, succumbs to the bigotry of those around her and their engagement is broken off.

What is true in literature is also true in life. In 1922, the non-Jewish but philosemitic Winston Churchill became the victim of an antisemitic libel brought by Lord Alfred Douglas, Oscar Wilde's former lover. Douglas alleged that immediately after the Battle of Jutland (the Anglo-German naval battle in 1916), a plot was engineered by a group of British Jews, led by Sir Ernest Cassel,

---

[9] Kenneth Marcus, *The Definition of Antisemitism* (Oxford: Oxford University Press, 2015), 47.

whereby they got the Admiralty to announce that Britain had suffered terrible reverses in the battle. This led to a dramatic fall in British stocks on the New York Stock Exchange whereupon, according to Douglas, Jewish speculators bought them up at cheap prices. The allegation then continued that Churchill, in return for a sum of money, got a second communiqué to be issued which gave a more positive reading of the Battle and downplayed Britain's losses. The stocks then rose in price and netted the Jewish investors a fortune. Eventually, the British government brought a case of criminal libel against Douglas and won, with the latter sentenced to a spell in prison. A more recent and harrowing case involved the CNN reporter Lara Logan who was covering the Egyptian coup against Hosni Mubarak in 2011. Standing in Tahrir Square, she was the victim of a mass sexual assault, the trigger for which was the (false) rumour that she was a Jew. Both cases show how easily a person can be a victim of antisemitism even though they are not themselves Jewish.

Antisemitism as misplaced virtue: It is sometimes said that we are witnessing a 'new antisemitism' and that what differentiates the new from the old antisemitism is that the former hides its hatred of or prejudice towards Jews by pretending to be morally virtuous. Whereas antisemitism from the past revelled in its orgiastic fury towards the Jews, today's more polite, post-Holocaust version wraps itself in the mantle of human rights and liberal values. This antisemitism opposes Jewish collective rights and Zionism in order to save humanity from colonialism and racism. It attacks 'pro-Israel' Jewish communities in the name of universal values such as equality, dignity and humanity. It discriminates against Jews in the pursuit of a better, nobler and more enlightened world. It advocates a genocidal attack on Israel as a form of self-defence, a way of saving the world from the Jewish state's sinister predations. It besmirches Jewish victimhood and Holocaust memory in order to sacralise those whom the Jews allegedly persecute. It is the racism of the virtuous, the hatred of the upright and the rage of the righteous. In the words of Daniel Jonah Goldhagen, antisemitism has become 'a program for righting the world.'[10]

But it is far from clear that this is unique to the modern age. Throughout history, antisemites have portrayed themselves as the victims of the Jews and carried out wanton attacks on Jewish communities in the name of universal righteousness. Jews were attacked during the Crusades as the 'enemies of God' who had committed a deicide. They were slaughtered during the Black Death in order to save mankind from the pestilence then raging. They were pilloried mercilessly by Enlightenment thinkers who believed that purging civilization of Jewish faith and culture was the path to a more progressive society. The enemies of Judaeo-Bolshevism pictured Jews as the enemies of humanity and saw their elimination as a moral necessity. They were slaughtered under Islamic rule in order to purify the *umma* of *haram* (forbidden) influences which undermined the

---

[10] Daniel Goldhagen, *The Devil that Never Dies* (New York: Little, Brown and Company, 2013), 36.

Muslim order. Antisemites have so often seen themselves as a virtuous vanguard doing God's work or as redeemers of their fellow man. It is a recurring motif in the history of antisemitism rather than a new phenomenon.

Antisemitism as a unique form of racism: As a unique form of racial prejudice and bigotry and as the longest lasting hatred in world, antisemitism needs to be understood and confronted on its own terms. It should not simply be lumped in with other forms of racism and attacked in purely generic terms. Yet that has sadly been the tendency among the more politically correct echelons of society. Following the antisemitic comments made by Rep. Ilhan Omar about the dual loyalty of those who support Israel, there were calls for the House of Representatives to condemn antisemitism. As Democrat Rep. Ted Deutsch put it: 'We are having this debate because of the language of one of our colleagues, language that suggests Jews like me who serve in the United States in Congress and whose father earned a purple heart fighting the Nazis in the Battle of the Bulge, that we are not loyal Americans.' Yet the resolution ended up condemning 'bigotry, discrimination, oppression, racism and imputations of dual loyalty' which 'threaten American democracy and have no place in American political discourse.'[11] It was an all-encompassing, all-inclusive resolution rather than one which singled out and responded to the very bigotry that had inspired it. In another example, the UK Labour party in 2016 issued its Chakrabarti report examining 'antisemitism and other forms of racism,' rather than the antisemitism that had necessitated the report in the first place. She claimed in the report that there could not be a 'hierarchy of racism' and 'no competition for victimhood,' sentiments which, while laudable in themselves, were inappropriate comments in the midst of Labour's antisemitism scandal.

In neither case does it follow that an investigation into one specific form of racism must become generic just because racism affects multiple communities. There is space for enquiries into specific forms of racism, each of which can deal with the unique forms of the prejudice in question. An added danger of taking the 'generic approach' to racism is that it can lead to the so-called deflection strategy, namely that when people wish to raise the issue of antisemitism, they are slapped down for ignoring other forms of racism in society. The end result is that antisemitism is not focused on as it ought to be and those who wish to investigate it are deemed to be acting wrongly unless they spread their concerns more widely. This is what the English University and College Union meant when they condemned a UK Parliamentary inquiry into antisemitism for its somewhat singular focus on this prejudice. The UCU claimed that it seemed 'inappropriate to have taken as a topic in isolation at a time when Islamophobia is also on the increase and when the two issues surely need a balanced approach.' As David Baddiel argues, the same tactic is used by the right when they use the term 'All Lives Matter' in responding to protests by Black Lives Matter.[12]

---

[11] House votes to condemn antisemitism after Ilhan Omar's remarks on Israel | House of Representatives | The Guardian.

[12] David Baddiel, *Jews Don't Count* (London: TLS Books, 2021), 89-90.

Antisemitism as conspiracy: Antisemitism is unlike other forms of prejudice in that it both looks *up* to the Jews and also looks *down* on them. For sure, antisemitism dehumanises the Jew, suggesting that he is a loathsome and malign creature whose appetites are bestial. It gives the Jew horns, distorted physical features and a fearful complexion so as to literally turn him into a beast. It pictures him as a malevolent sexual threat to a nation's women and an enemy of national purity. It turns Jews into a foreign presence in their own countries, a hideous unwanted 'other' that contaminates all that they come into contact with. But antisemitism is marked by something else: a palpable fear of what the Jews might do to the gentiles. In essence, antisemitism is a *conspiracy theory*, the oldest and darkest conspiracy theory in human history. It suggests that one should have a near hysterical fear of Jewish qualities (their purportedly superior power, guile and influence), ones which are designed to control and immiserate the lives of Gentiles. This was even true of Nazi ideology which was both unsparing in its venomous depiction of Jews as animals and bloodsuckers but which also regarded them as a major threat to German life and society.

In that sense, antisemitism can be contrasted with other forms of racism. The history of anti-black racism is littered with harmful prejudices and cultural tropes that have influenced attitudes and opinions across the ages, right until the present day. Black people have long suffered from disparaging representations which portray them as unintelligent, lazy, superstitious and ignorant. They have been dehumanised with comparisons to apes and beasts and depicted as powerful, menacing figures who represent a danger, especially a sexual one, to their white neighbours. All too often they have been the butt of jokes about their alleged sexual prowess. Sadly, these societal stereotypes still influence the way that some people see and respond to black people. Anti-Chinese racism has centred on the belief that Asians are carriers of deadly diseases, including sexually transmitted ones. The Roma, a long persecuted and marginalized community, have been stigmatised as socially backward criminals, liars and tricksters, worthy of nothing more than contempt and mistrust. They have attracted the most foul and odious hatreds and prejudices, ones which have been used to exploit, persecute and vilify them throughout history. For some, Arabs are unpatriotic and backward Middle Easterners who glory in terror and violence and can never contribute to wider society. All these stereotypes must be challenged whenever they surface, both by amplifying the voices of those who suffer from them and teaching about the harmful effects of stereotypes. But these appalling tropes rarely translate into a sense that the minority concerned is a global, politically connected threat to wider society. What is usually absent is the construction of a conspiracy, according to which a vanguard of the minority has plans to entrap and control the rest of society for their own evil purposes. The conspiracy evokes a sense that society is under the impending threat of destruction and that the only way to ensure its survival is to eliminate the minority in question.

Today there are many who engage in egregious forms of antisemitism denial, itself a form of antisemitism, by denying that it exists or downplaying its significance or, worse, engaging in a witch hunt against its victims. It is a double whammy for Jews, both to confront this virulent prejudice in all its forms and then to defend themselves against insidious charges of fraudulent victimhood. In progressive western circles, no other community is accused of fakery, deception and malevolence for protesting at the hatred thrown at them. Following the McPherson report in 1998, it is a British norm for minority communities to be heard with respect and dignity when outlining the prejudicial treatment they have received from others. It is those victims who get to define the forms of hatred they experience, even if there is no requirement to accept the veracity of each and every claim of racist treatment. Antisemitism denial regurgitates the tropes of traditional antisemitism by accusing Jews of being cunning, malevolent and scheming in their complaints, adding another sulphurous layer to their bitter experience. These forms of antisemitism denial too need to be spelled out, analysed and thoroughly deconstructed.

Denial 1 – The Semitism fallacy: The first form of denial is a *semantic* one – that the charge of antisemitism is false because it makes no sense or is linguistically invalid. One familiar variant of this argument, popular in much of the Arab and Muslim world, says that the term 'antisemitism' is a semantic contradiction because Arabs are Semites too and cannot hate themselves. Critically, it assumes that there is such a thing as a 'semitic people' and that Arabs, being part of that population, therefore cannot hate Jews. But it is as historically disingenuous to talk of a single 'semitic people' as it is to talk of an Aryan race. Instead, people talk about a group of semitic languages which are spoken in the Middle East and North Africa, principally Arabic, Amharic, Hebrew and Aramaic. As the great scholar Bernard Lewis points out, the term 'semitic' should be referred to as 'a linguistic and cultural classification, denoting certain languages and in some contexts the literatures and civilizations expressed in those languages.' [13] It is empirically false to state that no Muslims and Arabs are antisemitic in the sense that they hate or show prejudice towards Jews. Jew hatred is sadly endemic throughout the Arab and Muslim world, as the rest of this book will make clear. In any case, if there were a 'semitic people,' it would be wrong to think that they were collectively the target for antisemites. Certainly, Israelis and their supporters around the world are not attacked for being too 'semitic.' Instead, they are condemned for being western, pro-American and colonialist implants in the Arab and Muslim world, accused of subjugating and oppressing other people in the region. There are no significant 'semite haters' out there and the term antisemitism refers to only one group – the Jews. Throughout this book, I will follow other scholars by spelling the term 'Antisemitism' without a hyphen (so not 'anti-Semitism'). This is to emphasize that there is no opposition to 'semitism' as such, simply because the term itself is fairly meaningless when applied to a population as opposed to a collection of languages.

Denial 2 – The Jewish faith fallacy: There are others who hold that Jews are not a people or nation but members of a religion who freely choose to adopt

[13] Bernard Lewis, *Semites and Anti-Semites* (London: Phoenix Giant, 1997), 45.

its tenets, beliefs and values. In this voluntarist conception of identity, Jews are defined as a faith-based collective whose commitments do not impinge on any other aspect of their identity. One consequence of this view has been to reject as absurd any claim to national self-determination. How can those who dwell in the synagogues of many nations unite 'nationally' on the basis of their religious beliefs alone? But this is deeply problematic. Jewishness for many Jews is not about religious beliefs, practices or any faith-based narrative. Many Jews are secular and non-practising yet still cling to their Jewish identity with a deep and unbending strength of conviction. They feel that they are, in essence, Jewish but without making any explicit commitment to Judaic precepts and practices. In that sense, one can contrast Jews with other religious minorities whose sense of collective identity revolves far more around the acceptance of a set of core religious beliefs. What all Jews (religious and secular) retain is a sense of peoplehood, of belonging to a community and a wider civilization, past and present, with degrees of faith-based commitment. Jews are 'a people based on a religious civilization.'[14] This explains why the Bible does not refer to Jews in voluntarist terms but as *Am Yisrael* (the People of Israel). The vast majority of Jews today also recognise that they have a collective right to determine their future, either in a nation state called Israel or in the diasporic countries where they reside. Moreover, the vast majority identify with Israel and share a deeply felt concern for its survival, for some because of familial ties, for others because of pride in Jewish identity but for many, because Israel remains a safe haven and a guarantee of survival in times of crisis. Support for the existence of Israel, though not for all its policies, is fundamental to the identity of most Jews today. This is why it is naïve at best to draw a firewall between attacking the political ideology of Zionism and attacking the group identity of Jews. Most Jews will experience an entrenched assault on Zionism as a deeply hurtful attack on their Jewishness.

Denial 3 – Jews are not a race fallacy: Some argue that Jews cannot be victims of racism because they are not a race in any meaningful sense. Such a view *appears* to have a reasonable basis when one considers the nature of modern race theory, as well as salient facts about Jews as a people. First, race theory has undergone a transformation in the last 200 years. In the nineteenth century, race became a ubiquitous means of explaining human variation. Arthur de Gobineau's *Essay on the Inequality of Human Races* offered a paean to the Aryan race which was pictured as the progenitor of civilization and which railed against the 'evil' of miscegenation (race mixing). Around the same time, the Scottish anatomist Robert Knox wrote *The Races of Men*, a tome which lent support to pseudo-scientific racism by offering crude characterizations of various defined population groups. Both assumed that humanity could be divided into distinct racial types, that each race had distinct physical markers as well as identifiable social traits and, most disturbingly, that they could be placed on a racial hierarchy with Aryan whites at the top. The horrific legacy of Nazi race theory, with its emphasis on

---

[14] Garfinkle, *Jewcentricity*, 67.

biological superiority, eugenics and twisting of social Darwinism, discredited the field of pseudo-scientific racism. At the start of the twentieth century, the scientific studies of anthropologist Franz Boas were undermining the idea of pure races with their comparative analysis of the physical, cultural and intellectual characteristics of different population groups. Eugenics based race doctrines were discredited by the work of British biologist Julian Huxley, a key figure in exploding the idea of a unified African race. Later in the twentieth century, famed geneticist Richard Lewontin demonstrated that approximately 85% of genetic variation among people was between members of the same population and a further 9% between populations considered to have been part of the same race. What remained was phenotypical features (facial features, skull size, hair and skin colour) which scarcely denoted racial differences. The only conclusion was that providing a taxonomy of different races was near impossible, leading many to conclude that the term 'race' was redundant. Hence, it followed that there could be no separate Jewish 'race.' This is buttressed by the second point, namely that Jews come from a multiplicity of ethnic and racial backgrounds: there are white English, European and American Jews, Middle Eastern Jews, Indian Jews and Beta Israel (black Jews from Ethiopia). So whatever Jews are, they are not a race.

Yet those who deny Jews can be victims of prejudice because they aren't a race ignore the fact that other groups are demonstrably not racial and yet are still seen as victims of racism. To take an obvious example, it is hard to imagine a self-declared anti-racist denying that Muslims cannot be victims of hatred just because they are not a racially unified group. For this reason, many today invoke the notions of culture and ethnicity to widen the concept of racial prejudice. After all, racists attack various minority groups on the basis of allegedly immutable social characteristics, whether that is criminality and aggressiveness (black communities), deviousness and guile (east Asians) or avarice (Jews). When these traits are believed to be etched into the character of the populations concerned, they are treated as if they were a bio-cultural essence, a permanent marker of identity. The naturalising of social features is called essentialism, the attribution to a group of an unchanging essence. In the case of racism, that essence is usually a negative one and it undoubtedly applies to Jewish victims of prejudice and hatred.[15]

Denial 4 – The 'my best friend' fallacy: One of the most familiar defences against antisemitism is that the alleged perpetrator has a large number of Jewish friends. The 'Some of my best friends are Jewish' line has been endlessly trotted out as a defence to charges of racism and bigotry and has many variants depending on the racial or religious group concerned. The author remembers a speech given in Trafalgar Square by Azzam Tamimi, a leading Palestinian supporter of Hamas, marking 50 years of the Israeli occupation. Anxious to deflect criticism of antisemitism, he assured his audience that the Neturei Karta, an ultra-orthodox

---

[15] Sometimes, commentators speak of racisms rather than racism in an attempt to bypass this problem.

sect which asserts that Zionism is heretical, were among his 'best friends.'[16] This is a classic example of selective or token representation where the views of a heretical fringe group or sect are lauded as the voice of an authentic minority. Emanuele Ottolenghi sums up what he sees as a double standard: 'If someone quoted a black intellectual to support the theory behind slavery and apartheid or a woman to extol the benefits of infibulation (female genital mutilation), very few people would fall into the trap.' Actually, people do fall in the trap with more regularity than Ottolenghi imagines. A powerful way to deflect criticism of racism and bigotry is to find dissident voices from minority groups that support a racist or bigoted position (such voices can always be found), ignoring the agendas that might be at work. But he is right in referring to how progressive opinion works. Within that section of opinion, the 'renegade voice' fallacy would be exposed the moment it was attempted.

The defence is weak for another reason. Classical antisemitism expresses hate for an abstraction, a mythic racialized enemy who comes dressed in stereotypical garb, images and symbols. One need never encounter an actual Jew to believe that antisemitism is a real explanation for the ills of the world. It is not therefore surprising that even hardened antisemites form bonds with real Jews who don't accord with the mythic image they have imbibed. This principle extends even to the most hard hearted, ideological antisemites. For a number of years, Hitler built up a friendship with a young girl, Rosa Bernile Nienau, who is believed to have had an identical birthday to the Fuhrer. She and 'uncle Adolf' wrote to each other, despite the German leader finding out that she was of Jewish ancestry through her maternal grandmother and was considered to be Jewish under German race laws. Hitler also protected Ernst Hess, his former (Jewish) commanding officer from the First World War, until the middle of the Second World War while calling his former family doctor Eduard Bloch an *Ediljude* (noble Jew). In each case, he was thinking about individuals with whom he had built up a meaningful relationship rather than members of an abstract racial group. One can like individual Jews and yet be a committed, even genocidal, antisemite. Similarly, one can like black people, Muslims and gay people on an individual level yet still form attitudes or engage in actions that are harmful or insensitive to those groups.

The same logic applies to those who happen themselves to be Jewish and who parade this fact as proof positive that their deranged anti-Israel obsessions are not racist. Often, these individuals preface any letters to the newspapers which attack Israel with the words 'As a Jew,' a marker in advance that their epistolary diatribes are untainted by bigotry and come from a pure heart. One suspects this is why pro-Palestinian organizations, such as the Palestine Solidarity Campaign, actively seek the appointment of Jewish leaders, patrons and spokesmen. The presence of so many Jews appears to insulate them from bigotry because they provide their

---

[16] Enough Occupation: 40th Anniversary of the Occupation of large parts of Palestine, Demonstration & Rally, London 9th June 2007 (inminds.co.uk), accessed 10 June 2021.

organization with a kosher seal of approval. The fact that so many of these Jews are also bitter opponents of the Jewish communities from which they spring is of little interest. After all, why should it matter to gentile critics of Israel that their Jewish allies might be completely unrepresentative Jews? The rejoinder is obvious: such Jews can be antisemitic too and are easily capable of adopting positions that are deeply racist. In 2002, former World chess champion, Bobby Fisher, issued a rant on the radio in which he called Jews 'a filthy, lying bastard people' who murdered Christian children for their blood and invented the Holocaust to make money. Whether one calls this 'Jewish self-hatred' or 'Jewish antisemitism,' the hatred that some Jews can feel for their co-religionists is unmistakeable.

Denial 5 – Antisemitism as smear tactic: The fifth form of denial is that antisemitism allegations are essentially concocted by Jews in order to silence critics of Israel who are merely expressing legitimate criticism of the Jewish State. Here, antisemitism is regarded as an unseemly weapon of censorship, a smear to be hurled against people who merely wish to stand up for Palestinian rights. A classic version of this argument was supplied by French environmentalist Jose Bove in an interview in 2002. Bove, who had spent a day in Yasser Arafat's besieged headquarters in Ramallah, claimed that accounts of antisemitism were purely manufactured by Israel, stating specifically: 'Who profits from the crime? The Israeli government and its secret services have an interest in creating a certain psychosis, in making believe that there is a climate of antisemitism in France, in order to distract attention from what they are doing.'[17]

According to this activist, the psychosis affecting society was not the antisemitism itself, for which there was an abundance of evidence, but the accusation of antisemitism. Israel was effectively responsible for politically gaslighting the French nation with a fake accusation of racism, making the French question their sanity in the process. Another politician who blamed Israel directly in this way was British Green party leader Caroline Lucas who once claimed that Israel had 'been able to act with relative immunity hiding behind its incendiary claim that all who criticize its policies are antisemitic.'[18] Here, Lucas has constructed an imaginary Israel which lashes out at all accusers in bad faith but which also manages to get away with its charges, effectively turning gentile nations into a bunch of hapless dupes. For others, it is Israel supporters or the wider Jewish community that orchestrates false charges of antisemitism. Thus, Ken Livingstone once claimed, 'For far too long the accusation of antisemitism has been used against anyone who is critical of the policies of the Israeli government, as I have been.' When Jeremy Corbyn responded to the EHRC report into institutional antisemitism within the Labour party, he declared that accusations of racism had been 'dramatically overstated for political reasons by

---

[17] Gabriel Schoenfeld, *Return of antisemitism* (San Francisco, Encounter Books, 2004), 74.
[18] David Hirsh, *Contemporary left antisemitism* (London: Routledge, 2018), 34.

our opponents … as well as by much of the media,' ignoring the fact that the EHRC had been set up by the Labour party itself. Corbyn had earlier defended Stephen Sizer, a vicar who had long been accused of spreading antisemitic tropes, claiming that the attacks against the churchman were 'part of a wider pattern of demonising those who dare to stand up and speak out against Zionism.' [19] Illustrating the point that there is a convergence between left and right wing forms of antisemitism, David Duke of the KKK also indulged this formulation when he said: 'It is perfectly acceptable to criticize any nation on the earth for its errors and wrongs, but lo and behold, don't you dare criticize Israel; for if you do that, you will be accused of the most abominable sin in the modern world, the unforgivable sin of antisemitism!' [20] There are also religious versions of this secular smear against the Jews. The Catholic scholar E Michael Jones once declared: 'An antisemite used to be someone who didn't like Jews. Now it is someone whom the Jews don't like.' [21]

This form of denial works by refusing to take the accusation of antisemitism seriously. The person who is accused of antisemitism doesn't respond with an honest form of soul searching or intellectual engagement. Instead, there is a defensive counter-reaction in the form of a charge of bad faith. The person accusing the other of antisemitism is not regarded as being in error; they are accused of deliberating concocting a false claim in order to smear their opponent. The reason for the smear is that the accuser is so desperate to silence critics of Israel that they will use accusations of antisemitism to tarnish them. Moreover, it is crucial to this form of denial that the person accused of antisemitism is merely depicted as a 'critic' of Israel and that all they are doing is criticizing Israeli policy as they would the policy of any other country. In other words, they conflate respectable political discourse with demonization. Those who engage in this form of denial trivialize antisemitism, whether, in Duke's case, by putting an exclamation mark after the word (as if to mock it) or by dismissing the lived experiences of Jews who talk about it. It implies that the real vulgarity lies with those who accuse others of antisemitism, not those who make antisemitic statements. As David Hirsh says, the Livingstone formula treats the accusation of antisemitism as a 'vulgar, dishonest and tribal fraud.' [22] It triply damns Jews, firstly for the antisemitic content they are forced to endure and then denying them the right to call out the racism in question, furthermore accusing them of lying and manipulating others into believing there is antisemitism.

Those who accuse Jews of bad faith when making an accusation of this kind have devoted much of their time to attacking the IHRA definition of antisemitism. An oft mentioned criticism of the definition is that it is designed to silence

---

[19] Marcus Dysch, "Don't Vote for Jeremy Corbyn, urges new Labour Friends of Israel chair, Joan Ryan," *Jewish Chronicle*, August 10, 2015.

[20] Hirsh, *Contemporary Left Antisemitism*, 30.

[21] Michael L Brown, *Christian Antisemitism: Confronting the Lies in Today's Church* (Florida: Charisma House, 2021), 18.

[22] Hirsh, *Contemporary left Antisemitism*, 12.

criticism of Israel and hush up any public discussion of its alleged misdeeds. Thus, former Labour government minister Clare Short claimed that there had been a 'widening of the definition of antisemitism to include criticism of Israel' and that it was wrong to extend this definition 'to prevent people having any sympathy for the suffering of the Palestinians.'[23]

Yet this is wrong for several reasons. To start, the authors of the IHRA definition make this point explicit: 'Criticism of Israel similar to that levelled against any other country cannot be regarded as antisemitic.' Thus, if one wished to proportionately criticize the actions and policies of Israeli politicians, the human rights record of any of its governments, the policies associated with Israeli settlements or the occupation or the treatment of minorities in Israel, one would be free to do so without the taint of antisemitism. Some of the criticisms may be misguided but they are not antisemitic.

Second, many of the indicative examples of antisemitism contained in the definition have nothing to say about Israel's treatment of the Palestinians. They include the following:

Calling for, aiding, or justifying the killing or harming of Jews in the name of a radical ideology or an extremist view of religion.

Making mendacious, dehumanizing, demonizing, or stereotypical allegations about Jews as such or the power of Jews as a collective – such as, especially but not exclusively, the myth about a world Jewish conspiracy or of Jews controlling the media, economy, government or other societal institutions.

Accusing Jews as a people of being responsible for real or imagined wrongdoing committed by a single Jewish person or group, or even for acts committed by non-Jews.

The obvious rejoinder is that hardly anyone in the pro-Israel community says that mere criticism of Israel is antisemitic. More often, you will hear Israel supporters making frank and honest assessments of Israeli policy, perhaps disagreeing over settlement expansion, the issues of racism, discrimination and inequality that do sadly blight the lives of Israeli Arabs (despite their being the freest Arabs in the Middle East), the disproportionate influence of the religious right in Israel, and so on. To claim that this type of criticism is antisemitic is absurd and offensive. As Alan Dershowitz says, it would mean that the greatest collection of antisemites in the world would be in Tel Aviv, given that the Jewish state is hardly a place whose citizens are reticent about criticizing their own government. The conclusion will examine the many ways in which non-antisemitic criticisms of Israel are possible within a framework of fair, honest and robust debate.

---

[23] Simon Rocker, "'Anyone who is sympathetic to the plight of the Palestinians is called antisemitic,' says Clare Short," *The Jewish Chronicle*, May 29, 2019.

Denial 6 – The fallacy of 'no intent': The sixth form of antisemitism denial involves the idea that one cannot be guilty of antisemitism because one is not consciously hostile to Jews. This form of antisemitism denial was illustrated by figures within Jewish Voice for Labour, a group that was close to the UK Labour leader Jeremy Corbyn. They consistently rejected the claim that comparisons between Israel and Nazi Germany were 'inherently antisemitic.' They argued that 'such comparisons are only antisemitic if they show prejudice, hostility or hatred against Jews as Jews.'[24] In 2018, the NEC code of conduct on antisemitism stated: 'Discourse about international politics often employs metaphors drawn from examples of historic misconduct. It is not antisemitism to criticize the conduct or policies of the Israeli state by reference to such examples unless there is evidence of antisemitic intent.'[25]

But this offers a far too restrictive definition of antisemitism and, for that matter, every other form of racism. If intent becomes a necessary condition for a finding of antisemitism, this constitutes a major departure from decades of anti-racist practice and scholarly understanding. Racism functions when discourses about a minority reproduce age old forms of hatred, and when actions, processes and policies leave that minority humiliated, demeaned and discriminated against. With antisemitism, the objective tests are whether Jews are subjected to discourses of hatred replete with age old tropes of Jew hatred and whether, as individuals or as a community, they face second class treatment because their rights have been infringed. The test is not whether hateful thoughts motivated the interactions with Jews, a factor which would, in most cases, be impossible to prove. Political scientist Alan Johnson is therefore right to say that it is 'more productive to think about the structure and logic of the discourse' of any individual, and track 'the relation of that discourse to previous iterations of Jew hatred.'[26] Furthermore, as sociologist Keith Kahn Harris points out correctly in his book *Strange Hate*, 'For those who suffer it, the intent behind racial abuse is less important than the fact of the racist abuse.'[27]

Antisemitism cannot be discerned just by examining what goes on inside people's heads (their subjective intention). It is, as David Hirsh says 'an objective social phenomenon' because it has 'recognizable shapes and tropes,' it has 'been with us for a long time' and 'its symbols and memes are deep within us.'[28] People can genuinely say that they are not antisemitic because they feel no conscious animus towards Jews or Jewish institutions. Yet they may interact with the

---

[24]"Expelled activist tells JVL meeting that 'witchhunt' is plot to 'topple' Corbyn," *Jewish News*, November 11, 2018.
[25] Keith Kahn-Harris, *Strange Hate: Antisemitism, Racism and the Limits of Diversity* (London: Repeater Books, 2019), 41.
[26] Carey Nelson, *Israel Denial: Anti-Zionism, Antisemitism, and the Faculty Campaign Against the Jewish State* (Indiana: Indiana University Press, 2019), 14.
[27] Kahn-Harris, *Strange Hate*, 42
[28]Hirsh, *Contemporary Left Antisemitism*, 25.

cultural imagery of antisemitism and allow it to percolate into their way of thinking without any conscious realization.

Denial 7 – The 'Israel is to blame' fallacy: The seventh form of antisemitism denial states that attacks on Jews, while deplorable, are based on negative responses to Israel's behaviour. Israel, through its commission of crimes and misdemeanours, is therefore to blame for the antisemitism plaguing the world. This type of denial accepts the reality of modern antisemitism but takes issue with what causes it. A classic example came in a deeply disturbing interview on BBC News shortly after a lethal attack on a Parisian kosher supermarket in 2015. Broadcaster Tim Wilcox interviewed a Jewish participant on a rally against antisemitism who was complaining that the atmosphere for Jews in France was akin to that of the 1930s. He responded by saying: 'Many critics though of Israel's policy would suggest that the Palestinians suffer hugely at Jewish hands as well.' He then added: 'You understand everything is seen from different perspectives.'[29] Wilcox, who later apologised for his remarks, gave credence to the idea that French Jews were somehow part of the Middle East conflict and that they could be seen (from one perspective) as legitimate targets for attack despite being thousands of miles from the region. A similar claim was made by the veteran left wing activist Tariq Ali. In a speech outside Downing Street in 2018, he put forward this proposition: 'The purveyors of antisemitism today, those who have encouraged antisemitism are the Israeli government.' He added that 'killing Palestinians they way that they do it' and 'targeting children as they have done' is 'what produces a crude form of antisemitism.'[30] In *The Morning Star*, a columnist wrote about Israel's killing of Gazan protestors in 2018, arguing that 'no amount of protestations about the symptoms of rising antisemitism or anti-Israel sentiment in Britain and elsewhere will end the problem until its root cause – Israel's criminal behaviour – is dealt with.'[31] In 2019, Polish President Duda is believed to have argued that a comment made by the Israeli Foreign Minister (Poles suckle antisemitism with their mothers' milk) had 'encouraged' an antisemitic reaction from Poles.

The UK Liberal Democrat peer Baroness Tonge has given several egregious examples of this form of victim blaming. In response to a report of an alarming rise of antisemitic attacks at British universities, she claimed that the reason was the 'increasing violence in the West Bank and Gaza, the expansion of settlements and the occupation of east Jerusalem.' She went on: 'They (Jews) are victims because of the illegal actions of the Israeli government.'[32] In 2016, she responded

---

[29] Lucy Crossley, "BBC Reporter faces calls to resign after he tells daughter of Holocaust survivors after Paris attacks 'Palestinians suffer hugely at Jewish hands as well'," *Mail Online*, January 17, 2015.
[30] Lee Harpin, "Israel to blame for rise in antisemitism, left wing veteran Tariq Ali declares," *Jewish Chronicle*, April 9, 2018.
[31] Kahn-Harris, *Strange Hate*, 172.
[32] Lee Harpin, "Fury as Tonge blames rising UK campus antisemitism on the 'illegal actions of the Israeli government'," *The Jewish Chronicle*, January 22, 2021.

to a Home Affairs Select Committee report on antisemitism, pointing out that the rise in anti-Jewish prejudice reflected a 'disgust amongst the general public' for 'the way the government of Israel treats Palestinians.'[33] When a crazed neo-Nazi went on the rampage at the Tree of Life synagogue, murdering eleven people, she blasted it as 'absolutely appalling and a criminal act' but then asked: 'Does it ever occur to Bibi and the present Israeli government that it's (sic) actions against Palestinians may be reigniting antisemitism?'[34] The idea that a Jew hating Nazi had this conflict in mind before carrying out his murderous attack is almost too absurd for comment.

If Israel causes Jews to come under attack through its allegedly criminal deeds, it follows that Jews 'have it coming to them' if they do not dissociate themselves from the Jewish state. On December 27, 2008, the Jewish community of Malmo held a demonstration to express their sympathy for all civilian victims in both Gaza and Israel. A counter demonstration screamed abuse, including references to Hitler, and hurled a bottle and a homemade bomb towards the Jews. Malmo's Mayor, Ilmar Reepalu, chose to blame the Jews for coming under attack, saying 'I would wish for the Jewish community to denounce Israeli violations against the civilian population in Gaza. Instead, it decides to hold a [pro-Israeli] demonstration in the Grand Square [of Malmö], which could send the wrong signals.'[35] In fact, Reepalu argued that the mere exercise of Jewish collective rights would also be sending the wrong signals by declaring: 'We accept neither Zionism nor antisemitism. They are extremes that put themselves above other groups, and believe they have a lower value.'[36]

A similar sentiment was expressed by the French socialist leader Pascal Boniface. Citing the growing Arab population in his country, he warned French Jews that their linkage of antisemitism with 'all out defense of Sharon's Israel' would see them 'isolated' at 'a national level.'[37] At least Boniface acknowledged the role played by attitudes to Israel in framing antisemitic violence as well as the role played by Arab citizens in fomenting that violence. The mistake he made was in attributing blame to French Jews for holding entirely legitimate political opinions. For Jews in France were surely as entitled as any other citizens to endorse the actions of a foreign government and to act as cheerleaders for it. What unites these views is that Israel is responsible for spreading antisemitism and harming the interests of Jews and, that by supporting the state, especially in public, Jews have made themselves targets for attack.

---

[33] Hirsh, *Contemporary Left antisemitism*, 23.

[34] "Anti-Israel UK lawmaker who blamed antisemitism rise on Jewish groups retires," *Times of Israel*, February 7, 2021.

[35] Paulina Neuding, "Malmö's Mayor Blames Jews for Wave of Antisemitism," *Tablet Magazine*, April 5, 2012.

[36] "Swedish Jews raise issue of Malmö mayor's antisemitic comments with Social Democratic Party leader," *World Jewish Congress*, April 3, 2012.

[37] Wistrich, *A Lethal Obsession*, 292.

The feebleness of these explanations is evident the moment they are examined. For starters, they clearly ignore those manifestations of antisemitism that have little bearing on Israel's actions. The main themes of the antisemitic outpouring that accompanied Jeremy Corbyn's leadership had little bearing on Israeli actions or behaviour, focusing on these choice ideas: Jews have fabricated the Holocaust; they used to dominate the slave trade; the Rothschilds control the banking system and the global media; Jews are the drivers of a capitalist establishment which oppresses the working class for their own selfish ends; Jews are more loyal to Israel than to their own country and world leaders are puppets in the hands of their Jewish taskmasters. When attacks were made on Israel, it was often through deranged conspiracy theories, such as the notion that Israel planned the 9/11 attacks, that Jews and Israelis were part of a covert plot to infect the world with the Covid pandemic and that the Israel lobby or Mossad created ISIS to carry out false flag attacks. Views like this are part of an obsessional, unappeasable hatred that is impervious to any change in Israeli state policy.

The second problem with this 'Israel causes antisemitism' argument is that it is based on the false assumption that coverage about Israel is always fair, objective and unbiased. On the contrary, such reporting is scarcely an accurate barometer of Israel's character and conduct, especially during war. It is often sensationalistic, one sided and inflammatory, regurgitating Arab lies about Israel while ignoring the context for Israeli actions. One of the most egregious examples came in 2002 when much of the world's media swallowed whole the idea that Israel had carried out a massacre in the Jenin refugee camp. Many journalists who visit the West Bank and Gaza are convinced that Israel is a colonialist oppressor which subjugates innocent Palestinians, completely whitewashing the role of Fatah and Hamas.[38] Not surprisingly, much of their inaccurate reporting flows from this initial assumption.

Those who blame Israel for antisemitism make a third mistake by denying the moral agency of the perpetrators. They suggest that antisemitic crimes are an inevitable consequence of Israeli actions, a perverse view which depicts racists as automata acting without thought or reflection. It fetishizes the perpetrators, especially when they are Palestinians or Muslims, and denudes them of moral agency. It depicts the antisemites as puppets on a string, driven by political lusts over which they have no control and denies to them the capacity to make the sort of moral choices which are open to others. In short, it is a form of old-style colonial prejudice masquerading as progressive politics. There is of course a range of choices open to those who violently disagree with Israeli policy. They can protest Israeli behaviour in a democratic fashion, which is the right of any politically concerned citizen. They can write to their legislators, engage in demonstrations and launch petitions if they so wish. Attacking Jews is a choice

[38] For a fuller discussion about the complicity of the media in promoting a twisted version of the conflict, read Stephanie Gutmann's *The Other War: Israelis, Palestinians and the Struggle for Media Supremacy* (New York: Encounter Books, 2005).

born of prejudice, the warped actions of an agent who holds Jews accountable for the actions of Israel, which is itself an antisemitic judgment. Those who deny this fact are engaging in a morally obnoxious, anti-intellectual form of victim blaming. David Hirsh puts it well when he says that, 'other racisms are not normally analyzed by antiracists in terms of what it is that the victims of those racisms are doing to make people hate them.'[39]

Denial 8 – Jews as oppressors fallacy: Another form of denial pictures Jews as a sub-group of white people who share in the power and economic privilege of the wider establishment. This means that instead of being victims of racism, they are more likely to be seen as its progenitors, with Jews accused of reproducing the oppression of minorities that can be found in other western societies. This has come about because the way that racism is defined has undergone a seismic change in recent decades. Instead of seeing racism as a system of prejudice and discrimination directed towards members of a racial or ethnic group (a standard definition), it has come to be defined in terms of 'prejudice plus power.' In essence, racism is seen in terms of institutional webs of discriminatory power and the structural oppression of minorities/people of colour carried out by white people who dominate the societies of the 'Global North.' Much of modern identity politics and woke ideology finds manifestations of racial discrimination in immigration and asylum policy, anti-terror legislation, police brutality and misconduct as well as unequal outcomes in health and educational disparities. The only true racists are depicted as those who run these systems of racial inequality.

In one textbook on social justice from 1997, racism is defined as 'The systematic subordination of members of targeted racial groups who have relatively little social power in the United States (Blacks, Latino/as, Native Americans, and Asians), by the members of the agent racial group who have relatively more social power (Whites).'[40] Van Soest and Garcia see racism as 'a socio-political phenomenon that is characterized by social power.' They add: 'When discrimination is buttressed by social power it represents racism and oppression.'[41] Elsewhere, Beverly Tatum has stated that 'racism, like other forms of oppression, is not only a personal ideology based on racial prejudice, but a system involving cultural messages and institutional policies and practices as well as the beliefs and actions of individuals.' In one passage, she is explicit that if racism is seen as 'a system of advantage based on race,' then people of colour 'are not racist because they do not systemically benefit from racism' and 'there is no systematic cultural and institutional support or sanction for the racial bigotry of

---

[39] Hirsh, *Contemporary Left Antisemitism*, 204.
[40] Pat Griffin, Barbara Love and Charmaine Wijeysinghe, "Racism Curriculum Design," in *Teaching for diversity and social justice: A Sourcebook*, ed. Maurianne Adams, Lee Anne Bell and Pat Griffin (New York: Routledge, 1997), 88-89.
[41] Betty Garcia and Dorothy Van Soest, *Diversity Education for Social Justice: Mastering Teaching Skills*, (Virginia: Council on Social Work Education, 2008), 32-3.

people of color.'[42] She does acknowledge that people of colour can hold racist views but reserves the term racism for the behaviour of white people in the context of a white dominated society, simply because it is the best way of accepting the 'differential afforded Whites by the culture and institutions' of their society.

Similar assumptions are made in the modern manuals of critical race theory from such authors as Renni Eddo Lodge (*Why I am no longer Talking with White People about Race*) and Robin di Angelo (*White Fragility*). All assume that white people have privilege from being dominant within western societies and therefore have 'complicity in systemic racism.'[43] Those who disagree are simply in denial about the existence of systematic oppression and its effects within society. Similarly, Di Angelo argues that when white people disagree with her thesis, exhibiting emotions such as anger, fear or guilt, they display white fragility, a sign of weakness which results from their socialization through privilege and, in itself, a form of complicity in racism. Put simply, those who have power cannot be victims of racism but nor can the powerless be racist.[44]

Much of this reflects applied postmodern thinking which has always stressed the interplay between knowledge, language and power. Another key element here is standpoint theory, the concept that knowledge is dictated by one's position in a social hierarchy and that the subjective perspectives of minority groups give them insight not afforded to privileged and dominant groups in society.[45] This form of political positioning disregards rational, intellectual arguments made by people in favour of a judgment based on their immutable characteristics. These characteristics are one's skin colour, sexual orientation or genitalia and people are placed on a hierarchy of victimhood depending on which of those characteristics they possess.

In the words of one author, 'black beats white, woman beats man, trans beats cisgender, and gay...beats straight,' though a more recent mutation of identity politics has altered the rules so that 'Trans beats gay and Muslim beats black.'[46] The notion of disadvantaged groups showing solidarity with each other has been replaced with an Olympics of victimhood in which individuals are forced to acknowledge their relative privilege and place themselves correctly on an imagined pedestal of suffering. Moreover, identity politics toxifies whiteness and

---

[42] Beverly Tatum, *Why Are All the Black Kids Sitting Together in the Cafeteria? and Other Conversations About Race*, (New York: Basic Books, 2003).

[43] Barbara Applebaum, *Being White, Being Good: White Complicity, White Moral Responsibility, and Social Justice Pedagogy* (Minneapolis: Lexington Books, 2010), 31.

[44] John McWhorter, "The Dehumanizing Condescension of *White Fragility*," *The Atlantic*, July 15, 2020.

[45] James Lindsay and Helen Pluckrose, *Cynical Theories: How Activist Scholarship Made Everything About Race, Gender, and Identity - and Why This Harms Everybody* (London: Swift Press, 2020), 194.

[46] James Kirchick, "Rock, Paper, Scissors of PC Victimology," *Tabletmag*, February 26, 2015.

white cultural and political institutions, seeing the latter as irredeemably tainted by past racism and the exploitation of vulnerable, colonialized subjects.

Jews have not fared well from this modern trend. As a result of their assimilation and relatively high educational and economic status in western societies, they have come to be seen as essentially white. As such, they are deemed to possess 'white privilege' as much as any non-Jewish white person. Moreover, their purported association with wealth and power has led others to view Jews as part of a dominant establishment that is responsible for oppressing other minorities. The anti-colonialism inherent in the world of modern social justice scholarship has added another dimension to such racialized thinking. If colonialism is essentially about white racial dominance over people of colour, and if Israel is a colonialist power, indeed the world's last colonialist power, then Jews, who largely support Israel, are complicit in the oppression and subjugation of a racial minority. They are the chief bastions in the prolongation of a state that oppresses people of colour and which stands as one of the symbols of black protest against powerful white elites. For this reason, they cannot complain of antisemitism from the perspective of the powerful (they will be accused of manufacturing it anyway) and must be opposed *in the name of anti-racism*. This is, as one writer puts it, 'a form of antisemitism that denies its own existence.'[47]

The only way for Jews (and other groups) to respond to this twisted, anti-intellectualism is through a full throttled assault on its very foundations. They should treat social justice politics, especially its racial variant, as a flawed approach to understanding race relations. While it is important to understand how structural inequalities can arise from unjust systems of power, it makes no sense to think that only those with power can be racist. The logical extreme of such a view would be to hold that Adolf Hitler, while a mere orator on German streets, could not have been a racist. A powerless person filled with prejudice is still a racist. Secondly, Jews need to make it clear that their 'whiteness' is a matter of debate. A significant percentage of Jews who have come from the Middle East and Africa have darker shades of skin and so hardly count as white. But even Jews deemed to be white still experience the very worst forms of dehumanising racism and toxic bigotry, none more so than the victims of neo-Nazi and far right rampages. More importantly, the notion that racism only affects the poor, disadvantaged and disempowered falls apart the moment one starts examining it. Throughout history, the Jews who were subjected to pogrom, massacre, incitement and prejudice came from a variety of economic classes and rich and well-connected Jews were not spared from extermination under Nazi rule. Racism therefore simply cannot be understood in terms of a simplistic formula of power and prejudice.

Denial 9 – Muslim antisemitism denial: There is a particular form of denial attached to antisemitic acts carried out by members of the Muslim faith. When

---

[47] Philip Spencer, "Jews Behaving Badly," in *Looking for an Enemy: 8 Essays on Antisemitism*, ed. Jo Glanville (London: Short Books, 2021), 117.

Mohamed Merah carried out the killing of a Jewish school principal and three children at a school in Toulouse in 2012, mainstream commentators were at pains to explain the atrocity by reference to the killer's personal issues. For Tariq Ramadan, Merah was merely a 'French citizen frustrated at being unable to find his place' and 'young man adrift, imbued neither with the values of Islam, nor driven by racism and antisemitism.' Merah had been marginalized by society, a man without 'equality, dignity, security, a decent job and a place to live' and the 'victim of a social order that had already doomed him.'[48] For Stop the War's Lindsay German, the killings represented the 'terrible and disastrous outcome of the West's war policies and anti-Muslim racism.' Some French politicians blamed the immigration policies of the government while some other Western outlets provided analysis without mentioning antisemitism at all. The fact that Merah admitted to being an Islamist 'warrior' and that he had trained with Al-Qaeda, a terror group whose entire worldview was shot through with the most virulent antisemitic prejudice, was of no consequence to these apologists.

When a crazed Islamist killer went on the rampage in a Parisian kosher deli, President Obama responded by condemning 'a bunch of violent, vicious zealots who behead people or randomly shoot a bunch of folks.'[49] But there was nothing random about the victims for as the killer admitted at the time, the four people he killed inside the shop were targeted 'because they were Jewish.' In the aftermath of the killing of Ilan Halimi, there were multiple complaints about the police, in particular their assumption that the kidnappers and killers of the young Jewish Frenchmen were merely bandits motivated by money rather than antisemites hunting their prey. The EU has gone overboard to self-censor when confronted by the results of its own findings that a majority of antisemitic attacks on the continent are carried out by Muslim migrants. Thus, in the study called 'Manifestations of antisemitism in the EU 2002-03,' undertaken through the European Monitoring Centre on Racism and Xenophobia, mention of Muslim involvement in racist attacks was reportedly censored. This was confirmed in a roundtable conversation held in Brussels between the author and Katharina von Schnurbein, the first European Commission Coordinator on combating antisemitism.

Instead, the notion that Muslims are to be sacralized as victims has been reinforced by thinking of them as 'the new Jews.' According to Krishan Kumar, 'they have become the new 'other' of Europe, replacing the Jews of an earlier era.' Political scientist Amikam Nachmani has talked of the 'strong parallel...between Europe's Jewish question and its mirror image, the Muslim migrant question.'[50] India Knight, writing in the *Sunday Times*, has declared that

[48] Tariq Ramadan, "The lesson of Mohamed Merah," abc.net, March 23, 2012, https://www.abc.net.au/religion/the-lesson-of-mohamed-merah/10100692
[49] "Legitimate Concern When Zealots Randomly Shoot Folks in a Deli in Paris, Says Obama," *Haaretz*, February 10, 2015.
[50] Chad Alan Goldberg, "Have Muslims Replaced Jews as the Other of the Twenty-First Century?" Public Seminar.org, June 19, 2017.

it is 'open season on Islam' and that 'Muslims are the new Jews,' a view shared by Yasmin Alibhai and others.[51] Author and former advisor to Bill Clinton, Naomi Wolf, declared that Muslims were 'the new Jews' and that the 'violent rhetoric' of the anti-Muslim campaigning of President Trump felt 'like 1933.'[52] For another writer in *The Morning Star*, Islamophobia 'is the Jewish question of our day.'[53] What these views get wrong is not that there exists a virulent level of prejudice towards Muslims or that anti-Muslim stereotypes and canards exist; undoubtedly, they both do. What is wrong is the assumption that instead of looking for parallels between both prejudices, antisemitism and Jews are now to be replaced from anti-racist consciousness with hatred of Muslims.

There might be several motives for this refusal to correctly label these killers as 'Muslim antisemites.' One is an understandable concern to avoid instigating attacks on Muslims, the majority of whom are innocent, law abiding and patriotic. For attacks on Jews to be met with reciprocal attacks on Muslims or their communal property would indeed be reprehensible and it is right that governments do all they can to avoid this. The second motive, which also explains the refusal to believe that Islamist terror attacks spring from any interpretation of Islam, is political correctness. This can be summed up as a refusal to attribute negative motives or intent to members of an ethnic minority which is also beset with racism. When transplanted to the Middle East, Palestinian Muslim actors are seen purely as victims of a more powerful, colonial state, a factor which denies them moral responsibility for their actions. This refusal by (largely) white liberals to accept the real factors driving radicalized Muslims, replacing their stated motivations with a whitewashed veneer of respectability, is a form of latter-day colonialism. It imposes a mindset of tolerance on people who do not share such values, all so as to make liberal progressives feel better.

Instead, the truth must be told about Islamic antisemitism. It is that Muslims can be both victims *and* progenitors of racism. A significant percentage within the global Islamic community articulate a vision of radicalized Islam that is vehemently anti-Western, sexist, homophobic and authoritarian in its thinking, and which regards a jihad against the Jews as a supreme virtue. A larger number of non-radicalized Muslims has shown a predilection for antisemitic conspiracy thinking and extreme anti-Zionist lies. As a result, antisemitism is a major problem in many Muslim societies, both in the Middle East and beyond. One can acknowledge all this while also railing against anti-Muslim hatred and standing with moderate Muslims who oppose hatred in all its forms.

Denial 10 – Soft Holocaust denial: A final form of antisemitism denial involves the de-Judaization of the Holocaust which can also be termed soft-core Holocaust denial. This is not the same thing as denying the Holocaust which is a

---

[51] "Reasons why Muslims are not 'the new Jews'," *The Jewish Chronicle*, February 18, 2016.
[52] Mark Nuckols, "No, Naomi Wolf, America Is Not Becoming a Fascist State," *The Atlantic*, January 9, 2013.
[53] Rich, *The Left's Jewish Problem*, 210.

blatant attempt to deny the facts of history. Rather, it is a more subtle attempt to de-emphasize the Jewish element of the genocide by speaking instead of its 'victims.' A disturbing example of this trend occurred in 2017 when the White House issued a statement on Holocaust Remembrance Day that, instead of mentioning either Jews or antisemitism, spoke instead of 'innocent victims.' The justification, according to White House director of strategic communications Hope Hicks, was that the administration 'took into account all of those who suffered' and that they were 'an incredibly inclusive group.'[54] The problem was not that the Jews were the only people who suffered under the Nazis. Millions of people, including Jehovah's witnesses, Roma, gay people and mentally disabled were indeed murdered at the hands of the Nazis. Their suffering must be remembered in any memorialising of Nazism's evil upon humanity. But they were not murdered as part of an industrialized, scientific organised, state sponsored policy of total annihilation like the Jews. Moreover, the assault on Jews was not geographically limited in extent and would have been applied to the entire earth if the Nazis had conquered the globe. For this reason, the Holocaust should be referred to as the Jewish tragedy.[55]

Related to the de-Judaizing of the Holocaust are the persistent attempts to trivialize it, something that Deborah Lipstadt has termed 'soft core denial.' In 2019 Alexandra Ocasio-Cortez slated the policies of the Trump administration and declared: 'The US is running concentration camps on our southern border, and that is exactly what they are… If that doesn't bother you…I want to talk to the people that are concerned enough with humanity to say that "never again" means something.'[56] Ocasio-Cortez received a verbal barrage of criticism but chose to double down on her remarks, insisting that there was a difference between death camps and concentration camps and that the mass incarceration of children in cages made the analogy appropriate. She added: 'I will never apologize for calling these camps what they are. If that makes you uncomfortable, fight the camps - not the nomenclature.'[57] Yet her senseless comparison made it easy for her opponents, many of whom were indeed blind to the deep problems with the migrant policy, to focus on her language instead. Her comments were thus strategically foolish and self-defeating. A simple glance at a history book would have told Ocasio-Cortez that concentration camps were more than just centres of incarceration. They were an intrinsic part of a system of institutionalized mass murder, within which people were tortured horrifically, starved, abused and

[54] Alan Yuhas, "White House defends Trump Holocaust statement that didn't mention Jews," *The Guardian*, January 29, 2017.
[55] For a fuller discussion, see Katz, Steven. "The 'Unique' Intentionality of the Holocaust." *Modern Judaism* 1, no. 2 (1981): 161–83.
[56] Mark Moore, "AOC claims US is putting 'concentration camps' on border," *New York Post*, June 18, 2019.
[57] Emily Goodin, "I will NEVER apologize for saying Trump is building 'concentration camps' on the Mexican border says AOC after Republicans step up attacks on her Holocaust 'slur'," *Daily Mail*, June 19, 2019.

summarily executed – all on account of their ethnic origin. America clearly has no such policy of mass murder, even if its immigration policy is highly questionable.[58]

The same applies to the CNN anchor Christiane Amanpour and her own distortion of the historical record. In a show in 2020 on the anniversary of Kristallnacht, she made the following statement: 'This week 82 years ago, Kristallnacht happened. It was the Nazis' warning shot across the bow of our human civilization that led to genocide against a whole identity and, in that tower of burning books, it led to an attack on fact, knowledge, history and proof.' She then added: 'After four years of a modern-day assault on those same values by Donald Trump, the Biden-Harris team pledges a return to normal.' Unlike Ocasio-Cortez, Amanpour did express contrition for her remarks, though only after a barrage of condemnation from Jewish groups.[59]

The Holocaust and Nazi barbarity are regularly invoked by animal rights activists and anti-abortion campaigners, by those condemning outrages against ethnic groups and by the gun lobby in America in response to legislation to outlaw weapons. Invoking the genocide against the Jews, and the hatred that gave rise to it, to explain contemporary developments represents an egregious attack on Holocaust memory and an attempt to render Nazi crimes less serious than they ultimately were. Without denying the seriousness of Trump's policies towards migrant children or attacks on democracy or animal rights cruelty, the obvious rejoinder is simple: attack your enemies on their own terms rather than engage in gratuitously offensive and crass hyperbole.

When de-Judaising the Holocaust, the events become a symbol of universal misery. Every form of suffering to any ethnic group is designated in the same way, with talk of a 'black Holocaust,' an 'Indian Holocaust' and a 'Palestinian Holocaust.' This desire to expand the Holocaust to all manner of non-genocidal violence and injustice, whether in the form of slavery, famine, war or racism, reflects a deep standing utilitarian view of pain and adversity. This philosophical approach takes all human suffering to be evil, regardless of how it was perpetrated, and thus views the Holocaust as merely one particular instantiation of evil carried out by one group to another. Just take the twentieth century as an example. The reasoning goes that while 6 million Jews suffered during the Second World War, far greater numbers have perished since, including prisoners of war, victims of slavery, casualties of Allied bombing and the innocent victims of war. To have one Holocaust day to remember Jewish suffering would be to falsely prioritise one set of victims and one example of human misery over that of others. It would be to suggest a sectarian approach to suffering, that 6 million dead Jews matter more than 25 million dead Russians or countless millions of dead Africans who perished in the slave trade or the millions murdered in Rwanda or Cambodia.

---

[58] Marc LiVecche, "AOC's Holocaust Comparisons Are Stupid and Self-defeating – but Revealing as well," *Providencemag*, July 2, 2019, https://providencemag.com /.../holocaust-comparisons-stupid-self-defeating.

[59] Matt Matthers, "CNN Anchor says she regrets comparing Trump Presidency to Nazi's Night of Broken Glass," *The Independent*, November 18, 2020.

Attacks on the Jews for 'appropriating' genocide memory reflect 'Holocaust envy,' a belief that Jews and Zionists have monopolized the world's sympathy for their own suffering and have effectively stolen from others their 'right' to garner such sympathy for their own causes.

Yet the Holocaust was not merely part of the lamentable catalogue of evils carried out by one government against civilians. It was a unique example of the crime of racial genocide, the attempt by a government for the first time in history to wipe out all the members of a minority group for no other reason than that they were members of that group. It was not just a mass killing but an ideological project for racial extinction, wholly unique in human history. Reflecting on the enormity of this crime allows a subsequent generation to reflect on the horror of racial supremacism and the prejudices that allowed it to flourish. The Holocaust was a Jewish tragedy then, though it is also the case that other victims of Nazi mass murder are usually (and rightly) remembered during commemorative services.

Taken together, these forms of denial are themselves part and parcel of the antisemitism problem. They suggest that Jews are malicious fabricators of their own persecution, inventing claims of racism in order to promulgate insidious political or economic agendas. Such dangerous viewpoints merely reinforce a key stereotype of the Jew as a deceitful, tricksy and manipulative creature that cannot be trusted by the Gentile world.

Chapter Two

Antisemitism: the tropes of the world's oldest hatred

Antisemitism is thus seen to be at bottom a form of Manichaeism.
It explains the course of the world by the struggle of the
principle of Good with the principle of Evil.

Sartre, Anti-Semite and Jew

The demonization of the Jew has been a central feature of antisemitic thinking for more than two millennia, stretching from pagan times to the birth of Christianity, and from the Middle Ages to modernity. Every age has witnessed an ugly outpouring of hate against the Jewish people, with the outbreaks varying in extent and lethality, but each with an unmistakeable viciousness and intensity. Over two millennia, the charge sheet against Jews could hardly be more grave.

Let us summarise the lethal calumnies hurled in their direction: Jews have murdered God's son and shown unrelenting hostility to his faith; they are the enemies of God, the allies of the anti-Christ and desecrators of the new Christian faith; they are the devil made flesh, the allies of Satan and the poisoners and corrupters of all mankind; they have tried to thwart the prophet of Islam and shown enmity to all its co-religionists for a millennium and a half; they are insidious child killers who use the blood of innocents for sadistic, ritual amusement and they poison wells to attack their neighbours; they are eternal liars who debase the countries they live in for their own ends; they foment wars and international crises to pursue their own desire for power and money, inventing proxies to do their bidding; they are fifth columnists, detached from but willing to exploit every country they live in while falsely parading their patriotism; they are avaricious, insular, merciless and cunning.

All these charges are amply supported by a vast outpouring of literature, whether in the form of plays, novels, treatises, newspapers or pamphlets, as well as other forms of popular culture. Taken together, these calumnious condemnations have provided a rich cultural underpinning for centuries of gentile antisemitism, for waves of persecution that have deracinated Jewish communities in one land after another and for the unbridled hostility of vast numbers of novelists, cartoonists, poets, artists, academics, journalists, filmmakers, politicians and musicians. Indeed, there is probably no cultural form in which antisemitism has not found the deepest and most resonant expression through the ages. Summarising this charge sheet, it is possible to identify at least nine core tropes of antisemitism, all of which, in modified form, remain with us today.

1) The Jew as God killer.
2) The Jew as devil and beast.
3) The Jew as ritual murderer.
4) The Jew as disloyal.
5) The Jew as vengeful and chosen.
6) The Jew as avaricious.
7) The Jew as racial parasite.
8) The Jew as conspiring.
9) The Jew as a mendacious threat to Islam.

These constitute what I will call the 'archetypal antisemitic perspective,' a framework of understanding that sees Jews as fundamentally different to non-Jews, as a harmful, noxious and malign collective that arouses suspicion, fear, revulsion and hatred and for which the ultimate remedy is elimination.[1] The archetypal antisemitic perspective has produced ideological tropes against Jews, ones which, in turn, have yielded negative feelings that have gone on to 'outlive for generations the situations which (gave) birth to them.'[2] Each trope will be examined in turn.

The Jew As God Killer

The foundational trope of western antisemitism is the myth of deicide, an idea nearly as old as the Christian religion itself. It was the accusation that did the gravest damage to the Jewish people and the one which, more than any other, was 'apt to put the Jew outside the human pale' and prepare 'the ground for his moral defamation.'[3] In the decades following Jesus' death, a narrative was developed by Christian writers, theologians and polemicists which focused on the Jews' rejection of God's son, their collective responsibility for his death and their identity as an eternally apostate nation. Before the Gospels, the writings of the apostle Paul (the real founder of Christianity) bristle with anger and hostility at alleged Jewish animosity towards Christians. In *Thessalonians*, he spoke of the suffering that his religionists had endured 'from the Jews who killed both the Lord Jesus and the prophets.' These same Jews were 'enemies of their fellow men' who were 'hindering us from speaking to the Gentiles to lead them to salvation.' Here

---

[1] Elimination can take many forms, from eliminating their presence in society through ghettoization and severe social restriction, to forced conversion (so that Jews are transformed into a different religious entity) to physical expulsion and ethnic cleansing and finally, mass murder.

[2] Leon Poliakov, *The History of Antisemitism III: From Voltaire to Wagner* (Philadelphia: The University of Pennsylvania Press, 2003), 18.

[3] Jacob Katz, *From Prejudice to Destruction: Antisemitism, 1700-1933* (Cambridge: Harvard University Press, 1980), 116.

one finds the charge of deicide against collective Jewry, the demonization of Jews as humanity's enemy and the allegation that Jews have malicious designs against Christians and their faith. But what Paul also ushered in was the idea that the new Christian faith had superseded Judaism, that Christians were the 'new Israel' offering the only route to salvation and, more importantly, that Jews had to convert to this new faith in order to save themselves from the horrifying prospect of eternal damnation.

In the Gospel according to Matthew, the Jewish crowd bay for the blood of Christ and demand: 'Let him be crucified.' In one of the most insidious passages in the New Testament, they are quoted as saying: 'His blood be on us and on our children.' Pilate, unable to pacify this crowd, abjures responsibility for his fate and turns him over to the 'bloodthirsty' Jews. The passage makes clear that the Jews are eternally responsible for Jesus' death, not just at that fateful moment but in every future generation. They also reject the offer of eternal salvation represented by the Crucifixion and resurrection. In the Gospel according to John, a similar narrative emerges that demonizes the collective Jew. He too says that Jews demand that Jesus be put to death over and above Pilate's repeated entreaties for clemency and mercy. As with Matthew, John depicts the Jews as unyielding in their hostility to Jesus and holds them collectively responsible for his death.

Michael Cohen, a noted scholar of Christian antisemitism, is right to argue that the four Gospels 'bequeathed to the next generations of Christians an image of the Jew as the murderous enemy.' It was also a wildly inaccurate picture that barely survives scrutiny when examining the historical record. Contemporary historians depict Pilate as a hardened character who was determined to affirm the might and power of Roman rule and who would not have submitted meekly to the demands of others. If it is true that he rejected Jesus' guilt, as when he told the Jewish religious leaders that 'I find no basis for a charge against him' (John 19:4) and that he had the power to release him, it seems odd that such a strong and determined leader would allow others to subvert his judgment.

Early in the fourth century AD, the Roman Emperor Constantine was spurred to convert to Christianity after claiming to see the imprint of a cross in the sky, together with the words 'With this sign you shall conquer.' His patronage of the Church was a turning point in Christian-Jewish relations. The Jews were a conspicuous minority, educated and relatively wealthy, who stood out for their stubborn rejection of Christian dogma. It was the Nicene Creed, laid down in 325 following a challenge by an Alexandrian cleric, Arius, that solidified the charge of deicide against the Jews. It clarified the divinity of Jesus, declaring him consubstantial and the equal of God the Father, while setting out that the Jews had crucified 'Jesus Christ, the Word of God, God from God, Light of the Light, Life of Life, the only begotten Son, First born of all Creation.' For good measure, the Passover festival was banned and replaced by Easter, while keeping the Sabbath was condemned. As Constantine, the first Roman emperor to convert to Christianity put it: 'It is unbecoming beyond measure that on this, the most sacred of festivals, we should follow the custom of the Jews.' The Jews were outlawed as 'parricides and the murderers of our Lord.'

Later Christian writers would only go on to develop this theme of eternal Jewish responsibility for the death of God's son. Thus, the Christian writer Origen took up the theme of eternal Jewish responsibility for Christ's death when he wrote: 'Guilt for the blood of Jesus fell not only on those who lived then, but also on all subsequent generations of Jews, until the end of the world.'[4] Writing in the fourth century, the preacher John Chrysostom condemned 'the Christ killers' for denigrating the new faith, ridiculing God and rejecting the Holy Spirit. For Chrysostom, denigrating Judaism and the Jews (with their 'impiety' and 'madness') went hand in hand with affirming the truth of Christianity. 'If the Jewish rites are holy and venerable, our way of life must be false. But if our way is true, as indeed it is, theirs is fraudulent.' Similar fears were felt by St Jerome whose denunciation of the synagogue as worse than 'a brothel,' 'a den of vice' and 'the Devil's refuge' was bitter and vicious.[5] For Chrysostom and St Jerome, this was the crux: Judaism was a palpable affront to the new faith and had to be demonized so as to demonstrate the relevance of Christianity.

Similar invective fills the pages of Bishop Melito of Sardis in his 2nd century homily *Peri Pascha* (On the Passover). He too decides that Jewry as a collective murdered God in Jerusalem (with no mention of Pilate) and, as a result, 'dishonoured,' 'disgraced' and 'denied' him. Melito links the killing of Christ to the suffering of Jews in subsequent centuries, including their exile from the land of Israel. Indeed, in replacement theology, the Jewish rejection of Christ led God to repudiate the Jews as his chosen people, replacing them with the new Christian nation of Israel. Then there are the repugnant and obsessive calumnies hurled at Jews by Church Father Gregory of Nyssa. He described Jews as 'companions of the devil' and a 'race of vipers, informers, calumniators, darkeners of the mind' and 'a Sanhedrin of demons.'[6] In one of his hymns on unleavened bread, St Ephrem the Syrian railed against 'People with blood spattered hands' whose hands 'killed the Son.' The hands of the Jews were, he wrote, 'defiled with precious blood' and 'with the prophets' blood.'[7]

The venomous demonization of the Jew found its sharpest expression in the writings of St Augustine, the most influential thinker in early Christian theology. He too disparaged the notion that Pilate killed Christ, insisting that the Jews had to accept responsibility for their evil deed. He likened them to Cain, the murderer of his own brother Abel, and a man condemned to wonder the world in shame because of an ignominious act of fratricide. Augustine pictured the Jews as a blind and error strewn people who carried a murderous mark on their collective body and for whom redemption was possible only by turning to Christ at the Last Judgment. Just as Cain was turned into an outcast for his crimes, so too Augustine

---

[4] Jeremy Cohen, *Christ Killers: The Jews and the Passion from the Bible to the Big Screen* (Oxford: Oxford University Press, 2007), 32.

[5] Robert Wistrich, *The Longest Hatred* (London: Thames Methuen, 1991), 17.

[6] Schoenfeld, *The Return of Antisemitism*, 34.

[7] St Ephrem, *Three Hymns on Unleavened Bread* (translated from the edition of Beck, 1964), Hymn XVII.

believed that the Jews had to suffer permanent exile as a mark of condemnation for their sins.[8]

Not surprisingly, what followed from the demonization of the Jews was legislation designed to turn them into social outcasts who lived at the mercy of their rulers. Thanks to the laws of Constantine in the fourth century, the Latin Codex Theodosianus from 438 and the Justinian Code of 534, the rights of the Jews under Christian rule steadily deteriorated. Constantine forbade the Jews from proselytizing; he outlawed intermarriage and forbade Jews from owning slaves. Under the law of Theodosius, all manner of indignities were imposed on Jews, including preventing them from building synagogues and holding prestigious public positions. Under Justinian, Jews could not serve as witnesses in courts of law. The compulsory baptism of the Jews was a feature of life under Spain's Visigothic Church and compulsory conversion was occasionally perpetrated in the Frankish Kingdom. Over several centuries, Jews had been rendered second class citizens and such ill treatment would echo through the following centuries in Christian Europe.

Associated with the Christian belief that Jews were eternally guilty for Jesus' death was the legend of the Wandering Jew. The legend revolved around an alleged encounter that took place as Christ was making his way to Calvary bearing the cross. Stopping to rest on a man's doorstep, its owner (a Jew), taunted him by saying 'Walk faster.' Christ was led to respond: 'I go, but you will walk until I come again.' The Wandering Jew was born, a nameless, hapless figure who was cursed to walk the earth until the Second Coming. The figure cemented its place in literature, appearing in a German book called *A Short Description and History of a Jew Named Ahasuerus* (1602) and some years later in a French lyrical lament. It spawned folk renditions from the seventeenth century, not all of which related to Jews or their historical trajectory, though the figure of Ahasuerus was sometimes portrayed in antisemitic terms. A classic exposition of the Wandering Jew appeared in the antisemitic tract *Sur les juifs*, written by the French counter-revolutionary philosopher Louis de Bonald. He wrote of how the Jews, when they failed to recognise Jesus as their saviour, were 'dispersed throughout the whole world,' unable to combine with the nations and remaining 'always a stranger' and 'a people without power.'[9]

Certainly, there were periods of time when life for Jews in Christian Europe was much more tolerable. One example was under the Carolingian State when the Holy Roman Emperor Charlemagne and later his son, Louis the Pious, ensured that Jews had equal juridical rights as well as letters of protection. Many Jews were highly respected for their mercantile skills as well as their expertise in medicine and there were possibilities for integration. Jews could also practise their faith in the pre medieval period, the only non-Christian group thus tolerated. But

---

[8] For further reading, see: David Turner, "Foundations of antisemitism: Augustine and Christian Triumphalism," *The Jerusalem Post*, August 2, 2012.

[9] Katz, *From Prejudice to Destruction*, 115.

these periods of relative tolerance co-existed with a toxic and bitter legacy of theological hatred whose ramifications would resonate down the centuries and culminate in twentieth century mass murder.

For the record, Christianity has undergone a reformation and a move away from Biblical literalism towards a greater accommodation with other faiths. This includes greater tolerance towards Jews and Judaism and a willingness to overturn centuries of orthodoxy about Jewish responsibility for Christ's death. Thus, in 1965, the Vatican promulgated *Nostra Aetate: A Declaration on the Relationship of the Church to Non-Christian Religions*, a turning point in relations between the Church and the Jews. The declaration clarified that 'What happened in (Christ's passion) cannot be charged against all Jews, without distinction, then alive, nor against the Jews of today.' It also made clear that there could be no moral justification for the view that Jews were an accursed nation that had been rejected by God. But this should not gloss over the fact that the historical antecedents of modern Jew hatred reside, at least in part, in the foundational religious texts of the Christian faith. Deicide is the starting point of the archetypal antisemitic perspective.[10]

The Jew As Devil And Beast

For several centuries, Jews were seen as a benighted people whose ignorance blinded them to the truth about Jesus. Their blind faith came to be symbolized through the medieval iconography of a blind woman who stumbled around in the dark because of her ignorance. The Jews were not a people who had knowingly put their Lord on the Cross. It was in the twelfth and thirteenth centuries that commentators began to depart from this line. In the writings of Franciscan and Dominican theologians, including such venerated figures as Dons Scotus and St Thomas Aquinas, passages from the New Testament are invoked to argue that, far from being blind to Jesus' divinity, the Jews knew perfectly well that he was the messiah and were thus wilfully perfidious in their rejection. For these Christians, the violent repudiation of Christ was no intellectual error. Instead, it stemmed from the Jews' stubborn refusal to acknowledge the truth of the scripture and their unforgivable and unrelenting recalcitrance. The only explanation was that they were a less than human population living among Christians, and that the devil had implanted his evil into their willing ears.

The height of Christian hostility towards Jews was reached during the Middle Ages, a period up to and including the Renaissance in which the church was forced to confront the rise of Islam and deal with heretical challenges to the faith from within. The quest for ideological unity meant that Jews, viewed as the prime heretic and chief renegade within its European citadels, was the subject of

---

[10] Sadly, the belief in Jewish deicide remains alive among millions of people in 'progressive' Europe. The results of a 2012 ADL poll showed that 18% of Austrians 14% of Germans, 38% of Hungarians and 46% of Poles agreed with the statement that Jews are eternally responsible for the death of Christ.

hostility, suspicion and revulsion. During this period, Jews were depicted as a source of cosmic evil, as the agents of Satan and as the progenitors of misfortune. They were, quite literally, viewed as the devil made flesh. They were conceived as 'the abomination of abominations, the root and branch of all dissent...the adversary without peer of Christendom.'[11] The Jew was seen as a figure from whose every pore flowed a bilious torrent of anti-Christian hatred and resentment. Johann Eck summed up his denunciation of Jews by writing: 'Could they but drown all Christians in one spoon, they would eagerly do it.'[12] There are many Christian references to the devilish nature of the Jew, from John speaking of their 'father the devil' to the Book of Revelation referring to 'the synagogue of Satan,' from Chrysostom insisting that Jews sacrificed their sons and daughters to Devils' to Hilary of Poitiers arguing that Jews were 'possessed of an unclean devil.'[13]

Medieval literature too was unsparing in its contempt and hostility for Jews, painting them as figures of unbridled villainy, the fount of all sin and the progenitor of unspeakable crimes against the Church. In the Prioress' Tale, Chaucer blames the Jews for the death of a Christian child, writing 'our firste fo, the Serpent Sathanas, that hath in Jewes herte his waspes nest.' In *The Merchant of Venice*, Shakespeare's Shylock is referred to as 'a kind of devil,' as 'a cruel devil' and as 'the devil in the likeness of a Jew.' Turning to religious literature, Luther referred once to Jews as 'venomous, bitter, vindictive, tricky serpents, assassins, and children of the devil.'[14] He was backed in his view by Peter of Cluny, a religious leader for whom the Jew was no better than 'a brute beast.'[15] The great scholar of medieval antisemitism, Joshua Trachtenberg, wrote that medieval allusions to the Jew left an impression of 'a hatred so vast and abysmal, so intense, that it leaves one gasping for comprehension.'[16] Trachtenberg correctly observed that Jew hatred was 'one of the basic convictions of the Middle Ages'[17] and one which best illustrated the fundamental irrationality of this prejudice.

The comparison of Jews to the devil produced an outpouring of both intellectual and visual hate, the latter represented by the zoomorphic depiction of Jews as animals and wild beasts. Thus, we find Gregory of Nyassa likening Jews to a 'race of vipers' and 'companions of the devil' while John Chrysostom described the synagogue as a 'cave of pirates and the lair of wild beasts.' The Jews were a people 'living for their belly' and who behaved 'no better than hogs and

---

[11] Joshua Trachtenberg, *The Devil and the Jews: The Medieval Conception of the Jew and Its Relation to Modern Antisemitism* (Philadelphia: The Jewish Publication Society, 1995), 181.

[12] ibid 182.

[13] ibid 20-1.

[14] Goldhagen, *The Devil that never Dies*, 65.

[15] ibid. 65.

[16] Trachtenberg. The Devil and the Jews, 12

[17] ibid. 14

goats in their lewd grossness.'[18] Italian artists in the fourteenth century identified Jews with scorpions, with those creatures appearing on the shields and tunics of Jews. In German cities at the same time, Jews came to be associated with the sow and were sometimes shown fornicating with them. In his pamphlet *Vom Schem Hamephoras*, Martin Luther offers the following description of such a relief: 'Here in Wittenberg, on our church, a sow is carved in stone. Some young piglets and some Jews are suckling her; behind the sow is a rabbi. He raises the sow's right leg, with his left and he pulls his member, leans over and diligently contemplates, behind the member, the Talmud, as if he desired to learn something very subtle and special from it.'[19] This does not exhaust the negative visual depictions of Jews. In the Middle Ages, Jewish figures were also represented with horns, a common attribute of the devil.[20] Michelangelo's famous statue of Moses has two horns protruding from the patriarch's head, something that is often taken to be the result of an erroneous interpretation of a passage from Exodus 34 by St Jerome. However, some scholarly analysis suggests that the depiction of Moses (and Jews more widely) with horns was designed to highlight his ostensibly Satanic and monstrous nature, this serving as the definitive explanation of why his people had rejected the New Testament. Jerome himself expressed his animosity to the Jews in many of his letters, condemning them for their 'ignorance' and superstition.[21]

Moreover, for medieval Christians, Satan was not an abstract conception or a mere allegorical figure but a very real person whose diabolical machinations could be felt in the physical world. People took seriously the notion that the earth was divided into two realms, that of the Kingdom of Christ and the Kingdom of the devil, and that whoever did not believe in Christ belonged to his Satanic nemesis. The demoniacal conception of the Jew was that he was 'the devil's creature.' He was not a 'human being' but a 'diabolic beast fighting the forces of truth and salvation with Satan's weapons.'[22] Accompanying the belief that the Jews were in league with the devil was the view that the long-awaited Jewish messiah had to be the Anti-Christ. A belief took root among Christian thinkers in the Middle Ages that it would be this sinister figure that would rebuild the Jewish temple in Jerusalem and establish his throne there. He even had a Jewish parentage, like Jesus, and his supporters were Jews.

The coming of the Antichrist truly gripped the medieval Christian imagination. The alleged fear that it induced must be seen against the psychological anxiety of an age which was beset with an obsessional desire to

---

[18] Richard Rubinstein and John K Roth, *Approaches to Auschwitz*, (Louisville: Westminster John Knox Press, 2003), 52.

[19] Dan Cohn-Sherbok, *Antisemitism*, (Cheltenham: The History Press, 2011), 70-1.

[20] In ancient near eastern literature, horns had a different and more positive significance.

[21] Bertman, Stephen. "The Antisemitic Origin of Michelangelo's Horned Moses." *Shofar* 27, no. 4 (2009): 95–106.

[22] Trachtenberg, *The Devil and the Jews*, 18.

eradicate witchcraft and any other anti-Christian heretics. It was widely believed that when the Antichrist arrived on earth, he would be accompanied by a Jewish army and that he would raise up Judaism to a force powerful enough to destroy Christendom. The Anti-Christ is also associated with the heinous crimes that were ascribed to the Jews, such as the ritual murder of children and the mass poisoning of Gentile societies. As Trachtenberg sums it up so well, 'it seems as though half of Europe was enrolled in the endemic witch-cults which adored and served Satan, while the other half cowered in dread of these representatives of the devil and hunted and slaughtered them with a fanatical ferocity.'[23] Signs of the Jews' alleged devilish nature could reportedly be seen in the physical infirmities purportedly suffered by Jews, all of which derived from the original sin of the crucifixion. These included male menstruation, haemorrhages and haemorrhoids, scrofula, sores and various skin diseases. The fateful decision to put Christ on the cross had literally left its mark on the Jewish body.[24]

When it was possible to conceptualize the collective Jew through such a prism of metaphysical evil, there was no limit to the consequences that could ensue. Sure enough, in 1096, the First Crusade was marked by a spectacular explosion of violence towards Jews in Europe. Massacres took place across Germany and France as well as in Jerusalem, with an estimated 10,000 people perishing. The violence failed to abate in the Second Crusade (1146) though the number of Jews killed was mercifully lower. It seems impossible to explain this eruption of extermination and mob violence without paying reference to how the poison unleashed by theological antisemitism had softened up people for revenge against 'the Christ killers.' The 'bestial Jew' is an essential component of the archetypal antisemitic perspective.

The legacy of bestilization has persisted until the present day. In the twentieth century, Hitler's apocalyptic antisemitism built, in large part, on the demonological discourse of medieval Christian Europe. Indeed, there is some evidence that Hitler believed his war against the Jews was divinely mandated. In one passage from *Mein Kampf*, Hitler declares: 'The Jew goes his fatal way until the day when another power stands up against him and in a mighty struggle casts him, the heaven stormer, back to Lucifer.'[25] In another he says: 'Today I believe that I am acting in accordance with the will of the Almighty Creator: by defending myself against the Jew, I am fighting for the work of the Lord.'[26] An element of Christian diabolization, influenced by mysticism, can be found in the statement made by Hitler when he declared: 'There cannot be two Chosen People. We are

---

[23] ibid. 60.
[24] ibid. 50.
[25] Hitler, *Mein Kampf*, Berlin edition (1940) 751
[26] David Patterson, *A Genealogy of Evil: Anti-Semitism from Nazism to Islamic Jihad* (New York: Cambridge University Press, 2011), 34.

God's People...Two worlds face one another- the men of God and the men of Satan.'[27]

Then take a speech given by Goebbels in which he denounces the Jew in terms that would not have been unfamiliar to the early Church writers: 'Look, there is the world's enemy, the destroyer of civilizations, the parasite among the peoples, the son of Chaos, the incarnation of evil, the ferment of decomposition, the demon who brings about the degeneration of mankind.'[28] This was a case of nationalist fanatics secularising medieval superstition and demonology for their own dark purposes. These statements directly tapped into the apocalyptic language of Christian demonology, even though Hitler himself was an ardent foe of the Christian faith. As the author of a scholarly work in this area writes: 'However modern Nazism was, it planted its roots in the soil of age-old Church attitudes and a nearly unbroken chain of Church-sponsored acts of Jew hatred. However pagan Nazism was it drew its sustenance from groundwater poisoned by the Church's most solemnly held ideology – its theology.'[29]

Ritual Murder

The blood libel was a false accusation that the Jews had ritually murdered Christian children so that they could use their blood for religious purposes, especially the baking of Passover matzah (unleavened bread). Such accusations, made from the Middle Ages onwards, led to Jews being arrested and then tortured so as to extract confessions from them. The charge, which continued to be made despite the Biblical prohibition against consuming blood, would go on to become a cornerstone of antisemitism and a key justification for the hideous acts committed against Jews through the ages.

Despite being central to the medieval calumnies against the Jews, the accusation appears to have made its first appearance in antiquity. As recounted by Josephus,[30] the Egyptian grammarian Apion charged that every year, the Jews kidnapped a Greek boy and, after fattening him up for a year, offered up his body as a sacrifice before eating his internal organs. This accusation surfaced in the writings of another pagan, Democritus, who alleged that every seven years the Jews caught a stranger whose body they tore to shreds as part of their ritual sacrifice.

The first medieval appearance of the blood libel was the case of William of Norwich, a young English boy who, according to an account written by the monk Thomas of Monmouth, was found dead at the age of 12 after being murdered by

---

[27] Stephen E Atkins, *Holocaust Denial as an International Movement* (Santa Barbara: Praeger, 2009), 32.

[28] Quoted in Norman Cohn, *Warrant for Genocide*, (Middlesex: Pelican, 1970), 225.

[29] Marvin Perry and Frederick M. Schweitzer, *Antisemitism: Myth and Hate from Antiquity to The Present* (New York: Palgrave, 2002), 7.

[30] Ehrman, Albert. "The Origins of the Ritual Murder accusation and blood libel." *Tradition: A Journal of Orthodox Jewish Thought* 15, no. 4 (1976): 83–90.

local Jews. Spurred on by the Jewish convert Theobald, Monmouth wrote that the Jews had engaged in this brutal crime because of an ancient dictate which required them to shed human blood in order to obtain their freedom as a sovereign nation. In his gruesome account, the Jews had conceived a plan to torture the child in the same manner that they had crucified Christ, and were motivated by their enduring animus towards Christians. Roughly a century later, the mysterious death of another young child, Hugh of Lincoln, was falsely attributed to the Jews of that town. According to the contemporary account, the Jews tortured him, made him wear a crown of thorns, swore at him with blasphemous insults and called him Jesus. Under the orders of Henry III, one Jew who had confessed to the crime under torture was executed and a further ninety of his co-religionists were arrested and held in the Tower of London. Eighteen Jews were hanged with the King personally profiting from their deaths after expropriating their property.

England's most famous medieval writer, Geoffrey Chaucer, helped to immortalise this form of Jewish 'infamy' in his *Prioress Tale*. He tells the story of a boy who sings *Alma redemptoris* in order to express his devotion to Mary. The Jews are so outraged when they hear him singing in their quarter that they cut his throat and discard his body. Yet by a miracle, the boy's body continues to sing and is transported to an abbey whereupon the Christians apprehend the Jews and hang them for this crime. For Chaucer, the Jews are a force for evil, possessed by Satan who 'hath in Jewes' heart his waspe's nest.' At the end of her story, Chaucer invokes the case of 'yonge Hugh of Lincoln' who was 'slayn also with cursed Jews.'[31] The blood libel spread to the Continent too. In 1171, the Jews of Blois were accused of crucifying a Christian child on Passover and dumping his body in the river. Over 40 Jews were imprisoned and the majority, after refusing to convert, were burned to death.[32]

Another famous example was that of Simon of Trent, a young Italian boy whose murder was blamed on the local Jewish community. Fifteen members of the community confessed to his murder under torture and were executed. The specific charge that Jews not only sacrificed Christian children but consumed their blood is sourced to the thirteenth century. The Flemish Roman Catholic writer Thomas De Cantimpre (1201-1272) wrote the *Bonum universale de apibus* in which he said that Jews suffered from bleeding (male menstruation) and that in order to heal themselves, they were enjoined to use Christian blood (solo sanguine Christiano) in religious rituals.

As to why the Jews allegedly desired the blood of a Christian child rather than an adult, the answer might be best summed up by Johann Eck. He wrote: 'They desire innocent Christian blood, not that of an old Christian whose innocence, acquired through baptism, has been forfeited by his subsequent sin.'[33] It was certainly part of medieval folklore that the body parts of a human were of

---

[31]Langmuir, Gavin. "The Knight's Tale of Young Hugh of Lincoln."
[32] It is important to also stress that some Popes denounced the Blood libel, often citing the scriptural prohibition against defiling oneself with blood
[33] Trachtenberg, *The Devil and the Jews*, 146.

great value, but that children were especially 'virginal and uncontaminated' and thus had more potent blood. Another malicious legend stated that Jews needed to use the blood of a Christian child in order to heal their own maladies, primarily haemorrhoids and haemorrhages. From this arose an annual custom of hunting for Christian blood, a device to preserve Jewish life rather than to torture young Christians. Elsewhere 'confessions' extracted through torture suggested that Jews smeared unleavened bread with Christian blood in order to protect themselves against leprosy. The city of Tyrnau declared that Jews needed such blood to remedy the wounds inflicted at birth (circumcision) while elsewhere it was seen as medicine for Jewish menstruation or to aid the painful process of childbirth.[34] In Hungary, a superstitious belief held that Jews smeared blood on their genitalia in order to increase their fertility. These were but a selection of the irrational beliefs held within medieval and some later modern societies about Jewish perfidy and evil. But all built upon the guiding principle that the Jews were a satanic force within society, possessed by or in communion with the devil, and thus animated by the beastliest qualities. Others connected alleged ritual murder to religious rites carried out at Passover, specifically that Jews used the blood of a slain child to bake unleavened bread. A variant from 1329 was that Jews made a compound from the heads and entrails of dead Christian children in order to make charoseth (a paste made of fruit and nuts and which is eaten at the Jewish Passover seder).[35]

The accusation of ritual murder helped to shape medieval perceptions of the Jew as a malign influence in society. Joshua Trachtenberg is left in no doubt as to its haunting impact on how Jews were seen: 'It rendered him a figure of such sinister horror even in that blood stained, terror haunted period that it is little wonder that common folk came to despise and to fear and to hate him with a deep fanatical intensity.'[36] The terror fantasy connecting Jews with blood represented an amalgamation of traditional folk superstitions about blood sucking vampires with the satanic depiction of Jews in Christian theology.[37] What gave the accusations of ritual murder and poisoning added potency was the strong belief that Jews were sorcerers whose magical abilities kept them in touch with the powers of the underworld. Jews were seen to be in league with Satan, the figure of archetypal evil who used magical spells to seduce mankind. The fact that Hebrew appeared so incomprehensible only added to suspicions that it was a magical medium whose incantations were to a secret realm. Numerous legends, such as those revolving around King Solomon, made a strong impression on the medieval imagination. Thus, we can see how different tropes within the archetypal antisemitic perspective built upon one another. The Christ killer Jew, plagued by a visceral animus towards Christians, was depicted as lusting after Christian blood, in part to satiate his bestial nature and to avenge himself upon Christ. In

---

[34] ibid. p. 149.
[35] ibid. p. 135.
[36] Ibid. p. 124.
[37] Wistrich, *Antisemitism*, 30.

addition, such a devilish creature acted stealthily and in a sly manner, seeking out vulnerable members of society upon which to satisfy his carnal desires. Such creatures would naturally show no loyalty to any Christian society, preferring instead to maintain loyalty to each other (see 'dual loyalty').

Blood libels continued into the nineteenth and twentieth centuries. Between 1887 and 1891, there were twenty-two indictments of Jews in Europe based on the libel. In the Hilsner case, a young Jewish vagrant, Leopold Hilsner, was accused of murdering two young Czech girls in a forest, resulting in blood libel trials in 1899 and 1900. Representing the first victim's mother, Karel Baxa thundered against 'people of another race, people who acted like animals' who had 'murdered a virtuous Christian girl so that they could use her blood.'[38] Hilsner was eventually pardoned, having spent years in prison, but the whole episode provided yet a further stark reminder of this myth's enduring and demonic power.

The Muslim world has sadly not been free from this incendiary accusation. Cases of the blood libel appeared in a number of cities, among them Aleppo (1810), Antioch (1826), Tripoli (1834) and Jerusalem (1838). In a famous case from the nineteenth century, members of the Damascus Jewish community found themselves charged with kidnapping and killing a Christian priest in 1840. Several were tortured by the authorities and an unruly mob attacked and destroyed a local synagogue.[39]

Throughout this period, the frenzied demonization of Jewry and the extreme denigration of Judaism were accompanied by hostile depictions in medieval art. Some symbols with negative connotations became associated with Jews, including coins and coin filled bags that symbolized avarice, cats which symbolized heresy and crows which symbolized greed and usury. From the twelfth century onwards, Jews appeared in stained glass windows and manuscript illustrations as bearded creatures with pointed hats, marking them off from Christians and symbolizing their outdated nature. Eventually, these images gave way to more hostile depictions with Jews presented as having thick lips, large, protruding noses and lidded eyes. Jews (specifically Jewish males) were seen through the lens of grotesque distortion in a manner that became even more familiar in the twentieth century.[40]

A variant on the blood libel was that of host desecration. According to the doctrine of transubstantiation, the bread and wine offered in the Eucharist become the body and blood of Christ and the communion bread that was used was called the consecrated Host (or Host). From when the doctrine was first recognised in 1215 at the Fourth Lateran Council, it was widely believed that the Host could show supernatural powers and that the body of Christ could appear. For centuries, Jews were accused of profaning and desecrating the Host in a variety of

[38] Perry and Schweitzer, *Antisemitism*, 64.
[39] Madeline Schwartz, "The Origins of Blood Libel," *The Nation*, January 28, 2016.
[40] Robert Chazan, "Why medieval art is so unflattering to Jews," *Haaretz*, April 9, 2015.

chronicles, sermons, ballads and other forms of Gentile culture. One of the earliest examples in European history occurred in Paris in 1290 when a Jew was accused of stabbing the Host, throwing it into the fire and then submerging it in boiling water. From this point, the Host desecration libel spread rapidly across Europe, often being used as the pretext for arresting, torturing and killing Jews. The point of these accusations was clear enough: Jews could not confine their hatred of Jesus merely to his crucifixion. Instead, they had to re-enact their savage torture of the Messiah over and over again as a permanent reminder of their animosity and blind contempt for the faith he represented. As a result, Christians were in no doubt that Jews were the enemies of their Lord, as well as of their faith.[41]

The explanations given for Host desecration were as outlandish as those used to explain ritual murder. They ranged from a desire to re-enact the crucifixion, namely by torturing the wafer which represented the body of Christ, to outright mockery of the Host superstition, from seizing the Host so that Jews could use its reportedly magical qualities in their potions to the desire to use the wafer's 'blood' to cure Jewish ailments.

A related trope was that of the Jew as a poisoner. This was an archetypal representation of Jews as people who spread death and destruction to their neighbours and their environment, one which built on the demonic attributes imparted to Jews by centuries of theological persecution. The most notorious example from the Middle Ages was the accusations hurled at Jewish communities during the Black Death. From 1347 until about 1353, the Plague swept across Europe, India and the Middle East, engulfing entire nations and causing the deaths of between one third and one half of the population. It caused a devastation of unparalleled ferocity and one whose horror was exacerbated by the failure to comprehend it.

There were a variety of explanations put forward for why this disease was ravaging the world. Some invoked astrology and blamed the alignment of the planets. Others thought it was a divine punishment for blasphemy, heresy, and fornication, and that the only remedy was self-flagellation and repentance. Yet there were many who thought that the plague was the handiwork of the devil, acting in league with his earthly agents, the Jews. After all, had not the Jews been pictured as the devil incarnate and a pariah nation after centuries of frenzied theological brainwashing?[42] The central charge was that Jews had poisoned wells as part of a systematic plot to destroy Christian communities.[43]

Such was the depth of popular superstition about Jewish poisoning that it produced some remarkable statutes. In fourteenth century Tyrol, Jews had to point

---

[41] Stacey, Robert C. "From Ritual Crucifixion to Host Desecration: Jews and the Body of Christ." *Jewish History* 12, no. 1 (1998): 11–28.

[42] Dan Freedman, "Why were Jews blamed for the Black Death," *Momentmag*, March 31, 2020, https://momentmag.com/why-were-jews-blamed-for-the-black-death/

[43] Well poisoning accusations appeared quite frequently between the 13th and the 15th centuries and they were by no means all directed at Jews. Some were directed towards lepers, some towards Muslims and others towards foreigners in general.

out which items they wished to purchase in the market place and if they touched any item, they had to buy it. Moreover, if a Christian wished to buy meat that had been touched by a Jew, they had to be informed of this fact first so that their purchase was made at their own risk.[44]

Associating Jewish doctors with poisoning came naturally to Martin Luther, the father of the Reformation, who declared that 'Jews who pretend to be physicians rob their Christian patients of their lives and possessions with their drugs, for they believe that they serve God when they severely injure them and secretly bring about their death.' This theme surfaces within the society of German states in the sixteenth and seventeenth centuries. Thus, a clergyman from Frankfurt declared in 1652 that 'To appeal to Jewish physicians is to hatch serpents among us, to raise wolves in our house' while in Swabia, it was said: 'Rather die in Christ than be cured by a Jewish doctor and Satan!'[45] There seemed to be the strongest whiff of this antisemitism in the accusation levelled at Roderigo Lopez, Queen Elizabeth I's converso physician. He was tried and executed for attempting to kill the Queen, specifically to 'take away' Queene Elizabeth's life by poyson,' in return for 'fifty thousand Crowns.' In his trial, prosecutor Sir Edward Coke denounced Lopez as a 'Jewish doctor worse than Judas himself...not a new Christian but a very Jew.' Some years later in 1610, the medical school in Vienna made the absurd charge that Jewish law required physicians to poison one patient out of every 10 using poison. Ivan the Terrible turned down a request to allow Lithuanian Jews into Russia on the grounds that 'they import poisonous herbs into our realms, and lead astray the Russians from Christianity.'[46]

The accusations that Jews were poisoners surfaced in more modern societies. One of the most famous examples was in the Doctors Plot of 1951-3 when Soviet dictator Joseph Stalin accused many eminent doctors in Moscow, most of whom were Jewish, of taking part in a vast plot to poison members of the top Soviet political and military leadership. They were accused of being part of an international Jewish bourgeois nationalist organization and a media campaign whipped up a storm of abuse towards other prominent Soviet Jews. There were rumours that Jewish doctors were engaged in infanticide by poisoning Russian children and injecting them with diphtheria.[47] It was rumoured that this was but a prelude to the deportation of Soviet Jewry to the gulags and a second Holocaust, a catastrophe only averted by Stalin's death in 1953. It should never be forgotten that this vast conspiracy took place in a highly educated, albeit deeply autocratic, state and was promoted by the highest organs of the state.

---

[44] Trachtenberg, *The Devil and the Jews*, 100.

[45] Poliakov: *The History of Antisemitism I: From the Time of Christ to the Court Jews*, (Philadelphia: The University of Pennsylvania Press, 2003), 152.

[46] Simon Dubnow, *History of Jews in Russia and Poland volume 1* (Musaicum Books, 2020), 158.

[47] Jonathan Brent and Vladimir P. Naumov, *Stalin's Last Crime: The Doctor's Plot*, (London: John Murray, 2003), 3.

Dual Loyalty Trope

The charge of dual loyalty involves the idea that wherever they settle, Jews are never loyal to their 'adopted' country. Their loyalty is always to their own people and their own interests, ones which are frequently not those of the 'host' society. As Jews are scattered around the world, this means that their loyalties, concerns and values are parochial and selfish, something that makes them seem fundamentally disloyal, unpatriotic, untrustworthy and shifty. At most, they feign a love of their fellow citizens but this only adds to the sense that they are a deceitful people. It is essential to the archetypal antisemitic perspective to view Jewish pretensions to patriotism and liberal values as a charade, an illusion, a clever ruse by which to cover their treasonous tracks.

It would be a mistake to think that this trope is a product of modernity alone. In fact, it has ancient roots that reach back thousands of years and involves the first interactions that Jews had with their neighbours. In pre-Christian times, Jews were charged with disloyalty but this stemmed from a failure to see that their worship of different gods, customs and laws was compatible with the obligations of citizenship. One of the earliest examples of this intolerance can be found in the Biblical book of Esther. According to the Old Testament account, Haman the Agagite, the chief minister of King Ahasuerus, conspired to exterminate the Jews of Persia after Mordechai, his arch nemesis, refused to bow down to him. The Book of Esther (3:8-9) recounts the words of Haman to King Ahasuerus:

> There is a certain nation scattered abroad and dispersed among the peoples in all the provinces of thy kingdom; and their laws are diverse from all people; neither keep they the King's laws; therefore it is not for the king's profit to suffer them. If it please the King, let it be written that they be destroyed.

The Biblical account tells us that his murderous decree was thwarted by the actions of Esther, the King's wife, whose revenge on Haman saw the vizier hanged on the very gallows he had intended for Mordechai. Mordechai refused to bow to a man sporting a pagan symbol and thereby avoided compromising his monotheism. By contrast, Haman was an immovable symbol of intolerance, much as a number of Roman leaders would be centuries later.

Haman's genocidal intentions arose because he saw Jews as alien to their 'host' society. He perceived a people who dared to live among the Persians yet cleaved to their own set of customs, laws and values. He argued that, being disloyal and untrustworthy, they had forfeited any right to protection from the King and thus merited one simple punishment – their elimination.

In pagan times, the worship of multiple gods was the norm and different subjects paid tribute to the deities of alternate faiths. The Jews stood out for their insistence that they would worship just one god and their refusal to pay tribute to others marked them out as different and troublesome. Moreover, many interpreted their desire to have separate customs and practices, such as dietary laws, and their refusal to intermarry, as a sign that the Jews thought themselves superior to their neighbours. As will be seen later, this partly relied on a misunderstanding of the notion of chosenness.

In the Roman world, many shared this dislike of perceived Jewish exclusiveness and purported lack of respect for reverential custom. These feelings were accompanied by the growing fear that Judaism would win over many converts, undermining support for Roman rule through subversive ideological indoctrination. Certain Jewish customs, such as circumcision and the Sabbath day of rest, caused considerable resentment and helped to fuel the idea that Jews were undermining Roman values and the Roman lifestyle. Roman writers such as Seneca, Petronius and Juvenal mocked Jewish customs and were bemused by such institutions as the Sabbath and the refusal to eat pork. The Roman historian Tacitus was far more openly contemptuous of the Jews. In his *Histories*, he accused them of profaning everything that the Romans held sacred, branding their religious practices sordid and depraved, condemning them for scorning the gods and lambasting them as the basest of nations. He spoke of how the Jews had 'a stubborn attachment to one another, an active commiseration, which contrasts with their implacable hatred for the rest of mankind.'[48] In the words of Erich S. Gruen, Tacitus was 'the quintessential pagan anti-Semite.'[49]

In more modern times, the charge of dual loyalty was beginning to surface with alarming intensity and would become a centrepiece of nationalist attacks on Jews. Post-revolutionary France had promised an enlightened political landscape marked by liberty, equality and fraternity. But while Jews were liberated from the ghettos and granted political equality, there were question marks about fraternity. Napoleon himself, the great emancipator of European Jews, did more to advance Jewish civic interests on the Continent than any man in centuries. But that freedom came at a political cost, namely the abandonment of what made them distinctly Jewish. Napoleon posed the question: 'Do Jews born in France, and treated by the law as French citizens, consider France as their country? Are they bound to defend it? Are they bound to obey (its) laws?' He came up with his own answer. 'Once part of (the Jewish youth) will take its place in our armies, they will cease to have Jewish interests and sentiments.' In other words, Jews had to assimilate into French society or else they would be a nation cleaving to Jewish interests alone.

If one episode came to symbolise the new Republic's epic failure to uphold all three Revolutionary promises, it was the Dreyfus Affair of 1894-1906. The facts of 'L'Affaire' are well enough known. Captain Alfred Dreyfus was an artillery captain in the French army who was convicted of selling military secrets to Germany in 1894. He was court martialled and found guilty of treason, after which he was publicly humiliated by having the insignia torn from his uniform and his sword broken while a crowd screamed antisemitic abuse at him. As one

---

[48] Poliakov, *The History of Antisemitism I*, 9-10.
[49] Erich S Gruen, "Tacitus and the Defamation of the Jews" in *The Construct of Identity in Hellenistic Judaism* ed. Erich S Gruen (Berlin: De Gruyter, 2016), 266.

writer has observed, the ceremony appeared to belong to an 'older, medieval Europe, of public torture and autos-da-fé and Inquisitions.'[50] It was accompanied by vicious cartoons and caricatures, the worst appearing in Edouard Drumont's passionately antisemitic newspaper *La Libre Parole*.

Dreyfus was then sentenced to spend the remainder of his life behind bars on Devil's Island off French Guiana, the victim of a paroxysm of intolerance in which the charge of dual loyalty was paramount. Two years later, evidence emerged which pointed the finger of blame at another man, Major Ferdinand Esterhazy.[51] The man who uncovered this evidence was silenced and sent to Tunisia but the evidence against Esterhazy mounted up and began to surface in the media. He was later brought to trial but despite the damning evidence against him, was cleared of the charges. Enraged by the injustice, Emile Zola accused the French state of a cover up in his famous tract *J'Accuse*. The case had split France firmly down the middle with ministers forced to resign and there was even talk of civil war. Dreyfus went on trial for a second time but though he was again found guilty, received a Presidential pardon days later and was released. But it was not until 1906 that the French captain was exonerated, bringing to an end a decade of injustice and intolerance.

The charge of dual loyalty was made by reactionary conservatives who sought to roll back the advances in Jewish civic rights since the French Revolution. One such reactionary was the historian Friedrich Rühs who wrote the work *On the Claims of the Jews to Civil Rights in Germany*. In the book, he wrote:

> The Jews are in the nature of a nation; they have compatriots throughout the world, with whom they are bound by origin, outlook, duty, faith, language and inclination. Together with them they constitute a single unity, and they are necessarily obliged to be closer and more devoted to them than to the nation in whose midst they live and which will remain alien to them forever.[52]

Across Europe, the same charge of dual loyalty would surface in other contexts. In the late nineteenth century, Britain became embroiled in the Eastern Crisis. When Bulgarian Christians attempted to free themselves from Turkish Ottoman rule, the authorities responded by massacring them. Britain had traditionally allied with Turkey, seeing it as a useful counterweight to Russia. This was the position adopted by the Jewish Prime Minister Disraeli and it was opposed by the Liberal leader William Gladstone among others. One eminent Professor argued that if England was drawn into this conflict, it would be a 'Jewish war, waged with British blood to uphold the objects of Jewish sympathy or to avenge Jewish wrongs.' Goldwin Smith was little interested in the geo-strategic

---

[50] Adam Gopnik, "Trial of the century: Revisiting the Dreyfus Affair," *The New Yorker*, September 21, 2009.
[51] Letters were to surface in the French press from Esterhazy's mistress in which the officer expressed his hatred of France and its military.
[52] Katz, *From Prejudice to Destruction*, 79.

advantages of the Turkish alliance and how it might have secured British imperial interests, nor did he think that these factored into Disraeli's foreign policy. Disraeli was portrayed as a disloyal politician who could not uphold British national interests because he only favoured Jewish (read anti-Christian) ones. Others attacked Disraeli for his 'foreign mentality,' his 'Hebrew policy' and for being an 'Oriental dictator.'[53]

British critics of late Victorian imperialism offered wholly malicious and barely disguised denunciations of the 'Jewish' features of modern economics. One such critic was Henry M Hyndman, founder of the Social Democratic Foundation and its weekly newspaper, *Justice*. When the paper launched its antisemitic invective, it railed against 'capitalist Jews of the baser sort' who had 'poisoned the wells of public opinion' by controlling the press. Some of these 'base' capitalists were condemned as the root cause of Britain's involvement in the Second Boer War. The idea was that these financiers, in view of their exploitation of Boer land, were pulling the strings of the British government to seek their own financial gain and using the 'yellow Jew press' as cover for their nefarious activities. Using words whose resonance was immediately obvious to those with anti-Jewish prejudice, Hyndman wrote: 'Beit and Eckstein, Barnato and Oppenheim, Steinkopf and Levi, these are the true born Britons who are egging us common Englishmen into the war with the Transvaal.'[54] The fact that plenty of financiers were not Jewish and that many non-Jewish owned papers supported the war was of little consequence. These attacks came from other sections of the left. The Trades Union Congress passed a resolution in 1900 which looked on the war in South Africa as an attempt 'to secure the gold fields of South Africa for cosmopolitan Jews, most of whom had no patriotism and no country.'[55] The Jew, in other words, found home only in the pursuit of his own interests and if these soured international relations and embroiled their 'host' countries in war, it was of no consequence to them.

During the same period, such prejudice could also be found in the United States, a nation that promised Jews the greatest level of freedom found anywhere in the Western hemisphere. In response to a spike in antisemitic attitudes, the editors of a Jewish newspaper, *The American Hebrew*, asked dozens of notable public figures for their opinion on anti-Jewish prejudice. The President of Tufts College, E.N. Capen, declared that the Jews could never 'assimilate like other aliens' as they were always Hebrew and could 'never be Americans.'[56] In surveys carried out in the years preceding America's entry into WWII, between one

[53] Colin Holmes, *Antisemitism in British Society, 1876-1939* (New York: Holmes & Meier, 1979), 11-12.
[54] Claire Hirshfield, "The Anglo-Boer War and the Issue of Jewish Culpability." *Journal of Contemporary History* 15, no. 4 (1980): 619–631.
[55] Rich, *The Left's Jewish Problem*, 203.
[56] Pamela S Nadell, "A History of American antisemitism," *Quartz*, November 12, 2019.

quarter and one third of Americans believed that Jews were 'less patriotic than other citizens.'[57]

If Germany's highly assimilated Jews thought they were exempt from this tidal wave of antisemitic hysteria, they were mistaken. During the First World War, Prussia's War Minister Adolf Wild von Hohenborn (1860-1925) initiated a census of Jewish soldiers in the German army which came to be known as the *Judenzahlung*. Amid accusations that Jews were 'evading their obligation to serve' on the front line, the census was designed to ascertain the percentage of Jews in combat units compared to those in support roles behind the lines. Commanding officers of each regiment were asked to calculate the number of Jews killed in action and the number decorated for bravery as well as how many were behind the lines but fit to serve. Behind this census lay two pernicious stereotypes. One was of the Jew as a weak, cowardly shirker and the other, that he was unpatriotic with no loyalty to the fatherland. Despite its flawed methodology, which included a failure to account for Jews on leave or temporarily transferred from their units, it found no evidence of wrongdoing. The Ministry refused to disclose the results of the survey, an omission which would do nothing to dispel the charges of disloyalty levelled at Jews after the war.

Germany's shattering defeat in 1918 would give rise to the most notorious and damaging accusation of dual loyalty in the twentieth century, namely the Stab in the back myth (*Dollschosslegende*). In a desperate attempt to deflect blame for the military mistakes that led to Germany's surrender in November 1918, it was put about that the real reason Germany lost was because of plotting by defeatist and pacifist civilians who had stirred up unrest in a bid to end the war. Among the chief culprits were Jews, represented in the form of Weimar politicians such as Kurt Eisner and Walter Rathenau. The stab in the back myth became a central feature of Nazi propaganda and a dangerous canard used to attack Jews in Germany.

While some agitators blamed Jews for collapsing the German war effort in 1918, others believed that they were actively conspiring to bring about the next one. In his infamous Des Moines speech in September 1941, the celebrated aviator Charles Lindbergh assailed 'a small minority of our own people' who, together with 'foreign interests,' were forcing the United States into war. He specifically condemned Jews, as well as Britons, for seeking the defeat of Nazi Germany 'for reasons which are as understandable from their viewpoint as they are inadvisable from ours.' Rather chillingly, he added that these reasons were 'not American.' He accused Jews, among others, of plotting a foreign war under the guise of American defence and then involving the US 'without our realization.'[58] For

---

[57] Earl Rabb, "Attitudes towards Israel and Attitudes towards Jews: The Relationship," in *Antisemitism in the Contemporary World*, ed. Michael Curtis (London: Routledge, 1986), 289.

[58] Des Moines Speech," charleslindbergh.com, accessed 1 March 2022, http://www. charleslindbergh.com/americanfirst/speech.asp.

Lindbergh, Jewish concerns were automatically non-American and showed disloyalty to American values and interests.

The Holocaust did nothing to abate the pernicious charges of disloyalty and lack of patriotism. Under Stalin, Jews were hounded as rootless cosmopolitans as part of a campaign to promote Russian patriotism and expunge foreign influences in culture. In 1948, a group of Jewish drama critics were condemned for their 'antipatriotic views' and months later, denounced in the pages of *Pravda* for a rootless attitude in which 'the sentiment of Soviet national pride was foreign.' The majority of those who were identified were Jewish and the paper attacked these people for their 'clannishness' and 'tribelike solidarity.' While initially a bloodless campaign against Jews of culture, it soon segued into bloodshed as Stalin carried out a purge on what became known as 'the Night of Murdered Poets.' Shortly after, a group of doctors were arrested on charges of plotting to assassinate Soviet leaders.

Charges of dual loyalty played their role in the ethnic cleansing of close to one million Jews who lived in Arab countries prior to 1948. Arab Jews were suspected of being agents or collaborators with the 'Zionist regime' and subjected to a wave of pogroms and murderous assaults in the years leading up to Israel's creation. Hundreds of Jews were killed in Libya, Aden and Egypt. In 1967, Egypt rounded up Jewish men and arrested them as 'Israeli prisoners of war,' a reflection of how the state viewed its own citizens through the lens of dual loyalty. Iraqi Jews were barred from higher education, sacked from their jobs and placed under surveillance. In 1969, nine Iraqi Jews were executed for 'spying' for Israel.

Charges of dual loyalty founder on the basic facts of Jewish powerlessness throughout their history living in Gentile societies. The official position of the Jewish leadership was based, far more, on the need for accord and harmony than a flirtation with treasonous disloyalty. As Ruth Wisse points out in her book *Jews and Power*:

> It was politically illogical for Jews to betray the rulers whose protection they needed unless those rulers first betrayed them-and even then, how could Jews assume they would find any trustier alternatives? The advantages of power that rulers always enjoyed over their Jewish subjects made it far likelier that Jews would prove disloyal to their co-religionists than to those who could offer inducements for betrayal.[59]

The 'Vengeful Chosen People' Trope

The charge of dual loyalty was accompanied by the Jews' alleged belief in their own superiority. This reflected Judaism's oft stated belief that Jews were God's 'chosen people,' a people specially selected to receive divine blessing at the expense of the 'inferior' Gentiles whose lives were seen as worthless and expendable. At different times, the notion of chosenness was used to mock Jews for their perceived sense of superiority and arrogance. One can find pejorative

---

[59] Ruth Wisse, *Jews and Power* (New York: Schocken Books, 2020), 75.

references in the writings of Dutch philosopher Benedict Spinoza. In perhaps his most famous work, the *Theologico-Political Treatise*, he attacked his co-religionists for failing to understand the nature of true happiness. He wrote: 'He who thinks that his blessedness is increased by the fact that he is better off, or happier and more fortunate, than the rest of mankind, knows nothing of true happiness and blessedness, and the pleasure he derives from such thoughts, unless merely childish, arises only from spite and malice.' He believed that the Jews' belief in chosenness had incurred righteous hatred from their Christian neighbours, making Jews responsible for their own persecution. In turn, Spinoza argued that the Jews, being blind to how they were responsible for Christian hostility, hated the Christians in return.[60]

The antisemitic tract *The Talmud Unmasked*, written by the Lithuanian priest Justinas Bonaventure Pranaitis in 1892, attempted to prove that Jewish religious texts encouraged Jews to hate and kill Christians and see themselves as a chosen elect which could rule the world. He wrote this in Protocol 1 about the Jews: 'By the fact that he belongs to the chosen people, possesses so great a dignity that no one, not even an angel, can share equality with him.' Being chosen meant that he was 'considered almost the equal of God' and that the 'whole world is his and all things should serve him.'[61] That chosenness portended some great evil for mankind was also alluded to in other 'revelations' in the book. The prophets were quoted as saying that Jews were chosen by God to rule the earth and that God had endowed Jews with genius to be equal to the task. When this rule was complete, the Chosen would sweep away all other religions from the globe and slay all those who opposed Jewish rule. The book anticipated the arguments of the *Protocols of the Elders of Zion* with its dire warnings about a Jewish plot to seize control of the earth and all its institutions.

The English novelist G.K. Chesterton, an ardent opponent of theories of racial supremacy, interpreted the Jewish notion of chosenness in the most pejorative manner. In his book *The Crank*, he assailed Hitler's belief in Aryan supremacy but attributed it to the Jews. He wrote that if there was 'one outstanding quality in Hitlerism' it was 'its Hebraism' and added that 'the new Nordic Man (had) all the worst faults of the worst Jews: jealousy, greed, the mania of conspiracy, and above all, the belief in a Chosen Race.'[62] In his play *Geneva: A Fancied Page of History in Three Acts* (1938), George Bernard Shaw drew a contrast between Hebraic particularism and Catholic universality, assailing the Jewish spirit of parochialism as a form of rabid nationalism which conflicted with hopes of creating a better and more peaceful world. Indeed, like Chesterton, Shaw seemed to regard the

---

[60] It should not be forgotten that Spinoza had been excommunicated by Amsterdam's Jewish community for the unorthodox views he had espoused.

[61] Rev I. B. Pranaitis, *The Secret Rabbinical Teaching Concerning Christians* (Facsimiled Publisher, Delhi), 39.

[62] Quoted in Simon Mayers, *Chesterton's Jews: Stereotypes and Caricatures in the Literature and journalism of G. K. Chesterton* (CreateSpace Independent Publishing Platform, 2013), 86.

Jewish concept of a chosen people as a template for Nazi ideology, condemning Hitler for the irony of 'Hebraising' his nation. He argued that the Nazis might have dropped their offensive ideology if they had only detected its Jewishness.[63]

The idea that chosenness connoted a racist belief about Jews (and non-Jews) was at the heart of a shocking diatribe by the Soviet ambassador to the United Nations, Yakov Malik, in 1971. After warning Israel not to stick its 'long nose' into Soviet affairs and condemning Israeli policy for using 'Hitlerite' tactics, Malik likened Zionism to fascism and went on:

> The fascists advocated the superiority of the Aryan race (and the Zionist) racist theory is the same. The fascists advocated hatred toward all peoples and the Zionists do the same. The chosen people; is this not racism?[64]

In retrospect, we can say that these authors made the same error. They failed to understand that the notion of a chosen people had nothing to do with racial or religious supremacy. Instead, it connoted a belief that Jews carried the burden of transmitting a moral message to mankind, that they were chosen for the task of perfecting the world and serving mankind as a model community. This stemmed from the belief, deeply embedded in Jewish tradition, that Jews chose to accept divine commandments at Mount Sinai when other nations rejected them. Judaism is not, at its core, racist and neither is the notion of chosenness.

The Jew As Avaricious

One of the most insidious stereotypes that Christian Europe hurled at the Jewish population was that of being a greedy, money obsessed people. This accusation, which became a core feature of medieval antisemitic demonology, led to the widespread view of Jews as parasites who were exploiting the poorer and more vulnerable groups in society. The Book of Matthew (21:12-13) included the story of Jesus driving money changers out of the Temple in Jerusalem. He was quoted as saying: 'My house shall be called the house of prayer; but ye have made it a den of thieves.'

For millions of Christians, the prime symbol of treachery and greed was Judas Iscariot, one of the 12 apostles of Christ who betrayed Jesus in the Garden of Gethsemane in exchange for thirty pieces of silver (Matthew 26:15). The Gospels offered different interpretations as to Judas' motivation but by the Middle Ages, an 'ugly archetype of Judas' as a 'hunched figure with a large nose and red hair who would do anything for money' had become 'the personification of Judaism.'

[63] Bryan Cheyette, *Constructions of 'the Jew' in English Literature and Society: Racial Representations, 1875–1945*, (Cambridge: Cambridge University Press, 1993), 120.
[64] "Two Congressman Score Malik for Antisemitic attack on Israel," *Jewish Telegraphic Agency*, October 1, 1971.

In Passion plays of the time, he was shown in hell being tormented by demons.[65] Today, Judas lives on, a 'byword for traitor, the word Jew and Judas almost indistinguishable in several languages, including German.'[66] For Luther, Jews were 'Judas' kin' and Judas was 'the ringleader in guiding the mob against Christ.'[67] In *On the Jews and their Lies* (1543) he wrote: '[The Jews] let us work in the sweat of our brow to earn money and property while they sit behind the stove, idle away the time, fart, and roast pears ... with their accursed usury they hold us and our property captive. ... Thus, they are our masters and we are their servants, with our property, our sweat, and our labour.'[68] By contrast, other Protestant reformers had more positive attitudes towards Jews with Calvin expressing 'great affection for the Jews' and described the differences with them as 'purely theological.'[69]

However, a more likely explanation for why Jews have been associated with money derives from a particular set of historical circumstances connected to medieval Christian rule. In the Middle Ages, Jews were prohibited from owning land or being a member of guilds, something which excluded them from many trades. This meant that they could only engage in certain professions, such as trading goods across countries, as well as others which directly involved money, such as tax collecting and money lending. In Muslim countries without such restrictions, Jews engaged in many other trades and professions. Christians were forbidden from practising usury (lending money at high rates of interest) and faced severe punishment if found guilty. Medieval rulers made use of Jewish moneylenders, something which provided Jews with a degree of official protection, but which also subjected them to fierce hostility from the Church as well as from poorer sections of society.[70] These draconian restrictions cemented the image of the Jew as a 'bloodsucking profiteer' in the minds of many and led to violence and expulsion, as in 1290 when Jews were thrown out of England by Edward I. However, economic realities soon became inescapable and Christians took over the financial roles once played by Jews, establishing their own predominance.

---

[65] David Gibson, "Antisemitism's Muse: Without Judas, History Might Have Hijacked Another Villain," *New York Times*, April 9, 2006.

[66] Jonathan Freedland, "For 2,000 years, we've linked Jews to money. It's why antisemitism is so ingrained," *The Guardian*, March 9, 2019.

[67] Perry and Schweitzer, *Antisemitism*, 38

[68] Beth Griech-Lolelle, *Antisemitism and the Holocaust: Language, Rhetoric and the Traditions of Hatred* (London: Bloomsbury Academic, 2017), 36.

[69] W Lacquer, *The Changing Face of Antisemitism: From Ancient Times to the Present Day*, (Oxford: Oxford University Press, 2006), 64.

[70] Eventually Jews were squeezed out of usury by the development of banks. The reason why they could charge such high rates of interest was that the profession was extremely risky with the strong chance that the lender would not see money returned at all.

The association of Jews with avarice became a staple of English literature from medieval times to the modern era. In Christopher Marlowe's *The Jew of Malta*, the character of Barabas draws upon much of the classical demonology in regard to the Jews: he is devilish and motivated by blood lust, usurious, filled with avarice and represents a mortal threat to Christians. At the start, the Christian governor of Malta seizes Barabas' wealth, and that of all other Jews, in order to pay off the Turks. Barabas, motivated by Machiavellian cunning, embarks on a murder spree, poisoning his own daughter, an entire nunnery and his own servant. After successfully plotting with the Turks against the Christians, he is nominated governor but later switches sides, attempting to set a lethal trap for the Turkish soldiers. In the end, he falls victim to his own contrivance and burns just as his enemies agree to resolve their conflict. It is a classic tale of revenge and bloodlust though taken to almost farcical extremes. Much debate has ensued about authorial intention and whether Marlowe intended to highlight the hypocrisies of Barabas as well as his opponents.[71]

Shortly after Marlowe's play appeared, his contemporary, William Shakespeare, wrote *The Merchant of Venice*. In the play, the Jewish moneylender Shylock lends money to a merchant, Antonio, on condition that he can obtain a pound of Antonio's flesh if the merchant is unable to repay the loan. Shylock has long suffered antisemitism at Antonio's hands which explains the hardness of his position. Antonio later defaults on the loan and is taken to court by Shylock but in a twist, it is Shylock's daughter, Portia, who defends the merchant. She argues that the bond entitled Shylock to a pound of Antonio's flesh, not his blood, and thus repayment on the moneylender's terms would be impossible to fulfil. Shylock is charged with conspiring against a Venetian citizen and, in order to save some of his fortune, is forced to convert to Christianity.

Ever since, a fierce debate has ensued about whether *The Merchant of Venice* is an antisemitic play or instead a play about antisemitism. There is ample evidence to support the former interpretation. The character of Shylock builds upon tropes of avarice and vengefulness. He is a figure of archetypal greed, a devilish, merciless figure who hates Christians and has a single-minded determination to do them harm. Detractors suggest that Shakespeare humanised Shylock, putting into his mouth the most famous speech in the play (Hath not a Jew eyes?).

Arguably, the play attacks *both* Jews and Christians alike. When we examine the play closely, we can see that Shakespeare is critical, not just of Shylock and his lack of mercy, but of the hypocrisy of his Christian detractors. Shylock's lack of compassion is mirrored in the appalling manner in which Christians have treated him. Despite their professed love of mercy and love for their enemies, Christians attack Shylock unrelentingly, with Antonio calling him a dog, his own servant Launcelot cursing him as a devil and Gratiano wanting the moneylender

---

[71]Charles Nicholl, "The Jew of Malta: antisemitic or a satire on antisemitism?" *The Guardian*, March 27, 2015.

hanged. Shylock laments: 'You call me misbeliever, cut-throat dog.' His own daughter Portia tricks her father in court by disguising herself as a man and betrays him. Little wonder then for Shylock's complaint in Act 3: 'The villainy you teach me I will execute.' Nonetheless, the character of Shylock has become the literary embodiment par excellence of the avaricious Jew seeking his 'pound of flesh.'

Perhaps no Jewish character from nineteenth century English literature is better known than Fagin in Charles Dickens' *Oliver Twist*. Fagin is a vicious and miserly criminal who receives stolen goods and then grooms his child victims, among whom are the Artful Dodger and Bill Sykes, to become pickpockets. Oliver, a young orphan, arrives in London, is befriended by a pickpocket and is taken to see Fagin. He is hired to commit crimes for the villain but manages to escape his grasp on several occasions; at the end, Fagin is tried and sentenced for execution. It is the tale of an innocent child, set against the sordid reality of the criminal underworld and the cold and unfeeling hypocrisy of Victorian Britain. *Oliver Twist* is a Manichean work of melodrama populated by heroes and villains, the worst of which is a Jew whose sinister designs are confounded by the judicial system.

When he makes his first appearance in the novel, Fagin is described as 'a very old shrivelled Jew, whose villainous-looking and repulsive face was obscured by a quantity of matted red hair.' Indeed, he is referred to as 'the Jew' on 257 occasions in the novel. He is an archetypal, child abusing villain, a haunting, primitive figure who is compared to a reptile who 'glides stealthily along, creeping beneath the shelter of walls and doorways.' Fagin dredges up much of the folklore of antisemitic tropes – the Jew as a devilish, vampiric, deceitful and avaricious threat to society.

Dickens claimed that he meant no ill will towards the Jewish people of his time, claiming that Fagin's Jewish identity owed to the fact that, during the time in which the novel was set, 'that class of criminal almost invariably was a Jew.'[72] In later editions, he sought to remove references to Fagin being a Jew altogether, the first of many attempts to humanise the character. But the image has stuck with Fagin, like Shylock, serving as an inhuman icon of 'Jewish greed' and miserliness.[73] They are part of the rich literary underpinning for the archetypal antisemitic perspective.

European and Russian literature was no less susceptible to demonizing the Jew as a creature of avarice. One can find crude antisemitic stereotyping of Jews as greedy and miserly in the writings of Baudelaire,[74] Sand, Freytag and Turgenev, to name but a small selection. Vicious attacks on the Jewish economic character appear in the 1855 novel *Soll und Haben* (Debit and Credit) by German

---

[72] Israel Solomons, "Charles Dickens and Eliza Davis." *Jewish Historical Society of England* 1 (1925): iv-vi.

[73] Paul Vallely, "Dickens' greatest villain: the faces of Fagin," *The Independent*, October 7, 2005.

[74] Brett Bowles, "Poetic Practice and Historical Paradigm: Charles Baudelaire's Antisemitism." *PMLA* 115, no. 2 (2000): 195–208.

author Gustav Freytag. The work, one of the most widely read and popular German novels of the nineteenth century, deals with various segments and classes of German society with Jews represented by the greedy and mendacious Ehrenthal family. The novel's honourable Jew makes a speech on his deathbed in which he claims that Jews need to assimilate in Gentile society in order to shed their coarse, material values and adopt respectable forms of morality and culture. In *The Jew Among Thorns (Der Jude im Dorn)*, one of the tales in the collection written by the Brothers Grimm, a Jewish trader is cast in a negative light as a callous exploiter of the poor and is hanged at the end for his unscrupulous behaviour. In *The Good Bargain*, a Jewish man was portrayed as a greedy swindler because he substituted counterfeit for real coins in a transaction he carried out with a peasant.

Even the Enlightenment, that period in which barbarous ideas were supposedly being swept away in honour of creating a more rational and enlightened world, was not free from the taint of antisemitic prejudice. Voltaire, one of the Enlightenment's most ferocious antisemites, wrote in one passage: 'The Jew does not belong to any place except that place in which he makes money: would he not just as easily betray the king on behalf of the emperor as he would the emperor the king.' Elsewhere he wrote: 'The only thing that properly belongs to the Jews is their stubbornness, their superstitions and their hallowed usury.'[75] In a similar vein, Immanuel Kant, perhaps the most influential philosopher of the eighteenth century, said that the Jews owed 'their not undeserved reputation for cheating (at least the majority of them) to their spirit of usury...'[76] For Pierre-Joseph Proudhon, the Jews' economic policy 'was always negative' and as the Jew was neither an agriculturalist, industrialist or trader, was instead 'always fraudulent and parasitical,' operating in business through 'sharp practices.'[77]

Attacks on the Jews' alleged avarice fed into a view that they could not be productive and honest members of the wider society, given that they were 'consumed' by their inherited moral stagnation. Thus, the German physician and chemist Christoph Heinrich Pfaff, writing in the nineteenth century, spoke of the Jews' 'bent for speculation' and 'the concentration of all their mental forces on gain.' He concluded that Jews were 'a caste of tradesmen and hawkers who shun every serious and strenuous work, agriculture and handicraft.'[78] It led to his view that Jewish greed was a threat to the nation, given this people's alleged desire for economic dominance. Thus, the tropes of the avaricious Jew and the conspiratorial Jew were closely connected in the minds of many racists. Later in the nineteenth century, the German historian Heinrich von Treitschke, best known for formulating the words 'Die Juden sind unser Unglück' [The Jews are our misfortune), said that Jews had contributed a great deal 'to the dishonesty and deception and the bold greediness of the boom-time mischief' and bore much

[75] Arthur Hertzberg, *The French Enlightenment and the Jews* (New York: Columbia University Press, 1968), 303.
[76] Goldhagen, *The Devil that never dies*, 66.
[77] ibid. p. 67
[78] Katz, *From Prejudice to Destruction*, 149-150.

responsibility 'for the contemptible materialism of our age which regards every kind of work only as business.'[79] Such materialism and greed made Jews unworthy of medicine, according to the Austrian ophthalmologist Anton von Rosas, who argued that the spirit of 'mercantilism' in Jewish culture prevented Jews from adopting an 'ethical standard of self-abnegation.'[80]

For some, opposition to the Jews' allegedly nefarious economic conduct became a marker of conservative resistance to modernity in general. The English political philosopher Edmund Burke was not averse to the most pernicious forms of Jew baiting. He saw Jews as an 'economic and religious threat to English society,' believing that their influence was inextricably tied up with their 'moneyed-interest.'[81] He condemned Jewish brokers for 'contending with each other who could best remedy with fraudulent circulation and depreciated paper the wretchedness and ruin brought on their country by their degenerate councils.'[82] He believed that the spirit of usurious and corrupt calculation, which he attributed to Jews, was a threat to the landed class, and thus to the wider national interest of his nation. He also connected Jews with liberalism, a political ideology that he blamed for corrupting the old order, especially in revolutionary France. Progress, modernity, commerce and liberal values were elided with Jewishness to create an amorphous enemy that threatened tradition and order. Of course, Burke traded on multiple antisemitic stereotypes in his analysis, including that of the rootless Jew whose loyalty was to his co-religionists rather than to the nation of which he was a member.

The notion that Jews were rootless and worshipped the god of Mammon found its place in the writings of German thinkers such as Bruno Bauer and Karl Marx. In his *On the Jewish Question*, Karl Marx wrote: 'What is the secular basis of Judaism? Practical need, self-interest. What is the worldly religion of the Jew? Huckstering. What is his worldly God? Money.' 'Money,' he goes on to say, 'is the jealous god of Israel, in face of which no other god may exist.' The real god of the Jews has ceased to be a spiritual figure but is instead 'the bill of exchange.' Marx concluded that 'The *social* emancipation of the Jew is the *emancipation of society from Judaism.*'[83] In his *Semites and Antisemites*, Bernard Lewis understandably describes this essay as 'One of the classics of antisemitic propaganda'[84] because it bought into the age-old stereotype of Jews and financial

---

[79] Quoted in Marcel Stoetzler, *The State, The Nation & The Jews: Liberalism and the Antisemitism Dispute in Bismarck's Germany* (Nebraska: University of Nebraska Press, 2009), 313.

[80] Katz, *From Prejudice to Destruction*, 225.

[81] Rachel Schulkins, "Burke, His Liberal Rivals and the Jewish Question" *Otherness: Essays and Studies* 3:2

[82] Oliver Kann, "The baneful philosophical legacy of Edmund Burke," *Prospect Magazine*, January 1, 2020

[83] Avineri, Shlomo. "Marx and Jewish Emancipation." *Journal of the History of Ideas* 25, no. 3 (1964): 445–50, 445-6.

[84] Lewis, *Semites and Anti-Semites*, 112.

greed. Others point out that Marx supported full political emancipation for the Jews and that his real target was an economic system that he wrongly identified as being imbued with Jewish values (it was a common view at this time).

One finds echoes of such hostile stereotypical thinking in other economic writers of the late nineteenth and early twentieth century. Charles Booth, one of England's most important social investigators in the nineteenth century, put together the 17 volume *Life and Labour of the People in London* between 1889 and 1903. It was a fascinating and detailed survey which mapped both the extent and nature of poverty in London and closely examined the influence of religion on the lives of Londoners. He claimed that it was a neutral portrait of Victorian London which was free from bias and any form of class prejudice. Yet his description of the economic life of Jewish immigrant workers was replete with stereotypes, many of which were negative. For Beatrice Potter, one of the survey's contributors, the strongest impelling motive of the Jewish immigrant was 'love of profit.' The love of profit made the Jewish immigrant worker competitive and it was by competition that he sought success. But this competition was 'unrestricted by the personal dignity of a definite standard of life,' and was 'unchecked by the social feelings of class loyalty and trade integrity.'[85] In other words, because the immigrant Jews loved profit so much and had such a burning ambition to succeed, they were prepared to tolerate poor working conditions. For J A Hobson, the Jewish worker was 'admirable in domestic morality and an orderly citizen' but also 'almost devoid of social morality.' This was because his 'superior calculating intellect' was 'used unsparingly to enable him to take advantage of every weakness, folly and vice of the society in which he lives.'[86] These were cultural or essentialist rather than socio-economic explanations.

Some turn of the century social analysis in contemporary America was reaching similar conclusions about the alleged greed and competitiveness of Jewish immigrants. Writing in *The Century* magazine, Edward A Ross produced a theory about Jewish racial characteristics in which an 'inborn love of money-making'[87] was an important factor. He expressed nativist sympathies based on a belief in Anglo-Saxon supremacy as well as a disdain for certain ethnic groups, among whom were eastern European Jews, believing that they posed a threat to social stability. In his article 'The Jewish Invasion of America,' author Burton Hendrick, after surveying the economic activity of Jews in America, claimed 'there is not the slightest doubt that within a few years the Jew will own the largest part of Manhattan Island, the richest parcel of real estate in the world...' He gave a picture of Jews as relentlessly acquisitional, ignoring how their actions had transformed the industries in which they were immersed and enriched the country

---

[85] Ashley, W. J. "Booth's East London." *Political Science Quarterly* 5, no. 3 (1890): 507–19.

[86] David Robson, "So were we 'void of social morals'," *The Jewish Chronicle*, January 7, 2016.

[87] Talia Lavin, *Culture Warlords: My Journey into the Dark Web of White Supremacy* (New York: Hachette Books, 2020), 28.

as a whole.[88] Naturally, the trope of the avaricious, finance controlling Jew found resonance in the hateful screeds of Henry Ford and the *Dearborn Independent* in the years following WWI.

Such analyses examined Jewish economic behaviour in essentializing terms, ones in which Jews were depicted in negative stereotypical terms as avaricious, controlling and obsessed with profit. Jews were depicted as parochial, inward looking and selfish, lacking the social traits needed to join in collective enterprises for the common good. Such ways of thinking built upon and added another noxious layer to the original deicide myth and the bestializing depictions of Jews that accompanied it.

The Jew As Racial Parasite

The Christian religious heritage provided inexhaustible sources of antisemitic demonization and multiple tropes and ciphers of Jew hate. But Christian attitudes towards the Jews were always ambiguous; yes, they had to be hated because they had knowingly rejected their Lord in a fit of blindness that only Satanic possession could explain. Their status as a wandering nation had to continue on account of their original sin of rejecting the Messiah. But redemption too was possible. If the Jews only recognised the grievous sin they had committed, they would be welcomed with loving arms. The Jew may have had an inherited deicidal sin but it was also a stain he could remove through conversion. It was the faith that was the aberration, not the race.

By contrast, the modern era saw new iterations of Jew hate in which the inherent vices of the Jews were a permanent flaw and an eternal reminder of their threat to civilization. Modern secular societies in Europe, transformed by Enlightenment rationalism, witnessed an upsurge of antisemitism in the eighteenth and nineteenth centuries. Among leading intellectuals, Voltaire was the chief exponent of a virulent form of anti-Judaism which was transformed into a blinding hatred of Jews. There is little doubt that Voltaire saw in the Jewish faith an unlimited repository of ignorance, barbarism, fanaticism and superstition, one that was harmful to themselves and wider society. He came to see Christians too as being 'steeped in narrow-minded superstitious nonsense' as a result of their adopting a 'Jewish-imposed belief' that was fundamentally flawed and anti-intellectual. Yet the irony is that Voltaire, more than any other individual, helped shape the 'rationalistic trend that moved European society toward improving the status of the Jews.'[89]

But his vituperation was also extended to Jews, described by him in his *Philosophical Dictionary* as 'an ignorant and barbarous people, who have long united the most sordid avarice with the most detestable superstition and the most

---

[88] "Accuses Hendrick of caricaturing Jew," *New York Times*, March 15, 1913.
[89] Katz, *From Prejudice to Destruction*, 34.

invincible hatred for every people by whom they are tolerated and enriched.'[90] He thus came to believe that Jews were harmful and noxious by nature, foreshadowing the eliminationist antisemitism that was to come two centuries later. Fundamentally, he saw Christians as 'racially Europeans' with their faith 'an overlay on their basic noble character' whereas Jews were 'Asiatic' and were incapable of being saved because their 'corrupt nature' was 'part of their physical essence and thus could not be abandoned.'[91]

Thus, in his *Letter of Memmius to Cicero* (1771), Voltaire wrote of the Jews that they were 'all of them, born with raging fanaticism in their hearts, just as the Bretons and the Germans are born with blond hair.' He went on: 'I would not be in the least bit surprised if these people would not some day become deadly to the human race.'[92] Such detestable prejudice was not reserved for Jews alone. Voltaire entertained disparaging views on other nations and ethnic groups, declaring that Europeans seemed to him 'superior to Negroes as Negroes are to monkeys and monkeys to oysters.'[93]

The notion that Jews posed a grave threat to the European societies in which they were becoming steadily assimilated, a threat that would not necessarily be mitigated through their conversion, would gain more adherents in the nineteenth century as 'the Jewish question' began to be discussed with increasing urgency. It also coincided with the process of political emancipation by which Jews slowly gained political equality, escaped from the ghettos and began assimilating into European societies. Marx had argued that the only solution to the Jewish question was for Jews to abandon the religion of Judaism and adopt a universalist perspective that was aligned with socialism. In this way, they would merge as people into the political landscape without their particularist faith getting in the way.

But others saw the Jews as a threat regardless of how they altered their appearance, religion or customs. Jews *as* Jews were a problem, given that they were deemed to be an inherently alien and parasitical presence in society that could not be tolerated under any circumstances. In this sense, they shared Voltaire's view that Jews, by virtue of their 'abhorrent' qualities, had an irredeemable nature. One was Karl William Grattenauer whose pamphlet *Wider Die Juden* (Against the Jews) appeared in 1803. Grattenauer, the son of a pastor, burned with hatred and loathing for Jews. He asserted that they had alien characteristics so pernicious and malodourous, including a unique odour, that their continuing presence in Europe was intolerable. He sought to replace a bust

---

[90] Leon Poliakov, The History of Anti-Semitism III: From Voltaire to Wagner, (Philadelphia: The University of Pennsylvania Press, 2003), 88.
[91] Maxine Schur, "Voltaire and the Jews," https://www.reed.edu/gls/Maxine.Schur. pdf, p. 9.
[92] "Lettre de Memmius a Ciceron from The Complete Works of Voltaire," as quoted in Arthur Hertzberg, The French Enlightenment and the Jews (New York: Columbia University Press, New York, 1968), 303.
[93] Litvinoff, The Burning Bush, 145.

of Mendelssohn that adorned Berlin with that of the Jew hater Voltaire. The mathematician and philosopher Jakob Fries launched a similarly destructive invective at German Jews in his pamphlet 'On the Danger Posed to the Welfare and Character of the German People by the Jews.' He accused Jews of being bloodsuckers of the German people who contaminated the purity of the nation. He wanted laws to prevent intermarriage between Jews and Gentiles and insisted that Jews bear a mark on their clothing to distinguish themselves. Furthermore, he wanted the German states to encourage Jews to emigrate and to prohibit Jewish immigration.

These may have been the ethnological rantings of an obscure figures but that did not mean that Jews could ignore them. The winds of history had taught Jews to be vigilant of fanatics, given how easily their thoughts could segue into the most extreme violence. As Barnett Litvinoff wrote, Jews 'hugged a perennial fear of even the most hollow fragment of Judaeophobic literature.'[94]

At the same time, the nineteenth century witnessed an explosion of interest in racial categorization and notions of white supremacy. In Count Arthur de Gobineau's *Essai sur l'inegalite des races humaines* (1853), the author divided the human race into three groups: white, yellow and black and asserted that the white (or Aryan) race was alone capable of creativity and greatness. He warned that due to miscegenation (mixing of races), whites were in danger of degenerating.

In old age, De Gobineau spent time as a guest of the German composer Richard Wagner, a figure notorious for his antisemitic prejudice. Wagner believed that Jews were an unfeeling people who were incapable of true creative greatness. In his *Das Judenthum in der Musik* (Jewishness in Music) (1850), he wrote that the Jew was 'incapable ... of artistic expression, neither through his outer appearance, nor through his language and least of all through his singing.' Wagner saw Jews as 'the most heartless of all human beings'[95] and a people who could only be apathetic to the societies they lived in. Being divorced from the *Volksgeist*, they lacked the soul or passion for true art; they were mere imitators. This viewpoint resonated with those of his contemporaries who identified the worst excesses of industrial capitalism and modernity with Jewish influence.

Houston Chamberlain, the son of a British admiral, would adopt some of de Gobineau's ideas about white supremacy in his major work *Die Grundlagen des neunzehnten Jahrhunderts* (Foundations of the Nineteenth Century). In the book he lauded the Aryan race for laying the foundations for all the great economic, scientific and technological advances of modernity. He claimed that the canon of Western art, literature and music was the product of Aryans and drew a sharp contrast between them and Jews, the latter depicted as 'the inverse of the Aryan.' For Chamberlain, Jews were the focus of all negative attributes and posed a menacing threat to the societies they lived in. Invoking the conspiratorial theory

---

[94] ibid.146.
[95] Wistrich, *A Lethal Obsession*, 103.

of the Jew as poisoner, he warned that Jews were trying to infect Indo-Europeans with Jewish blood through intermarriage just as Jewish miscegenation in ancient times was the cause of the Roman Empire's decline and fall. The aim of the Jewish people was to create 'a single people of pure race' with the rest being 'pseudo-Hebraic mestizos' who were 'beyond all doubt degenerate physically, mentally and morally.' In this way, the Jew would 'put his foot upon the neck of all nations of the world and be Lord and possessor of the whole earth.' [96] Chamberlain bristled with contempt for the Catholic Church, in part because he believed that the Papacy was controlled by Jews.

Hostility to Jews continued in the writings of ideologues such as Wilhelm Marr, Eugen Duhring, Heinrich Von Treitschke and Theodor Fritsch. These writers produced books that attempted to 'solve' the Jewish question, a euphemism for removing Jews from society. The economist Eugen Dühring published *Die Judenfrage als Racen-, Sitten- und Culturfrage: Mit einer weltgeschichtlichen Antwort* (The Jewish Question as a Question of Race, Customs and Culture: With an Answer Relating to World History) in which he pictured Jews as irredeemably evil and argued that their depraved nature stemmed from their inherent characteristics. Similar diatribes were penned by propagandist Theodor Fritsch, author of *Handbuch der Judenfrage* (Handbook of the Jewish Question) and German agitator Wilhelm Marr, who wrote *The Way to Victory of Germanicism over Judaism* (1879). None of these authors believed that Jews could be redeemed by conversion and all pictured them as a sinister race whose machinations threatened the stability of western societies.

Perhaps the most extreme voice of German nationalism and antisemitism belonged to the radical Austrian politician Georg Ritter von Schönerer (1842-1921). Von Schönerer advocated the pan German union of Austria and Germany (the Anschluss) and was an uncompromising foe of the Hapsburgs, the Catholic Church and the Jews. He came to believe that the struggle for Austria was really a struggle against Jews and, in 1885, proclaimed that antisemitism was 'the main pillar of a true folkish mentality and thus as the greatest achievement of this century.' [97] His influence grew among the working class in Vienna, with supporters addressing him as 'Fuhrer' and using the term 'Heil.'

These racial doctrines were being propounded during an era of resurgent nationalism. Originally, nationalism was seen as entirely compatible with liberalism. If one fought for a national state free from foreign overlords, it would enhance the rights of all its citizens and be a blessing to other nations. But as the rancour for liberation grew louder and as support for authoritarian figures grew stronger, it began to drown out support for liberty and, with it, any tolerance for minority populations within the national boundaries. Minorities were scapegoated, marginalized and reviled because they were deemed to be barriers

---

[96] Quoted in Geoffrey G Field, *Evangelist of Race: The Germanic Vision of Houston Stewart Chamberlain* (New York: Columbia University Press, 1981), 189.

[97] Robert Wistrich, *Hitler and the Holocaust*, (London: Weidenfeld & Nicolson, 2001), 41.

to national progress. The most extreme forms of reactionary nationalism stressed the organic unity of blood, soil and people, turning loyalty to the nation state into something akin to mystical belief. Racist mythologies and philosophies were eagerly seized upon by nationalists who saw them as useful vehicles to attract new supporters.

Racist diatribes helped to shape an ethno-nationalist völkisch antisemitism that was becoming more prevalent in nineteenth century German circles. Völkisch thought was romantic and nationalist, seeking to bind the German ethnic community through a common literature, language and fatherland and decrying influences from modernity, primarily urbanization, materialism and class conflict. It believed that the modern capitalist system, depicted as rootless and alienating, posed a threat to a simpler life which was based on rural simplicity, traditional virtues and communal ties. Völkisch thinkers yearned for a pre-industrial age of rustic virtue in which the worship of soil would go hand in hand with a return to roots. In their excoriating critique of modern capitalism, these thinkers saw the hidden hand of the Jew, a figure who was perceived to be undermining the organic unity of the German nation with his alleged corruption, materialism and scheming. Volk culture regarded the Jews as an alien biological 'other,' a representative of the modern order that sat at odds with rural purity and simplicity. As an urban dweller who had long abandoned farming, the Jew was seen as the enemy of the German peasant. Sentiments such as these appear in the writings of Paul de Lagarde, a German Bible scholar who believed in creating a German form of Christianity purged of Jewish 'vermin' and 'parasites.'[98] He argued that the Jews could be resettled or assimilated but if these alternatives were impossible, advocated their destruction. He thus foreshadowed the eliminationist antisemitism of National Socialism.

This völkisch tradition of antisemitism did not have a uniform influence on Germans in the nineteenth and early twentieth centuries. Those classes of German society that had secure economic and social positions, such as the nobility or the industrialized classes, were relatively immune to it. But the lower middle-class artisans and shopkeepers, and some university graduates, needed a convenient scapegoat on which to hang all their discontents, fears and anxieties. This was despite the fact that Jews formed a tiny minority of the population, many of whom were subjected to the same economic crises as anyone else. Among those propagating Völkisch theories were a large number of nineteenth century German writers whose pens were dripping with racist venom. A study by researcher Klemens Felder of 51 antisemitic German writers from 1861 to 1895 found that over one third (19) advocated 'physical extermination' of Jews.[99]

In the twentieth century, Hitler would become the principal political disciple of Völkisch racism. He came to believe the fundamental premises of this racialist

---

[98] Albert S Lindemann, "Review of Germany's Prophet: Paul de Lagarde & the Origins of Modern Antisemitism, by Ulrich Sieg." *Holocaust and Genocide Studies* 29, no. 1 (2015): 126-129.
[99] Perry and Schweitzer, *Antisemitism*, 105-6.

philosophy. He believed that the conflict between races was the motivating force in all human history, culture and social relations, fusing Marxist determinism with a twisting of Social Darwinism. From de Gobineau, he took the view that the Aryan nation was the most perfect race on earth and that the German nation was essentially of Aryan stock. For Hitler, Aryan man was the fount of civilization and culture, the source of great spiritual energy and the progenitor of art, science, and technology. In Hitler's words, without the Aryan, 'the dark veils of an age without culture (would) again descend on this globe.'[100] Yet he believed that world civilization and German greatness were on a precipice and that the ascendancy of the Aryan race in the world was under threat. This was because Aryan blood, the source of all racial greatness, had been contaminated by an inferior race, namely the Jews. In his own words, 'The mightiest counterpart to the Aryan is represented by the Jew.'[101] For Hitler, the task of the Jew was to dominate the world and this could be achieved through blood poisoning, the contamination of a higher-grade race. The primary tools at the Jews' disposal, according to this theory, were miscegenation, the mixing of racial blood through the sexual rape and exploitation of Aryan girls, and the Marxist policy of mass immigration which led to the importation of racially inferior groups. For Hitler, ancient and modern history were seen through the lens of racial theory, as a cosmic global battle between the Aryans and the Jews. In order to restore the 'rightful' supremacy of the Aryan nation, Hitler's fundamental task was to eliminate the Jews, initially from German life but, in the long run, from human existence.

This fanatical depiction of Jews as an existential threat to Germany, and the wider Aryan race, was accompanied by a relentless stream of dehumanizing imagery. Cartoons that appeared in the main Nazi newspaper, Der Sturmer, delighted in likening Jews to vermin and bestial animals. One Nazi cartoon from 1933 compared the Jews to a giant frog which had opened its mouth in order to consume the human race while its amphibian hands clutched onto gold. In September 1934, the Jew was represented as a worm seeking 'to creep up on what he wants.' In March 1935 Jews were depicted as a poisonous serpent, complete with grotesque facial features, that was being strangled by a German hand. In 1944, Jews were likened to vermin, with readers told that 'Life is not worth living when one does not resist the parasite.'

In addition, Nazism presented Jews as a morbid sexual threat to the German nation. In an effort to indoctrinate young German children, Julius Streicher introduced books into Germany's schools replete with antisemitic images. In one such book, 'Trust No Fox on His Green Heath and No Jew on His Oath,' a cartoon showed a grotesque image of a Jewish male dressed in black preying on an innocent, blond haired German girl. The Jew was unmistakably represented as a lecherous and devious figure whose predatory lust posed a grave threat to the

---

[100] Hitler, *Mein Kampf*, trans. Ralph Manheim (Boston, 1943), 339.
[101] ibid. p. 300.

nation's youth. Just as black American men were depicted as despoilers of white American women, so too were Jewish males pictured as rapacious sexual exploiters seeking to defile Aryan girls. Such images were designed to inspire fear and paranoia among German men, in turn encouraging them to burn with hatred at world Jewry.

The point of all this imagery was to 'to dehumanize the Jews in order to frame an anti-Jewish public consensus and to insist on the need for action taken against the "Jewish problem."' [102] Indeed when the Second World War loomed in Europe, the notion that this coming conflict would see a German drive to solve the 'Jewish problem' was readily apparent. In January 1939, Hitler himself declared that if 'the international Jewish financiers in and outside Europe should succeed in plunging the nations once more into a world war, then the result will not be the Bolshevization of the earth, and thus the victory of Jewry, but the annihilation of the Jewish race in Europe!' [103]

The notion of the Jew as an alien racial parasite, a lurid threat to his society and to civilization in general, emerged at a time when another virulent trope had infected the Zeitgeist. It was one that would fuse with earlier forms of dehumanization and culminate in the greatest tragedy in the history of the Jewish people.

The World Jewish Conspiracy

The myth of the Jewish world conspiracy focused on the idea that Jews were a secret and shadowy cabal, acting behind the scenes to exercise their control of events with the ultimate aim of achieving world domination. The Jew was no longer just a creature to be despised and mocked, a figure of ridicule and hatred, the bearer of all that was most insufferable in mankind. Now, the Jew was to be feared too, his notorious plotting and conniving seen as a threat to the safety of society and the continuation of civilization. In this type of conspiratorial antisemitism, Jews acted 'malevolently in the background, pulling strings, controlling events, acting as an all-powerful force backing and enabling the other targets of their hate.' [104] The most infamous exposition of this view was the notorious forgery *The Protocols of the Elders of Zion*, a book that cast a dark shadow on twentieth century antisemitism and which ultimately served as a 'warrant for genocide.' [105]

---

[102] Gregg Hunt, "Framing Consent: Nazi Antisemitic Imagery, 1933-1945," yumpu.com, accessed 10 February 2021, https://www.yumpu.com/en/document/ view /23388647/gregg-hunt.

[103] This is an excerpt from a speech given by Hitler to the Reichstag on January 30, 1939.

[104] Emma Green, "Why the Charlottesville Marchers Were Obsessed with Jews," *The Atlantic*, August 15, 2017.

[105] After the Bible, the *Protocols*, in its many translations, was the most widely circulated book in the world during the interwar years.

The enduring myth of global Jewish control and influence, a vital component of the archetypal antisemitic perspective, should be seen as a form of 'political antisemitism,' according to which Jews constitute 'a malign and conspiratorially minded political entity: an entity whose nature, once that nature was exposed, and understood, must compel the patriotic citizen to combat and expel it, lest the host body politic be irretrievably harmed, corrupted, or both.' [106] It is contrasted with social antisemitism which essentially consists of a series of hatreds and prejudices about Jews as individuals, picturing them as avaricious, unpatriotic, clannish, untrustworthy, among other negative attributes, but not necessarily acting in concert as a harmful *collective* force. Political antisemitism has seen the Jews as a global threat to humanity, operating on an international level, rather than a merely local threat to whichever society they reside in. For more than two centuries, it has resulted in truly fantastical notions of Jewish malevolence and conspiratorial power and served, in the warped minds of antisemites, as the ultimate justification for mass murder.

But the trope of conspiratorial antisemitism did not start with the *Protocols* and nor has it ended with it. Antisemitism as a whole is a malevolent conspiracy theory, a key part of which revolves around the purportedly nefarious plans of world Jewry for the domination and enslavement of Gentiles, whether the Jews are in league with the devil or acting on their own accord. At the heart of Christendom's tirade against Jews is a belief in their diabolical, conspiratorial powers. The Jews are pictured as manipulators who somehow conspire to force Pilate, and the might of Rome, to do their bidding. During the Black Death, such fears of Jewish world domination surfaced among Gentile societies who thought that the Plague was 'but a first step in a Jewish plot to take over the world.' [107] It was also foreshadowed in the myth of ritual murder, the blood libel, which was accompanied by the belief that a remote conclave of Jewish sages decided the time and place where a Gentile child would be snatched and murdered. So, the predilection for conspiracy theories is long lasting in the history of the human race and has affected Jews as much in medieval times as the modern.

The modern fears, frustrations and resentments that gave birth to anti-Jewish conspiracy mongering can be traced to the aftermath of the French Revolution, the seminal event at the end of the eighteenth century that heralded profound economic and social changes across Europe. These changes involved the abolition of a feudal monarchy, the upending of aristocratic privileges, the surge in industrialization and the consequent rise of a dynamic, entrepreneurial capitalistic class intent on increasing its wealth. Above all, the Revolution ushered in an age of nationalist fervour with calls for liberal and democratic reform. It would be a profound mistake to believe that this century long clarion call for change was seen

---

[106] Paul Harrison, *The Resurgence of Antisemitism: Jews, Israel and Liberal Opinion* (Lanham: Rowman & Littlefield, 2006), 27-8.

[107] Friedman, Jerome. "Jewish Conversion, the Spanish Pure Blood Laws and Reformation: A Revisionist View of Racial and Religious Antisemitism." *The Sixteenth Century Journal* 18, no. 1 (1987): 3–30.

universally as a sign of progress. For some, this revolutionary fervour was disconcerting and hateful, an interference in the natural order of society.

Jews came to be seen as the prime agents and symbols of modernity and the embodiment *par excellence* of the forces of change. Having been liberated from the ghettos and allowed to enter the universities and professions, they were in a position to take advantage of all these social and economic changes. Their drive, entrepreneurship, scholarship and dynamism made many Jews successful in business and enterprise, with a certain number dominating in several professions. Moreover, as a despised minority that had long suffered the depredations of autocratic rule, they readily embraced the liberal and democratic values that would allow them to live freely. All these factors made Jews visible to their enemies, among whom were the aristocracy, the church and conservatives. They saw in the onset of modernity the hidden hand of the Jew, a human enemy whose sinister machinations were well known from medieval times.

One of the earliest expositions of the conspiracy theory about global Jewish control came from French Jesuit writer Augustin Barruel (1741-1820). Barruel set out a theory whereby the French Revolution had resulted from a secret plot hatched by Freemasons, Enlightenment thinkers and the Order of the Illuminati with the ultimate aim of overthrowing the Christian order. He claimed that the heirs of their conspiracist thinking were the Jacobins, the left wing, revolutionary movement that played an important role in the Revolution. Later, Barruel received a letter from a 'Jean Baptiste Simonini,' purporting to reveal a secret conversation that he had had with a group of Jews from Piedmont. In this conversation, Simonini claimed to have been told that the Jews founded both the Freemasons and the Illuminati and that they were plotting to take over the world, abolish the church and effectively turn Christians into their slaves. Naturally, there was no truth to the claim that Jews founded either organization. But the Judaeo-Masonic conspiracy was given rocket fuel by Napoleon's decision to free the Jews of Europe from the ghettos and convene a Sanhedrin (an assembly of Jewish elders). For some, this was proof that Napoleon (for some a secret Jew himself) was heralding the age of the Anti-Christ at the behest of world Jewry. Barruel did not publish the letter but he did pass it around circles in France, though its influence is believed to have been limited.

The notion of a political Judaic conspiracy to control world affairs might have been consigned to history had it not resurfaced in the writings of German writer Hermann Goedsche (1815-1878), a minor official in the Prussian postal service and later a novelist. One of his novels, *Biarritz* (1868), contained a chapter titled 'In the Jewish cemetery in Prague.' It described a night-time meeting between a secret Council of 13 Jews assembled around the tomb of Rabbi Simeon Ben Jehuda, 12 of whom represented each of the twelve tribes of Israel.

The opening speech talks of how Jews have been 'trampled' and 'humiliated' by their enemies and suffered for eighteen centuries under Christendom. The assembled are told that the power of the Jews is rising in the world. Jews will soon possess all the global reserves of gold, 'the instrument of every power' and 'the sum of everything that man fears and craves.' In virtue of the Rothschild dynasty, the Jews are said to be the financial masters in every major European city and the controllers of all capital, ensuring that all kings, emperors and princes are in debt to the cabal. As the Jews' global control is not yet secured, further plans for world domination are discussed. The elders are told they must weaken the influence of the church by promoting doctrines of scepticism and free thought which will widen religious schisms within Christianity. Jews must also become legislators so that they can abrogate the laws promulgated by 'sinners' and 'infidels.' They must dominate the world of trade and speculation but only in professions which bring honour and power. Jews must also attain 'supreme control over all the industrial, financial, and commercial operations' while avoiding legal action in the country's courts. Jews are told to master the sciences, especially medicine as this will mean that 'the health and life of our mortal enemies, the Christians' are in Jewish hands. Intermarriage with Christian families is to be encouraged because this will make Jews 'the arbiters of their fate.' Jews are told they must master the means of mass communication because becoming 'the arbiters of public opinion' will enable them to dominate the masses. One consequence is that the Jews will deal a blow to the sanctity of the family and 'extirpate all belief and faith in everything' that Christians have sworn by. In case it was not already clear, the ultimate aim of these plans is to achieve 'world domination.'[108]

In the coming years, the chapter was published as a pamphlet and in newspapers in cities across Russia and Europe, except that it was treated as if the rabbi's speech was authentic and not fictional. When Germany began to dominate the production and dissemination of antisemitic ideas in the last two decades of the nineteenth century, the myth of the world Jewish conspiracy was a dominant feature.

Before the *Protocols* were published, similarly dire views about the power of Jewry had been expressed in one of the nineteenth century's most famous antisemitic tracts, *The Way to Victory of Germanicism over Judaism (1879)*. It was written by the activist Wilhelm Marr, a man known as 'the father of antisemitism.' In it, he issued a dire warning that 'the Jewish spirit and Jewish consciousness have overpowered the world' and demanded that action be taken against 'this foreign power.' This power had 'corrupted all society with its views' and now possessed 'the controlling position in commerce, as well as infiltrating into state offices and ruling the theatre.' Marr was anxious to avoid dressing up his Jew hatred in religious terms, hence the need for a new term that was devoid of theological elements: antisemitism.

In France, the Catholic priest Emmanuel Chabauty (1827-1914) produced his own version of the myth in *Les Juifs nos maitres* (1882). He claimed to have discovered authentic letters, 'The Letter of the Jews of Arles' and 'The Reply of the Jews of Constantinople,' both of which purported to reveal a fifteenth century

---

[108] Quotes from The Rabbi's Speech, "In the Jewish Cemetery in Prague," from the novel *Biarritz* (1868).

plot to force Christians into poverty, destroy the church, kill Christians through medicine and achieve the summit of power.

For Chabauty, these documents were proof of a secret Jewish government existing through the ages, one to which all Jews showed fealty, which was conspiring to ensure a Jewish takeover of the world. He came to see the Jews as agents of Satan who were preparing the world for the reign of the Anti-Christ. The sinister document was reprinted by the notorious French antisemite Edouard Drumont and later appeared alongside the *Protocols*, providing for antisemites additional proof of the 'Judaic-Masonic' machinations that threatened to overwhelm the world order.

In Russia, the idea that Jews were engaged in a subversive conspiracy to overthrow the Christian order came naturally to the autocracy's ruling elite. Russian Jews, an unassimilated minority numbering some 5,000,000 by the turn of the twentieth century, were blamed for fomenting revolutionary and terroristic violence against the country's imperial rulers. They were a convenient scapegoat, hated by Tsars such as Nicholas II, as well as the clergy, the peasantry and many of the Jews' commercial rivals. The Russian political police were only too happy to distribute antisemitic propaganda to incite violence and hatred towards the Jews. Among the leading propagandists was a Polish priest Hippolytus Lutostansky (1835–1915). His three volume work *The Talmud and the Jews* (1879-1880), together with earlier writings that directly invoked the blood libel, were seized upon by The Black Hundreds, a right wing ultra-nationalist group responsible for violence against Jews and other groups. Later in the century, Jacob Brafman (1825-1879), a Jewish convert to the Russian Orthodox Church, would pen a seminal antisemitic text called *The Book of the Kahal: Materials for the Study of the Jewish Life* (1869). In it, Brafman contended that the kahal, an institution governing the Jewish world, had been brought to life in the form of five organizations, among which were the Paris based *Alliance Israélite Universelle*. He described these organizations as 'a state within a state' and alleged that they formed part of a universal Jewish conspiracy to control the lives of Jews and non-Jews alike. The book received glowing reviews and became one of the bibles of the Russian antisemitic movement.

Another obscure contribution to the myth of global Jewish domination was provided by Major Osman Bey (real name Frederick Millingen) in his slim volume *Conquest of the world by the Jews*. Jews, he declared, were in 'everlasting antagonism to the rest of mankind.'[109] This is because they had discovered the 'principle of Material Interests,' one which impelled them to save wealth as a means of obtaining supremacy over other nations. He proceeded to trace the growth in Jewish plunder from Biblical times to the modern era, arguing that no matter how dispersed Jewish communities found themselves, they were always part of a 'united and fearful body.' He condemned Jews as 'unproductive

---

[109] Major Osman Bey, *The Conquest of the World by the Jews: An Historical and Ethnical Essay* (European Freedom Foundation, 2019), 7.

parasites'[110] whose means of acquiring wealth was based on appropriating the productions of others. At the time he wrote, Jewish domination was apparently an established fact with Jews 'the wealthiest and most influential class of men.' With this vast financial power, they threatened to 'crush all other nations.' He went on to say: 'There is not a man amongst us, who is not in some way tributary to the Jewish power.'[111] For Millingen, this power was manifested in the means by which Jews controlled public opinion, a feat achieved after they 'flooded the professions of law and journalism.' Using their ability to 'make the world believe anything,' the Jews had 'appropriated the right of intervention in all foreign affairs.'[112] In politics, the overall Jewish goal was 'conquest of the world,' achieved by the manipulation of parties and nations through capital.[113]

In nineteenth century French literature, many works were imbued with fear and loathing of the Jew, mirroring the phobias, prejudices and obsessions of French society. Jews were depicted as 'strangers, intruders, as unassimilable parasites arriving from other lands to despoil the French nation.'[114] Their ascent from the ghetto to the halls of power was deeply resented, as was their ability to outwit rivals without mercy. Characters like Monach in Robert de Bonniere's *Les Monach* use vast wealth and unscrupulous means to make it into high society. In *Le Baron Vampire*, the Jewish protagonist similarly rises from ghetto squalor after learning the means by which to ruin Christians and enrich his own people. The novel, which was replete with accusations that Jews were responsible for the financial ruin of European peasants and for war profiteering, was written amid rumours that the Union Generale bank had crashed due to illicit speculation by Jews. In *Le Baron Jehova*, Sidney Vigneux described an alleged secret meeting of Jewish conspirators as 'a cancerous tumour' which was designed to create 'an empire of the world' throughout its nefarious control of politics, the judicial system and the press. Similar literary references appeared in Guy d'Orcet's *La Comtesse Schylock*. The notion that Jews were conspiring to dominate France and Europe undoubtedly appealed to the ultra-conservative, Jew-baiting French journalist Edouard Drumont. In his notorious two volume work *La France Juive*, Drumont pictured Jews as racially inferior creatures who used capitalism and materialism as vehicles with which to undermine the French nation and drive a stake through the heart of Catholic culture. His book passed through 100 editions, was translated into a number of languages and aroused considerable influence and interest.

Few of these relatively obscure tracts had the power to move history or shape popular attitudes towards the Jews. What gave rocket fuel to the myth of global Jewish domination was a pamphlet whose sentiments would echo across the twentieth century and provide the Nazi totalitarian regime with a 'warrant for

---

[110] ibid., 36.

[111] ibid., 45.

[112] ibid., 53.

[113] ibid., 58.

[114] Weinberg, Henry H. "The Image of the Jew in Late Nineteenth-Century French Literature." Jewish Social Studies 45, no. 3/4 (1983): 241–50.

genocide.' Its name was *The Protocols of the Elders of Zion*, though it is also known by the title *The Protocols of the Meetings of the Learned Elders of Zion*. According to the testimony of Henri Bint, a Frenchmen who worked for the Tsarist regime, it was put together on the orders of Pyotr Ivanovich Rachkovsky (1853-1910), the chief of the Okhrana, the Russian secret police. He had a history of forging documents in the service of seeking to destroy radical and revolutionary movements inside and outside Russia as well as a history of making antisemitic pamphlets.

There are many different versions of this text but the one most familiar to modern readers was produced by Russian mystical writer Sergey Nilus (1862-1929). He printed the *Protocols* as chapter 12 of his book *The Great within the Small and Antichrist, an Imminent Political Possibility. Notes of an Orthodox Believer*, and an abridged version of the document appeared in the literary magazine *Znamya*. The document was then distributed across Russia and millions of copies found their way across the capitals of Europe.

The main themes in the *Protocols* borrow much from Goedsche and the other authors already cited. A member of a secret government called the Elders of Zion outlines a sinister plot to ensure Jewish domination of the globe. The Elders of Zion believe that gentile states have been undermined and that it is their task to abolish them altogether. This will be achieved by fostering the ideas of liberalism and democracy, philosophical doctrines which by their nature sow confusion and unrest among the populace. The Elders will encourage Presidential systems in order to create puppet leaders and foster conflict between states so as to undermine international understanding. They will encourage wars which will lead to increasing global strife and economic chaos. The Elders will undermine Gentile morality by encouraging atheism, drunkenness and all manner of depravity. Moreover, to ensure that the Gentiles do not defeat the Jews, they will create revolutionary unrest which sees workers everywhere rise up against their governments and destroy private property. They believe that rulers everywhere are demoralized already, afraid to appear in public because of assassinations and aware that they do not command the consent of those that they rule. Once this demoralization becomes critical, the Elders will step in to rule Gentile societies.

Their vision for rule is plutocratic and based on their possession of gold, the true basis for all wealth in the world. But they also seek to control all the instruments for shaping public opinion from the education system to the law, from Parliament and the media to the Freemasons. All political parties are their tools and they will manipulate them as they see fit. The Elders will ensure that society is run on a totalitarian basis. Thus, there will be strict censorship of publications with limitations on freedom of speech and association, all of which can be enacted through emergency powers that will become permanent. To ensure compliance, a secret police will spy on citizens and it will become obligatory to report criticism of the regime. However, in order to keep the masses contented, the Elders will provide a full range of economic benefits, such as full employment and fair taxation, while peace and justice will prevail. This is a vision of a pseudo-Messianic age concocted by the Jews, pacific and idealistic in some respects, deeply sinister and autocratic in others. Such is the message in the *Protocols*.

In the early years of the twentieth century, the *Protocols* were exploited by fanatical, demagogic right-wing groups such as The Black Hundreds to incite against Jews. Their propaganda portrayed the Duma (the National Assembly), set up in the aftermath of the 1905 revolution, as a Jewish creation designed to overthrow the royal court. Members carried out waves of pogroms and assassinations and in their unrelenting hatred of Jewry and their belief in Judaeophobic conspiracies, represented a virulent strand of Russian proto-Nazism.

The *Protocols* found a new lease of life at the end of the First World War. In the intervening four years, the world had faced an unprecedented level of political and economic convulsion. Millions had been plunged into the horrors of global war; families had been torn apart, the landscape had been ravaged and the threat of hyperinflation was stalking many countries. Amid this seemingly senseless upheaval, the West was also confronted by a new Bolshevik regime that was intent on imposing its revolutionary dogmas on European societies. Supporters of the ousted Tsar distributed the *Protocols* in an effort to discredit the Bolshevik revolutionaries, some of whose leading ideologues were Jewish.

Suddenly, it appeared that there was a Bolshevik-Jewish conspiracy designed to overthrow empires, monarchs and governments in the service of their revolutionary ideals. As Paul Hanebrink argues, 'counterrevolutionaries everywhere cast "Judaeo-Bolshevism" as a threat to European civilization' with Europe imagined as 'a community of Christian nations' threatened by an eastern invasion.[115] The alleged connection between Bolshevism and international Jewry mesmerised many on the political right. A headline in *The Chicago Tribune* gave credence to the *Protocols* when it proclaimed 'Trotsky Leads Jew Radicals to World Rule. Bolshevism only a tool for his scheme.' It went on to denounce Bolshevism as a movement 'aiming for the overthrow of existing society' whereas the other 'world revolutionary movement' as described by the *Protocols* was about 'the establishment of a new racial domination of the world.' Such a racial movement, it reminded its readers, was profoundly 'anti Anglo-Saxon.'[116] The American moment was ripe for such conspiracist hatemongering. It was the time of the Red Scare when America was convulsed by a widespread fear of subversive anarchism, immigration and Bolshevism. Shortly afterwards, Henry Ford was to popularise the notion of the world Jewish conspiracy for an American audience in a long series of articles for his paper *The Dearborn Independent*. In 1920, the first of three French translations of the *Protocols* appeared.

News of a nefarious Jewish plot to dominate the world reached London in 1920. It was duly announced by *The Times* with an article headlined 'The Jewish peril: A Disturbing Pamphlet: A call for inquiry.' The paper took an ambiguous line on this document, neither confirming nor denying its authenticity and

---

[115] Paul Hanebrink, *A Specter Haunting Europe: The Myth of Judeo-Bolshevism* (Belknap Press, 2020), 8.
[116] Cohn, *Warrant for Genocide*, 172-3.

providing no proof of authorship. It asked: What are these '*Protocols?*' Are they authentic? If so, what malevolent assembly concocted these plans and gloated over their exposition? Are they forgery? If so, whence comes the uncanny note of prophecy, prophecy in part fulfilled, in part so far gone in the way of fulfillment. The paper warned that, having just escaped a 'Pax Germanica' there was a danger of falling into a 'Pax Judaica.'[117] But its credibility as one of the world's leading papers brought this document to the attention of scholars and political figures.

A year later, the document was exposed for the transparent forgery that it was, a piece of writing so clearly plagiarised that its duplicitous nature could hardly be doubted. This was discovered in 1921 by Times' journalist Philip Graves, the paper's Constantinople correspondent, and the paper subsequently issued a retraction. He found that whole passages of The *Protocols* were copied from *Dialogue aux enfers entre Machiavel et Montesquieu ou la politique de Machiavel au XIXe siècle (The Dialogue in Hell Between Machiavelli and Montesquieu)*, a brilliant work of political satire written by French lawyer Maurice Joly (1829–1878). Joly's dialogue was intended as a biting critique of the authoritarian policies of Napoleon III with Montesquieu putting the case for liberalism and Machiavelli, the case for despotism. His work had nothing defamatory to say about the Jews or Judaism. Yet a good portion of Joly's text, together with its format, was reproduced by whoever first wrote the *Protocols*. What ought to have been even more obvious was that the majority of Jews did not support Bolshevism and that the majority of Bolshevik leaders and thinkers were Gentile.

Of course, for some antisemites, the idea that this document was a fake merely provided further proof of its authenticity. Thus in 1921, Catholic prelate Monsignor Ernest Jouin responded to claims that the *Protocols* were forged by saying: 'The Jews fight against the *Protocols*, first with suppression and then with denial. That double attitude induces us to believe in the authenticity of this famous document.'[118]

By the end of the First World War, the virulent messages of racial Judaeophobia and Jewish-Bolshevik global control had been transmitted to a young Austrian agitator and former corporal in the German army, Adolf Hitler. Like millions of others who had fought for imperial Germany, he was at pains to understand how his country had been defeated by the Allied powers. For those who could not accept conventional perspectives, there was a simple and seductive explanation to hand. Germany had been defeated, not by the mistakes of its high command or by the successes of the Allies, but by a cabal of internal enemies who had sold the country to its opponents. According to the legend of the 'stab in the back' (*Dolchstoßlegende)*, these 'November criminals' had conspired to end the war, bring down Wilhemine Germany and instigate a new pacific regime based

---

[117] Henry Wickham Steed, "A Disturbing Pamphlet: A Call for Enquiry," *The Times*, May 8, 1920.

[118] William Brustein, *Roots of Hate: Antisemitism in Europe Before the Holocaust* (Cambridge: Cambridge University Press, 2003), 277.

on liberal democracy. Those allegedly committing such treasonous behaviour consisted of pacifists, strikers and Bolsheviks, though central blame was directed towards the Jews. Books were produced purporting to reveal the full scale of the conspiracy directed against Germany and its interests. They included the first German edition of the *Protocols*.

Hitler assumed control of the German National Socialist party in 1921 and became seduced by the notion that Jews posed an existential threat to the German nation. In *Mein Kampf*, he adopted a twisted form of social Darwinism in which each nation or racial grouping faced a life and death struggle for its existence. He pictured the German *Volk* as an embattled nation which was forced to confront the predatory Soviet Union, its ideological arch nemesis. To survive, the German nation needed *Lebensraum* (living space) and thus to expand to the east, at the Soviet Union's expense.

But crucially he saw Bolshevism as an inherently Jewish creed, an ideology that the Jews had used to annihilate the Russian intelligentsia and commit genocide against ordinary Russians. He thus pictured the Soviets and the Jews as part of a noxious anti-Aryan alliance. For Hitler, Jewish egalitarianism and liberal democracy contradicted 'the significance of nationality and race' and represented a negation of 'the eternal laws of nature.' Using the kind of apocalyptic language that presaged the Holocaust, Hitler declared: 'If, with the help of his Marxist creed, the Jew is victorious over the other peoples of the world, his crown will be the funeral wreath of humanity…'[119] For Hitler, Germany's war against the Jews had a redemptive, almost utopian, quality. He saw their removal from Germany, and later their mass murder, as a means not just of saving the German nation from defilement and extinction but of rescuing the world order. Hence the Manichean vision outlined in a statement from 30 January 1942 in which he declared that the Second World War would end 'either in the extermination of the Aryan peoples or in the disappearance of Jewry in Europe.'[120]

Hitler acknowledged the role that the *Protocols* played in his thinking, repeating the canard that Jewish claims that it was a forgery constituted the surest proof that they were genuine. Already in *Mein Kampf*, he spoke of how Jews were using Bolshevism to dominate the masses and overthrow the existing order. In the book, he produced a philosophy of history in which, time and again, social revolutions and rebellions occurred because of the Jews' radical, egalitarian ideas. In each society, there was a dominant, pure-blooded elite that was chosen to rule on account of its innate strengths. The Jews, lacking the same physical prowess, incited unrest by mobilising the discontented lower orders to revolt. In his worldview, Paul's introduction of egalitarian, pacifist thinking in Christianity corrupted the Roman Empire's belief in martial supremacy. All subsequent revolutions, from the French Revolution to the birth of liberalism, from the Russian Revolution to the birth of Weimar, revealed the subversive, hidden

---

[119] Extracts From Mein Kampf by Adolf Hitler (yadvashem.org).
[120] Cohn, *Warrant for Genocide*, 210.

hand of the Jew. It was a hidden hand because the Jew was envisaged as 'the invisible wirepuller.'[121] For Hitler, this hand manipulated the lower orders into overthrowing the strongest forces in society, all of which was done in the service of his diabolical aim of global domination. He pictured world civilization as teetering on the edge of disaster and the Jew as the cause of its decay and decline. The destruction of the biological basis of Jewry was thus envisaged as an existential necessity. It was the only way to restore the natural order, namely the supremacy of the world's naturally strong racial stock (i.e. the Nordic race). Mass murder was the logical end point of eliminationist antisemitism, warranted by centuries of relentless demonization that chipped away at the basic humanity of Jews. It was made possible only by culturally brainwashing millions of people with the archetypal antisemitic perspective in generation after generation.

There are postwar variants of this apocalyptic belief in Jewish global domination. The notion of a world Jewish conspiracy has also become a feature of modern black nationalist thought, especially within the Nation of Islam (NOI) and the BLM movement. Malcolm X spawned a radical, hard hitting black nationalism which rejected any notion of integration and eschewed the non-violence of Martin Luther King. Associated with this was a toxic perception of Jewish power in the US. He once wrote: 'Anybody that gives even a just criticism of the Jew is instantly labelled anti-Semite. The Jew cries louder than anybody else if anybody criticizes him. You can tell the truth about any minority in America, but make a true observation about the Jew, and if it doesn't pat him on the back, then he uses his grip on the news media to label you anti-Semite.'[122]

The NOI's leader, Louis Farrakhan, has a history of Jew baiting and of making virulent claims about America's Jewish community. Farrakhan once claimed that the Jewish lobby had 'a stranglehold on the government of the United States.' In an interview with *The Washington Post*, he claimed that 'Jews were part of a small clique who use their power and their knowledge to manipulate the masses against the best interests of the people.' He clearly believed that fellow American blacks were the targets of this Jewish manipulation when he declared that Jews were sucking the blood of the black community, a phrase that evoked both the blood libel and the *Protocols*.[123] The theme of black people being pawns in the grubby hands of their Jewish overlords was reiterated by another prominent black nationalist leader in the NOI, Khalid Abdul Mohammad (1948-2001). In a hate filled tirade from 1993, Mohammed claimed that Jews had 'our athletes in the palm of our hand' and that they controlled prostitution and 'white slavery.' Mohammed's invective was so deranged that even Farrakhan distanced himself from it and Mohammed went on to lead the virulently antisemitic New Black Panther party.

---

[121] Patterson, *A Genealogy of Evil*, 38.

[122] Baddiel, *Jews Don't Count*, 84.

[123] "Excerpts of Interview with Louis Farrakhan," *Washington Post*, March 1, 1990.

The NOI was responsible for a historical myth of Jewish conspiratorial control when, in 1991, it published *The Secret Relationship between Blacks and Jews*. This work, which had no identified author, purported to prove that Jews dominated the centuries old transatlantic slave trade and were its principal beneficiaries. In its words, there was 'irrefutable evidence that the most prominent of the Jewish pilgrim fathers (sic) used kidnapped Black Africans disproportionately more than any other ethnic or religious group in New World history.' In a calculated attempt to attack Jewish victimhood, it called slave vessels 'holocaust ships' and labelled black slaves 'holocaust survivors.'[124] As if to emphasize the point, it stated that Jewish slave traders were 'much like the Nazis at the concentration camps of Auschwitz, Treblinka or Buchenwald.'[125] Thus, like those who liken Palestinian victims of Israel to Holocaust survivors, the authors of this book were trying to appropriate the memory of the Holocaust from Jews by launching a spiteful attack on Jewish historical memory. The book accused Jews of continuing to exploit black people post emancipation. It pictured them as spiteful and venal store owners, as cruel and oppressive landlords, as school teachers responsible for infecting young black minds with pernicious ideas, as insensitive social workers and as activists opposed to affirmative action. The clear message was that Jews were (and in the present day remain) the enemies of black people. If there was a guiding hand that kept black people oppressed and which robbed them of life chances, it was a Jewish one. Thus, black liberation required an ongoing struggle with the Jewish oppressor, using violent means if necessary. With its quotations, indexes and bibliography, the book came across as an intellectually respectable, evidence-based tome.

Yet, close analysis of this work reveals that many of the quotations are inaccurate, the works cited are secondary sources (some are out of date) and the methodology is suspect. In essence, the authors focus on every Jewish name as if to prove that they and they alone were responsible for racism, exploitation and slavery, a clear form of confirmation bias. It is perhaps rather like those who list every Jewish banker and financier in the world to prove there is a global conspiracy to control the money supply. It is mendacious and utterly fraudulent. In any case, the factual case is simply incorrect. Historian Saul S Friedman cites figures which destroy the myth that Jews dominated the slave trade. He wrote: There were 697,681 slaves in America in 1790, 1,538,022 slaves in 1820. According to official census records, Jews owned 209 slaves in 1790, and 701 in 1820. During the formative years of the United States…when the import and sale of Africans was at its peak *Jews owned less than three one hundredths of a percent, 0.03 per cent of all the slaves in America.*[126]

It is undeniable that the enslavement of millions of black Africans over several centuries was a monstrous and inhuman crime and those that took part in

---

[124] The Nation of Islam, *The Secret Relationship Between Blacks and Jews* (Chicago: The Final Call, 1991), 191.

[125] ibid p. 207.

[126] Perry and Schweitzer, *Antisemitism*, 246.

it were guilty of reprehensible behaviour. It is right that we memorialize the death and suffering of innocent people and use our efforts to end modern day slavery. But to single out Jews in this crime when all the evidence shows their role to be marginal is nothing better than noxious Jew baiting and such gutter racism has no place in respectable academic circles.

The modern far right has spawned its own, equally noxious, conspiracy theory about Jewish global control, called the Great Replacement theory. The basic idea is that western identity, framed in terms of racial whiteness, is under threat by policies of mass immigration and multiculturalism. The demographic changes that are portended are designed to replace white dominated societies with those of darker skin and to bring about the genocide of white people. It is claimed that this replacement has been orchestrated by a shadowy elite as part of a dastardly plan to rule the world. The guiding mantra of those who subscribe to this paranoid view can be summed up in 14 words: 'We must secure the existence of our people and a future for white children.' This white supremacist slogan was coined by the American neo-Nazi leader David Lane in his White Genocide Manifesto. That manifesto also contains these chilling words: 'All Western nations are ruled by a Zionist conspiracy to mix, overrun and exterminate the White race.' [127]

The idea has been popularised by fascists across Europe. It was a belief that prompted the psychotic acts of mass murder committed by Anders Breivik when he killed 77 people in Norway in 2011, though his primary motivation was to stop 'the Islamic colonization of Europe.' It also underpinned the actions of New Zealand shootist Robert Bowers and it has been central to the ideology of the American alt right. Many have identified Jews as the shadowy elite responsible for this nefarious plan, bringing the theory in line with all the essential elements of the *Protocols*. Thus, in their Declaration of Independence, the neo-Nazi group Aryan Nations accused Jews of seeking 'the eradication of the white race and its culture' and, in the US, of waging war against the inhabitants of the South. [128] In 2017, far right protestors at a rally in Charlottesville shouted that 'Jews will not replace us.' [129] What they meant was not that Jews were trying to take the place of whites themselves but that they were instigating a takeover of white dominated society by promoting policies of mass immigration. This was also the reason why shooter Robert Bowers went into the Tree of Life synagogue in Pittsburgh in 2019 and shot dead 11 people. He claimed that Jews were behind the influx of Central American migrant caravans and immigrants and, justifying his actions, said: 'I can't sit by and watch my people get slaughtered.' [130] In Hungary, anti-immigrant

---

[127] Jonathan Sarna, "The Symbols of Antisemitism in the Capitol Riot," *Brandeis Now*, January 11, 2021.
[128] "Declaration of Independence: Aryan Nations," March 12, 1996, accessed 20 March 2020.
[129] Rosa Schwartzburg, "The 'white replacement theory' motivates alt-right killers the world over," *The Guardian*, August 5, 2019.
[130] Masha Gessen, "Why the Tree of Life Shooter Was Fixated on the Hebrew Immigrant Aid Society," *The New Yorker*, October 27, 2018.

rhetoric that is cited by the alt-right has often used antisemitic canards associated with the *Protocols*.

However, the most noxious theory of Jewish conspiratorial theory is the one most readily identified with the extreme right, namely Holocaust denial. The denial of the most egregious crime in modern history has been inspired by the writings of a small cadre of committed ideologues, among them Harry Barnes, Arthur Butz, David Irving, Fred Leuchter Jr., Paul Faurisson and Ernst Zundel. A summary of just one of these figures is enough to understand the dynamics of this appalling assault on truth and memory.[131] In 1975, Arthur Butz, an American electrical engineer, wrote *The Hoax of the Twentieth Century: The Case Against the Presumed Extermination of European Jewry*, a book which has since become one of the bibles of Holocaust denial. His central thesis was that the Nazi mass murder of 6 million Jews was nothing but a Zionist hoax and that the gas chambers did not exist.

He claimed that Zyklon B, the deadly gas used at Auschwitz and other camps, was purely an 'insecticide' rather than a deadly weapon used to kill Jews and others.[132] He dismissed the gas chambers as a hoax, providing seemingly credible scientific and engineering data to disprove the idea that millions of bodies were cremated at that and other camps. He stated that deaths at Belsen were because of a 'typhus epidemic' and were the result of 'a total loss of control, not a deliberate policy.'[133] As regards Belzec, Chelmno, Majdanek, Sobibor, and Treblinka, the evidence for an extermination program at those camps was 'fairly close to zero.'[134] Statements from both Hitler (in his will and before the war) and Himmler which, *ceteris paribus*, revealed an intent to eliminate European Jewry were similarly explained away either as forgeries or wilfully twisted to pervert their meaning. Instead, he took contemporary Nazi documents with all their euphemisms at face value, suggesting that 'German policy was to evacuate the Jews to the East' rather than exterminate them.[135]

He dismissed the clear and obvious demographic evidence for a Jewish population fall in Europe by claiming that it was impossible to check the accuracy of the Jewish or Communist sources, adding the additional problem that there is a 'lack of any legal, racial, or religious basis for defining a "Jew."'[136] He stated that it would 'appear excessively brazen to claim the virtual disappearance of Polish Jewry.'[137] The war crimes trials at Nuremberg were also dismissed in cavalier fashion as a case of victor's justice, carried out in an 'atmosphere of

---

[131] The subtitle of Deborah Lipstadt's book *Denying the Holocaust* (2000) was 'The Growing Assault on Truth and Memory.'
[132] Arthur Butz, *Hoax of the Twentieth Century: The Case Against the Presumed Extermination of European Jewry* (Uckfield: Historical Review Press, 1975), 138.
[133] ibid. p. 55.
[134] ibid. p. 215.
[135] ibid. p. 260.
[136] ibid. p. 32.
[137] ibid. p. 30.

unreality and hysteria' that the author compares to 'the witchcraft trials of Europe's younger days.'[138] In short, the book dismissed all the evidence for a mass extermination program in the strongest and most pejorative terms.

The hoax, for Butz, was carried out by many groups and agencies but led by the Jews, one of 'the most powerful groups on earth,' with all their powers of manipulation and control of the media and government. Among those who were duped were the German people themselves and the defendants at Nuremberg, though Butz claimed their acceptance of guilt came about because of the wave of post-war hysteria that swept Europe. Yet, as Deborah Lipstadt points out, these were the same Jews who made no impression on Allied powers prior to WWII in their request to open borders to Jewish refugees. Central to this manipulation was the ability to forge an untold number of documents that gave proof of Nazi plans to murder Jews, documents which had to be created at breakneck speed after the war and then planted so as to deceive Allied governments. For some reason, these skilful forgers forgot to produce the most vital proof of all, namely an order from Hitler authorizing the mass destruction.

It is not just white westerners, such as Arthur Butz, Roger Garaudy, David Irving and Robert Faurisson, who have denied the Holocaust. The belief has also become part of the discourse in the Middle East where the racist demonization of Jews is permeated with the notion that this people has swindled the West in order to extort sympathy for their 'anti-Arab' Zionist project. The belief ultimately comes from the very top. Egypt's Abdel Nasser once claimed that 'no person, not even the most simple one takes seriously the lie of the six million Jews who were killed.'[139] In his book *The Other Side: The Secret Relationship Between Nazism and Zionism* (1983), Mahmoud Abbas, later the PA President, wrote of the 'Zionist fantasy, the fantastic lie that six million Jews were killed' and cited a figure of 890,000 Jews who were murdered. He would later revise his attitude towards the tragedy. Holocaust denial conferences have been organised by the Iranian government with President Ahmadinejad claiming not to believe in the mass murder of Jews. Supreme leader Khamenei has also claimed: 'The Holocaust is an event whose reality is uncertain and if it has happened, it's uncertain how it has happened.'[140]

Denying that the Nazi Holocaust took place combines all the noxious elements of the *Protocols* – that the Jews are liars and covert manipulators, that they have sufficient control of the media, government and organs of public opinion to actively manipulate others, friends and foes alike, that they force gentiles to bend to their will in order to extort money or political favours from

---

[138] ibid. p. 233.

[139] Laqueur, *The Changing Face of Anti-Semitism*, 141.

[140] Joshua Levitt, "Iran's Ayatollah Khamenei Says Reality of Holocaust is 'Uncertain'," *Algemeiner*, March 21, 2014.

them and that they hate non-Jews enough to spread appalling lies about them.[141] Like those who are obsessed with Jewish power, these deniers twist, manipulate and wilfully misinterpret evidence so as to defame their enemies. It stands to reason that people like Butz and Irving have the same burning hatred of Jews as the Nazis.

Holocaust denial has been a central plank of the white supremacist onslaught against the Jews from the mid twentieth century onwards. While today's white supremacists are at the forefront of attacks on Muslims and other racial, ethnic, religious and sexual minorities, seeing them as dilutors of a 'pure' white society, they also have a paranoid obsession about Jews which underlies the rest of their worldview. In general, white supremacists see Jews as being 'adjacent to whiteness' yet involved in an insidious plot to destroy it through policies of mass immigration, asylum and refugee policy. This is because the racial minorities 'invading' western societies are not seen as clever or agile enough to advocate for themselves, a belief that is itself based on a series of malign racist tropes. Instead, their cause is guided by the 'the cunning, world-controlling, whiteness diluting Jew' whose omnipresence provides 'the intellectual foundation of the white supremacist movement.'[142]

The belief in the power of Jews to control world events has even reached Japan and South Korea, countries that have barely any Jews at all.[143] Talking of Korea, Jason Lim has said that 'There is a widespread belief that Jews supposedly control the world through shadowy governments and institutions, fanned by best-selling books and exposes.' In Japan, a series of bestsellers on this theme has appeared in recent decades with titles such as *The Jewish Plot to Control the World, To Watch Jews Is to See the World Clearly* and *The Next Ten Years: How to Get an Inside View of the Jewish Protocols*, while articles have appeared blaming the Jews for the world's financial woes. The Chinese bestseller *The Currency War* argues how Jews are 'planning to rule the world by manipulating the international financial system.'[144] At the same time, this form of antisemitism differs from its European counterpart in that there is a simultaneous desire to emulate the Jews' supposed control. Thus, one can find books in Korean bookshops with titles like *How to Succeed like Jews* and *The Wisdom of the Talmud*.

Notions of Jewish conspiratorial control have been revitalized in South America via the Andinia Plan, a conspiracy theory alleging that Jews are trying to create a Jewish state in Patagonia, the continent's southernmost region.

---

[141] Holocaust denial is also referred to as a form of secondary antisemitism, a phenomenon whereby Jews are blamed for being victims of persecution and trying to deviously exploit the Gentile world by talking about their role as wartime victims.

[142] Lavin, *Culture Warlords*, 25.

[143] Such views filtered through from Japan during the period of colonization in the twentieth century, after the Japanese began to distribute the *Protocols* following the Russo-Japanese war in 1905.

[144] Ian Baruma, "The 'Jewish conspiracy' in Asia," *The Guardian*, February 9, 2009.

Proponents of this theory seize on the fact that the early Zionists, Herzl among them, were looking to create a Jewish state outside of Palestine and that large waves of Jewish immigrants entered Argentina in the early part of the twentieth century. The plan was taken seriously by Argentina's right-wing junta and is referred to by neo-Nazis. In 2012, antisemitic conspiracy theories appeared on Chilean websites accusing Jews and Israel of deliberating starting a fire in the Torres del Paine Park in Chilean Patagonia. Chilean politicians poured fuel on the flames by suggesting that the Israeli tourist who accidentally caused the fire had been sent deliberately.

All of these hateful theories are variants on a common theme: an obsession with the supposedly demonic power and influence of Jews on world events, with an ensuing fear of what Jews are capable of doing if their power is left unchecked.

The Jew as a mendacious threat to Islam

Thus far, we have looked at the development of antisemitism in the Christian West. But today, there is a three-pronged assault on the Jews that comes not just from the far left and far right but also from the Muslim world. The Islamic dimension of antisemitism must therefore be explored too. In recent decades, a debate has raged between those who see Islamic antisemitism as a European or western import, brought to indigenous Arab populations by Christian missionaries in the nineteenth century, and those who see it as homegrown, an inherent feature of Islamic civilization. There is much historical evidence for the first view, particularly given the presence of European tropes in Arab and Muslim antisemitic discourse. But there is an indigenous tradition too which will be outlined.

Like early Christianity, Islam is a supersessionist faith. Just as early Christian theologians claimed that the Christian Church had supplanted the Jews as the true people of God, so too Islam preaches that the teachings of Mohammed are the most authentic version of the original Abrahamic monotheism, presenting the world with a purer version of God's message for mankind. The Quran is regarded as the infallible message of God that expresses the divine intent, an immutable and eternal truth for mankind.[145] Those reformists who argue today for a more enlightened Islam are frequently denounced as infidels and *kuffar*.

Islam too has an early history and mythology which invokes the Jews of Arabia and their relations with the faith's founder. In the seventh century, Jews were living in all the major Arabian towns as well as the peninsula. Many were the descendants of exiles who had fled Judaea after the Roman conquest or had converted. When Muhammad began to preach the basics of his new faith, he was certain that the Jews would be among his first converts. After all, he adopted a monotheistic outlook of submission to one God, prayed in the direction of Jerusalem, adopted the practice of circumcision and introduced a set of dietary

---

[145] The comments of Islam scholar Rashad Ali were invaluable for this section.

restrictions similar to those in Judaism. He also saw Moses, the great Jewish lawgiver, as a prophet and Abraham, the first Jewish patriarch, as the father of Jews and Arabs. But Jewish tradition held that prophets would arise with the return of Jews to Zion and, as a result, could not accept Muhammad's religious leadership. A series of battles ensued, after which Muhammad expelled the Jewish tribes of Banu Nadir and Banu Qainuqah and later killed between 600 and 900 Jews from the tribe of Banu Qurayzah.[146] In popular mythology, the Jews had sided initially with Muhammad and then later broke their agreement in order to side with his enemies. With the exception of the Red Sea port of Jeddah, Arabia was effectively rendered *Judenfrei*, denuded of its Jewish population. This was in keeping with Muhammad's decree: 'Let there not be two religions in Arabia.' It is these varying relations with Jews that help explain the divergent attitudes towards them in the Quran.

One of the central themes in the Quran's depiction of Jews was that this people had rejected God's prophets because of their treacherous and deceitful character. They denied Muhammad even though they knew he was the prophet, much as in Christianity, and thus attempted to lead humanity astray. The punishment of God was to impose abasement and poverty on the obstinate Jews for their heretical ways, the latter including the imposition of the jizya tax.[147]

The Islamic scholar Qadi Baydawi spoke of the Jews 'intense obstinacy' and 'multi-faceted disbelief' as well as 'their addiction to following their whims.' Another Muslim commentator from the fourteenth century, Ibn Kathir, condemned the Jews' 'rebellion, defiance, opposing the truth' and 'belittling other people.'[148] In the Quran, Jews are accused of rejecting the revelation of Allah, of unjustly killing his prophets, (Sura 4:155) and are condemned for their disbelief (4:46). Jews are asked: 'Why did you kill the prophets of Allah if you are true believers?' (2:91). As a result, they were said to be (with polytheists) 'the people most hostile towards the believers' (5:82). They stand accused of confounding truth with falsehood (3:71), of usury (4:161) and misleading others (3:69). Jews were said to have hearts as hard as rock (2:74), of being blind and deaf to the truth (5:71) and to be an envious people (2:109). Due to these various flaws which seem to be permanently etched in the Jewish character, the Quran warns that a 'humiliating punishment' awaits them (58:14-19), that their faces will be obliterated (4:47) and they will burn in hellfire (4:55). As Scholar Ronald L Netter

---

[146] It is fair to point out that these figures are disputed, together with the identity of the tribe of Banu Qurayza.

[147] The jizya tax was not specifically for Jews but for non-Muslim males who were judged sane and permanently residing in a state governed by Islamic law. Many classes of people were excepted from paying the tax.

[148] Andrew Bostom, *The Legacy of Islamic Antisemitism: From Sacred Texts to Solemn History* (Amherst, N.Y.: Prometheus, 2008), 37

put it, the overriding theme in the Quran was that Jews were 'arrogant renouncers and falsifiers of God's truth.'[149]

Mohammed also railed against those monotheistic peoples who had rejected his revelation, saying, 'O Lord, perish the Jews and Christians. They made churches of the graves of their prophets. There shall be no two faiths in Arabia.'[150] In essence, Jews were depicted as rejecting God's message and his messenger (Muhammad) in a stubborn denial of the truth and had ever since been conspiratorially minded, mortal enemies of the Muslim world. For this cardinal sin of rejecting the Muslim message, it was essential that the Jews faced continuing disgrace and submission to Islam. The most visible manifestation was that the Jews were forced to pay the jizya tax (9:29) as a permanent mark of their subordination and as a stark reminder of their error strewn ways. Never again could they be a sovereign people within a Muslim jurisdiction.

There were clear elements of demonization in the early Islamic attitude to Jews. Just as early Christian texts picture the Jews as a devilish force embodying evil, so too did the Quran. A verse in the text specifically associates them with Satan and suggests that they are consigned to hell for their sins (4:60). Numerous pieces of anecdotal evidence attest to the ubiquity of the association between Jews and hellfire in Muslim societies. Elsewhere Allah has the Jews transformed into 'apes and pigs' (5:60).[151] The pigs and apes reference is a staple of modern Muslim antisemitism, a pejorative reference often cited by Islamists when they demonize Jews and Zionists.

Rendering the Jews as animalistic, as less than human, is one of the most grievous forms of demonization and leads to an inescapable belief in eliminationist racism. In this sense, there are strong elements within Islam and Christianity in which Jews are described and pictured as something less than human, as a monstrous element in the world population. All these verses, ones whose negative interpretation has been backed up by leading Muslim authorities, are then taken to offer scriptural justification for antisemitic atrocities. One can largely agree with this statement by historian Andrew G Bostom: 'Basic Islamic education in the Qu'ran, hadith and sura...may create an immutable superstructure of Jew hatred on to which non-Muslim sources of Jew hatred are easily grafted.'[152]

But there is a positive side too. Unlike Christianity, there is no deicide in Islam. The faith pictures Jews as renouncers of Mohammed's message but instead of conquering and killing him, they are decisively defeated. Instead, it is the Islamic creed that is in the ascendant, subduing all those who doubted his divinity. It was precisely because Mohammed's prophetic message and his chosen faith

---

[149] Ronald Netter, *Past Trials and Present Tribulations: A Muslim Fundamentalist's View of the Jews* (Oxford: Pergamon Press, 1987), 7.

[150] Hadith Malik 511: 1588.

[151] Some early exegetes like Mujahid, the student of Ibn Abbas, stated this was not literal but among Islamists, it is a common expression which seems to be taken literally.

[152] Bostom, *The Legacy of Islamic Antisemitism*, 33.

triumph over the unbelievers that there is less of an emotional need to espouse Jew hatred in early Islam. Jews like Christians were regarded as 'peoples of the book' (Ahl al-Kitab). The great figures of the Judaeo-Christian narrative, such as Abraham (Ibrahim), Moses (Musa), David (Daud) and Jesus (Isa), are prophets in Islam, albeit they are referred to by Arabic names. Allah is said to have helped the Israelites cross the Red Sea (10:90), sent manna and quails to the Jews (20:80), resettled Jews in a sanctified land (10:93), delivered them from 'humiliating torment' (44:30) and given Moses (Musa) the Holy Book as guidance to the children of Israel (17:2). The Jews are said to have had wisdom and prophethood bestowed upon them and they are granted Scriptures (45:16). It is said that those believers (Jews and Christians included) who understand the Quran's revelation will enjoy the blessings of Paradise (27:76-81).[153]

Over the coming centuries, the ambivalent attitudes towards Jews were manifested in an equally ambivalent experience of Muslim rule. During the much-lauded Golden Age in the Iberian Peninsula, al-Andalus became a central place for Jewish culture where poets and philosophers thrived. There were also significant periods of prosperity for Palestine's Jews during the era of Ottoman rule. Despite certain limitations and restrictions, Jews were largely not confined to ghettos[154] as they were in Christian Europe and they could engage in various trades. They had a defined political status in the developing Islamic societies, enjoying rights and protections that were absent in Christian Europe. In addition, they were largely free to practise their faith and enjoyed formal representation before the authorities of the states they lived in.[155]

But at the same time, Muslim rule could be deeply injurious. 5,000 Jews were massacred in Granada in 1066 and many Jews, as well as Christians, were killed under the Almohads in Spain and North Africa in the twelfth century. There were decrees ordering the destruction of synagogues in Egypt (1014), Iraq (1344) and Yemen (1676) and Jews were forced to convert to Islam or face death in many countries. Jews faced pogroms on many occasions, including Safed in 1834, Damascus in 1848, Aleppo in 1853, Marrakech and Fez in 1864 and Alexandria in 1870 and 1881.

Jews living under Muslim rule were also subjected to *dhimmitude*, a form of governmental 'protection' which came in exchange for subordination to Muslim overlords. Anyone subject to *dhimmitude* faced various forms of discriminatory treatment in their social and economic life. They were, in effect, second class citizens. Restrictions included a prohibition on arms, restrictions concerning the building of churches and synagogues, inequality in tax laws, and a requirement that Jews and other non-Muslims wear special clothes and walk on a certain side of the road. In Yemen, in the late eighteenth and early nineteenth centuries, decrees

---

[153] All references are from an online translation of the text at www.clearquran.com.
[154] From the fifteenth century, the Jews in Morocco were confined to mullahs (segregated quarters).
[155] David J Wasserstein, "So, what did the Muslims do for the Jews?" *The Jewish Chronicle*, May 24, 2012.

were issued that forced Jews to remove human waste and filth from Muslim areas. In nineteenth century Morocco, Jews in major cities such as Fez were forced to salt the heads of decapitated rebels, a humiliation enacted even on the Sabbath.[156] All of this reflects the Quaranic injunction that 'humiliation and wretchedness were stamped upon them and they were visited with wrath from God' (2:61).

Taken as a whole, however, Jewish populations fared better under Islamic than under Christian rule. It is also true that the truly obsessive and demoniacal thinking associated with Christian antisemitism entered the Middle East only in the first half of the nineteenth century. Its worst manifestations could be seen in 1840 when thirteen members of the Damascus Jewish community were arrested after being accused of murdering a monk for ritual purposes. The local consul Ratti-Menton, together with the Governor-General Sharif Pasha, conducted a brutal investigation whereby they tortured a Jewish man until he 'confessed' to the crime. Others among the accused died from torture while 63 Jewish children were also seized to put pressure on the community. The resulting international outcry led to the release of the prisoners. This was the most prominent of the blood libels that spread around the Arab world at this time and though most were initiated by Christians rather than Muslims, they would come to gain increasing acceptance in the twentieth century.

Antisemitism has certainly been a ubiquitous feature of Islamist thinking in recent centuries and has led to a discourse of demonization matching anything produced in the West. Ibn Taymiyya insisted that the strictures on Jews regarding their clothing and religious practice be strictly enforced and issued a fatwa allowing Muslims to curse and insult Jewish holy books.[157] In *Kitaab at-Tawheed*, ibn Abd-al-Wahhab venomously denounced Jews for their alleged betrayal of Muhammad and their idol worship. He regarded some Christians and Jews as 'sorcerers' who believed in devil worship and accused both groups of turning the graves of their prophets into places of worship. A key theme in his writings was the danger of Jewish unbelief which was seen as the inevitable result of their untrustworthiness and 'deceitful' nature.[158]

The archetypal image of the Jew as treacherous, deceitful and untrustworthy resonated with twentieth century Islamists who sought to rationalize the civilizational collapse of Muslim power in the modern era. Sayyid Qutb, the leading theoretician of violent jihad in the twentieth century and arguably one of the most famous personalities of the Muslim world in the modern era, directed a litany of abuse towards Jewish people, accusing them of 'wickedness,' 'deception,' 'mercilessness' and 'moral shirking.' For rejecting the message of Muhammad, he accused them of 'perpetrating the worst sort of disobedience [against Allah], behaving in the most disgustingly aggressive manner and sinning

---

[156] Bostom, *The Legacy of Islamic Antisemitism*, 46.
[157] Daniel Benjamin and Steven Simon, *The Age of Sacred Terror* (New York: Random House, 2002), 67-68.
[158] Dore Gold, *Hatred's Kingdom: How Saudi Arabia Supports the New Global Terrorism* (Washington: Regnery Publishing, 2004), 25.

in the ugliest way.' This essentialist perspective roots the enmity between Muslims and Jews in the perceived negative traits of the 'Jewish character.'[159]

In his book *Our Fight Against the Jews* (1951), Qutb depicts Jews as the natural enemy of Muslims everywhere and as a people animated by revenge after their defeat by Muhammad. He wrote: 'The Jews want no more no less than to exterminate the religion of Islam.'[160] One of his most incendiary claims was that the Jews had engineered the split between Sunni and Shia Muslims in order to weaken the Muslim community by a process of divide and rule. He believed that Jews had sown dissension within Muslim ranks and claimed that they had installed puppet regimes in the modern Muslim world in order to conspire against the community. These paranoid conspiracy theories bore all the hallmarks of the *Protocols*. Furthermore, he believed that the Jews had established the philosophical principle of rule based on secular law and legislative assemblies. For Qutb, the rule of man was anathema because it contradicted the idea that God's commandments were the only valid basis of all laws. For this reason, he condemned modern Jewish and Christian societies as being in a state of pre-Mohammedan ignorance, using the term *jahiliyyah* deriving from the Arab root *jahala* (to act stupidly) to describe them. For Qutb, this was no mere coincidence but was intrinsically rooted in an essentialist reading of Jewish character. The Jewish propensity to paganism reflected their 'wickedness' and 'deception,' traits which had 'accompanied the Jews in every generation and remain typical of their behaviour even today.'[161]

Qutb's antisemitic diatribe reflected the virulent prejudice that became rife in the Muslim Brotherhood before WWII. The Muslim Brotherhood, founded by Hassan al-Banna, advocated *jihad* against the British and the Jews and demanded a Nazi- style anti–Jewish boycott campaign. Its newspaper *al-Nadhir* blamed Egyptian Jews for the country's ills. In the years leading up to the Second World War, Nazi antisemitism in the 1930s would go on to find a receptive ear in various Arab countries, ranging from Egypt (the Muslim Brotherhood) to Iraq (the Futuwwa). Al Banna and other members of the Brotherhood were professed admirers of Hitler and during the war, Banna encouraged Muslims to join the SS Handschar, Kama and Skandberg divisions. Haj Amin el Husseini, Grand Mufti of Jerusalem, was an enthusiastic supporter of the Nazis who embraced Nazi race theory fervently in the pre-war years. During the Second World War, he spent a number of years in Berlin from where he helped inspire a pro-Nazi coup in Iraq and gather thousands of Bosnian Muslims to kill Jews in Yugoslavia. Husseini continues to be feted by Palestinian and Arab leaders to this day, despite his atrocious support for the Final Solution. In October 1956, the Muslim

---

[159] Quoted in Schoenfeld, *Return of antisemitism*, 41.

[160] Sayyid Qutb, *Our battle with the Jews* (Cairo: Dar al-Shuruq, 1989), 33.

[161] Sayyid Qutb, *In the shade of the Quran*, vol. 1 (Leicester: The Islamic Foundation, 1999), 17.

Brotherhood in Damascus declared that Hitler occupied 'a respected place in the Arab world' and his name aroused 'sympathy and enthusiasm.' [162]

Yusuf Al-Qaradawi (1926-) is one of the most influential Sunni Islamic scholars alive today. Lauded by figures such as Ken Livingstone, Al-Qaradawi has written some 120 books and broadcast on *Al Jazeera* to an audience close to 60 million. Qaradawi has been a vehement critic of Salafi Islam (the doctrine propounded by the religious establishment in Saudi Arabia), issued a fatwa denouncing the Islamic State and called for a dialogue with non-Muslims. But he has issued diatribes against Jews and Israelis that are every bit as bad as the antisemitic venom of Sunni Islamists. He has supported suicide bombings against Israelis, declaring them to be 'heroic martyrdom operations.' [163] In 2009, he appeared on Al Jazeera where he declared: 'Throughout history, Allah has imposed upon the (Jews) people who would punish them for their corruption. The last punishment was carried out by Hitler. By means of all the things he did to them – even though they exaggerated this issue – he managed to put them in their place.' [164] To leave no doubt about his position, he declared in 2013 that he would not participate in an interfaith rally if Jews were present.

It is not just Muslim extremists and radicals who give vent to antisemitic diatribes. If it was, it would be so much easier to isolate and ostracize the more radical elements in the Muslim community. One can also find respectable and feted leaders of the Muslim world who engage in incendiary Jew baiting, often citing holy texts to buttress their noxious prejudices. Muhammad Sayyid Tantawy (1928-2010), the former Grand Imam of al-Azhar, was often taken to be an Islamic moderate because of his opposition to suicide bombings, his condemnation of the 9/11 attacks, his opposition to female genital mutilation and his apparent support for normalized ties with Israel. But earlier in his life he had written a long treatise called *Jews in the Quran and the Traditions* in which he wrote: '[The] Quran describes the Jews with their own particular degenerate characteristics, i.e. killing the prophets of Allah, corrupting His words by putting them in the wrong places, consuming the people's wealth frivolously, refusing to distance themselves from the evil they do, and other ugly characteristics caused by their deep-rooted lasciviousness ... only a minority of the Jews keep their word. ... [A]ll Jews are not the same. The good ones become Muslims, the bad ones do not.' [165] In 2002, he referred to Jews as 'the enemies of Allah and descendants of apes and pigs,' directly citing Quaranic verses.

Another Muslim scholar feted in some western circles is Abdul Rahman ibn Abdul Aziz al-Sudais, the imam of the Grand Mosque in Mecca. Like Tantawy, Sudais has delivered sermons which have denounced terrorism and violence in

---

[162] Wistrich, *Hitler's Apocalypse*, 177.

[163] *Al Raya*, April 2001, quoted in Michael Slackman, "Islamic Debate Surrounds Mideast Suicide Bombers," *The Los Angeles Times*, May 27, 2001.

[164] Oren Kessler, "Analysis: Yusuf al-Qaradawi – a 'man for all seasons'," *The Jerusalem Post*, February 20, 2011.

[165] Bostom, *The Legacy of Islamic Antisemitism*, 33.

the name of the faith and he has made encouraging noises about interfaith work. Yet in a speech in 2002, he issued a fiery invective against Jews throughout time. He declared: 'Read history and you will know that yesterday's Jews were bad predecessors and today's Jews are worse successors. They are killers of prophets and the scum of the earth.' The Jews, he added, were a 'continual lineage of meanness, cunning, obstinacy, tyranny, evil and corruption.'[166]

The *Protocols of the Elders of Zion* is widely available in many Arab countries and has been regularly quoted by scholars and politicians. 'The (*Protocols*) is the most important source' in how Indonesian Muslims define Jews, according to Ibnu Burdah, director of the Centre for Islamic and Middle East Studies at the State Islamic University in Yogyakarta.[167] The ranting conspiratorial themes in the *Protocols* must have influenced Malaysia's most notorious antisemite, Mahathir Mohamad. He declared in 2003 that 'the Jews rule the world by proxy' and added that 'they invented socialism, communism, human rights and democracy' and have 'now gained control of the most powerful countries.'[168] The subsequent silence of Muslim leaders was itself a damning reflection of how an antisemitic culture could take root and form assumptions and worldviews. In 2002, a number of Arab television channels, as well as Egypt's state television, aired a 41-part series called *Knight without a horse*. Much of the show was an attempt to vindicate the *Protocols* by showing Jews throughout history as scheming global manipulators. A year later, Syrian television aired a 29-part series called *Ash Shatat* (The Diaspora) which reproduced the blood libel and alleged a vast Jewish conspiracy to rule the world. Even crazier conspiracy theories abound. One Iranian academic has said that the Tom and Jerry cartoon is a Jewish conspiratorial creation designed to enhance the image of mice, creatures that were associated with Jews and seen as unclean.[169] Indeed many Islamists consider not just Disney but the whole of Hollywood to be a Jewish manipulated capitalist conspiracy.

So how widespread are antisemitic attitudes and perspectives in the Muslim world? Of course, there is no completely accurate guide as to how people think. All survey data should be treated with due caution, given the nature of the questions posed and the risk that in autocratic societies, the responses one receives might not truly convey what people think. That said, the Pew Global Attitudes Project for 2010 showed that 'more than 90% of Egyptians, Jordanians, Lebanese and Palestinians express unfavourable views towards Jews' while in non-Arab Muslim countries (Turkey, Pakistan and Indonesia), the figure is around 70%.[170] However, what was interesting was the more positive view of Jews expressed by

---

[166] Howard E Negrin and Martin Perry (eds.), *The Theory and Practice of Islamic Terrorism: An Anthology*, (New York: Palgrave Macmillan, 2008), 211.

[167] Neil Kressel, *The Sons of Pigs and Apes: Muslim Antisemitism and the Conspiracy of Silence* (Lincoln, Potomac Books, 2012), 39.

[168] John Aglionby, "Fight Jews, Mahathir tells summit," *The Guardian,* October 17, 2003.

[169] ibid. 45

[170] ibid. 91

Muslims who knew Jews best: those living in Israel. Here the percentage expressing negative views fell to around 35%, suggesting that direct acquaintance with Jews was an antidote to the noxious, conspiracy driven fear that populates antisemitic fantasies. Muslims in many western countries are far more likely to hold antisemitic views compared to the rest of the population. According to a 2015 ADL survey, antisemitic views are held by 56% of German Muslims, as opposed to 16% of the population as a whole while the corresponding figures in France are 49% to 17% and in the UK, 54% to 12%. In the Netherlands, Muslims carry out 70% of the antisemitic attacks according to CIDI, its top watchdog for hate crimes. Yet Europe officially prefers to tell itself that there isn't a Muslim antisemitism problem and that the overwhelming majority of attacks come from the right wing.

The evidence from a number of outspoken Muslim writers suggests that such attitudes are widespread. To take some examples, Nonie Darwish said this about her upbringing in Gaza and Cairo: 'As a child, I was not sure what a Jew was. I had never seen one. All I knew was they were monsters. They wanted to kill Arab children, some said, to drink their blood.'[171] The British journalist Mehdi Hasan has talked of antisemitism being 'routine and commonplace' in his community and described it as 'our dirty little secret.' In his words, 'The virus of antisemitism has infected members of the British Muslim community, both young and old.'[172] In his book *The Jew is not my enemy*, Muslim moderate Tarek Fatah has spoken about how a billion Muslims are 'constantly being told by clerics about the essential deviousness of the Jew and the global conspiracies he weaves.' He has written of the 'growing number of Islamists and Muslim intelligentsia' who 'accept that the Jews control the world' and of their use of the word Jew as a slur.[173] He spoke of how hatred of Jews was 'aired on television talk shows' and among intellectual circles in Pakistan and was rife in school textbooks. The disease of antisemitism, he concludes 'has become endemic in the Islamic world.'[174] Canadian journalist Irshad Manji recalls a childhood at a school in Canada where she was told that Jews worshipped 'moolah, not Allah' and decried the foul brainwashing to which fellow Muslims were subjected.[175]

One feature of Islamic antisemitism is that it dehumanises and debases its victims. By describing Jews as the sons of 'pigs and apes,' Muslim extremists repeat the tropes of Christian theologians who depicted Jews as Satanic and the Nazis who likened them to rats and vermin. Dehumanization softens people up to rape, mass murder and other crimes against humanity. Such intellectual

---

[171]Nonie Darwish, *Now They Call Me Infidel: Why I Renounced Jihad for America, Israel, and the War on Terror* (New York: Sentinel, 2006), 3.

[172]Mehdi Hasan, "The sorry truth is that the virus of antisemitism has infected the British Muslim Community," *The New Statesman*, March 21, 2013.

[173] Tarek Fatah, *The Jew is not my enemy: Unveiling the Myths that Fuel Muslim Antisemitism* (Toronto: McClelland and Stewart, 2011), xv-xvii.

[174] ibid. 21-2

[175] Irshad Manji, *The Trouble with Islam* (Edinburgh and London: Mainstream Publishing, 2004), 23.

brainwashing is a preliminary stage before genocide, the means by which perpetrators justify their infamous deeds by pretending their victims lack humanity. That is another reason why we cannot ignore those who peddle such poisonous language.

It cannot be stressed enough, however, that there are also a huge number of Muslim voices, both from individuals and religious organizations, which decry this poisonous prejudice within their midst. Groups such as the UK based Muslims against Antisemitism, the Council of Muslims against Antisemitism, the Quilliam Foundation, the German based Muslim Alhambra Society, the Islamic Network Groups, together with many millions from the Ahmadiyya communities right across the world, have expended considerable energy, not just in condemning various manifestations of antisemitism but in promoting tolerance as an antidote to extremism. They endorse a pluralist platform that shuns radicalism and promotes dialogue and mutual understanding, making them role models in their societies. All of these voices should be applauded for their brave stand against prejudice. It must equally be made clear that those who spread harmful bigotry against Muslims or who threaten Muslim communities with violence are guilty of the same prejudice, and should face the full consequences of the law. The vast majority of Muslims reject jihadism and the assault on western values, with radical Islam merely one interpretation of the faith at present. But there is equally little benefit in denying that antisemitism is a real and growing problem in many Muslim societies.

Conclusion: In essence, the demonization of the Jews across Christian, Islamic and secular European cultures was based on a set of tropes: in virtue of the Jews' malevolent nature, due to some inherent fault in their makeup, they were constitutionally motivated to immiserate, impoverish and deceive non-Jews for their own ends. The most fundamental ideas expressed in this narrative are as follows:

1) Jews are responsible for the death of Christ, the saviour. They are also the primary enemy of Mohammed, though they did not kill him. They have sought to destroy the foundations of both Christianity and Islam.
2) Jews are prepared to immiserate the lives of non-Jews, engaging in malevolent behaviour (such as murder and poisoning) to achieve their cruel ends.
3) Jews have a deceitful, untrustworthy and malign character, disguising their hateful or spiteful nature to kill or harass their enemies.
4) Jews target children, the most innocent of victims, for their own sadistic, ritual purposes.
5) Jews are avaricious and money obsessed, denuding them of all social conscience and trustworthiness.
6) Jews regard themselves as chosen and superior to non-Jews.
7) Jews are more loyal to their own kind than to the nations they live in.
8) Jews are an alien race who live parasitically off their host societies.

9) In virtue of their alien, perfidious and exploitative nature, the Jews do not deserve to exist and must be destroyed.

But as we shall see in the next chapter, this is but one side of antisemitism.

Chapter Three

Antisemitism as outcome: inequality and adverse treatment

He who allows oppression shares the crime.

Erasmus

Thus far, the book has explored one side of how antisemitism is manifested, involving attempts to construct the Jew according to a set of racist tropes that are embedded in a variety of religious and secular cultures. The other side of the coin involves the multifaceted nature of discrimination, double standards and, in general, adverse treatment of Jews throughout history and across multiple societies. For centuries, Jews were disregarded as human equals in society and subjected to a series of discriminatory measures that underpinned their sense of difference, as well as inferiority to, gentiles. Such discrimination covered a broad spectrum of life's experiences, from how Jews dressed to where they lived and from the jobs they performed to the taxes they paid. The restrictions imposed by gentile rulers were frequently painful, demeaning and debilitating. In the worst cases, they could prove catastrophic for the survival of Jewish communities.

Yet, it would be a mistake to see the entirety of Jewish history as an unceasing tale of woe, persecution and despair. For much of their history, Jews have thrived in a relative atmosphere of enlightenment and prosperity. Often, they found themselves under the rule of benevolent caliphs, emperors and governors who were well disposed to the Jews and who valued the community for their business acumen and intellectual gifts. Whether this was in the Golden Age in Spain, ancient Alexandria, sixteenth century Poland, post Enlightenment Europe or modern Britain and America, Jews were able to live without undue hindrance and in an environment of relative tolerance. From the French Revolution onwards, the gradual emancipation of the Jews took root in Napoleonic France and spread to Germany and Austria-Hungary. Though reactionary conservatives challenged the naturalization of the Jews, the guiding principle that they should live as free and equal citizens took root in many nations. While it did not bring full freedom to the

Jews, it provided for a significant measure of progress and civic betterment.[1] It would therefore be a mistake to view the Jewish past through the monolithic lens of gentile hatred and one would do well to be wary of what the great historian Salo Wittmayer Baron called the 'lachrymose conception of Jewish history.' But it would be equally foolish to ignore the effects of poisonous antisemitic dogma and how it helped foster policies that discriminated against Jews over many centuries. Such discriminatory treatment has come in many forms and includes the following:

1) The denial of the right to life – a history of massacres and subjection to violence.
2) The denial of religious liberty to the Jews, including forced conversion and restrictions on religious practice.
3) Denial of the right to domicile.
4) Restrictive rules on Jews' external appearance, such as the type of clothes they could wear.
5) Restrictions on the types of profession Jews could engage in.
6) Restrictions on the Jews' legal rights in court.
7) Restrictions on Jews' financial freedom and rights, including the payment of special taxes to get protection.
8) Restrictive quotas on admission to universities.

1. Denial of right to life

The most blatant abuse of human rights is manifested by the denial of the right to life. History records innumerable instances in which Jewish communities have faced sporadic and organised violence from their neighbours, whether in the form of individual acts of violence, pogroms, torture, synagogue burnings and genocide, the ultimate crime against humanity. Far from occurring in a vacuum, such frenzied outpourings of rage have instead been encouraged and incited by demagogues and autocrats, whether in the service of religious dogma, nationalist zealotry, financial self-interest or other nefarious ends.

Perhaps the first pogrom against the Jews came in Alexandria in 38 CE during the reign of Emperor Caligula. Spurred by envy at Jewish wealth and success, the Greek community accused the Jews of being unpatriotic and manifesting dual loyalties, a pretext for which was the clash between Judaic monotheism and the erection of altars and statues to the emperor. Riots subsequently erupted, though whether they could be compared to later pogroms has been questioned by historians.

Europe's dark descent into murderous pogroms began with the massacres perpetrated during the First Crusade in 1096. Armed with a vengeful attitude towards the 'infidel' Jews and an economic incentive to seize their wealth, the

---

[1] For a useful summary of the process of emancipation, see Katz: *From Prejudice to Destruction* p. 2-4

Crusaders put thousands of Jews to death and forced others into conversion or suicide. The religious pretext had its own cruel logic: the Jews were viewed as the foremost enemy of God, indeed far more so than the infidels who had settled in the Holy Land, and thus had to be eliminated as a matter of sacred duty. Massacres took place in Rouen, in a number of German towns, including Speyer, Worms, Mainz and Cologne, and in Prague. Many Jews chose to commit suicide rather than face extermination by their foes while a small number chose conversion instead. These massacres took place despite the exhortation of local bishops for them to desist.[2]

During the Third Crusade, launched following the capture of Jerusalem by Saladin, local pogroms broke out in England after King Richard I left the country. Attacks against Jews and Jewish properties occurred in King's Lynn, Colchester, Lincoln and Bury St Edmonds. The worst event in these religiously inspired killings took place in York in 1190 after the entire community was forced by a baying mob to seek shelter in the local castle. Many hundreds of Jews, facing certain death or forced baptism, chose to take their own lives instead. The rioters burnt the record of their debts to the Jews, proving that there was a clear financial incentive for the events that transpired.

These were mostly localized massacres inspired by impassioned demagoguery. But in 1298, the Rindfleisch massacres, which started with an incendiary accusation that the Jews had desecrated the Host, set off a catastrophic wave of attacks that decimated one German Jewish community after another. Murderous squads roamed cities with Jewish populations, butchering their inhabitants (but sparing converts) and looting and burning properties. The total number of victims has been estimated at up to 100,000. A similar wave of massacres swept the Jews of Spain in 1391. Inspired by the fiery preaching of Ferrand Martinez, Archdeacon of Ecija, mobs attacked multiple Jewish communities, commencing with Seville where 4,000 Jews were put to death. It brought to an end a long period in which Jews, despite official antisemitic doctrine, had lived with a degree of protection from the authorities. What it prefigured was the dark period of intolerance that would lead to the Jews' expulsion a century later.

Between 1648 and 1649, Polish Jews suffered fearfully in the so called Chmielnicki massacres. These took place during the Cossack and peasant uprising against the Polish–Lithuanian Commonwealth, led by a nobleman called Bogdan Chmielnicki (who has come to be known to Jews as Chmiel the wicked). He aimed to establish an independent Ukraine, free from Polish rule, while also cleansing the country of Jews. Polish Jews had played an important role as administrators of the Polish noble estates and had helped to develop towns in times of danger. In his book *The Abyss of Despair*, Nathan Neta Hanover provides a chronicle of the unremitting savagery that unfolded against the Jews who fell into Cossack hands. They were tortured and butchered in the most sadistic fashion with the bodies of

---

[2] Poliakov, *The History of Antisemitism* I, 45.

some victims sliced open and their limbs removed. Perhaps as many as 40,000 Jews fell victim to this orgy of violence, a number that would not be equalled until the pogroms of the post WWI era. As historian Simon Dubnow points out: 'The number of victims exceeded that of all the catastrophes of the Crusades and of the Black Plague in Western Europe.'[3]

In the late nineteenth century, Jewish communities in Russia fell victim to a wave of violent pogroms. When they erupted in 1881, the catalyst was the assassination of Tsar Alexander II by a group called Narodnaya Volya (People's Will). For some, this was the handiwork of foreign agents (Jews), an idea purportedly lent credence by the fact that one of the twenty two conspirators was a Jew. Large scale rioting occurred in the city of Kiev and a number of other cities, leading to the death of 40 Jews. From 1903 to 1906, a more violent series of pogroms was launched against Jews in hundreds of towns, many of them incited by clerics and the secret police and spurred on by the rabid hatred of the authorities. The pogrom of 1905 in Odessa, which came in the wake of Tsar Nicholas II's October Manifesto, led to the deaths of many hundreds of Jews.[4] However, it was the turbulent aftermath of the First World War that saw the most sustained waves of violence against Russian Jewry. During the Civil War, which pitted the Whites against the Reds, tens of thousands of Jews were massacred across Ukraine by various factions in the conflict, some of whom blamed the Bolshevik Revolution on a Jewish conspiracy.

The Holocaust, the most tragic series of events in all Jewish history, was the logical end point for the murderous antisemitism that had long consumed European societies. What differentiated it from previous massacres was both its scale and its totalizing nature. This was an industrialized, scientifically organised, bureaucratically driven and utterly methodical attempt by one of the world's leading states to destroy all Jewish life in Europe and beyond. The logic of the Nazi killing machine was clear - no Jews could be spared in the areas conquered by National Socialism. Hitler's all-consuming ideology demanded the eradication of the 'biological basis' of Jewry and, by 1945, two thirds of European Jews had succumbed to the Nazis' genocidal fury. The Holocaust was the apotheosis of racial destruction, the culmination of centuries of Jew hatred, cultural brainwashing and incitement by both religious and secular demagogues.

It would be a mistake to think that the liberation of the death camps put an end to the slaughter. In 1946, a rumour spread that Jews had been responsible for the abduction of a young Polish boy in the town of Kielce. The boy in question said he had been held in the basement of a building which was owned by the Jewish Committee. Later, officers from the state militia and local police approached the building and dragged Jews into the courtyard where townspeople attacked them savagely. Later, a group of metalworkers, armed with iron bars and other weapons, arrived at the building and attacked those inside. In total, 42 Polish

---

[3] ibid. 258.
[4] Some estimate that as many as 2,500 Jews were killed in Odessa.

Jews were murdered. The previous year, a series of blood libel rumours led to a violent mob assault on Jewish worshippers in the Kupa synagogue of Krakow, leading to one death. These atrocities happened in a country whose Jewish population was almost entirely decimated in the previous six years. Yet the horrors of the Holocaust did not induce the kind of deep national mourning or contrition that might have prevented them. Instead, underlying reserves of hatred and resentment that had welled up deep in Polish society were unleashed after the war on the oldest of their scapegoats. As Adam Garfinkle aptly observes: 'Like amputee victims who feel pain in their severed limbs, Poles…felt the unsettling presence of the Jews even after the vast majority of them had already been murdered.'[5]

The Arab world was not immune to such large-scale killings. One of the most famous was the 1066 Grenada massacre whereby a Muslim mob stormed the city's royal palace, murdered the Berber king's Jewish vizier, Joseph ibn Naghrela, and proceeded to slaughter around 1,500 Jewish households (maybe 4,000 people). It has been claimed that the massacre was inspired by an antisemitic poem written by Abu Ishaq of Elvira, one of the vizier's enemies. Such massacres were far rarer in the Arab than in the Christian world but smaller scale pogroms did occur more frequently in the nineteenth century, such as the terrible mob violence that engulfed Safed in 1834. Of course, the twentieth century would see appalling attacks repeatedly unleashed against Jewish communities in Palestine and the wider Arab world. The hateful incitement and incendiary rhetoric of Palestine's Sunni Grand Mufti, Mohammed Amin Al-Husseini, lit the spark for pogroms against Jews in 1920 (Jerusalem), 1929 (Hebron and Safed) and in 1936 (across Palestine). In 1912, a Muslim mob, outraged by a treaty which turned Morocco into a French protectorate, turned on Fez's Jewish population and killed 51 people. In 1934, the outburst of a reportedly drunken Jewish tailor in the Algerian town of Constantine led to a massacre of 25 Jews. Some 200 Jews were massacred during the Farhud which engulfed Baghdad in 1941 and in the aftermath of the UN Partition plan that would have created a Jewish and an Arab state in mandatory Palestine, hateful mobs massacred Jewish communities in Aleppo, Aden, Tripoli and the Moroccan towns of Oujda and Jerada.

2. Denial of religious liberty

In most societies for the last two millennia, Jews have been free to practise their faith without excessive hindrance, even in societies where they have been second class citizens. But this has not always been the case. At certain moments, the practice of Judaism put Jews in grave danger and conversion became an overriding, existential imperative.

The Emperor Constantine, who converted to Christianity in 313 AD, repressed Judaism as a faith and prevented the Jews from proselytising. Under the Theodosian Code (404-527), Jews were banned from building new synagogues

---

[5] Garfinkle, *Jewcentricity*, 61.

and denied the chance to gain any public office. The Byzantine Emperor Flavius Heraclius issued an edict calling for the forced conversion of Hebrews to Christianity, which though it covered the whole Empire, was applied only in Cartagena (632). The Twelfth Council of Toledo, initiated in 681 by King Erwig, contained a number of repressive measures against the Jews, including banning *conversos* from returning to Judaism. He was not the first King of the Visigoths to turn against the Jewish faith. Earlier, King Sisebut forced Jews who had converted from Christianity to become Christians once again or go into exile. He later forced other Jews to convert to Christianity, sending many into exile.[6]

Forced conversions are recorded at Merovingia (582 CE), Byzantium (628 CE) and Toledo (633CE). There were also innumerable cases of forced conversion during the early years of the First Crusade. Christians attempted to convert Jews to the Christian faith in a number of German towns. Jews opposed forced conversion and many died as a result, though a small number did choose forcible conversion as a survival strategy.[7] Forced baptism too is believed to have occurred at different times, especially when doing so was the only route to obtaining some form of social advancement. One of the worst cases of forced conversion was in Portugal following the edict of expulsion. After the marriage of Manuel I to the infanta of Spain, the kingdom was Christianised but as expulsion would have been financially prohibitive, the solution was forced baptism for Jews. Many thousands were dragged to the baptismal fonts and for those who would not submit, the only option was suicide. The policy would later be described by one nineteenth century commentator as "a sacrilegious farce, motivated by the most vile and sordid material interests."[8]

History records numerous occasions when synagogues containing the holiest Jewish texts were burned to the ground and others ransacked. There were also times when Jews were forbidden from building new synagogues, such as the edict issued by Stephen Langton, the Archbishop of Canterbury, in 1222. Even Jewish holy texts were put on trial. In the so-called Disputation of Paris (the trial of the Talmud as it is also known), a group of rabbis were summoned to appear at the court of French king Louis IX where they faced charges that the Talmud blasphemed against Christianity. What followed was a mass book burning in which thousands of volumes of Hebrew manuscripts were destroyed.

The violent campaign against the Talmud and other Judaic literature continued throughout the Middle Ages. The religious authorities sincerely believed that the Talmud contained the seeds of Jewish antipathy towards Christianity as well as a host of strange religious superstitions. In 1242, some 12,000 volumes of Jewish literature were publicly destroyed in Paris and

---

[6] Bachrach, Bernard. "Reassessment of Visigothic Jewish Policy, 589-711." *The American Historical Review* 78, no. 1 (1973): 11–34, 16.

[7] Simha Goldin, *Apostasy and Jewish identity in High Middle Ages Northern Europe: 'Are you still my brother?* (Manchester; New York: Manchester University Press, 2014), 22-30.

[8] Poliakov, *The History of Antisemitism II*, 202.

thousands confiscated. In 1248, Jews were forbidden to own copies of the Talmud, an edict upheld by Louis X when he allowed Jews to return to France in 1315. In the middle of the sixteenth century, copies of the Talmud were seized and destroyed in some Italian cities while a Venetian commission decried any Hebrew work which rested upon the authority of the Talmud.

It is generally accepted that Jews faced less oppression living under Islamic rule than under European Christian rule, at least until the onset of the secular revolution in the seventeenth century. As dhimmis (literally protected persons) living under Islamic caliphs and rulers, Jews, like Christians and many other groups, received the state's protection in matters of life, property and freedom of religious practice in return for payment of the jizya tax. Jews were generally able to practise their religion and live according to their own laws, something owing to the more general fact that Islamic law 'allowed most conquered peoples to retain their religions.'[9] American historian Mark R Cohen concurs with this view, arguing that it was easier for Jews to practice their religion under Islamic rule than in Christian Europe.[10]

Nonetheless, they were still subject to a variety of social restrictions, including the law that prevented them from building a place of worship higher than a mosque and being forced to give right of way in the street to Muslims. Under other rulers, they fared worse. The Sassanian King of Persia, Yazdegerd II, is believed to have persecuted the Jews, prohibiting them from observing the Sabbath. In 720, Caliph Omar banned Jews from worshipping on Temple Mount, despite its status as the holiest Jewish site on earth. Jewish cemeteries, so fundamental for remembrance of the dead, were flattened by Ahmad ibn Tulun, founder of a dynasty that ruled Egypt and Syria in the ninth century. These are a sample of episodes which illustrate the difficulties often faced by Jews under Muslim rule.

3. Where Jews could live

At different times in history, Jews were denied the fundamental right of domicile, the idea that one could establish permanent roots in a place called 'home.' Instead, the history of anti-Jewish persecution is littered with the horrors of expulsion and ethnic cleansing, with Jewish communities bearing the brunt of oppressive legislators and overlords intent on making their lands *Judenfrei*.

In ancient times, Jews were threatened with expulsion by the emperor Tiberias if they did not convert. They were expelled from Rome in 50 CE by Emperor Claudius and were then prohibited from entering Jerusalem by the Romans after the Bar Kokhba revolt. Expulsion then became a regular feature of life under Christian rule. In 1290, Edward I issued the Edict of Expulsion against

---

[9] Coope, Jessica A. "Religious and Cultural Conversion to Islam in Ninth-Century Umayyad Córdoba." *Journal of World History* 4, no. 1 (1993): 47–68.

[10] For a fascinating comparative analysis, see Mark R. Cohen, *Under Crescent and Cross: The Jews in the Middle Ages* (Princeton: Princeton University Press, 2008).

the Jews of England, a royal decree which built upon decades of restrictions and punitive taxation and which remained in force until Cromwell re-admitted Jews in 1656. Edward I had already expelled Jews three years earlier from the duchy of Gascony. Contemporary French rulers were little better. Jews were expelled from parts of France by Phillip II as well as by John I, Duke of Brittany and Louis IX. Jews also faced a number of expulsions, albeit temporary in many cases, during the terrible convulsions caused by the Black Death. For example, Jews were expelled from Hungary during the Plague, before being readmitted, and then expelled again by King Louis the Great in 1360. Much later, Louis XIV would issue his *Code Noir* (1685), a document which set out a series of rules about the treatment of slaves in France's overseas empire but which also ordered the expulsion of Jews in those colonies. They faced numerous threats of deportation at the hands of Austrian monarch Maria Theresa, whose hatred of Jews was only matched by her fervent dislike of Protestants.

The most infamous example of expulsion was the Alhambra decree issued on 31 March 1492 by King Ferdinand II and Queen Isabella I ordering the removal of Jews from Spain. It was the culmination of the Spanish Inquisition, a determined attempt to frame the converso, the Jew who had converted to Christianity, as a Christian heretic. In a series of tribunals, these 'heretics' were invited to hand themselves in via the so-called Edict of Grace. They had to admit that they were covertly practising Judaism before going on to denounce all those others who were also practising the old faith. While spared torture, they were ritually humiliated in public and forbidden to hold office. To aid in identifying the sinners, an edict listed dozens of ways to recognise them, including their observance of dietary laws and their omission of certain words in reciting psalms. Those who confessed were spared while those who declared their innocence were burnt to death. Most were reconciled with the church but many hundreds were executed for refusing to confess.

It was the belief that Spain's Jews were seeking to 'seduce' the New Christians, such as by bringing them prayer books, procuring unleavened bread at Passover and teaching them the holidays, and thus debasing the Catholic faith, that led to the Edict of Expulsion by Ferdinand and Isabella in 1492. Jews were given four months to liquidate their businesses and sell their possessions with only baptism enabling them to remain in the country. According to one estimate, up to 100,000 Jews were expelled while 50,000 accepted conversion.

Expulsion orders were even issued in America. On December 17, 1862, Major General Ulysses S Grant issued Order no 11, which expelled Jews from Grant's military districts of Tennessee, Mississippi, and Kentucky. The Jews in those areas stood accused of 'violating every regulation of trade established by the Treasury Department.' It was later countermanded by President Lincoln but was widely condemned as a gross violation of civil liberties.

The forced expulsion of Jews from Arab lands was a notable feature of modern persecution. In the twentieth century, Jews faced expulsion or enforced departure from communities across North Africa and the Middle East. Jewish communities in Egypt, Morocco, Algeria, Tunisia, Iraq, Aden, Libya, Iran and

Syria were many centuries old and had long played a vital role in the commercial, political, cultural and social life of those countries. From 1947 onwards, these communities were forced to flee their homes either because of the threat of Arab violence and intimidation, or because they were physically expelled.

The Jewish exodus from the Arab world was an enforced one, brought about by the scarring effects of antisemitic incitement and murderous violence. For example, a series of riots in Tripoli and other Libyan cities in 1945 led to the murder of over 140 Jews. In 1947, a Muslim mob in British controlled Aden carried out a three-day rampage in the Jewish quarter killing 82 people. Dozens were killed in attacks on Cairo's Jewish quarter and in Tripoli in June 1948, as well as in a number of Moroccan cities. Anti-Jewish violence in Aleppo led to the exodus of most of its 7,000 Jews while the Muslim Brotherhood whipped up a frenzied hatred of Jews and Zionists in Cairo. Articles in the Lebanese press even accused Jews of poisoning wells. In Egypt, a mass exodus of Jews came about following the government's response to the Suez Crisis of 1956. Some 24,000 received deportation notices and were forced to leave Egypt within days. Thus, the former Canadian minister of justice, Irwin Cotler, is right when he says: 'The displacement of 850,000 Jews from Arab countries is not just a "Forgotten Exodus" but a "Forced Exodus."' [11]

If Jews were not always forcibly moved from one place to another, they could still face innumerable restrictions on where and how they could live. To keep Jews isolated from their Christian neighbours, the logic of separation dictated that physical distance was necessary to keep the communities apart. This came in the form of the European ghetto. A papal bull (*cum nimis absurdum*) issued in 1555 by Pope Paul IV instituted the ghetto in Rome (the word 'ghetto' is Italian in origin). The Jews of that ancient city, then numbering some 2,000, were ordered to live in a walled quarter with gates that were locked at night. The Jews were forced to pay for its construction and experienced a multitude of restrictions: they could not own property; they could only work in unskilled jobs (being ragmen or pawnbrokers); they had to pay yearly taxes to live in the ghetto and were forced to wear yellow cloths if they left the ghetto. As ghettos became overcrowded, conditions became dire with poor hygiene and inadequate water the norm. The idea was to ensure the triumph of the Christian doctrine and 'the intransigent purity of its own principles,' as summed up by one publicist who wrote: 'One ghetto of Jews is better proof of the truth of the religion of Jesus Christ than a school of theologians.' [12] Another famous ghetto was the one in Venice, instituted in 1516, while the one in Frankfurt dated from the fifteenth century. In the latter case, the Jewish Code of Residence dating from 1616 restricted Jewish marriages to 12 per year while Christians could marry as long as they could prove their wealth. In these and other cases, Christian Europe heavily restricted the lives and

---

[11] Irwin Cotler, "The forgotten exodus." accessed March 10, 2020, https://www.jewish refugees.org.uk/2007/11/forgotten-exodus-by-irwin-cotler.html.

[12] Leon Poliakov, The History of Anti-Semitism III, 39.

activities of Jewish inhabitants, forcing upon them a second-class existence that was demeaning and discriminatory.

Throughout the eighteenth and nineteenth centuries, Russian Jews faced a set of strict legal restrictions on domicile. In the treaty signed by Tsar Feodor III and John III Sobieski in 1678, it was expressly stipulated that Jewish merchants could not settle in Moscow, an edict that had been enforced by Tsar Michael. Even though Peter the Great was one of the most enlightened of Russian rulers, he too chose not to admit the Jews. In 1791, Catherine II set limits for where Jews could legally reside in the borders of Tsarist Russia, an area later known as the Pale of Settlement. It consisted of a series of provinces in Ukraine, Lithuania, Belorussia, Crimea, and the part of Poland annexed to Russia in 1772. Despite its vast size, life in the Pale was characterised by poverty, given the increasing size of the Jewish population and the absence of widespread employment in many trades. Within the Pale, the Jewish population (numbering some 5 million at its height), faced a number of restrictions at different times. Jews faced limitations on residence in certain cities, such as Kiev and Sebastopol, restrictions on residence close to international borders and were forced to live in small urban communities, now known as shtetls.

Certain classes of Jews, such as wealthy merchants, people with degrees and those with specialist skills, did have the privilege of living outside the Pale, though this was not possible for the majority. In the late nineteenth century, the communities faced the threat of pogroms and restrictive legal decrees, such as the May Laws of Tsar Alexander III.

4. Restrictions on Jews' physical or external appearance

Medieval rulers emphasized the subservient status of Jews by ordering them to wear distinctive clothing. At the instigation of Pope Innocent III, the Fourth Lateran Council in 1215 stated that Jews, together with Saracens (Muslims), had to be 'marked off in the eyes of the public from other peoples through the character of their dress.' It would be up to the secular authorities to decide on the nature of this distinct clothing. In France, the authorities decided upon a special insignia in the form of a circular, yellow coloured 'Jew badge,' which would serve as a permanent reminder of Judas' betrayal of Jesus. It would enable an easy way to identify Jewish heretics and prevent social intercourse between Jew and Gentile. But at the same time, it was a humiliating and permanent reminder of the Jew's subservient position in Christian society, etched literally into his appearance.

The badge was imposed by Francophone kings down to Charles VI and was compulsory for men and women. Fines were imposed for those who did not wear the badge though on some occasions, a Jew could be given permission to remove it in return for payment. At times, it was enforced in Spain, particularly following the Bull of Benedict XIII in 1415 and it made its appearance in some Italian states and German cities. The Statute of Jewry, enacted under the rule of England's England I, decreed the same:

'Each Jew, after he is seven years old, shall wear a distinguishing mark on his outer garment, that is to say, in the form of two Tables joined, of yellow felt of the length of six inches and of the breadth of three inches.'

Jews were also distinguished by wearing the so called *Judenhat*, a pointed hat which was either white or yellow and which was worn by them both in Europe and the Middle East. Initially, this appears to have been a voluntary form of dress but it was later imposed as a compulsory form of discrimination. Thus did the Synod of Breslau in 1267 decree that Jews 'should resume wearing the horned hat which they had been wearing in those regions and which in their temerity they dared abandon.' [13] For Leon Poliakov, this degrading, second class treatment created a powerful impression in the minds of gentile society that the Jew was 'a man of another physical aspect, radically different from other men.' [14]

As dhimmis, Jews were forced to wear distinctive clothing in order to further separate themselves from their Muslim masters and in order to emphasize their inferior status. Under the Islamic Pact of Umar in 637, Jews, and other non-Muslims, had to wear a yellow seam on their upper garments while in 1005, the Egyptian authorities ordered Jews to wear bells on their garments and a wooden calf (in memory of the golden one).

5. Restrictions on type of employment

The history of Jews in medieval Christian society was marked by draconian restrictions on employment. For much of this period, Jews were denied citizenship and were not allowed to hold posts in either the government or the military. They were also barred from owning land which meant that they were forbidden to engage in agriculture, their chief occupation during Biblical times. They could not take part in crafts and in manufacturing but they nonetheless performed important roles in trade and commerce, especially in the sphere of money lending and tax collecting. These professions were resented by the peasant class who, in turn, bought into a prevailing negative image of Jews as avaricious and dishonest.

It is often assumed that, following Europe's moment of Enlightenment after 1789 which swept away the ghettos, such restrictions were removed, giving Jews the freedoms they had long craved in secular society. In practice, some countries, such as the UK and Italy, did loosen their restrictions much more quickly than others while in imperial Russia, most Jews had to wait a century before seeing the tangible benefits of Western emancipation. Social discrimination continued even in those liberated countries where Jews had become relatively acculturated. After the Napoleonic wars, some German states imposed draconian restrictions on Jews. Their right to work and settle was taken away and they were barred from certain professions, unless they had letters of protection. For some, this meant taking menial positions, such as peddling. In the more tolerant atmosphere of late

---

[13] For a full discussion, see Straus, Raphel. "The 'Jewish Hat' as an Aspect of Social History." *Jewish Social Studies* 4, no. 1 1942), 59–72.

[14] Poliakov, *The History of Antisemitism* I, 67.

nineteenth century imperial Germany, Jews had more formal equality but their path to senior positions in the army, diplomatic service, academia and judiciary was effectively blocked. Often, conversion to the Christian faith provided the only route to success.

During the interwar period, the Second Polish Republic witnessed escalating levels of antisemitism with Catholic trade unions of doctors and lawyers barring all those who were not Christian and taking a hard line on Jewish employment. Of course, it was in the fascist autocracies of Europe that Jews faced the gravest onslaught of legal restrictions. In the 1933 Law for the Restoration of the Professional Civil Service, Germany barred 'non-Aryans' from a swathe of professions, including teaching, law, academia and other government positions. Apart from WWI veterans, those who had lost a father or son in the war or those who had served continuously in the civil service since 1914, most Jews were affected by the legal restriction. Italy implemented its own Manifesto of Race in 1938 which similarly excluded Jews from the civil service as well as the armed forces.

It would be a grave mistake to think that such employment restrictions ceased to apply in more relatively free and liberal countries. The United States has provided Jews with the warm embrace of democratic and liberal values for the best part of two centuries but this has co-existed with the harsh reality of social discrimination. Historian Laura Weber has written that until a decade after World War II, 'economic discrimination against Jews was a problem in virtually every United States metropolitan area.' According to one source, 90 percent of the general office jobs in New York City were closed to Jews. [15]

An article in *Forbes* for 1936 called *Jews in America* showed that there were many sectors of the American economy which were exclusively non-Jewish, among them transportation, commercial banking, coal, rubber, petroleum and mining. Jews instead found employment in areas such as medicine and dentistry, ones where they were not subject to discrimination by an employer. There is also multiple evidence of overt job discrimination in the job market around this time. The Chicago Bureau of Jewish employment problems carried out a survey of 20,000 job orders placed by commercial employment agencies in Chicago in 1953-4 and found that 20% were closed to Jews. 142 of the companies with discriminatory orders held government contracts. The Bureau found that Jewish job seekers had less than half the opportunity to be placed by employment agencies as those who were not Jewish. [16]

Discrimination against Jews also extended to the legal profession. After the Second World War, the American legal industry was 'segregated along religious and cultural lines between WASP and Jewish law firms' and Jews found themselves shut out of major Gentile dominated law firms. In New York,

---

[15] Weber, Laura. "Gentiles Preferred: Minneapolis Jews and Employment 1920-1950." *Minnesota Historical Society* (Spring 1991).
[16] Waldman, Lois. "Employment Discrimination against Jews in the United States - 1955." *Jewish Social Studies* 18, no. 3 (1956): 208–216.

the doors of most law offices 'were closed, with rare exceptions, to a young Jewish lawyer.' Even Jewish law review editors, those who reached the pinnacle of academic achievement, were excluded from partnerships in prestigious corporate law firms. This reflected a wider truism that entrance to the legal profession was so often a reflection of individuals' racial, religious and ethnic backgrounds.[17]

This is backed up by the findings of a survey carried out by the B'nai B'rith Vocational Service Bureau in 1950. It found that proportionately more Jews than non-Jews failed to go into legal work following graduation from law school. 63% of all Jewish lawyers in legal work were employed in firms with all Jewish partners, suggesting that this was the route that Jews had to take to escape Gentile discrimination in the legal world. Jews also faced discrepancies in pay. Only three Jewish accountants out of a total of 286 were employed in the fifteen largest public accounting firms, and only 11 had been employed by them in the previous thirty years. There is evidence suggesting that rampant discrimination also affected the employment of Jews in the insurance industry.

Such institutional discrimination could also be found in Britain, especially between the wars. In the 1920s and 1930s, many newly qualified Jewish doctors had to Anglicize their names in order to gain advancement in their careers. One advert that appeared in the *British Medical Journal* in 1930 stated: '*Wanted, Midlands, Assistant [doctor] ... male. Panel 1,950. Receipts £2,700. Good House and garden available. No Jews or men of colour.*' Many Jews had to purchase their own practices, often starting in working class neighbourhoods. After the war, prejudices died hard and it became 'almost impossible' for Jews to obtain a senior surgical post in the Central London teaching hospitals. [18] These are but a small sample of such restrictions in even the most liberal of modern nations.

6. Unequal in court

In the Middle Ages, the subordination of Jews to their Christian masters was reflected in debilitating inequality in the courts. The reign of Justinian I (527-565) was marked by the negative impact of his new legal Code, which remained in force in the Eastern Empire until the 9th century and which contained 33 articles that affected Jews. Jews were branded as heretics, alongside others who were 'not devoted to the Catholic Church and to our Orthodox and holy faith,' and there were severe restrictions on the Jewish ownership of Christian slaves as well as penalties on the circumcision of slaves. In 531, Justinian ruled that Jews, like heretics, could not give testimony against orthodox Christians, though they could

---

[17] Auerbach, Jerold. "From Rags to Robes: The Legal Profession, Social Mobility and the American Jewish Experience." *American Jewish Historical Quarterly* 66, no. 2 (1976): 249–284.
[18] Cooper, John. "Jews who helped make the health service." *The British Journal of General Practice: the Journal of the Royal College of General Practitioners* 69,678 (2019): 32-33.

do so against fellow Jews or those that they deemed 'heretics.'[19] It should be noted that Jews were higher in the legal hierarchy than certain other non-Christians, such as Samaritans, who could not give testimony at all.

The medieval *Oath More Judaico* (on/by the Jewish custom) was a special type of oath that Jews were forced to declare when in a lawsuit with non-Jews, often with the intention of humiliating and degrading them as well as portending punishment if it was falsely taken. One of the more extreme examples was contained in the German Schwabenspiegel (c. 1275) and contains some of the following verses:

> 'So help thee God, who created heaven and earth, valleys and mountains, wood, foliage, and grass, that was not before;
>
> So help thee the Law that God wrote with His hand and gave to Moses on Mount Sinai;…
>
> And that so [if] thou eatest something, thou will become defiled all over, as did the King of Babylon; And that sulphur and pitch rain upon thy neck, as it rained upon Sodom and Gomorrah;
>
> …And that the earth swallow thee as it did Dathan and Abiram;
>
> So art thou true and right.
>
> And so help thee Adonai; thou art true in what thou has sworn.
>
> And so that thou wouldst become leprous like Naaman: it is true...'

A further verse made reference to the Jew as a decide:

> 'And so that the blood and the curse ever remain upon thee which thy kindred wrought upon themselves when they tortured Jesus Christ and spake thus:
>
> His blood be upon us and upon our children: it is true.'

Some of the rituals associated with the oath were also designed to demean and intimate Jewish witnesses. One ritual involved a Jew standing on a sow's skin, and, in another, a Jew was made to stand on a stool, wearing a cloak and his Jew's hat and facing the rising sun. In the Byzantine empire of the 10th century, a Jew was made to wear a girdle of thorns around his loins before standing in water and swearing that if he told any lie, he would be swallowed by the earth. The municipality of Breslau stated in 1455 that a Jew had to swear while bareheaded and spell out the Tetragram. As dhimmis under Muslim rule, Jews too suffered legal discrimination as they could not give evidence in court against Muslims.

It is fair to point out that not all courts went along with these debilitating restrictions. The Carolingian Kings of the ninth century placed the testimony of Jews and Christians on an equal footing, a point stated in the charter of Henry IV,

---

[19] This changed with a new law introduced in 537.

and in legal jurisdictions, such as that of Duke Frederick II of Austria, a Jew was merely required to swear by the Torah. One should also mention the Statute of Kalisz (General Charter of Jewish Liberties), issued by Boleslaw the Pious, a thirteenth century Duke of Greater Poland, which gave to Jews a set of legal rights and privileges not seen elsewhere in Europe. This piece of legislation was subsequently upheld by later rulers of the Polish-Lithuanian Commonwealth.

7. Financial double standards

On many occasions throughout history, Jews were exploited by avaricious rulers who viewed these 'heathens' as a convenient cash cow for their needs. Special taxes were imposed on Jews over and above the tax burdens imposed on society as a whole. Following the destruction of the Second Temple in 70CE, the Romans imposed the *Fiscus Judaicus*, a Temple Tax equivalent to two denarii on all Jewish men, women and children (as well as slaves) throughout the empire. Those who abandoned Judaism were exempt from the tax.

The financial exploitation of Jews continued into the medieval era. Kings of England were more than happy to act on a whim towards their Jewish subjects and nullify previous obligations. In 1189, a tallage (land tax) known as the Saladin tax was levied against England's Jews, among others, to pay for the crusade to the Holy Land. Again in 1210, King John imposed the tallage on England's Jews, amounting to the princely sum of £40,000. Tallages were made by later English kings. Such disproportionate treatment reflected the unique extra-legal status that the Jews held in England: they were both '*both* legal persons *and* negotiable property' and could be sold and mortgaged.[20] In the year that King John signed the *Magna Carta*, the Fourth Lateran Council of 1215 imposed economic restrictions on Jews, such as the demand that they pay tithes on property (Canon 67) which was formerly owned by Christians.

Some medieval European rulers charged Jewish populations for their own protection. One example was Louis IV, the Holy Roman Emperor, who ordered all Jews above the age of 12 to pay the *Opferfennig*, one gulden for protection, so long as they possessed at least 20 gulden. Similar to King John, Louis IV had stated the same principle in regard to the Jews: 'You belong to us, body and belongings, and we can dispose of them and do with you as we please.' European Jews also had to pay a special poll tax called the *Leibzoll* which enabled them to have safe passage or a limited stay in an area, providing local rulers with an invaluable form of additional income. In the same spirit, Jews in eighteenth century Hungary were forced to pay a tolerance tax by Empress Maria Theresa, a virulent Catholic antisemite who threatened Jews with expulsion if they refused. Jews continued to pay the tax under the benign rule of her son, Joseph II, and also paid special taxes on marriage, synagogues, cemeteries and kosher meat. In 1571, Jews in the Polish city of Kolo were similarly provided with protection on

---

[20] Anthony Julius, *Trials of the Diaspora*, (Oxford: Oxford University Press, 2010), 105.

payment of a municipal tax while they were required to pay an annual poll tax in the eighteenth century. Taxes on kosher meat were not uncommon with Russian Jews paying the *korobka*, a humiliating and burdensome tax paid for each animal slaughtered according to the laws of kashrut and for each pound of the meat sold. Similar taxes were imposed in Galicia and Moldova. In the Islamic world, the jizya too was a financial burden which free adult Jewish males (together with many other non-Muslims) paid for their own protection, not that they were always protected.

In the twentieth century, Nazi Germany imposed draconian taxes on Jews. In 1934, they altered and extended the Reich Flight Tax, targeting the vast number of German Jews who were forced to flee the country due to religious persecution. Following Kristallnacht (Night of the broken glass) in 1938, the Jews of Germany were fined one billion Reichsmark for the damage. The government also confiscated all insurance payouts to Jews whose homes had been looted or destroyed, ensuring that the property owners had to bear the full costs. Following the Decree Concerning the Atonement Fee for the Jews of German Citizenship, the country's Jews were forced to pay 20 percent tax on all their reported assets above 5,000 Reichsmarks as declared on April 16, 1938. By the end of 1938, a Jew leaving Germany would be 'stripped of anywhere from 96.5 percent to more than 99 percent of his fortune.[21] Such measures deracinated the wealth of the Jewish community, robbing them of financial independence in a naked act of state sponsored theft. Naturally, this was one of the least of their problems.

Another notable example of discriminatory taxation came via the Soviet imposed diploma tax, introduced to counter the brain drain from Soviet Jews emigrating from the USSR. The demand was for would-be emigrants to repay the costs of higher education prior to departure, something that led to a sustained outcry in the West.

8. Restrictive quotas on admission to universities

Nineteenth century European societies put in place heavy restrictions to limit the number of Jewish students who could attend universities. This was carried out by means of the Numerus Clausus (closed number), a quota system which set a maximum number of students that could be admitted to institutions of higher education as well as professions and professional associations. In Russia, the restrictions that were introduced in 1887 allowed Jews to enter secondary and higher education at a rate of no more than 10% of overall places within the Pale and 5% outside it and with smaller percentages in Moscow and Saint Petersburg.

Jews experienced segregation in the 1930s in Polish universities, following a campaign of unrelenting pressure from right wing student bodies. Thus, Jewish students at medical schools were supplied with Jewish cadavers after two far right ultranationalist Polish groups objected to them practising on Christian ones.

---

[21] "Nazi restrictions, Special Taxes Strip Jews of Wealth," *Jewish Telegraphic Agency*, December 25, 1938.

The numerus clausus laws that were introduced had a severe impact on the numbers of Jewish students at universities, especially in the faculties of law, medicine and engineering. In Hungary, the Numerus clausus had an explicitly antisemitic character as it was designed to screen all Jewish applicants to university, either by assessing their religion or birth, and fix the number of entrants at a maximum of 6%. This corresponded with the number of Jews in Hungary. Despite many Hungarian Jews undergoing decades of acculturation and Magyarization, they were still classed as a non-Hungarian nationality, as were other national and ethnic minorities. For educational purposes, it removed the Jews' status as equal citizens. In 1928, Hungary amended the legislation at the request of the League of Nations but it was re-applied in the following decade.

Elsewhere in eastern Europe, Jews suffered discrimination even without restrictive laws. Though numerus clausus laws were not introduced in Romania, social pressures led to many Jewish students studying abroad. In 1933, professors who supported such a law introduced special entrance exams for Jewish students and then deliberately failed almost all of them, though the few who were successful were prevented by Christian students from participating in university life. In 1940, the pro-Nazi regime of Ion Antonescu saw Jewish students expelled from schools and universities. In the same year, the Yugoslav government introduced its own numerus clauses law called 'Decree on the Enrolment of Persons of Jewish Descent at the University, Secondary School, Teacher Training College and Other Vocational Schools.' As Jews made up less than one half of one percent of the population but 16 percent of students of the faculties of medicine and law, this had a drastic effect.[22] This continued during the Soviet period. A study by Prof. Nicholas DeWitt of Indiana University in 1964 showed that the USSR employed a quota system 'as a direct discriminatory device against the admission of Jews to institutions of higher learning.'[23]

In the history of American education, Jews faced heavy discrimination. Harvard University President Abbott Lawrence Lowell introduced a quota on Jewish students at the university in the early 1920s, limiting their intake to 15%. It was to last until the 1960s. He had expressed grave concerns that the high percentage of Jews would drive away a generation of Anglo-Saxon Protestant students and claimed to have 'foreseen the peril of having too large a number of an alien race.'[24] Yale too shared in these ignominious practices by implementing an informal admissions process which restricted Jewish enrolment to 10%. In 1922, the admissions chairman had urged limits on accepting 'the alien and unwashed element.' As with Harvard, the discriminatory policy remained in place

---

[22]"The Jews in Yugoslavia 1918-41: Antisemitism and the Struggle for Equality," http://web.ceu.hu/jewishstudies/pdf/02_goldstein.pdf, accessed 18 August 2020.

[23] "Percentage of Jewish Students IN Soviet Union Smaller than under Czar," *Jewish Telegraphic Agency*, April 29, 1964.

[24] Ben Sales, "Harvard once capped the number of Jews. Is it doing the same thing to Asian-Americans now?" *Jewish Telegraphic Agency*, October 17, 2018.

for four decades.[25] Jewish entrance into American medical and dental schools in the US was also limited by the quota system, as discovered in a report by the President's Committee on Civil Rights called *To Secure These Rights* (1947). According to Edward Halperin, these quotas were in place 'at most U.S. medical schools in the 1920s' and they were 'well-entrenched by 1945.'[26] In Canada, discriminatory measures against Jews were put in place by McGill University, limiting Jewish enrolment to 10%.[27] In recent decades, Jewish success in tertiary education is taken for granted and is one of the shining successes of the community. But this was far from the case in the past.

These examples are not designed to be a completely comprehensive examination of the adverse treatment of Jews throughout the ages. But it hopefully provides an indication of the ways in which Jewish communities have been singled out, discriminated against and treated as second class subjects by many different societies during the last two millennia.

---

[25] Dirk Johnson, "Yale's Limit on Jewish Enrollment Lasted Until Early 1960s, Book Says," *New York Times*, March 4, 1986.

[26] Halperin, Edward. "Why did the United States Medical School Admissions Quota for Jews End?" *The American Journal of the Medical Sciences* 358, issue 5 (2019): 317.

[27] Valérie Beauchemin, "McGill University Quota," accessed 25 March 2020, http://imjm.ca/location/1565.

Chapter Four

Turning Israel into the devil among nations

In short, that which the demonized Jew once was in older forms of antisemitism, demonized Israel now is in contemporary antisemitic anti-Zionism: all-controlling, the hidden hand, tricksy, always acting in bad faith, the obstacle to a better, purer, more spiritual world, uniquely malevolent, full of blood lust, uniquely deserving of punishment, and so on.

Professor Alan Johnson

Given the depth, persistence and longevity of antisemitism, it is no surprise that its classic tropes have resurfaced in attacks on Israel. They include deicide, the charge that the Jewish state is once again killing the son of God, the 'child killer' blood libel which pictures Israel as feasting on the blood of innocent Palestinians, the 'vengeful Zionist,' the notion of the poisoner Israeli who deliberately infects humanity with germs, the avaricious Zionist and the disloyal supporter of Israel. These specific tropes form part of a climate of opinion which has become increasingly prevalent in the Middle East and much of the Muslim world, as well as dominant sections of left/liberal opinion in the West.

At the heart of the anti-Zionist narrative is a belief that Israel is a nation without parallel in evil, malevolence and infamy; that it is a pariah state whose global machinations are a threat to its neighbours, to the region and the world as a whole; that Israel has committed such foul deeds that it is deserving of the most execrable labels, indeed, that it is so devilish that it must be depicted visually using the crudest, foulest and most violent imagery. This overarching narrative builds upon centuries of Christian and Islamic theology which sought to dehumanise the Jew, to render him an object of contempt and ridicule, which blamed him for all the ills of the world and which sought either his conversion, expulsion or destruction.

How then might anti-Israel hostility be considered antisemitic? Kenneth Marcus writes of four ways in which this might be the case. The first is the intentionality principle, which broadly states that negative anti-Israeli attitudes can be considered antisemitic if 'based on hatred of Jews.' The second is the 'tacitness principle', which states that hostilities 'may be motivated by unconscious or tacit anti-Jewish prejudice.' The third is the memetics principle, the notion that some tropes of antisemitism 'have come to transmit cultural information about Jews even when the speaker is unaware of their impact.' The fourth is the ethnic 'ethnic traits principle', which states in essence that some anti-Israel hostility is antisemitic due to the 'foreseeable impact of this hostility on reasonable Jewish listeners or targets.'[1]

There is considerable merit in this analysis. It is undeniable that some of the hatred and vitriol directed towards Israel comes from a deep well of contempt, fear, paranoia and suspicion of Jews and Jewish institutions. When one listens to the levels of vituperation heaped upon Israel, with incessant calls to destroy the country, kill Israelis and re-enact Nazi atrocities on its Jewish population, there is little doubt that this is often motivated by antisemitic malice. That doesn't mean that all those who express such extreme views will admit to disliking Jews, as survey data often shows. Nonetheless, the belief in one's own progressive credentials can often mask more hidden levels of prejudice, as the second principle tells us. Often people are reluctant to spell out what they really think about Jews, perhaps because it might reveal that their attitude to Israel is not entirely innocent after all. For this reason, an entire industry has been created that is designed to uncover 'unconscious bias.' This book doesn't attempt to find evidence for either of these two, in large part because they revolve around subjective assessments and interpretation of mental states. The third principle forms the heart of Chapter 4, which assesses how deeply embedded tropes of historic antisemitism have been reproduced by those engaged in campaigns against Israel. It is indeed true that the speaker or writer need not be aware of the cultural information they are transmitting, even though one must suspect it to be a conscious choice for many others. The fourth principle is relevant to Chapter 5 which examines the impact of anti-Israel positions, both on Jewish citizens outside of Israel (who find themselves discriminated against) and on Israelis themselves. Organizations that adopt militant anti-Israeli positions can create an institutionally racist and unsafe environment for a Jewish minority, whether that be in a trade union, a university or a political party. Similarly, the argument will be advanced that on an international level, an endless drumbeat of anti-Israeli bias and disproportionate attacks creates an unsafe environment for Israel and Israelis, regardless of what motivates those attacks.

Throughout this chapter, there will be a strong emphasis on visual images used to depict Jews and Israelis, among them newspaper cartoons from the Middle East. There are several reasons for this. In Arab and Muslim societies where political criticism carries significant risks, cartoons provide an invaluable outlet for political expression. They are more than merely comical commentary on contemporary events. They can be seen as a 'reflection of the problems in the Middle East,'[2] one where there is a need to find a scapegoat for the ills of contemporary society, with 'the Jew' fitting the bill for many. Cartoons speak to their societies' deepest anxieties and prejudices by objectifying their enemy as a feared 'other,' though in a manner which simplifies and vilifies their target. As

---

[1] Marcus, *The Definition of Antisemitism*, 175, 176, 178, 181.
[2] Flores-Borjabad, Salud. "Political Cartoons in the Middle East: a New Form of Communication and Resistance."*US-China Foreign Language* 16, no. 6 (2018): 326.

non-discursive visual representations, they are designed to provoke extreme emotional reactions, such as shock and outrage, by concretizing in visual form the allegedly malign qualities of Jewish subjects, thus making those evil qualities seem more real and more threatening. Moreover, such cartoons do not appear in fringe publications, as would be the case in the West, but in mainstream newspapers which are read by millions of people on a daily basis. As such, they have widespread reach and significant potential influence in an area of the world where attitudes to the conflict with Israel are already volatile. As in Nazi Germany, these dehumanizing images are capable of poisoning the minds of entire populations.

1. Israel as a Christ killing state

The ancient Christian charge of Jews killing Jesus has resurfaced with venom in the Holy Land, the land where Christ was born. Now it is Israel, the Jewish nation, that stands accused of deicide and of embodying the original Jewish crime from two thousand years ago.

This idea has featured in the writings of Naim Ateek, the founder of Sabeel, a radical Christian theology outreach centre in Jerusalem. In his Easter message of 2001, he declared:

> Here in Palestine Jesus is again walking the Via Dolorosa. Jesus is the powerless Palestinian humiliated at a checkpoint, the woman trying to get through to the hospital for treatment, the young man whose dignity is trampled...In this season of Lent, it seems to many of us that Jesus is on the cross again with thousands of crucified Palestinians around him.[3]

In a few sentences, Ateek restated the long- repudiated charge that Jews killed Jesus, but put this into a modern context.[4] Ateek's depiction of Israelis as a nation of latter-day Christ killers stemmed from a belief in Palestinian replacement theology. This supersessionist philosophy stresses that the Jewish Old Testament and Covenant have now been supplanted by the New Testament and that the Christian Church has replaced the Israelites as God's Chosen people. Much Christian theological anti-Zionism has emerged from replacement theology. According to Dexter van der Zile, Ateek 'has created a powerful international anti-Zionist infrastructure' which has turned anti-Zionism into 'a competing religious practice in American mainstream churches and a persistent element in Protestant thought.'[5]

---

[3]Paul Wilkinson, "A Goliath in the Church," *The Jerusalem Post*, July 4, 2011.

[4] Daniel Swindell, "How Palestinian Activists Manipulate Western Activists," *Times of Israel*, May 30, 2018.

[5] Manfred Gerstenfeld, *The War of a Million Cuts: The Struggle Against the Delegitimization of Israel and the Jews, and the Growth of New Antisemitism*, (New York: RVP Press, 2015), 207.

Replacement theologians, together with non-Christian anti-Zionists, seek to portray Jesus as the original Palestinian or imply that the same Jewish mentality that led to Christ's crucifixion is being visited upon his Palestinian 'heirs.' This is reflected in visual images and discourse. In 2002, a Lutheran bishop in Copenhagen compared Sharon's anti-terror policies during Operation Defensive Shield to those of King Herod, the monarch who, according to legend, ordered the murder of all male children under two in Bethlehem. A cartoon published during the Second Intifada showed an Israeli soldier pointing a gun at a Palestinian baby. The infant was designed to represent the baby Jesus and it was accompanied by a caption that read 'Oh, you're doing it to me all over again.' In April 2002, the website Arabia.com showed an Israeli soldier (wearing a green jacket with the Star of David) about to bayonet a Christ like figure wearing a keffiyeh. A female figure, perhaps modelled on Mary Magdalene, was raising her hand in protest and the words 'Do not kill him TWICE' appeared above. Not for nothing did Palestinian television once describe Jesus as 'the first Palestinian shahid (martyr).'[6]

Other cartoons make the point that it is Palestine as a whole that is being murdered and that the Jewish killers of Christ are to blame. In 2002, Stavro Jabra in *Daily Star*, drew an image of Jesus with a thought bubble 'Father, forgive them because they know what they make.' Underneath in dripping red paint, was the word 'Bethlehem.' Similarly, in a cartoon from *Al-Quds* from 2002, Nasser Al-Ja-afari drew an image of Bethlehem on a cross with barbed wire in the foreground, emphasising current Jewish brutality and past perfidy. The fact that Bethlehem was Jewish at the time of Christ was seemingly lost on the cartoonist.

The fantastical claim that Jesus was himself a Palestinian and that the Palestinians are his Jesus like heirs surfaced in a comment made by Mustafa Barghouti in 2009. He said: 'We always remember that Jesus was the first Palestinian who was tortured in this land.'[7] Palestinian prisoners more recently still have been called 'the sons of Nativity, the sons of Jerusalem, and the sons of Jesus, the Palestinian, the first prisoner and the first martyr.'[8] It should not be forgotten that a significant percentage of Palestinian Arabs are Christians, meaning that they will not be unfamiliar with the demonological tradition within the Christian faith.

Such vicious iconography is by no means confined to the Arab press. Palestinian leader Yasser Arafat was likened to Jesus in a cartoon produced by Willem for French paper *Liberation* in 2001. Ariel Sharon was standing over a cross and, with a title Pas de Noel Pour Arafat (No Christmas for Arafat), Sharon muttered 'Mais Pour Paques Il est Le Bienvenu' (But for Easter he is welcome).[9] In a cartoon from April 2002 at the height of the second intifada, Giorgio Forattini

---

[6] Goldhagen, *The Devil that Never Dies*, 444.

[7] Palestinian Authority MP, Mustafa Barghouti. Palestinian TV (Fatah), December 24, 2009.

[8] ibid. 384-5

[9] Joel Kotek, *Cartoons and Extremism: Israel and the Jews in Arab and Western Media* (London: Vallentine Mitchell & Co. Ltd., 2008), 120.

drew an image for *La Stampa* of an Israeli tank firmly pointing its turret at a baby in a manger with the infant crying out 'Are they going to kill me again?' In a cartoon by Carlos Latuff, Che Guevara was idolized as a Palestinian, though the image was redolent with religious imagery. In another, he showed the Virgin Mary covered in blood having been 'wounded by Israeli soldiers.'[10] When Israel carried out a targeted assassination of Hamas leader Sheikh Ahmed Yassin, the popular Greek newspaper published a cartoon in which a woman was asking: 'Why did the Jewish government kill a religious leader?' The response was: 'They are practising for Easter.'[11]

World leaders have not been immune to making the antisemitic charge of deicide. In 2001 during a Papal visit to Damascus, Syrian president Bashar Assad echoed the ancient calumny when he complained that Jews were trying 'to kill all principles of divine faiths with the same mentality of betraying Jesus Christ and torturing Him, and in the same way that they tried to commit treachery against Prophet Mohammed.[12] Here, Assad achieved a double whammy. He firstly created a linkage between present day Israeli 'crimes' and the killing of Christ, arguing implicitly that a strain of treachery and cruelty ran perpetually through the Jewish character. Secondly, he connected their perfidy towards the Muslim prophet to their betrayal of Jesus. Similarly, the idea of Israel as a Christ killer state clearly resonated with the notorious anti-Israel hater, Father Miguel d'Escoto Brockmann, President of the United Nations General Assembly, who declared in 2008 that 'our brothers and sisters (the Palestinians) are being crucified.'[13] It hardly needs pointing out that Brockmann, far from being a fringe lunatic, occupied one of the most prestigious positions in world diplomacy.

2. Israel as a demoniacal state and racial threat

Just as Christian art portrayed Jews as a devilish and Satanic force, so too much of the discourse within both the Arab and Islamic world and among leftist commentators portrays Israel in dehumanizing terms, likening it to an irredeemably bestial nation, a Nazi state and a force for evil in the world. The state can shapeshift, in line with its shadowy nature, but it remains an object that inspires fear and revulsion no matter how it is manifested. In other words, just as centuries of anti-Jewish hatred led to the construction of the Jew as a force of demonic power, so too decades of anti-Israel hatred have constructed the Jewish state as a place of unparalleled bloodlust and cruelty, ripe for cleansing and extermination.

Zoomorphic imagery: One key motif in this bestialization is the use of zoomorphic imagery: the comparison of a state or its citizens to animals, to vermin

[10] ibid p. 138.
[11] Goldhagen, *The Devil that Never Dies*, 317.
[12] Bostom, *The Legacy of Islamic Antisemitism*, 41-2.
[13] Daniel Luban, "Gaza Tensions Shadow U.N. Holocaust Ceremony," *Interpress Service*, January 27, 2009.

and to microbes. The point of such comparisons is to suggest that Israel is an inhuman force among the nations of the world and, as such, needs to be destroyed in order to save humanity. The Nazi proclivity to represent the global Jew as a controlling octopus has become a staple of anti-Israel propaganda. In December 2001, the Greek cartoonist Stavro drew an image of an octopus (complete with Star of David) enveloping a number of figures marked 'Hamas,' 'Jihad' and 'Faith.' Such incendiary iconography has not been lost on Carlos Latuff, who once depicted Israel as a Nazi like octopus enveloping the Mavi Marmara flotilla in 2010. It captured the essential element of demonization well while adding the notion that Israel was intent on controlling its subjugated adversaries.

Elsewhere, Israel has been represented by a monstrous dragon, as in a Yemeni cartoon by Mohammad Massod.[14] In one Qatari cartoon from 2018, Israel was depicted as a bloodthirsty wolf (with a Star of David earring) with blood dripping from its fangs and a pocket President Trump cleaning its teeth. The caption stated: 'Exonerating Israel from the Gaza massacre.'[15] Sometimes, Israel has been depicted as a snake, a creature that in folklore is often associated with lies, vindictiveness and vengefulness. In 2001, Emad Hajjaj drew a cartoon for the Jordanian paper *Ad Dustour*, depicting Ariel Sharon and Ehud Barak as a two headed snake like monster. Just as arachnids inspire paranoia and fear, so too depictions of the Jew as a spider are not uncommon. A Lebanese paper from October 2000 featured an image of then Israeli Prime Minister Ehud Barak as a spider weaving a web that said 'War.'

Israeli leaders have frequently been likened to devilish creatures. A typical example was a cartoon published in Egyptian daily *Al Wafd* in May 2001 which featured Ariel Sharon as a devil with a swastika in his tail and with the Israeli leader holding a blood-stained knife. Unbelievably, the paper was connected to the liberal-democratic *Al-Wafd* party, yet that was no barrier to producing such incendiary imagery. In the Durban Conference held in the same year, the Union of Arab lawyers distributed a cartoon in a brochure which showed a menacing goose with blood-stained claws and a Star of David symbol on its back, in the process of killing a Palestinian child. In a 2002 cartoon from Qatari paper *Al-Watan*, an Israeli devil was holding a pitchfork while walking on skulls as hellfire raged in the background.[16]

The zoomorphic representation of Jews as illnesses, microbes or viruses was a core feature of Nazi and Soviet demonology.[17] So it is too throughout the Islamic world. According to Hamas' Deputy Minister of Religious Affairs, Abdallah Jarbu: 'The Jews suffer from a mental disorder, because they are thieves

---

[14] Kotek, *Cartoons and Extremism*, 106.
[15] "Antisemitic Cartoons: A Hallmark of Qatari News," *Anti-Defamation League*, December 26, 2018, https://www.adl.org/blog/anti-semitic-cartoons-a-hallmark-of-qatari-newspapers.
[16] Kotek, *Cartoons and Extremism*, 74.
[17] Manfred Gerstenfeld, *Demonizing Israel and the Jews* (New York: RVP Press, 2013), 37.

and aggressors.' Using Nazi animalistic terminology and quoting from the Quran, he described them as 'foreign bacteria – a microbe unparalleled in the world.' For good measure he continued: 'They are not human beings. They are not people. They have no religion, no conscience, and no moral values.' What followed in this diatribe was the eliminationist logic inherent in antisemitism; he called on 'Allah' to 'annihilate this filthy people.'[18] In one Arab cartoon, Ariel Sharon was represented as a microbe on a hospital bed with the title 'This is the germ that Arafat has.'

Fatah, the more secular branch of the Palestinian national movement, has not held back from repeating these appalling tropes of Islamist antisemitism. On the eve of the third millennium in December 1999, the Palestinian Authority newspaper *Al Hayat al-Hadida* published a cartoon showing an old man that represented the twentieth century together with a young boy that represented the coming century. A Jewish man with a Star of David stood between them with an arrow, pointed to him, saying he was 'the illness of the century.' The PA's official views have found resonance in Egypt, one of the countries with which Israel has signed a peace agreement. For Egyptian writer Fatma Abdallah Mahmoud, the Jews, a people 'accursed from the day the human race was created,' were 'the virus of the generation,' 'the plague of the generation' and 'the bacterium of all time.'[19]

Iran's leaders have many times indulged in the same dehumanizing comparisons. Thus in 2008, President Ahmadinejad described Israel as a 'germ of corruption' which would be 'wiped off.'[20] Again in May 2011, he said of Israel that like 'a cancer cell that spreads through the body, this regime infects any region,' adding, 'it must be removed from the body.'[21] This ominous and threatening language was repeated by Iran's Supreme Leader Ali Khamenei in 2012. At Friday prayers, he said that Israel was: 'a cancerous tumour that should be cut and will be cut.'[22] The demonology of Israel, which has taken on an obsessive quality, has been a constant even for alleged Iranian political moderates. Thus in 2018, Rouhani called Israel 'a fake regime' and likened its creation to 'the formation of a cancerous tumour in the region.'[23] The leader of Iran's proxy, Hezbollah, has repeated the trope several times, once describing Israel as a 'cancerous body in the region' which had to be 'uprooted.'[24] He then added that peace and co-existence with the Jews was impossible because they were 'a

[18] Goldhagen, *The Devil that Never Dies*, 227.
[19] Quoted in Schweitzer and Perry, *Antisemitism*, x.
[20] "Ahmadinejad: Israel is a germ of corruption that will be removed," *Haaretz*, August 20, 2008.
[21] "Israel is a cancer cell, says Iran," *Herald Sun*, May 16, 2011.
[22] "Iran: We will help 'cut out the cancer of Israel'," *The Telegraph*, February 3, 2012.
[23] "Iran's Rouhani Calls Israel a 'cancerous tumour' established by West," *Times of Israel*, November 24, 2018.
[24] Schoenfeld, *Return of antisemitism*, 23.

cancer...liable to spread again at any moment.' A spokesman for Iran's ally, the Taliban, once called the Jewish state 'a tumour in the body of the Islamic Ummah' on Arabic language television.[25] By likening Israel to a cancer, these figures have legitimised the notion that the Jewish state is a threat to humanity requiring extermination.

One of the most infamous of all the Nazi antisemitic images came in the 1940 film *Der Ewige Jude* (The Eternal Jew) where Jews were frequently shown as rats as they wondered around the world spreading their criminality. Photos were shown of Jews languishing in Polish ghettos, surrounded by vermin and dirt. At one point the viewer saw an image of rats escaping from a sewer, followed by a shot of malnourished and sickly Jews in the Lodz ghetto. As if the point of the juxtaposition was unclear, the narrator told the audience that just as rats were the vermin of the animal kingdom, so too the Jews were humanity's vermin. In the Saudi paper *Arab News*, cartoonist Amjad Rasmi drew an image of rats bearing the Star of David escaping from a sewer labelled Palestine House. The cartoon appeared to be an unmistakeable attempt to capture the demonology of the Nazi film.

Mohamed Morsi, the former President of Egypt, made another attempt to 'animalise' Jews, inspired directly by Quranic verses. In January 2010 he told Egyptians that there could be no 'accommodation with Israel' because the 'occupiers of the land of Palestine' were 'the descendants of apes and pigs.'[26] Therefore, just as the Middle Ages conjured up the image of the Jew as Satan, a bestial creature whose corrupting presence inspired fear among Gentiles, so too the Muslim world has seen an explosion of zoomorphic hatred for Jews.

Secular bestialization: If one thinks that the better educated elites of the secular West have been immune to this demonological discourse, one would be wrong. In fact, their own visceral distaste for Israeli nationhood and Zionist values has created its own vocabulary of unremitting hatred which leaves little doubt about the hostility that underlies it.

On a number of occasions, the entire Israeli nation has been described in the most pejorative terms. In 2001, while serving as Ambassador of France to the UK, career diplomat Daniel Bernard was quoted as saying: 'All the current troubles in the world are because of that shitty little country Israel.... Why should the world be in danger of World War III because of those people?'[27] For Bernard, Israel represented a grave and lethal liability to the planet, making remarks (which he did not deny making) that were gravely dehumanizing.[28] There was a firestorm of outrage after his words were revealed but he did have one defender: The *Independent* columnist Deborah Orr. 'Ever since I went to Israel on holiday,' she wrote, 'I've considered it to be a shitty little country too.' Later she qualified her comments by saying that 'the daily trauma it undergoes in defending its right to

---

[25] Neuer, Hillel, Twitter Post, 2 September 2021, 3.38PM.
[26] Goldhagen, *The Devil that Never Dies*, 237.
[27] ibid. 44.
[28] "Daniel Bernard (obituary)," *Telegraph*, May 3, 2004.

exist is the main thing that makes the place so shitty.' She then claimed that the comments were merely anti-Zionist, which involved 'disliking the existence of Israel and opposing those who support it.'[29] One should reflect on this sentiment for a minute. Orr was admitting that the Israeli nation had undergone 'daily trauma' because others were denying its right to exist while subjecting it to attacks on multiple fronts. Yet instead of paying tribute to the fighting fibre, resilience and patriotism of the Israeli people, she chose to label the country as 'shitty.' As an *ex post facto* rationalization, it was transparently fatuous.

Then there was the former (and disgraced) *Independent* journalist Johann Hari who reflected on Israel's achievements on its 60th birthday. While listing some of its qualities, he claimed that it was impossible to rid himself of a 'a remembered smell' which filled his nostrils. 'It is the smell of shit.'[30] He was specifically referring to the smell of raw sewage that, according to Hari, was being pumped out of Jewish settlements onto Palestinian land. The purported actions of some settlers pumping sewage during certain moments of the Israeli-Palestinian conflict made Hari think of a vile smell when trying to sum up an entire country on its birthday. Anti-globalization activist Carlos Latuff has similarly depicted Israelis using the dehumanizing image of excrement while also accusing Israelis of being child murderers.[31]

Hamid Dabashi, Professor of Iranian Studies and Comparative Literature at Columbia, took his demonization of Israeli Jews a stage further by attacking their very physical characteristics. In an article for *Al Ahram*, he wrote: 'Half a century of systematic maiming and murdering of another people has left its deep marks on the faces of these people. They way they talk, the way they walk, the way they handle objects, the way they greet each other, the way they look at the world.' He went on to speak of a 'vulgarity of character' which was 'bone-deep and structural to the skeletal vertebrae of its culture.'[32] This is destructive essentialism of a most pathological nature. For Dabashi, Israelis cannot even be conceived without seeing them in terms of gross physical deformities, a quality making them less than human. It is a grotesque, Nazi like frenzy masquerading as political commentary. Even babies are not spared the frenzy of demonization. Thus, the speaker of the Lebanese Parliament, Nabih Berri, in an article titled 'How to Recognise a Jew' wrote: 'If you see a pregnant woman, get close to her and toss a piece of gold near her or at her feet. If the fetus jumps out from his mother's womb and grabs the gold, you know he is a Jew.'[33]

[29] Deborah Orr, "I'm fed up being called an anti-Semite," *Independent*, December 21, 2001.
[30] Johann Hari, "Israel is suppressing a secret it must face," *Independent*, April 28, 2008.
[31] Kotek, *Cartoons and Extremism*, 142.
[32] Hamid Dabashi, "A Fistful of Dust: A Passage to Palestine," *Al Ahram*, September 23, 2004.
[33] "How to recognise a Jew according to the Lebanese parliament speaker," *The Jerusalem Post*, May 31, 2019.

Yet for Roger Waters, such demonization does not go far enough. In a somewhat bizarre rant during the Eurovision Song Contest in 2019, he claimed that the competition had been taken over by aliens akin to a scene from *Invasion of the Body Snatchers* and mocked those who condemned antisemitism. Whether this was a comparison of Israel with aliens is not clear but it was demonology all the same.

The head of Amnesty International in Finland, Frank Johansson, once described Israel as a 'scum state' in Finnish tabloid newspaper *Iltalehti*.[34] It is hard to imagine that any other nation or state would be labelled in such insulting terms, no matter how reprehensible or demeaning its government's policies. Indeed, he claimed that he would also apply the term 'scum' to some Russian officials, though not to Russia alone, a distinction which was naturally designed to avoid charges of Russophobia. For Norman Finkelstein, Israel was 'an insane state' because, 'while the rest of the world wanted peace, this state (wanted) war, war, and war.' He went on to characterise this belligerent country as 'Genghis Khan with a computer.'[35]

The readiness to describe Israel in such calumnious terms reflects the media's cartoonish representation of the conflict, one where Israelis and Palestinians play out their allotted roles in a Wild West fantasy of good and evil. Palestinians are shown as virtuous but downtrodden, Israelis as malevolent and brutish and each acts according to an unchanging nature. As Seth Franzman points out, many visitors to the region have 'an emotional, romantic and fetishistic connection to Palestinians that turns them into objects of affection, often seen as incapable of doing wrong.'[36] It is true that television news craves the juxtaposition of heroes and villains and seduces an audience into adopting a blinkered, simplistic view of the conflict. It is also true that journalists fall in with this tendency, ensuring that good copy is replete with scarred bodies, bombed out buildings and the suffering of victims. The extent to which antisemitism informs such narratives is open to question, but it surely cannot be discounted. What seems less disputable is that the frenzy of hatred inspired by such malevolent misrepresentation plays into subsequent attacks on Jews and creates a climate of fear affecting wider Jewish communities.

The Nazi connection: Israel's enemies have found an even more effective way to bestialize the Jewish state, namely by likening it to Nazi Germany, the principal persecutor of the Jewish people in the modern era. In the twentieth century, Nazi Germany was the ultimate pariah state, one which put its diabolical plan of industrialized mass murder into operation in order to systematically wipe out every Jewish man, woman and child. The aim was to erase the biological basis

---

[34] Jennifer Lipman, Amnesty head calls Israel 'sum state' *The Jewish Chronicle*, August 25, 2010.

[35] Goldhagen, *The Devil that Never Dies*, 25.

[36] Seth J Frantzman, "A Dangerous Obsession – The Press and Israel," in Alex Ryvchin (ed.), *The Anti-Israel Agenda: Inside the Political War on the Jewish State* (Jerusalem: Gefen Publishing House, 2017), 201.

of Jewry. By enacting a policy of mass extermination, it violated every norm and principle of international law, the laws of war and accepted principles of morality and human rights. Thus, when any nation today is compared with Nazi Germany, it is effectively accused of unspeakable criminality, bestiality and cruelty. It hardly needs stating that the Palestinians have not been subjected to genocide by any Israeli government. Israel has never created or sought to implement a policy of mass extermination, either of the Palestinians or its own Arab population. If it had, there would scarcely be any Palestinians in existence as the population would quickly have been decimated.

Background: The comparison of Israel with Nazi Germany was a staple of Soviet propaganda from the 1950s onwards. In the early years of the Cold War, Zionists and 'rootless cosmopolitans' were hounded across Eastern Europe (Hungary, Czechoslovakia and East Germany) and in the infamous show trials of the early 1950s, Jews featured heavily among those shot for alleged treason. Soviet Cold War antisemitism, symbolized above all by the Doctors' Plot of 1952, might have led to a mass pogrom against the Jews of the USSR had it not been for Stalin's death in 1953. Though that dastardly plan was dropped by his successors, state sponsored antisemitism continued and was ratcheted up after Israel's victory in the 1967 Six Day War. The guiding ideological principle was that due to Israel's alliances with 'imperialist' western nations after 1948, international Zionism was a malignant conspiratorial force designed to destroy socialism and the Soviet Union. Zionism was seen as a natural bedfellow of those forces that had nearly destroyed the USSR – Nazism and fascism. Thus was born the notion that the Zionists had been allied to and helped facilitate Nazism.

The antisemitic campaign involved the production of a vast plethora of anti-Israel books, articles, lectures, documentaries and films, the production of which was overseen by ideologues within the Communist party. The Soviets had a vast media apparatus and its main carrier of foreign propaganda, the Novosti Press Agency, worked in over 100 countries around the world. Given its relationships with local media and pro-Soviet front organizations, this agency helped ensure that Soviet anti-Zionist messages could be disseminated to tens of millions of people at the drop of a hat.

Cartoons denouncing Zionism featured the kind of imagery that regularly appeared in *Der Sturmer*. A book by Ukrainian author Trofim Kichko called *Judaism Without Embellishments* condemned Jews as inherently racist and alleged that they had conspired to help the Nazis attack the USSR in 1941. It led to a storm of protest in many countries and though the Soviets temporarily disavowed Kichko, he continued to write anti-Zionist tracts. The book *Caution Zionism* (1968) by Yuri Ivanov pursued some of these themes. It was obsessed with the alleged links (business, financial, political) between Nazi Germany and Zionist leaders over several decades and painted a lurid picture of Jewish nationalism in supposed cahoots with national socialism. He argued that 'Israeli militarism and West German neo-Nazism' were 'fed from the same source.'[37] In 1967, a cartoon in the *Berliner Zeitung* showed Moshe Dayan flying with his arms outstretched towards both Gaza and Jerusalem (two areas that were captured during the Six Day War). Next to him was the decayed Adolf Hitler, encouraging him with the words 'Carry on, colleague Dayan!'[38]

In 1985, the Anti-Zionist Committee of the Soviet Public (AKSO) published a brochure that outlined the alleged Zionist facilitation of Nazi expansion, accusing Zionist leaders of making it easier to unleash the Second World War through the transfer (Ha'avara) agreement and colluding in the genocide of the Slavs as well as fellow Jews. In short, it aimed to associate the movement for Jewish national liberation with the worst excesses of fascism, Nazism and tyranny.

Some have argued that this was a mere exercise in propagandistic hyperbole, one that reflected an era of profound Cold War tensions between the superpowers, rather than antisemitic ideology. But this is to miss the point. Such poisonous outpourings *both* reflected an era of Cold War rivalry and showmanship as well as the venom expressed by Soviet officialdom towards Jews and Zionists. To emphasize the political motivation of such vituperative attacks on Zionism at the expense of their content is to fall foul of a blatant false dichotomy. Ideological hate can resurface for political ends as and when it is needed.

Nazifying Israel: One of the worst outpourings of Soviet inspired demonology came during the Lebanon War of 1982. According to Nick Thimmesch of *The Los Angeles Times*, Begin was spouting 'the language of Hitler' by invoking the right of Jews to live in the West Bank.[39] At the height of the 1982 war, the *Morning Star* called for the 'genocide' to stop while cartoons in the *Arizona Republic* showed 'goose stepping Israelis in German helmets guarding cattle cars and patrolling concentration camps.' Peter Taylor likened the mass crowds in Tel Aviv who came out to support Israel's war to the mass German rallies of the 1930s. Novelist John Le Carre condemned Begin and his generals for 'inflicting upon another people the disgraceful criteria once inflicted upon themselves' while American journalist Nicholas von Hoffman said that as a result of this war, people could see that the Israeli government was 'pounding the star of David into a swastika.'[40] In one *Morning Star* cartoon, titled 'Holocaust: Begin style,' two Israeli soldiers were shown holding two men who were wearing striped clothing with one saying to the other: 'It's funny how well those old uniforms of your grandads (sic) fit these PLO terrorists.'[41] One British literary legend who

---

[37] Yuri Ivanov, *Caution Zionism: Essays on the Ideology, Organisation and Practice of Zionism* (Moscow: Progress Publishers, 1970), 133.

[38] Brinks, J.H. "Political Anti-Fascism in the German Democratic Republic." Journal of Contemporary History 32, vol. 2 (1997): 207-217.

[39] Edward Alexander, "Stealing the Holocaust," in Michael Curtis (ed.) *Antisemitism in the contemporary world*, 233.

[40] ibid p. 235

[41] Rich, *The Left's Jewish Problem*, 219.

doubtless agreed with this analysis was children's author Roald Dahl, a man notorious for his dark depictions of women and minorities. In a review of a book written for *Literary Review*, Dahl said this of Jewish people: 'Never before in the history of man has a race of people switched so rapidly from being much-pitied victims to barbarous murderers.'[42] For Dahl, the perceived ruthlessness of the Israeli army gave him free rein to vent his pre-existing animus against Jewish people, and in a manner that was barely disguised.

One of the Soviet Union's most enthusiastic disciples was veteran Labour politician and former London Mayor, Ken Livingstone. During the Lebanon war of 1982, a cartoon appeared in *The Labour Herald* which was being edited at the time by Livingstone. It showed a picture of Menachem Begin dressed up as a SS officer and performing a Hitler salute while standing on the skulls of dead Palestinians. Begin issued the words: 'Shalom? Who needs Shalom with Reagan behind you.'[43] Livingstone had a long track record of making offensive comments that either trivialized the Holocaust or which insulted the Jewish community in Britain. Thus, in 1983 he made a ludicrous comparison between British troops in Northern Ireland and the Nazi persecution of Jews. He attacked the Board of Deputies, the UK's main communal organization, claiming that it had been 'taken over by Jews who hold extreme right-wing views' while also suggesting that there were Jews in London and Britain who were 'organizing...into paramilitary groups which resemble fascist organizations.'[44] In 2005 he was suspended from office after comparing the Jewish journalist Oliver Finegold to a German war criminal. The journalist, who had doorstepped the Mayor, told Livingstone that he was a Jew but Livingstone doubled down on the offensive remark, telling him that he was behaving like a 'concentration camp guard.'[45] Such spectacular insensitivity would be unthinkable if applied to any other minority.

The level of demonization, using the Nazi trope, has only increased in fury and intensity in the last two decades. The Portuguese Nobel Prize winning novelist, Jose Saramago, during a visit to Yasser Arafat's compound in Ramallah, which was under Israeli siege, said these words: 'What is happening in Palestine, is a crime we can put on the same plane as what happened at Auschwitz... A sense of impunity characterises the Israeli people and its army. They have turned into rentiers of the Holocaust.' He later provided further clarification of his remarks, claiming that while Ramallah was not Auschwitz, 'the spirit of Auschwitz was present in Ramallah' and that while plenty of novelists had made criticisms of Israeli policy, 'it was the fact that I put my finger in the Auschwitz wound that

---

[42] Megan McCluskey, "What to Know About Children's Author Roald Dahl's Controversial Legacy," *Time*, March 18, 2021.

[43] Robert Wistrich, *From Ambivalence to Betrayal: The Left, the Jews, and Israel* (Nebraska: University of Nebraska Press, 2012), 542

[44] Keith Dovkants, "Anti-Semitism – and a timely question for Ken," *Evening Standard*, April 17, 2008.

[45] Matt Born, "Livingstone borrows Disraeli defence," *Telegraph*, February 23, 2005.

made them jump.'[46] When he was asked by an Israeli journalist to point out the gas chambers, he replied 'I hope this is not the case. There are so many things being done that have nothing to do with Nazism, but what is happening is more or less the same.'[47]

Saramago's words represented a perverse and unforgivable trivialization of the Holocaust, a belittling of a historical tragedy in order to score political points. Of course, novelists speak in metaphors and allusions but no other profession knows better the haunting power of words. Saramago, fuelled by righteous hate, no doubt intended to hurl a grave insult at the heart of the Jewish nation rather than stir liberal Israeli consciences. In that he succeeded, even if the price was to remind people about his own prejudice.

Others too barely disguise the hatred that appears to gnaw away at their soul. Take the case of Northern Irish poet, essayist and academic Tom Paulin who wrote a poem which included a reference to Palestinians being 'gunned down by the Zionist SS.'[48] In an interview with the Egyptian newspaper *Al Ahram* in 2002, he called for Jewish settlers in the West Bank to be 'shot dead,' adding, 'I think they are Nazis, racists, I feel nothing but hatred for them.'[49] Leaving aside the legal implications of his call for murder, his words were those of a self-righteous fanatic intoxicated by his own hatred. Paulin later fell back on the time-honoured canard that his words had been distorted and that he actually favoured a peaceful, two state solution to the conflict. The problem is that there was no reference to any of this in the *Al Ahram* interview where Paulin, after sympathising with the motives of suicide bombers, called on Palestinians to attack non-civilians because those attacks would be more effective.

Another academic who claimed that it was justified to kill and attack Israelis was Ted Honderich, a Professor at University College, London, who wrote as follows: 'To claim a moral right on behalf of the Palestinians to their terrorism is to say that they are right to engage in it, that it is permissible if not obligatory.'[50] Nor was he the only philosophical supporter of murdering Israelis. Gianni Vattimo, one of Italy's most famous modern philosophers, claimed in a radio interview in 2014 that he wanted 'to shoot those bastard Zionists' and that he was launching a fund-raising campaign to buy better weapons for Hamas because the terrorists were 'fighting with toy rockets that don't really kill anyone.' Comparing Israel to Franco's regime, he called on Europeans to form international brigades to fight alongside Hamas.[51]

---

[46] Julian Evans, "The militant magician," *The Guardian*, December 28, 2002.

[47] Theodore Dalrymple, "Trivializing the Holocaust II," *City Journal*, April 12, 2002.

[48] Tom Paulin, "Killed in Crossfire," *The Guardian*, February 18, 2001.

[49] Sarah Hall, "Death to Jewish settlers, says anti-Zionist poet," *The Guardian*, April 13, 2002.

[50] Jonathan Kay, "Hating Israel Is Part of Campus Culture," *National Post*, September 25, 2002.

[51] Anna Momigliano, "Well-known Italian philosopher: 'I'd Like to Shoot Those Bastard Zionists'," *Haaretz*, July 23, 2014.

No iconography is too sacred for these malevolent commentators. In 1988, the Kuwaiti paper *Al-Rai Al-Aam* drew an image of an Israeli soldier (with a clearly visible Star of David on his helmet) shovelling a baby into a furnace, a clear allusion to the crematoria in the death camps. In April 2002, a Greek paper showed a cartoon by Greek activist Stathis Stavropoulos in which a soldier (possibly Israeli) was screaming: 'Whoever was killed by bad Ariel Sharon and bad George Bush should go to the right...whoever was killed by good Shimon Peres and good Colin Powell should go to the left.' In other words, Israel was worse than the Nazis because there was no possibility of redemption or survival. The message was that all Israelis were fundamentally evil and inhuman, a point reinforced by the image of crucifixions in the background. The same cartoonist depicted Ariel Sharon as a Nazi.[52] In 2009, during the Gaza offensive, Yasmin Alibai-Brown asked, 'How many Palestinian Anne Franks did the Israelis murder, maim or turn mad?'[53] By her logic, the Israelis were a people who gloried in shedding innocent blood and a nation defined by boundless sadism and brutality. It was a clear attempt to picture Gaza as an extermination camp that had been built on the memories of the last Holocaust.

She was not alone in thinking this. The noted philosopher Slavoj Zizek once claimed that Gaza was 'the greatest concentration camp in the world.'[54] UN Special Rapporteur for the Palestinian territories, Richard Falk, compared conditions in Gaza to the Warsaw Ghetto. In his article from 2009 called 'Slouching towards a Palestinian Holocaust,' he wrote that the 'dire and worsening situation in Gaza threatens to produce a new holocaust' and denied that it was an 'irresponsible overstatement to associate the treatment of Palestinians in Gaza with this criminalized Nazi record of collective atrocity.'[55] A cartoon from *Al Quds Al Arabi* in 2004 by Emad Hajjaj pictured the iconic image of Auschwitz with its rail tracks, but emblazoned with Israeli flags, and underneath the title: 'Welcome to Gaza Strip or the Israeli Extermination Camp of Palestinian Refugees.' The Chilean communist journalist Luis Sepulveda wrote: 'In Auschwitz and Mauthausen, in Sabra, Chatila, and Gaza, Zionism and Nazism go hand in hand.'[56]

During Operation Pillar of Defence in 2012, Professor John Ashton, a former regional director of public health for north-west England, was using his twitter

---

[52] Leon Saltiel, "Antisemitic caricatures that appeared in Greece press, 2001-2003", accessed 5 March 2021, https://www.academia.edu/7693093/Antisemitic_caricatures_that_appeared_in_Greece_press_2001_2003.
[53] Yasmin Alibhai-Brown, "Israel's friends cannot justify this slaughter," *The Independent*, January 19, 2009.
[54] Slavoj Zizek, "Quiet slicing of the West Bank makes abstract prayers for peace obscene," *The Guardian*, August 18, 2009.
[55] Richard Falk, "Slouching Towards a Palestinian Holocaust," Countercurrents (blog), July 7, 2007, https://www.tni.org/my/node/9132.
[56] Pascal Bruckner, *The Tyranny of Guilt: An Essay on Western Masochism* (Princeton: Princeton University Press, 2012), 71

account to vilify Israel and Zionists in the same pejorative terms. In 2012, he wrote that it was 'sickening to see Zionists behave like Nazis.' Commenting on a report about post-traumatic stress disorder in the enclave two years later, Ashton tweeted: 'Can anybody begin to imagine the impact on the mental health of survivors of the Gaza Ghetto? Surely time for Jews to reflect.'[57] Comments such as these were doubly egregious and doubly reprehensible.

For veteran Australian journalist John Pilger, a man obsessed with picturing Israel as a racist, colonialist implant in the Middle East, Israel's war in Gaza in 2009 was a 'Holocaust denied.' Indeed, it was the culmination of a 'holocaust in the making' which started in 1948 with David Ben-Gurion's Plan D and continued as 'a joint US-Israeli project.'[58] Israeli journalist Gideon Levy has depicted Israel as a nation intent on spilling Palestinian blood, arguing that it was 'well prepared to massacre hundreds and thousands, and to expel tens of thousands.' He claimed that this resulted from 'dozens of years of brainwashing, demonization and dehumanization.'[59]

Comparisons of Israel's Gaza policy with Nazi genocide are the stock in trade of Brazilian freelance cartoonist Carlos Latuff. One of his cartoons showed a man in a keffiyah, dressed in concentration camp uniform (identified as a Palestinian), with the Israel security fence in the background. In another cartoon, he has compared the Gaza conflict to Nazi atrocities. He shows two Palestinians discussing what Israel will do next to the enclave following 'power and fuel cuts, food and medicine shortages, air strikes and border closure.' One says to the other 'gas chambers?'[60] Perhaps the most iconic image of the Warsaw Ghetto is that of a young Jewish child with his hands up in the air with Nazi soldiers behind him. Latuff reproduced this with the words 'Gaza ghetto' and a Palestinian child with his arms aloft and surrounded by Israeli soldiers. In a similar view, Palestinian television took an image of Nazi death camp victims and used it to suggest that they were victims of the attack on Deir Yassin.[61] Another depicted two individuals impaled on an electrified fence, the first a Jew from a concentration camp set against the words 'Never Again' and the second, a Palestinian wearing a uniform with the words 'Gaza' and the words underneath saying 'Over again.' It received second prize in the Iranian Holocaust cartoon competition that was launched in 2006. The first prize was given to Abdellah Derkaoui who produced an image of the security barrier that contained an image of Auschwitz. In one of Pat Oliphant's cartoons, a figure representing Israel resembled a goose-stepping

[57] Lee Harpin, "Top public health expert compared 'Zionists' to Nazis," *The Jewish Chronicle*, April 28, 2020.

[58] John Pilger, "Holocaust denied," *Green Left*, January 17, 2009.

[59] Gideon Levy, "60 dead in Gaza and the end of Israeli conscience," *Haaretz*, May 17, 2018.

[60] Adam Levick, "Anti-Semitic Cartoons on Progressive Blogs," *The Jerusalem Centre for Public Affairs*, September 2, 2010.

[61] "PA TV presents image of Nazi camp victims as taken from 'Deir Yassin massacre'," *Times of Israel*, April 11, 2018.

Nazi monster marching towards a tiny beleaguered figure representing Gaza. The cartoon appeared in the *New York Times* and *The Washington Post*.

Holocaust as a learning experience: One theme in the Nazi demonology is that Israel has somehow managed to imbibe lessons from the Holocaust to the detriment of their Arab 'victims.' In 2002, the Greek paper *Ethnos* carried this theme. In a cartoon, two Israeli soldiers, wearing Nazi style uniforms, were shown stabbing two Arabs to death with one saying to the other: 'Don't feel guilty, brother, we were not in Auschwitz and Dachau to suffer but to learn.' Worse still was an image by the Indonesian cartoonist Abdurahman Alattas for the Iranian Cartoon Festival on occupation in 2006. One half of his cartoon showed a Nazi thug attacking a Jew (who was depicted as a monster) while the second half showed the 'Israel army' as an identical beast attacking a Palestinian. In 2019, the Nova Scotia Human Rights Commission was forced to rescind a human rights award given to Rana Zaman after evidence emerged of hateful tweets against Israel. She had tweeted that in its attempts to exterminate Palestinians, Israel was 'aiming higher than 6 million,' adding, 'I wonder if #Israel borrowed this from the #Nazis after they saw how successful they were?' '#Gaza,' she wrote, 'is the new #Auschwitz.'[62]

This point is *de rigueur* in the Arab press. A 2006 cartoon from Jordanian paper *Ad Dustour* showed Ehud Olmert performing a Nazi salute as a Hitler portrait with an identical gesture was hanging behind him. Several recent cartoons depicted Hitler congratulating Israeli leaders on carrying out acts of murderous violence, echoing a theme found among Arab commentators that the Israelis had somehow used the Holocaust as an educational experience. It would be wrong to think that such egregious defamations occur only in the Arab press. In 2006, Norwegian illustrator Finn Graff drew an image of Ehud Olmert strutting around a death camp scene with a gun in hand, a caricature of the notorious Amon Goth, commandant of the Plaszow concentration camp. In May 2001, Clio, the muse of history, was shown delivering a Hitler style moustache to the face of Ariel Sharon on the pages of *El Pais*, Spain's most famous daily.

Major world politicians are not averse to making these odious Nazi-Zionist analogies. Former Swedish Prime Minister Olaf Palme once lamented the 'extraordinary reversal of roles' whereby it was 'the Palestinians, not the Jews,' who were being persecuted and threatened by 'liquidation.' The Palestinians, he went on to say, were 'locked up in a new Warsaw Ghetto.'[63] Venezuelan President Nicolas Maduro said that Israel had 'initiated a higher phase of its policy of genocide and extermination with the ground invasion of Palestinian territory, killing innocent men, women, girls and boys.'[64]

At the height of the Gaza offensive in 2014, former Labour Deputy Prime Minister Lord John Prescott likened Gaza to a 'concentration camp'. In a

---

[62] Jesse Synder, "Former NDP Candidate stripped of human rights award after comparing Israel to Nazi Germany," *National Post*, December 20, 2019.
[63] Schoenfeld, *Return of antisemitism*, 98.
[64] Gerstenfeld, *War of a Million Cuts*, 113.

subsequent telephone conversation with the author, Prescott claimed that the concentration camps he was referring to were those constructed by the British in the Second Boer War. As was pointed out to him, the connotation of a term and its context were crucial and the term concentration camp was overwhelmingly associated in the public mind with World War II and the Holocaust. Prescott was unmoved. One might have thought that if one nation's politicians were immune to regurgitating Nazi language, it was Germany. Sadly, this is not entirely the case. The former German minister Norbert Blüm caused a storm when he accused Israel of carrying out a *Vernichtungskrieg* (war of destruction), the Nazi term for war that implies genocide. The notoriously antisemitic Malaysian Prime Minister Mahathir Mohamad once claimed: 'The Nazi oppression of Jews' had turned them 'into the very monsters that they condemn so roundly in their propaganda material.'[65] For Mohamad, the Holocaust was less a tragedy for the Jews than a preparation for their future state, a learning experience in which they utilized Nazi dark arts to oppress another people. Conceiving of the Holocaust in this way inverts the role of victim and victimiser and destroys any sympathy for its Jewish victims.

Some believe that comparisons of Israeli policy to the Holocaust are an excess too far and prefer to compare the Jewish state's policies to those of pre-war Nazi Germany. This way they can argue that while no Holocaust has occurred in the West Bank or Gaza, the suffering of Palestinians mirrors that of Jews until 1939. Thus in 2001, Erkki Tuomioja, the then Finnish Foreign Minister, said he was 'appalled' by Israel's policy to 'crush, humiliate, subjugate and impoverish the Palestinians.' He went on: 'It is rather shocking that some people advocate towards the Palestinians the same kind of policy as they themselves were victim to in the 1930s.'[66] The former Pink Floyd songwriter and singer Roger Waters echoed identical sentiments in a piece for *The Guardian* where, talking of Israeli policies, he wrote: 'The parallels with what went on in the 1930s in Germany are so crushingly obvious.'[67]

Marches laden with swastikas: The sickening and intellectually baseless Nazi comparison is not solely the staple of misguided intellectuals. It is also an ever-present feature of anti-Israel marches and demonstrations, many of which have descended into violence, thuggery and criminality. The United Nations World Conference Against Racism held in Durban, South Africa only days before the 9/11 attacks provided a bitter foretaste of this in 2001. One of the central themes in this conference was the demonization of Israel, which was perversely labelled an apartheid state and the central locus of evil in the world. Antisemitic

---

[65] Eli J Lake, "U.S. slaps ally Malaysia for antisemitism," upi.com, October 16, 2003, https:// www.upi.com / Defense-News / 2003 / 10 / 16 / US-slaps-ally-Malaysia-for-antisemitism/86701066339802/.
[66] Robin Shepherd, *A State Beyond the Pale*: *Europe's Problem with Israel* (London: Weidenfeld & Nicolson, 2009), 56.
[67] Vanessa Thorpe and Edward Helmore, "Former Pink Floyd frontman sparks fury by comparing Israelis to Nazis," *The Guardian*, 14 December, 2013.

literature was on open display outside the main hall with one leaflet showing a resurrected Hitler declaring, 'If I had not lost, Israel would not exist today.' In addition, 'booths with posters equating Zionists with Nazis were set up' and Jews were depicted 'with 'with hooked noses, blood dripping from their hands, and fangs.' At the UN Youth Summit, Jewish participants were told they were 'a cursed people' who 'don't belong to the human race.'[68] A conference designed to protest racism turned into 'a grotesque spectacle of modern antisemitism.'[69] The UN Human Rights Commissioner, Mary Robinson, lamented 'the horrible antisemitism present.'[70]

A year later, as the Second Intifada raged in the Middle East, demonstrations erupted across Europe. In the Bosnian town of Tuzla, some demonstrators carried placards which read 'Sharon and Hitler: Two Eyes in the same head.' In Paris, the placards read 'Hitler has a son: Sharon' while in Italy and Ireland, Nazi swastikas were superimposed over the Star of David. In 2009, during the next phase of the conflict between Israel and Hamas, pro-Nazi imagery appeared at a rally attended by notorious firebrand Labour MP Jeremy Corbyn. With banners brandishing the Jewish state as a nation of 'child killers' another called Gaza a '21st Century Concentration Camp.'[71] The swastikas came out in an anti-Israel event in 2017 organised by Palestine Solidarity Campaign.[72] In October 2018, a Dutch local politician tweeted his support for artists who had flown kites in solidarity with Gaza. What made his support so incendiary was that one of the kites featured a swastika in green while another showed Nazi Germany's Imperial Eagle symbol.[73] These are but a tiny sample of cases in which this vile calumny has been indulged.

Attacks on Jewish memory: To ratchet up the offensiveness of these comparisons, these anti-Israel ideologues have chosen to launch their noxious attacks during one of the most sacred moments of the Jewish calendar: Holocaust Memorial Day. In 2013, Liberal Democrat MP David Ward caused outrage with remarks posted on his blog. He expressed sadness that the Jews, 'who suffered unbelievable levels of persecution during the Holocaust' could, 'within a few years of liberation,' go on to inflict 'atrocities on Palestinians in the new State of

---

[68] Bayefsky, Anne. "The UN World Conference against racism: a racist antiracism conference." *Proceedings of the Annual Meeting (American Society of International Law* 96 (2002): 67.

[69] Gerald Steinberg, "NGOs and the Battle Plan for the Political War on Israel," in Ryvchin (ed.) *The Anti-Israel Agenda*, 2.

[70] Gerald Steinberg, "NGOs and the Battle Plan for the Political War on Israel," in *The Anti-Israel Agenda*, ed. Alex Ryvchin, 3.

[71] "Corbyn blasted for speaking at 2009 protest likening Israel to Nazi Germany," *JNS*, August 2, 2019.

[72] "Utterly disgusting swastikas at Palestine event condemned," *Jewish News*, December 12, 2017.

[73] "Dutch politician praises pro-Palestinian kite show featuring Nazi symbols," *Jewish Telegraphic Agency*, October 26, 2018.

Israel and continue to do so on a daily basis in the West Bank and Gaza.' [74] His belief in collective responsibility, blaming 'Jews' for Israel's actions, sparked widespread anger. In 2013, Lee Jasper, a race relations activist and candidate for the Respect party, exploited the commemoration to launch his own spiteful attack. Israel, he declared, had 'failed to learn the lessons of its own tragic history having evolved into a racist oppressor.' He added: 'Israel has...allowed itself to turn into the very thing that it despises the most, a political ideology that seeks to oppress people on the basis of race or religion.' [75] For Jasper, the most crucial thing about Holocaust Memorial Day was not to remind the world about remembering and honouring the Holocaust victims or the need to battle antisemitism. The crucial message was to remind people about the purported infamy of the Jewish state and to tarnish its (mostly Jewish) supporters by association.

This desecration of sacred Jewish memory has taken an even uglier twist in recent years with Memorial Day events used as a mouthpiece for extreme Palestinian views. In 2009, Scottish Palestine Solidarity Campaign hosted an event on Holocaust Memorial Day called 'Resistance to Genocide and Ethnic Cleansing: from Europe in the 1940s to the Middle East today.' The main speaker, Azzam Tamimi, had previously expressed his support for suicide bombings in Israel. [76] In 2018, members of Students for Justice in Palestine at Columbia University held an anti-Israel demonstration opposite an event that marked Holocaust Memorial Day. Students could be heard chanting: 'From the river to the sea, Palestine will be free.' In 2020, a group of BDS activists in Germany interrupted an online memorial for Holocaust Remembrance Day with 'images of Hitler, pornographic content and anti-Israeli and antisemitic slogans.' [77] In the same year, on the eve of Israel's Holocaust Memorial Day, a tree that was planted to honour Anne Frank was desecrated. [78] In 2010, journalist Ewa Jasiewicz daubed a wall of the Warsaw Ghetto with the words 'Free Palestine' and 'Liberate all ghettos,' later describing it as 'a small act of unarmed resistance.' [79] All these people might have taken inspiration from earlier attacks on sacred days of Jewish memory. In 1969, the Marxist organization Schwarze Ratten/Tupamaros West-Berlin carried out an antisemitic attack on the Berlin Jewish Community Centre

---

[74] "Lib Dems condemn MPs criticism of Israel ahead of Holocaust Memorial Day," *BBC News*, January 25, 2013.

[75] ""Lee Jasper shows no respect for Israel or HMD," *The Jewish Chronicle*, January 24, 2013.

[76] Johnny Paul, "Scottish group accused of hijacking Holocaust Memorial Day," *The Jerusalem Post*, January 24, 2009.

[77] Itamar Eichner, "BDS activists disrupt Holocaust event with Hitler imagery," *Ynetnews*, 21st April, 2020.

[78] "Anne Frank Memorial desecrated days before Holocaust Memorial Day," *The Jerusalem Post*, April 16, 2020.

[79] Justin Cohen and Jenni Frazer, "Activist who daubed 'Free Palestine' at Warsaw Ghetto quits Momentum panel event," *Jewish News*, September 12, 2018.

on Pogrom Night (9th November) which commemorated Kristallnacht. Those who carried it out used a justification that would resonate with people like Jasiewicz:

> Every ceremony in West Berlin and in Germany suppresses that Zionists repeat the Kristallnacht from 1938 every day in the occupied territories, in refugee camps and in Israeli prisons. The Jews expelled from fascism have themselves become fascists.

There have been other antisemitic desecrations of Holocaust memorials that do not appear to have been made with the same political intent. Thus in 2019, a Holocaust memorial in Rome was daubed with an inscription in German that read 'The murderer always returns to the scene of the crime.'[80] Fascists were believed to be behind an attack on a similar memorial in Belarus in 2008 when vandals burnt the flowers and wreaths that had been laid at the monument. These are familiar examples of far-right extremist attacks that aim to inflict maximum wounds on the Jewish community and their examples could be multiplied many times over.

This tendency to politicize the Holocaust has even appeared in respectable outlets. In a recent BBC report on the 75th anniversary of the liberation of Auschwitz-Birkenau, the broadcaster's veteran Middle East reporter, Orla Guerin, followed an interview with a Holocaust survivor with these words: 'The state of Israel is now a regional power. For decades it has occupied Palestinian territories. But some here will always see their nation through the prism of persecution and survival.' One former BBC executive condemned the report as 'unnecessary, insensitive and particularly ugly.'[81]

Naturally, if one believes that the Jewish state has morphed into a version of Nazi monsterdom, then it is likely that they deride as fake or phony a *Jewish* commemoration of this atrocity. On this view, Jews as Zionists have no moral right to see themselves as victims. Until they unequivocally denounce the infamy of Israel, they are scarred by its sins and tainted by its racism. This is because, according to one commentator, there is an 'indelible link between the Holocaust and the current situation of the Palestinian people' and that 'Palestinians are part of the post-Holocaust narrative.'[82] This smear is related to the accusation that Zionists collaborated with Hitler before the war, helping to bring about Nazi plans of expansion and conquest and either manipulating (in one version) or facilitating the mass murder of Jews for political ends. In a now infamous BBC radio interview in 2016, Ken Livingstone, rushing to the defence of Labour MP Naz Shah (herself embroiled in a scandal over antisemitism on social media), claimed the following: 'He (Hitler) was supporting Zionism before he went mad and ended

---

[80] "Holocaust Memorial desecrated in Rome's Jewish ghetto," *Wanted in Rome*, May 30, 2019.
[81] Mark Sweeney, "Former BBC executives criticize Orla Guerin's Holocaust report," *The Guardian*, January 24, 2020.
[82] Yvonne Ridley, "On Holocaust Memorial Day, remember too that the Nakba is an indelible part of Israel's history," *Middle East Monitor*, January 26, 2020.

up killing six million Jews.' Livingstone, aware of the torrent of fury that his comments produced, simply doubled down on his remarks. He cited the Trotskyite writer Lenni Brenner whose book *Zionism in the age of dictators* (1983) argued that there was extensive co-operation between Zionists and the Nazis during the 1930s.

This is not the place to debate the rights and wrongs of what happened at the birth of Israel or the subsequent vicissitudes of the conflict. Needless to say, it is a complex and multifaceted picture which does not reduce to simple formulas of Israeli wrongdoing and Palestinian benignity. But it is the view that Jews must pass some anti-Zionist loyalty test to the progressive community before they can represent Holocaust victims that is so grossly offensive and noxious.

Yet until Jews wholeheartedly disown Zionism, some anti-Israeli zealots argue that they do not deserve the honour of commemorating the Holocaust. One university professor has even gone on record as saying that 'the heritage of the victims of the Holocaust belongs to the Palestinian people. The state of Israel has no (legitimate) claim to the heritage of the Holocaust.'[83] Another academic has written: 'Today, the Palestinians are the heirs of the Jewish sufferings, the sufferings of Treblinka, Dachau and Auschwitz. The Jews were the direct victims of Nazism. The world recently discovered that the Palestinians were the Nazis' indirect victims.'[84] Professor John Ashton would doubtless agree, having tweeted: 'Shame on you Israel and Damn your custodianship of the victims of the holocaust.'[85] This is buttressed by the view that Jews and Zionists engage in something as egregious as Holocaust denial, namely denial of the nakba, seen as the Palestinian Holocaust. One commentator has said that 'Naqba denial' is 'as pernicious as Holocaust revisionism.'[86]

Why the Nazi comparison? So, why are people so ready to call Israel a Nazi state? For some, this is an instance of Godwin's rule of Nazi analogies: The law states that as an online discussion grows longer, the probability of a comparison involving Nazis or Hitler approaches 1 (that is to say it will happen in any discussion eventually). Such comparisons, sometimes made in the heat of the moment, are an example of the kind of rhetorical exuberance and hyperbole that enters discussions, especially when they are conducted online. Holocaust comparisons occur frequently in discussions about war, abortion and animal killing where zealots talk of the genocide of animals and children. Western politicians are also vilified by egregious comparisons to fascists and Nazis. One suspects that these comparisons are not always meant literally and are designed

---

[83] Mitchell Bard, *The Arab Lobby: The Invisible Alliance That Undermines America's Interests in the Middle East*, (Northampton: Broadside Books, 2011), 314.

[84] Afif Safieh, *The peace process: From Breakthrough to Breakdown*, (London: Saqi Books, 2010), 14.

[85] Ashton, John. Twitter Post. 7 August 2014, 3.53PM.

[86] Anthony Loewenstein, "Why aren't Jews outraged by Israeli occupation?" *Haaretz*, June 17, 2009.

to increase attention through the outrage they attract, though they also reflect a modern predilection for anti-intellectualism and vulgarity.

Yet, if the goal is to express anger and outrage at something Israel has done, why denounce the whole of Israeli society? Why compare all of Israel with Nazism, or excrement or a virus? Why depict all Israelis or all Zionists as animals or as some evil, Satanic force? Secondly, there are many countries that these critics could compare Israel to if they so wished, including Bolsonaro's Brazil, Putin's Russia, Orban's Hungary or any number of other regimes. Yet those who most passionately denounce Israel choose just one: Nazi Germany. Thirdly, if the aim here is to stir the liberal consciences of Israeli left wingers, the Nazi analogy is entirely misplaced. It has usually had the opposite effect: to turn a tin ear to the burning zealots. Thus Amos Oz, responding to the Nazi comparisons made by Jose Saramago, responded: 'The Israeli occupation is unjust - but to compare it to the crimes of the Nazis is like comparing Saramago to Stalin.'[87]

But there is something purposive and intentional when these same critics compare Israel with Nazi Germany or allege close Nazi-Zionist links: they are trying to systematically blacken and demonize the world's only Jewish state. They want it to become the world's chief pariah state, a country isolated in the halls of international opinion and ripe for dissolution.[88] After all, a state that mandates the deliberate mass slaughter of innocents is an abomination, a state beyond the pale. The insidious genocide comparison is an attempt to even up the score between the Nazis and the Jews by suggesting that the victims of hatred and racism have now become its progenitors. For Germans and for many other Europeans, it is a psychic mechanism for relieving the endless burden of culpability by imagining 'Jewish behaviour so heinous that the Jews no longer deserve German guilt.'[89] Attributing Nazi methods to Israel thus serves a cathartic purpose by shifting the focus from perpetrators to victims.[90]

There is also the insidious suggestion that we should feel less pity for those who were murdered, given that they would have gone on to become Nazis themselves. If so, then the Jewish claim to victimhood is phoney and the true heirs of Jewish suffering are the Palestinians instead. Thus, interrupting Holocaust Memorial Day events in order to make a political statement has become *de rigueur*

---

[87] Evans, "The militant magician."

[88] Some anti-Zionists claim that they do not want Israel to be destroyed, merely replaced with a one state of all its citizens, including all the Palestinians in the West Bank and Gaza (and those in the diaspora). But given the population sizes, this would instantly mean the demographic disintegration of a Jewish state as the country would have an Arab majority.

[89] Garfinkle, *Jewcentricity*, 240.

[90] What is worrying is that such views find resonance among educated populations. A famous study in 2011 conducted by the University of Bielefeld for the German Social Democrat Friedrich Ebert Foundation found that 42% of the British people – and a percentage similar to that in some other European countries – took the view that Israel was conducting a war of extermination against the Palestinians.

for pro-Palestinian activists. Alternatively, it is simply a way to launch spiteful and vicious attacks against the Jews of Israel, knowing how deeply ingrained the memory of the Holocaust remains in the country's psyche. In essence, it is malodorous Jew baiting.

The response to these accusations should be to point out the manifest absurdity of the accusation, given that the Arab population, both inside Israel's pre-1967 boundaries and in the West Bank and Gaza, has rapidly multiplied over the last half century. Between 1960 and 2020, the Palestinian population has increased from 1.1 million to 5.1 million, a near fivefold increase. Given the vast strength of Israeli military forces, any attempted genocide would have wiped out the Arab inhabitants of the territories rather than allowing it to multiply so continuously. Secondly, one should point out that talk of genocide brings to mind the insidious connection between Palestinian leader Hajj Amin al-Husseini and the Nazi leadership during the Second World War. It is undeniable that al-Husseini was a fervent supporter of the Final Solution, that he bears responsibility for a multitude of Jewish deaths during the war and that he sought the elimination of Palestine's Jewry in the event of a Nazi victory. One can further point out that there was considerable wartime support for Nazism in a number of Arab countries, that there was a pro-Nazi coup in Iraq and that several Arab countries offered refuge to Nazi war criminals after 1945.

3. Chosenness, vengefulness and a belief in racial superiority

Some of Israel's most demented critics have condemned the state's real or alleged excesses by reference to the notion of Jewish 'chosenness' According to this interpretation of 'the chosen people,' Jews see themselves as set apart from the rest of humanity by dint of their superiority to other peoples. A related idea is that Jews are a vengeful people who seek the destruction of their enemies, invoking a plethora of Biblical verses where God is said to have avenged his people with bloodshed. This conveniently ignores the express prohibitions on vengefulness in the Talmud and those verses that espouse love for all humanity. Nonetheless, in some of Israel's recent wars, some commentators have invoked these notions within the character of the Jewish state to explain its behaviour.

In 1982, following Israel's invasion of Lebanon, a Swedish columnist saw fit to condemn the Jewish state for adhering to an 'Old Testament ideology' and implied that this was the primary impediment to peace. A similar hate filled invective filled the columns of the Swedish newspaper *Vastgota-Demokraten*. It contrasted Christianity with Judaism, claiming that the latter was a 'composed story' that was suited 'to military and warlike adventures.' It added: 'If one believes the old source texts, Israel was God's chosen people. It is therefore perhaps not a difficult choice for such a people, using all the means at its disposal, especially military options, to strive to extend its chosen property and territory.'[91]

---

[91] Schoenfeld, *Return of antisemitism*, 93.

This is a direct attempt to normalise Israel's alleged misdeeds in terms of the negative behaviour associated with Jews rather than geopolitical reality.

A similarly passionate denunciation of Israel was offered by Nobel Prize winning novelist Jose Saramago in 2002. In an article for *El Pais* he penned a diatribe so toxic and so saturated in prejudice that it seems scarcely believable it was printed.

He accused Jews of being 'intoxicated mentally by the messianic dream of a Greater Israel which (would) finally achieve the expansionist dreams of the most radical Zionism.' He said they had been 'contaminated by the monstrous and rooted "certitude" that in this catastrophic and absurd world there exists a people chosen by God' which allowed them to justify 'all the actions of an obsessive, psychological and pathologically exclusivist racism.' He went on: 'Israel seizes hold of the terrible words of God in Deuteronomy: 'Vengeance is mine, and I will be repaid.' Israel is 'a racist state' because it has been infected by 'Judaism's monstrous doctrines' which are racist not just towards the Palestinians but 'against the entire world.'[92]

For Saramago, Judaism's original sin was the belief in a vengeful and destructive God who had conferred chosenness on one people. That too became Israel's original sin, the factor that turned it into a leper among the nations and a malign force in the international order. Israel was reduced to being an 'illegitimate' state whose diabolical nature stemmed from a religious heritage of pure infamy.

Not only does this narrative misinterpret the basis of Jewish law, one which stresses the brotherhood of man, the equality of all human beings under the law and tolerance towards the stranger, not only does it assume that Jews justify their behaviour according to Biblical doctrines (which for the majority is not true) but it assumes without evidence that Jews as a community are more racist than any other. Saramago *et al* read the Israeli-Palestinian conflict as a sorry tale of hyper vindictive Jews meting out racialized Biblical justice to Palestinian victims while using the Holocaust 'banner' to deflect criticism from Gentiles. As for the notion that antisemitism remains a problem today only because the Jews endlessly 'scratch their own wound,' one only needs to look at the plethora of evidence gathered in this volume to see that those wounds are being scratched by others all too willingly.

These diatribes have only continued in the last two decades. In 2006, Israeli soldier Gilad Schalit was kidnapped by Hamas terrorists and taken to Gaza. In the intervening years, Israel tried its level best to capture him but failed and, as a result, faced a series of unconscionable demands by the Islamists for his release. In 2011, the Netanyahu government agreed to the release of more than 1,000 Palestinians in return for Schalit, many of whom were murderers or terrorists whose crimes had killed dozens of Israelis. It was a painful action, precisely

---

[92] Quoted in: Paul Berman, "Bigotry in Print. Crowds chant murder. Something's Changed," *Forward*, 24 May 2002.

because it militated against the idea that such wanton criminals would face justice for what they had done. Yet the *Independent's* Deborah Orr commented that this lack of proportion was somehow 'abject' because it acknowledged 'that the lives of the *chosen* (author's emphasis) were of hugely greater consequence than those of their unfortunate neighbours.' In other words, Israel's decision to hand over so many prisoners did not reflect the country's desperate love for its own soldiers and its willingness to meet unreasonable demands. Instead, it was all about a chosen people thinking that Arab lives were so worthless that they could be traded with impunity.

A similar argument was made by Tariq Ali in 2006 during the height of the Lebanon war. He decried many elements of 'hubris' in the Jewish state, including 'a belief in its racial superiority' and used this to explain why 'the loss of many civilian lives in Gaza and Lebanon' mattered 'less than the capture or death of a single Israeli soldier.'[93] Orr and Ali believed that what was animating Israel was a sense of superiority over Gentiles and a primitive desire for vengeance, both of which were built on pre-existing prejudices.

In 2012, Professor John Ashton referenced a racist interpretation of the Old Testament in his indictment of Israel's behaviour. He tweeted: 'Fundamentalist Zionist old testament interpretation of 20 eyes for 1 eye will produce a new generation of militant jihadists, so it goes on.'[94] Elsewhere he tweeted: 'If disease breaks out in Gaza Israel will not be exempt. Very Old Testament.'[95]

In 2019, the Belgian writer Dimitri Verhulst penned a vitriolic piece ('There is no promised land, only stolen land') that was so hateful in its depiction of Jews it could have appeared in *Der Sturmer*. After inaccurately quoting a French Jewish singer as having said, 'Being Jewish is not a religion, no God would give creatures such an ugly nose,' Verhulst wrote: 'Because God has His favorites and they have their privileges, Palestinians were driven out of their homes in 1948 to make place for God's favorites.' He went on to invoke the Livingstone defence, claiming that 'speaking with [the] chosen' was impossible because 'as soon as you mention Israel and the fate of the Palestinians, they look at you like you masterminded the Holocaust yourself.' The defence was duly accepted by Bart Eeckhout, *De Morgen's* editor in chief, who suggested that the piece was 'a harsh criticism on Israel's politics towards the Palestinian people.'[96]

But perhaps the most infamous indictment of Israel as a nation animated by superiority and vengefulness was penned by philosopher Jostein Gaardner. In his article 'God's chosen people,' Gaardner sought to attack Israel's policies on the basis of their 'archaic, national and warlike religion' which, unlike Christianity, had no belief in 'compassion or forgiveness.' He pulled no punches. Israelis, he said, were animated by 'blood vengeance' that was based on the principle of 'an

---

[93] Tariq Ali, "A protracted colonial war," *The Guardian*, July 20, 2006.
[94] John Ashton. Twitter Post. November 25, 2012. 06.08AM.
[95] John Ashton. Twitter Post. August 9, 2014. 12.52AM.
[96] Cnann Liphshiz, "Belgian editor defends publication of column saying Jews have 'ugly noses'," *Jewish Telegraphic Agency*, August 7, 2019.

eye for an eye.' They supported their country in war 'in the same manner they once cheered the plagues of the Lord as "fitting punishment" for the people of Egypt.' He went on: 'To act as God's Chosen People is not only stupid and arrogant, but a crime against humanity. We call it racism.' In sanctimonious fashion he intoned, 'We do not believe in divine promises as a justification for occupation and apartheid. We laugh uneasily at those who still believe that the god of flora, fauna and the galaxies has selected one people in particular as his favourite and given it silly, stone tablets, burning bushes and a license to kill.'[97] There was no attempt here to treat Israel as a normal country. Indeed, its very abnormality, its pariah status among the civilized Christian nations on earth, stemmed from the abnormally cruel nature of its Jewish population whose attitudes to non-Jews had not changed in two thousand years. He invoked the idea that there was a timeless essence to Jewry marked by belligerence, cruelty and arrogance, first revealed in its holy texts and now played out again on the battlefronts of the Middle East. It is an example of destructive, racist essentialism.

The notion that the Jewish religion has spawned racism towards other nations has found a ready audience across the Arab and Muslim world. A number of cartoons depict Judaism as an inherently discriminatory faith whose criminal religious pronouncements are seized upon gratefully by a bloodthirsty Israeli regime. The cartoonist Stavro Jabra typified this trend when he drew an image in the Lebanese *Daily Star* of an Arab man bleeding to death from a wound inflicted from a Talmud containing a gun. An Egyptian paper in 1992 displayed even more gut-wrenching anti-Judaism when it featured a cartoon of a menacing figure, identified as a Jew but drawn as a devil, holding up a menorah as if it was a pitchfork. *Al Ahram*, Egypt's most widely circulated daily, attacked Judaism in equally explicit terms in August 2001. In the cartoon we see a rabbi, standing among Jewish congregants in Jerusalem, holding up a stone tablet inscribed with the word 'racism.' Finally, in *Al Quds Al-Arabi*, a cartoon from 2004 showed Ariel Sharon drawing up plans for disengagement from Gaza, plans which were contained in a scroll, one section of which formed the turret of an Israeli tank. The less than subtle messages of all these cartoons is that the Israeli threat to the Arab world is mandated by Judaism with its 'racist' doctrines.

4. Avaricious Jewish state

Another pernicious stereotype associated with Jews is greed or avarice and this too occasionally surfaces in narratives that attack Israel. To take one example, an article in *The Economist* described conditions in the Jenin refugee camp following an Israeli incursion. It warned that there was a danger of epidemic in the camp as Palestinians were 'shovelling their decomposed dead' and needed 'massive humanitarian aid' which the Israelis were hindering. Israel, the article concluded, 'is a superior land' and needs to 'abate its greed for other people's

---

[97] Jostein Gaardner, "God's Chosen People," *Aftenposten*, August 5, 2006.

land.' [98] Leaving aside the fact that the only reason for the Israeli incursion was the incessant terrorist activities that were taking place in Jenin, the piece is simply echoing an antisemitic canard by attributing avarice to the political DNA of the Jewish state. If greed was the reason for the incursion, it is also strange that Israel later withdrew its forces from the Palestinian town rather than cementing a land grab. This is not the way that colonialist powers behave when they greedily capture another nation's land, as the recent behaviour of the Russian Federation all too clearly attests. The Swedish paper *Vasgota-Demokraten* wrote a piece during the 1982 Lebanon War that made damning references to traditional antisemitic tropes. After attacking Jews for their status as a 'chosen people,' it continued with an attack on the Jewish economic character:

> Jews and pawnbrokers used to be virtually synonymous concepts, but things have moved on and they now invest their assets in the West Bank, which pays a higher dividend. [99]

In these cases, a traditional antisemitic trope of 'Jewish avarice' has been transposed to the conflict between Israel and the Arab world to describe the behaviour of the Jewish state.

5. The blood libel

Sometimes, the actual content of the demonization almost entirely duplicates that of medieval times. Nowhere can this be better observed than with the blood libel accusation that has been flung at Israel by her enemies. There have been occasions when the medieval blood libel has been stated as if it were a factual truth and an inescapable part of Jewish and Zionist history. In 1983 Mustafa Tlass, Syria's Minister of Defence, published '*The Matzah of Zion*.' The book attempted to validate the Damascus blood libel of 1840 and argued that at the heart of Judaism was 'a black hatred against all humans and religions.' He concluded that 'no Arab country should ever sign a peace treaty with Israel.' [100]

The Second Intifada brought a vast tidal wave of antisemitic images and commentary that directly reproduced the ancient idea of the blood libel. They were given rocket fuel by coverage of the story of Mohammed al-Dura, a young Palestinian boy who was reported to have been shot by IDF troops in September 2000. Subsequent investigation by the Israeli authorities strongly disputed this account of events, suggesting that the shooting was in fact staged. While the death of any child in a war zone is tragic, what followed was an inexcusable torrent of anti-Jewish racism from the Arab press.

At the height of the Second Intifada, Egyptian paper *Al Ahram* produced a cartoon showing two Israeli soldiers wantonly killing children in a meat grinder

---

[98] "The Road to War?" *The Economist*, October 7, 2000.
[99] Schoenfeld, *Return of antisemitism*, 93.
[100] Rawan Osman, "New Forms of Old Hate: Confronting Assad's Anti-Semitism in Germany." Fikra Forum, February 6, 2020.

while another Jewish figure held out a cup to catch the blood of those being killed. The toast was: 'Here's to peace.'[101] On October 28 2001, the same paper ran an article explaining how 'bestial' Jews murdered Arab children in order to use their blood for Passover matzah. Mixing Christian allegory with traditional blood libel, the Qatari newspaper *Al Watan* in 2002 showed a cartoon of Ariel Sharon holding what appeared to be the Grail and inscribed on the cup were the words 'Palestinian children's blood.'

In 2002, Carlos Latuff drew an image of Israeli soldiers as bestial and inhuman figures who were 'born to kill' and collect the eyes of their victims in ghoulish fashion. In April 2002, another cartoon showed a demented Israeli soldier pointing a weapon at the head of a blood-soaked Palestinian baby while screaming 'Who did commit the Jenin massacres?' A Bahraini cartoonist in June 2002 showed an Israeli, possibly a Jewish settler, holding a bayonet with a baby impaled on it, harking back to the British anti-German propaganda of World War 1. Meanwhile, in May 2002, students at San Francisco State University produced posters showing a graphic image of a dead baby and titled 'Made in Israel: Palestinian Children Meat, slaughtered according to Jewish rites.'[102]

At times, the blood-soaked conspiracy of Jews murdering Palestinians is seen as the result of a lethal collaboration between the US and Israel. Thus, Palestinian cartoonist Omaya Joha showed the Statue of Liberty embracing 'child murderer' Ehud Barak in one hand while holding up a dead Palestinian child in the other.

The blood libel was rekindled with spectacular venom during Israel's counter terrorist operations in Jenin in 2002. Commentators lined up to accuse Israel of committing grotesque crimes against humanity. A N Wilson talked of the Jewish state having carried out a 'massacre' and a 'genocide.' The attack on Jenin was 'every bit as repellent' as the 9/11 attacks.[103] Peter Beaumont of *The Guardian* spoke of 'an act of ferocious destruction against an area of civilian concentration.'[104] Phil Reeves of *The Independent* wrote of 'A monstrous war crime that Israel (had) tried to cover up for a fortnight' and, invoking the genocide of Cambodia, spoke of 'killing fields.'[105] *The Evening Standard* lamented Israel's 'staggering brutality and callous murder' while Yasmin Alibhai-Brown declared that Ariel Sharon 'should be tried for crimes against humanity.'[106] *The Economist* opined that, as the Palestinians were 'shovelling out their decomposed dead, the

[101] Kotek, *Cartoons and Extremism*, 63.
[102] John Podhoretz, "Hatefest by the Bay," *New York Post*, May 14, 2002.
[103] Daniel Treiman, "Guardian Editor: Sorry About That 9/11-Jenin Comparison," forward.com, March 6, 2008, https://forward.com/life/12849/guardian-editor-sorry-about-that-9-11-jenin-compa/.
[104] Peter Beaumont, "Not a massacre, but a brutal breach of war's rules," *The Guardian*, April 25, 2002.
[105] Sharon Sadeh, "How Jenin battle became a 'massacre'", *The Guardian*, May 6, 2002.
[106] Yasmin Alibhai-Brown, "Why I'm Boycotting Israel," *The Independent*, April 15, 2002.

danger of epidemic (was) real.'[107] As Tom Gross has pointed out, the sinister accounts of Israel's alleged misdeeds were largely based on the words of a Palestinian labourer called Kamal Anis. Anis claimed to have seen Israelis pile bodies into a mass grave, bulldoze buildings and flatten the area. Of course, when it was finally made known that no massacre had taken place, that the Israelis had actually gone door to door to root out terrorists, costing the lives of 23 servicemen, and that the majority of Palestinian dead were actually terrorists hunted by Israel, it was too late to correct these flagrant misrepresentations.

A ubiquitous feature of anti-Israeli blood libels is that the victims are uniformly children. This reinforces the narrative that the Israelis are bestial, subhuman killers who target only the most innocent members of society. It ties in with the notion that Jews have a noxious appetite for the blood of Gentiles, an idea reinforced by the wanton glee on the faces of Israeli leaders when confronted by the result of their 'sport.' Image after image from Arab papers shows Palestinian infants impaled and murdered by Israelis, of Israeli leaders wading in blood or, in one case, displaying Palestinian body parts on their military uniform. For Lebanese cartoonist Stavro Jabra, a nation that is so willing to engage in vicious bloodletting is best represented as the Grim Reaper, pouring blood down his throat while surveying a ruined, blackened Gazan landscape. Israelis are literally shown lusting after the physical remains of children. The reality is that the vast majority of Palestinians killed by Israeli forces are adults not children, moreover, adults who are engaged in warfare against Israel.

The British media has by no means been immune to this tidal wave of blatant prejudice, even if it appears less frequently than in the Arab press. In 2003, *The Independent* published a cartoon by Dave Brown that featured Ariel Sharon, then Israeli Prime Minister, eating a baby in a satire of Goya's famous painting 'Saturn devouring one of his sons.' The subtext underneath said: 'What's wrong? You never seen a politician kissing babies before?'[108] The British Political Cartoon Society went on to award it cartoon of the year. Was the painting a version of the blood libel, of Jews sacrificing children for their nefarious purposes, or merely an attempt to reproduce a famous artwork in the context of political elections?

In one sense, it could have been both. Clearly, the cartoon looked sufficiently similar to Goya's great masterpiece as to remove any doubt that it was the inspiration for the cartoon. Of course, the big difference was that Goya depicted Saturn devouring *his own* babies whereas Sharon was seen consuming Palestinian ones. Few, however, would deny Brown his right to use mockery and satire in his cartoons. Crucially, Sharon was not a proxy for the Jewish people as a whole and the cartoon was shorn of Jewish imagery, such as the Star of David. That said, antisemitic images rely on historic iconography and the image of the Jew eating a child (or drinking its blood) is a central feature. The cartoonist, unwittingly it may be added, may have tapped into this iconography to produce his cartoon.

---

[107] "After the Assault," The Economist, April 25, 2002.
[108] "Idiots call me a Nazi over a cartoon," *The Times*, December 3, 2003.

An even more blatant example of a blood libel cartoon appeared in the highly respected *Sunday Times* in 2013. Cartoonist Gerald Scarfe decided to mark Holocaust Remembrance Day with an image of Benjamin Netanyahu building the security wall but using the blood and bodies of Palestinians as cement. The caption was 'Israeli elections - will cementing peace continue?' Of course, the whole point of the wall was that it was designed to *prevent* Palestinians freely spilling Jewish blood in lethal suicide bombings rather than the other way round, a point which made the cartoon an absurd inversion of reality. But this cartoonist chose to depict the Israeli leader as having a vengeful and insatiable lust for Palestinian blood. Its combination of blood libel imagery, political illiteracy and appalling timing was sufficiently damaging for *The Sunday Times* to issue a fulsome apology. The paper later agreed that it was unacceptable to 'reflect in a caricature, even unintentionally, historical iconography that is persecutory or antisemitic.'[109]

In 2007, Raed Salah, the leader of the Israeli Islamic movement, made a speech in east Jerusalem where he declared: 'We have never allowed ourselves to knead [the dough for] the bread that breaks the fast in the holy month of Ramadan with children's blood.' He added: 'Whoever wants a more thorough explanation, let him ask what used to happen to some children in Europe, whose blood was mixed in with the dough of the [Jewish] holy bread.'[110] In 2014, Yahya Rabah, a columnist for the official PA daily *Al-Hayat Al-Jadida* and a member of the Fatah Leadership Committee in Gaza, wrote that Jews offered their God 'sacrifices during Passover in the form of matzah made from the blood of our children.'[111]

In 2020, a blood libel rapidly swept through Palestinian media and society. In January of that year, the body of a seven-year-old Palestinian Boy, Qais Abu Ramila, was found in a pit after he had apparently drowned the night before. It appeared to be a terrible and tragic accident and the Israeli authorities co-operated to find his body. Almost immediately, a Twitter account belonging to 'Real Seif Bitar' accused a 'herd of violent Israeli settlers' (note the animalistic language) of kidnapping the child and throwing his body into a well. Palestinian leader Hannan Ashrawi immediately re-tweeted this lie, adding the words, 'The heart just shatters, the pain is unbearable, no words,' and she was joined by Democratic Congresswoman Rashida Tlaib. Tlaib would later retract her action, claiming that she had re-tweeted something that was 'not fully verified.'[112]

The massacre of Palestinians in the refugee camps of Sabra and Chatila in 1982 was one of the most shocking acts of the Lebanon war. Though Israel had indirect responsibility for the crime, given that it allowed bloodthirsty Phalangists

---

[109] "Netanyahu cartoon: an apology," *Sunday Times*, February 3, 2013.
[110] Yoav Stern, "Islamic Movement Head Charged with Incitement to Hatred," *Haaretz*, January 29, 2008.
[111] Melanie Phillips, "How the West is complicit in Jew hatred," *The Jerusalem Post*, July 17, 2014
[112] "The death of a Palestinian boy shows blood libels are born," *The Jerusalem Post*, January 26, 2020.

into the camp, its troops did not kill any Palestinians as is often wrongly stated. Nonetheless, Arab propaganda has attempted to depict the massacre as another example of bloodthirsty Jews attacking innocent Arabs. In 2018, an egregious cartoon appeared in the Qatari media showing an orthodox Jew drinking blood from goblets with the text above the cartoon in Arabic saying: 'The 36th anniversary of the Sabra and Chatila massacre and the text on the goblets reading: Massacres and the Palestinian people.'

One might have thought that NGOs, dependent on western funding, would think twice about producing images replete with antisemitic motifs. Apparently, this did not matter for Badil - Resource Center for Palestinian Residency and Refugee Rights, a Palestinian NGO which has in the past received money from European countries. In 2010, it produced a cartoon of a Hasidic Jew standing with a blood-stained pitchfork in his hand and standing triumphantly on a stone marked 1948, underneath which lay a prostrate Palestinian holding a key. Nor did it matter for the Belgian branch of Oxfam which, in 2003, released a poster showing a Jaffa orange dripping with blood with the title 'Israeli fruit taste bitter. Say no to the occupation of Palestine. Don't buy any fruit from Israel.'[113] It did not occur to Oxfam that such essentializing imagery suggested that Israel was a nation tainted by blood, and one whose bloody crimes warranted a boycott of all its products.

If people believe that Israel has a blood lust for children, they will naturally liken it to a dangerous predator or psychopath. That was exactly the line taken by anti-Israel comedian Alexei Sayle who, at the height of the Gaza war, described Israel as 'the Jimmy Saville of nation states,' adding 'It clearly doesn't care about damaging the lives of children.'[114] A candidate for the UK Labour party stood down when it emerged that she had written: 'To me the Israeli state is like an abused child who becomes an abusive adult.'[115] On July 2 2013, the German paper *Suddeutsche Zeitung* published a cartoon which depicted the Jewish state as a Moloch, a Canaanite god that is associated with child sacrifice. The hideous monster was lying in bed, knife and fork in hand, while being waited on by a woman (presumably representing Germany).[116] The cartoon dredged up all the worst elements of antisemitic canards: Jewish avarice in the form of monstrous appetites, the control of gentiles, a predatory lust for children, to say nothing of the bestial presentation of a collective Jew that harked back to the imagery of *Der Sturmer*.

A variant on the blood libel is that Israel has deliberately killed Palestinians in order to harvest their organs and body parts. This is a myth that has spread with pernicious speed in the Middle East and which has been disseminated on Arabic

---

[113] Oxfam denies anti-Semitic allegation," *Irish Examiner*, July 11, 2003.
[114] "Alexei Sayle: Israel is Jimmy Saville of national states," *Belfast Telegraph*, July 16, 2014.
[115] Rowena Mason, "Labour candidate steps down after comparing Israel to 'abusive adult'," *The Guardian*, November 7, 2019.
[116] Lazar Berman, "German daily slammed for depicting Israel as Moloch," *Times of Israel*, July 3, 2013.

media channels. In 2010, while Israel was desperately trying to save the lives of people affected by the earthquake in Haiti, rumours surfaced that Israelis were trying to harvest the organs of Haitians to use in transplants. The allegations appeared in a Gaza based web page called *The Palestine Telegraph* and were repeated on other outlets, including Press TV, the state-funded Iranian TV news channel, the Izzedine al-Qassam Brigades, an armed wing of Hamas and the site of conspiracy theorist Alex Jones. In an article called 'Dark Echoes of the Holocaust' written for the *Daily Record*, George Galloway drew attention to claims that the body parts of Palestinian prisoners had been harvested by Israeli doctors without their families' consent. For this Galloway accused those responsible of 'playing mini–Mengele on Palestinian prisoners in Israeli jails.'[117]

One of the most graphic portrayals of this vile accusation came from the Iranian Sahar 1 TV broadcaster. In 2004 it ran a weekly series called Zahra's Blue Eyes. It was directed by an Iranian education ministry official and was filmed in Persian and subsequently dubbed in Arabic. In the first episode, Israelis, who are disguised as UN workers, visit a Palestinian school on the pretext that they are examining children's eyes for diseases. In reality, they are there to select which eyes to steal for transplant. In the next episode, the audience discovers that the Israeli president is being kept alive only with stolen Palestinian organs and that the Israeli military commander of the West Bank is kidnapping Palestinians.

A related charge made by officials within the Palestinian Authority is that Israel is conducting gruesome medical experiments against Palestinian prisoners. On July 6 2008, the paper *Al-Hayat Al-Jadida* issued this statement: 'The method employed by the Israeli Occupation in which they [are] instigating slow death ... doctors in Israeli prison clinics use the prisoners as guinea pigs for clinical drug testing under the pretence of "treatment".' They said that the inmates had received injections which 'caused their hair and facial hair to fall out permanently' while 'others lost their sanity.' Another report in the same paper claimed that prisoners were being used as 'guinea pigs for clinical testing of drugs and treatment-methods.'[118] This is a variant on the blood libel, the idea that innocent civilians (that is how prisoners are seen by the PA) are ripe for exploitation by Jews.

The poisoner Jew: The trope of the poisoner Jew, a variant on the blood libel, has found a new lease of life within the anti-Israel movement. Today, it is rife across the Arab and Muslim world. One of the most notorious examples of this accusation came in March 1983. Some days before Pesach, it was reported that hundreds of Palestinian girls in different towns on the West Bank had suddenly fainted for no apparent medical reason. Rumours began to spread that they had been poisoned by the Israelis as part of a secret plot to arrest Palestinian fertility. One of Israel's leading epidemiologists carried out an investigation and

---

[117] George Galloway, "Dark echoes of the Holocaust," *Daily Record*, December 28, 2009.

[118] "Wiesenthal Center: Palestinian Authority's Big Lie Campaign Alleging Nazi-like experiments by Israelis," wiesenthal.com, accessed 27 February 2022, https://www.wiesenthal.com/about/news/wiesenthal-center-7.html

found the accusations to be baseless; he concluded that it was a case of mass hysteria. Yellow powder on school window sills was found to be from local pine trees. Yet, the Palestinians continued to disseminate this hoax to a gullible international media and to the visiting International Red Cross.[119]

In 1997 the Palestinians accused Israel of trying to 'suppress Arab population growth' by exporting strawberry flavoured gum to schoolhouses in the West Bank and Gaza. It was claimed that the gum was laced with sex hormones (progesterone) and would arouse sexual appetites in Palestinian women before sterilising them. Palestinian supply minister Abdel Aziz Shaheen said that the gum was capable of 'completely destroying the genetic system of young boys.' *The Washington Post* took the story seriously enough to carry out a test by a professor of pharmaceutical chemistry. Using a mass spectrometer, he could find no progesterone in the gum.[120]

The most lethal virus in recent years has been HIV which has killed nearly 40 million people to date. It comes as little surprise to learn that Israel has been accused of spreading this virus for political purposes. In 1997, the PA's representative to the UN Human Rights Commission in Geneva claimed that 'the Israeli authorities infected by injection 300 Palestinian children with the HIV virus.'[121] At the same time, the head of the Criminal Division of the Palestinian Police in Nablus accused the Israeli security services of running a ring of HIV infected prostitutes to infect Palestinians. It has also been picked up by the Egyptian media. *Al-'ilm*, a science monthly, carried a story that 'Jewish tourists infected with AIDS are travelling around Asian and African countries with the aim of spreading the disease.'[122]

In 1999 Suha Arafat, the wife of the Palestinian President, made an incendiary accusation in the presence of Hillary Clinton: 'Our people have been subjected to the daily intensive use of poisonous gas by the Israeli forces, which have led to an increase in cancer cases among women and children.' She accused them of contaminating 80% of the PA's water sources.[123] Her husband accused Israel of killing Palestinian children in order to get their internal organs while Mohammad Baraka, Head of High Follow up Committee for Arabs in Israel, said that Palestinians in Israeli jails were being used as guinea pigs in medical trials.[124] A similar incendiary claim was made by Palestinian academic and activist Nadera

---

[119] Raphael Israeli, "Poison: The Use of Blood Libel in the War Against Israel," *Jerusalem Centre for Public Affairs*, April 15, 2002.

[120] Barton Gellman, "Pop! Went the Tale of the Bubble Gum Spiked with Sex Hormones," *Washington Post*, July 28, 1997.

[121] The charge was made by Nabil Ramlawi, the PLO representative to the United Nations Commission on Human Rights in Geneva.

[122] Schoenfeld, *The Return of Antisemitism*, 16.

[123] William A Orme Jr., "While Mrs. Clinton Looks On, Palestinian Officials Criticize Israel," *New York Times*, November 12, 1999.

[124] "Committee: Israel testing medicines on Palestinian prisoners," *Middle East Monitor*, April 3, 2019.

Shalhoub-Kevorkian, the Lawrence D. Biele Chair in Law at the Hebrew University, who claimed in a lecture that 'Palestinian spaces' were 'laboratories for the Israeli security industry' which was 'using them as showcases.'[125]

For good measure, the director of the PA's Committee for Consumer Protection once accused Israel of supplying Palestinian markets with chocolates causing mad cow disease. The PA's Deputy Minister of Supplies, Abdel Hamid al-Qudsi, alleged a plot 'under the auspices of the Israel Defence Forces' to stunt Palestinian growth, claiming that Israel was distributing to the Palestinians 'food containing material that causes cancer and hormones that harm male virility' in an attempt to 'poison and harm the Palestinian population.'[126]

Given the predilection for labelling Jews as mankind's poisoner in chief, it was perhaps hardly surprisingly that Israel was blamed for the death of Yasser Arafat. A 2009 Fatah convention in Bethlehem passed a resolution stating that Israel was responsible for Arafat's death and many officials said that the IDF or Mossad had killed him by poisoning. A subsequent exhumation of Arafat's body found traces of polonium 210, though experts disagreed on whether this was the cause of death. Of course, the accusation that Israel poisoned Arafat was not *per se* antisemitic, just as accusations of Russian state sponsored poisoning are not *per se* Russophobic. But given the sinister role that this trope plays in modern antisemitism, it does seem antisemitic to revert to the accusation so readily and without any substantial evidence.

In 2016, in the European Parliament, Mahmoud Abbas accused Israeli rabbis of telling their government to poison Palestinian water supplies in order to 'commit mass killings against the Palestinian people.'[127] According to officials in the PA, a 'Rabbi Mlma,' chairman of the 'Council of Rabbis in the West Bank settlements,' had issued the call for mass poisoning. Yet investigation showed that there was no such rabbi nor was there any known rabbinic organization by that name.

The Palestinian daily *Al-Quds*, in an article titled 'Herds of Wild Boars: The Settlers' New Tool for Seizing Agricultural Lands,' claimed that Israeli soldiers and Jewish settlers had been releasing wild boars in parts of the West Bank in order 'to destroy Palestinian crops and intimidate Palestinian villagers and farmers.' The head of the Palestinian Commission for Resisting the Wall and Settlements in the Northern West Bank accused settlers of 'waging a war of wild boars against residents.' Interestingly, no footage has emerged to back up this incredible claim, despite the presence of both Palestinian and foreign photographers throughout the region. Veteran Palestinian journalist Khaled Abu

---

[125] "Hebrew U: Prof, who claims arms tested on Palestinian kids doesn't represent us," *Times of Israel*, February 17, 2019.

[126] Rafael Medoff, "'Poisoning' accusations are a Palestinian tradition," *STL Jewish Light*, June 29, 2016, https://stljewishlight.org/opinion/poisoning-accusations-are-a-palestinian-tradition/.

[127] Diaa Hadid, "Mahmoud Abbas Claims Rabbis Urged Israel to Poison Palestinians' Water," *New York Times*, June 23, 2016

Toameh sums up the absurdity of the accusation when he says: 'Needless to say, none of the Palestinians interviewed for the report managed to provide evidence that Israeli soldiers or settlers were behind the spread of wild boars in the West Bank. It is hard to find one Palestinian who does not carry a smartphone that he or she could use to document the alleged practices of the soldiers and settlers.'[128] The PA has spent a quarter of a century since Oslo engaging in this outpouring of irrational hatred, despite pledging to abstain from incitement and hostile propaganda. Indeed, one could write a whole book on conspiracy theories which allege that Israel has tried to poison its neighbours.

During 2020, while the Coronavirus pandemic was spreading around the world with lethal force, the virus of antisemitic conspiracy theory followed in its wake. Hateful conspiracy theories began to proliferate which encouraged the view that Israel had either engineered the virus in order to destroy its neighbours or target other countries, or that Jews had done so for financial reasons. A commentator on Turkish television, Coskun Basbug, said that 'Jews, Zionists have organized & engineered #Corona virus as biological weapon just like bird flue & Crimean–Congo hemorrhagic fever (CCHF)…They want to design the world, seize countries, neuter the world's population.'[129] An Iranian academic charged that 'Zionist elements' had 'developed (a) deadlier strain of coronavirus against Iran.' Others have alleged a sinister plot co-ordinated between these 'malicious' Jews and their allies, especially in Washington. A Saudi writer called Sa'ud Al-Shehry claimed that the coronavirus was a plot hatched by American and Israeli drug companies aimed at increasing their profits. He wrote: 'A 'wonder' virus was discovered yesterday in China; tomorrow it will be discovered in Egypt, but it will not be discovered either today, tomorrow or the day after tomorrow in the U.S. or Israel.'[130]

Islamists have no monopoly on such repugnant views. Philip Giraldi, Executive Director of the Council for the National Interest, said that it was possible that the US 'had a hand in creating the coronavirus' at a research centre and it was 'very likely that Israel was a partner.' The US/Israeli intent was to engineer a 'biological weapon' that would damage their enemies (China and Iran).[131] Alain Mondino, a far right local election candidate in France, posted a video on social media which was titled 'Corona virus for goy' which claimed that the virus had been put in place by Jews with the aim of 'establishing their

---

[128] Abu Khaled Toameh, "Palestinians Revive Blood Libels as Israel Saves Their Lives," *Gatestone Institute*, March 9, 2020.

[129] Alyssa Weiner, "Global Trends in Conspiracy Theories Linking Jews with Coronavirus," ajc.org, May 1, 2020, https://www.ajc.org/news/global-trends-in-conspiracy-theories-linking-jews-with-coronavirus.

[130] "Arab writers: The Coronavirus is part of biological warfare waged by the U.S against China," *MEMRI*, February 6, 2020.

[131] Philipe Giraldi, "Who made Coronavirus? Was it the US, Israel or China itself?" *Strategic Culture Foundation*, March 5, 2020.

supremacy.'[132] The group 'Organic Christian Generation,' founded by Swiss cult leader Ivo Sasek, distributed a flyer claiming that coronavirus was a biological weapon unleashed by Jewish financier George Soros. The Austrian extremist Martin Sellner, who leads Identitäre Bewegung Österreich (Identitarian Movement of Austria) and who has a conviction for antisemitic hate, has similarly claimed that the virus has come from the Soros Open Society Foundation.[133]

Florida pastor Rick Wiles, a man who claimed that the 'synagogue of Satan' was pushing the US to fight wars on its behalf, said that God was spreading Coronavirus in synagogues because Jews opposed Jesus. He added: 'Repent and believe in the name of Jesus Christ, and the plague will stop.'[134] An American academic tweeted in response to news that Israel was taking stringent measures to protect her population from the virus: 'Israel will – I am sure – have different medical procedures for Jews and non-Jews. Non-Jews will be put in mass prisons.'[135] On social media, people posted on texting platforms like Telegram that this virus was a Jewish plot, either to manipulate the stock market so that they would make a lot of money or that it was part of a partnership between Zionists and the deep state to undermine and ultimately unseat President Trump.

Summing up these incendiary accusations, Moshe Kantor, president of the European Jewish Congress, was led to say: 'Since the beginning of the COVID-19 pandemic, there has been a significant rise in accusations that Jews, as individuals and as a collective, are behind the spread of the virus or are directly profiting from it.'[136] Taken as a whole, the sinister age old notion that Jews are behind plots to poison and immiserate mankind has been unleashed with full fury by Israel's most vociferous opponents.

6. The all controlling Zionist lobby

In the twentieth century, the myth of the world Jewish conspiracy has endured and found new life in the anti-Israel movement. It is no exaggeration to say that Israel's enemies have become obsessed and deranged over the spectre of Zionist power. They have pictured the Jewish state as a conspiratorial and malign entity, exercising its devious tentacles to manipulate the region and the wider world in its own interests. In the fervid imaginations of its enemies, Israel and its supporters work behind the scenes to plot terror attacks, censor opponents, create terrorist organizations and stage 'false flag' operations, all of which are designed to bring

---

[132] "Classic antisemitic allegations arise over coronavirus, says gov't report," *The Jerusalem Post*, March 25, 2020.

[133] Manfred Gerstenfeld, "Anti-Jewish Coronavirus Conspiracy Theories in Historical Context," *The Begin-Sadat Centre for Strategic Studies*, March 31, 2020.

[134] Marcy Oster, "Conservative pastor says spread of coronavirus in synagogues is punishment from God," *Jewish Telegraphic Agency*, March 29, 2020.

[135] "California State University Professor Claims Israel Will Place Arab Coronavirus Patients in 'Mass Prisons'," *Algemeiner*, March 11, 2020.

[136] "Coronavirus crisis stoking antisemitism worldwide – report," *Reuters*, April 20, 2020.

to heel 'subservient' western politicians who will be made to do Israel's bidding.[137]

Since 9/11, an obsession with the Israel lobby has gradually moved into the mainstream of western political thought. The spectre of radical Islamic terror has come to haunt western policy makers and in their unbending refusal to accept the reality of global jihadism, some commentators have reflexively blamed the Jewish state for stoking up Muslim anger against the West. Israel's 'crimes' against the Palestinians, its 'aggression' against the Arab world and its alleged anti-Muslim racism have been cited as the alleged cocktail of grievances rousing an angry Muslim world and the chief causes of Islamist and Salafi violence. Given that Israel is pictured as a strategic threat to the West, and given that western nations normally act in their interests, it seems that the only explanation for the close support given to the Jewish state is that its overseas lobbies (run from Jerusalem) force those governments to do its bidding, using every underhand tactic available.

The charges made against the Israel lobby fall into a number of categories:

1) It silences opponents, whether in the media or in academia.

2) It controls the agenda of western politics, forcing Gentile politicians to do Israel's bidding.

3) It manipulates and conspires against the West by launching false flag attacks under cover of Islamist enemies.

4) The lobby controls the world through international institutions.

Silences media, academia: For some, the Israel lobby has such a demented hold over Gentile institutions that it effectively silences them from criticizing Israel. Five days after the 9/11 attacks, the journalist Richard Ingrams, surveying the British media, lamented the 'reluctance throughout the media to contemplate the Israeli factor' that lay behind the attacks. The reason for this silence was due to 'pressure from the Israel lobby in this country' which has made 'even normally outspoken journalists...reluctant to refer to such matters.' That Ingrams was not solely concerned with Israeli wrongdoing was made clear later in his piece when he complained about the presence of Lord Levy, an 'unelected, unknown Jewish businessman' in the government of Tony Blair, a government then planning to intervene in the interminable conflicts of the Middle East.[138] Some journalists were making equally lurid allegations that the British political establishment had been silenced in a somewhat McCarthyite fashion. For the anti neo-conservative journalist Peter Oborne, the pro-Israel lobby had 'coordinated campaigns and denunciation' to quieten their opponents. Many people, he declared, 'just don't

---

[137] This terrifying vision of unstoppable power and insidious influence was a staple of Soviet propaganda.

[138] Richard Ingrams, "Who will dare damn Israel?" *The Guardian*, September 16, 2001.

want to speak out about the Israel lobby.' [139] A former BBC Middle East correspondent, Tim Llewellyn, at a book launch hosted by Middle East Monitor in October 2012, denounced Zionist propaganda as, at times, 'extremely intense,' 'bitter,' 'angry' and 'violent' and went on to say that it is something that 'the suits at the BBC find very hard to resist.' The result is that the BBC and ITV have engaged in 'a kind of self-censorship.' [140] He found a kindred spirit in the radical left wing journalist John Pilger who lamented the BBC's failure to show his documentary, *Palestine is still the issue*, saying that the organization 'would never have dared to incur the wrath of one of the most influential lobbies in this country.' For Pilger, the pro-Israel lobby 'intimidates journalists to ensure that most coverage remains biased in its favour.' [141]

At the same time, the Israel lobby has been accused of silencing academics, whether in the UK, Europe or America. Among those obsessed at the apparently malevolent power of the global Zionist movement is Professor David Miller, a former Professor of Sociology at Bristol University. [142] In an online meeting in 2021, Miller launched a somewhat hysterical rant, calling for an end to Zionism as a functioning ideology of the world. He accused Jewish students at the university of being 'political pawns' of a 'violent, racist foreign regime engaged in ethnic cleansing' [143] and raised the prospect that because Zionism was a purportedly anti-Arab and Islamophobic ideology, 'Arab and Muslim students, as well as anti-Zionist Jewish students, (were) particularly unsafe.' [144] Miller is not the first British academic to make the claim that Jews and Zionists have made it impossible to speak out against Israeli 'crimes.' What is uniquely dangerous here is his suggestion that Jewish students (who may or may not be Zionists or interested in Middle East affairs) are actively threatening harm to other students, thus stirring up an incendiary identity war on campus. To single out Jewish students in this way, treating them as warriors in a political battle simply because they are Jews, is not only vile but dangerous.

Before Miller, a former head of the National Union of Students, Malia Bouattia, had referred to Birmingham University as 'something of a Zionist

[139] Peter Oborne and James Jones, "The pro-Israel lobby in Britain," opendemocracy .net, accessed 5 March 2022, https://www.opendemocracy.net/en/opendemocracyuk /pro-israel-lobby-in-britain-full-text/
[140] Richard Millett, "Former BBC Middle East correspondent Tim Llewellyn: Zionists are scattered at strategic points throughout British business." richardmillett.wordpress. com, accessed 19 January 2021, https://richardmillett. wordpress.com/2012/10/19/tim -llewellyn-zionists-are-scattered-throughout-british-business/
[141] John Pilger, "Why my film is under fire," *The Guardian*, September 23, 2002.
[142] Miller was sacked by Bristol University in 2021.
[143] Lee Harpin, "Academic calls Bristol JSoc 'Israel's pawn'," *Jewish Chronicle*, February 18, 2021
[144] Lee Harpin, "Bristol mayor backs Jewish students in row over 'end Zionism' academic," *The Jewish Chronicle*, February 18, 2021.

outpost' given that it had 'a very sizeable Jewish society on campus.'[145] In a speech given in September 2014, she said: 'The notion of resistance has been perhaps washed out of our understanding of how colonised people will obtain their physical emancipation...With mainstream, Zionist-led media outlets ...resistance is presented as an act of terrorism.' The government's Prevent strategy had come about because of pressure from the 'Zionist lobby.'[146] Bouattia's worldview is informed by radical left First Worldism and identity politics, a worldview in which Muslims are almost uniformly victims of powerful colonialists in the 'racist' West. There was little wonder that her candidacy for President of the NUS was supported by the extreme Islamist group MPAKUK.

Controls politics: A related charge is that the Israel lobby has a vice like grip on politics in each of the countries where it operates. For Labour MP Tam Dalyell, British Prime Minister Tony Blair had fallen under the spell of a 'cabal of Jewish advisers,' among which was Lord Levy. The word 'cabal' usually refers to a group of people contriving secretly to bring about their political aims and thus directly taps into the language of the *Protocols*. He was joined in his conspiratorial thinking by the veteran Liberal Democrat politician Baroness Jenny Tonge, who complained that the pro-Israel lobby had 'got its grips on the western world, its financial grips' and they had 'probably got a grip on our party.'[147] Her political colleague, Chris Davies, warned in 2006 that he would 'denounce the influence of the Jewish lobby that seems to have far too great a say over the political decision-making process in many countries.'[148] That the Israel lobby was trying to influence British elections was alleged by the Labour MP Martin Linton, a man who claimed that there were 'long tentacles of Israel in this country who are funding election campaigns and putting money into the British political system for their own ends.'[149] His fellow Labour MP, Gerald Kaufmann, simultaneously claimed that 'right wing Jewish millionaires'[150] owned large parts of the Conservative party. Of course, one can find much cruder and darker references to the Zionist lobby if one delves into the world of the far left. Thus, one finds a Labour candidate for office declaring that it was 'the super rich families of the

---

[145] "Malia Bouattia stands by Birmingham 'Zionist outpost' comment," *The Jewish News*, September 28, 2016.

[146] Maajid Nawaaz, "Malia Bouattia is symbolic of the poison of the regressive Left," *The Jewish Chronicle*, April 20, 2016.

[147] "Tonge condemned for Israel remark," bbcnews, accessed 5 March 2022, http://news.bbc.co.uk/2/hi/uk_news/politics/5366870.stm

[148] Greg Hurst, "Email tirade against Israelis costs Lib Dem leader his job," *The Times*, May 5, 2006.

[149] Martin Bright and Robyn Rosen, "MP: Israel's tentacles will steal the election," *The Jewish Chronicle*, March 29, 2010.

[150] Andrew Porter and Rosa Prince, "Labour MP accuses Tories of being too close to Israel," *The Times*, March 31, 2010

Zionist lobby that control the world.'[151]

When the UK Labour party was convulsed by genuine accusations of antisemitism within its ranks, some chose to interpret this as reflecting the powerful Israeli lobby in action. Typical was a cartoon in the Dutch daily *De Volkskran* from 2019. It depicted Benjamin Netanyahu with a stone in one hand, on which was written 'antisemitism charges,' and an indictment in the other. Opposite him was Labour leader Jeremy Corbyn who could be seen saying: 'Let him who is without sin cast the first stone.'[152] The implicit suggestion was that Netanyahu was the source of complaints against the Labour leader, not the British Jewish community, who were merely the vehicle through which the Israeli lobby intended to silence criticism of Labour policy.

Such insidious allegations of Israeli/Jewish power haven't just emerged from within left-liberal British parties. The former Conservative MP and government minister, Sir Alan Duncan, launched a scathing attack on Israel and the Israel lobby in a speech to the Royal United Services Institute in October 2014. He said that there were rules in the UK that 'political funding should not come from another country or from citizens of another country, or be unduly in hock to another country.' This rule, he added, 'seems to apply to every country except when it comes from Israel.'[153] What Duncan appeared to suggest was that the Israeli state and its associated lobby in the UK were illicitly funding British political parties, with the further implication that the UK based lobby of British Jews was more loyal to Israel than to the UK. Alternately, he might have been suggesting that the financial tentacles of the Israeli state were subverting the politics of the UK and twisting the priorities of its political parties. Cartoonist Steve Bell would doubtless have sympathised with the notion that a secret Israeli hand was guiding a former British administration. Commenting on the war in Gaza, Bell produced a cartoon with Netanyahu in front of a 'Vote Likud rally poster' and with puppets in his hand representing William Hague and Tony Blair.

Left-wing Israeli journalist Mira Bar Hillel denounced the 'guiding hand' behind the strategy of silencing British politicians who would otherwise be critical of Israeli policy were it not for fear of 'being accused of antisemitism.' She declared the pro-Israel lobby to be 'incredibly powerful,' an equivalent to AIPAC in the UK.[154] In 2020, a faction within the UK's BLM movement suggested that it was British politics which had been gagged of the right to critique Zionism.[155]

---

[151] Justin Cohen, Labour drops council candidate who posted about 'rich families of the Zionist lobby',", *Jewish News*, November 15, 2017

[152] Cnann Lipshiz, "Dutch daily cartoon shows Netanyahu behind UK Labour antisemitism scandals," *Times of Israel*, November 30, 2019.

[153] Jerry Lewis, "British MP condemned for anti-Israel comments," *The Jerusalem Post*, October 19, 2014

[154] Mira Bar Hillel, "The truth about the UK's pro-Israel lobbies," *The Independent*, September 1, 2014.

[155] Jack Mendel, "Black Lives Matter UK: 'Politics is gagged of the right to critique Zionism'," *Times of Israel*, June 28, 2020.

They issued an incendiary tweet, just weeks after the controversial killing of George Floyd, which was timed to coincide with Israel's proposed annexation of part of the West Bank. There was form among radical black groups for this kind of racialized, conspiratorial anti-Zionism. In 1967, the Student Non-violent Coordinating Committee (SNCC) published a cartoon in which a Star of David and a dollar sign were pulling a noose round the necks of black African leader Nasser and Muhammed Ali. The theme of Jews using their financial clout to silence their opponents and gain control of the world's resources is never far from the surface.[156]

Accusations that the Jewish and pro-Zionist lobby engineered US foreign policy were never more in evidence than in the run up to the second Iraq war. In 2002, former German defence minister Rudolph Scharping commented that President Bush needed to overthrow Saddam Hussein because he had to curry favour with 'a powerful – perhaps overly powerful – Jewish lobby' in the coming US elections. Germany, which did not have this problem, would therefore not face the pressure to intervene militarily.[157] One lecturer at the University of California at Irvine, discussing the war, said: 'If you have any questions why we're in Iraq, ask the Jews in the audience.'[158]

The reality is that the 2003 Iraq war did not come about because of the concerted efforts of a pro-Israel lobby or pro-Israel strategists. Similarly, America did not go to war because of pressure from the then Israeli government, one which was focused far more on the threat from the Islamic Republic of Iran. None of the prime architects of the war were Jewish, although they were also staunch allies of Israel. That starts with George Bush Junior, the man who made the ultimate decision to declare war against Saddam. It included non-Jews like the Vice President, Dick Cheney, Secretary of Defence, Donald Rumsfeld, Secretary of State, Colin Powell, and Karl Rove, Bush's chief strategist. All these figures were deeply enmeshed in America's financial, defense and oil industries and understood better than most the fundamental interests of their government and nation. It is simply stupefying to believe that a tiny clique of Jewish advisors and lobbyists, wedded to the interests of a foreign power, could have so unsettled these power brokers that they were duped into advocating a war they would not otherwise have sought. Yet stupefying blindness to reality is the hallmark of an antisemitic worldview.

In 2006, two American academics, John Mearsheimer and John Walt, wrote a book *The Israel Lobby and US Foreign Policy* which became a *New York Times* bestseller. The book contained two principal arguments. Firstly, the authors contended that the strong economic, military and political support given by the United States to Israel over the preceding few decades did not serve US national interests, embroiling the country in Israel's own alleged breaches of international

---

[156] Rabb, 'Attitudes Toward Israel and Jews,' 293-4.
[157] William Safire, "The German Problem," *New York Times*, September 19, 2002.
[158] Marcus, *The Definition of Antisemitism*, 25.

law and eating away at the goodwill that the US would have otherwise obtained from Arab governments. Secondly, they believed that the only explanation for why the US was acting so contrary to its interests was that the Israel lobby was incredibly powerful and effective in being able to sway otherwise sensible politicians to do its bidding. In support of the second assertion, they argued that the Israel lobby was incredibly effective in Congress where Israel was 'virtually immune from criticism.' They described this apparent largesse as 'remarkable' given that Congress rarely shied away from 'contentious issues' but as far as Israel was concerned, 'potential critics fall silent.' The leading organization within the lobby, AIPAC, was said to have a 'stranglehold' on Congress and was described as a 'de facto agent for a foreign government.'[159] The authors argued that were it not for groups like AIPAC, America would be holding Israel more at arm's length and that its stance would be more even handed in the region. They criticized the Israel lobby for throwing around the false charge of antisemitism in order to smear anyone who merely wanted to criticize Israel. Mearsheimer went out of his way to deny that he was an antisemite masquerading as a political activist. Yet that claim was badly undermined when he wrote a favourable review of *The Wandering Jew*, a book by the notorious antisemitic author Gilad Atzmon which was full of hateful language and toxic accusations against Jews. He described it as 'a fascinating and provocative book on Jewish identity in the modern world' which ought to be 'widely read by Jews and non-Jews alike.'[160]

The arguments of Mearsheimer and Walt were not new. A number of authors produced books that inveighed against the supposedly nefarious power and influence of the lobby, among them Paul Findley's *They Dare to Speak Out: People and Institutions Confront Israel's Lobby* (1985), Noam Chomsky's *The Fateful Triangle* (1983), Edward Tivnan's *The Lobby* (1987) and George Ball's *The Passionate Attachment* (1992). Findley, who served in the US House of Representatives for Illinois for over 20 years, was convinced that that the Israel lobby, which he described as 'the 700-pound gorilla in Washington,' dominated American foreign policy. He described himself as 'Arafat's best friend in Washington' and became convinced that Israel, not the PLO, was the main barrier to peace in the Middle East. He also argued that the absence of a Palestinian state was down to AIPAC's 'stranglehold on American politicians' which was also the reason for his own ejection from Congress. As he wrote in a subsequent book: 'Thanks to a flow of hostile dollars from both coasts and nearby Chicago, I became 'the number one enemy of Israel and my re-election campaign the principal target of Israel's lobby.'[161] During a speech in 2015, Findley reflected

---

[159] The quotes above are taken from the article that formed the basis of their book: John Mearsheimer and Stephen Walt, "The Israel book," *The London Review of Books*, Vol. 28 No. 6 23 March 2006

[160] Jeffrey Goldberg, "John Mearsheimer endorses a Hitler Apologist and Holocaust Revisionist," *The Atlantic*, September 23, 2011.

[161] Katharine Q Seelye, "Paul Findlay, Congressman Behind War Powers Act, Dies at 98," *New York Times*, August 13, 2019.

on what he saw as the reticence of President Obama and the American media to criticize Israel's conduct in its 2014 war with Hamas. He claimed that this reticence was due to Obama being muzzled by 'higher authority' and that 'the reporters of the major media in this country are just as overwhelmed and paralyzed by the Israel lobby.' He described the decision to invite Netanyahu to Congress in 2015 as 'shocking evidence of AIPAC's towering political clout over our government'[162] and proof that the 'lobby for Israel has sufficient power to gain control of the House chamber.' He went on: 'It's as if a blanket, a suffocating blanket, had been spread across the entire nation.'[163] So, these arguments are not new. But Mearsheimer and Walt were distinguished academics at Ivy League universities and this lent credibility to the arguments they put forward.

In 2011, Helen Thomas, the doyenne of the White House press corps, created deep controversy when she told an Orthodox rabbi that Jews had to 'get the hell out of Palestine' and 'go home' to 'Poland, Germany and America and everywhere else.' The idea that Jews were not 'home' in Israel and were mere colonial usurpers who had stolen someone else's home has been a ubiquitous and defining feature of anti-Zionist Arab and Palestinian discourse. Her comments, which reflected a prior belief in the illegitimacy of Jewish self-determination and communal self-definition, were widely condemned at the time. While some may have seen this as an egregious aberration from a respected figure, Thomas removed all doubt with the comments that followed. She spoke of the Jews possessing 'power over the White House, power over Congress,' stating: 'It's real power when you own the White House.' She added: 'Everybody is in the pocket of the Israeli lobbies which are funded by wealthy supporters, including those from Hollywood.'[164]

A year later, Ilhan Omar tweeted about Israel that it had 'hypnotized the world' and called on 'Allah' to help the world 'see the evil doings' of Israel. She later regretted the offensive use of the term 'hypnotize.'[165] She then claimed that American politicians' support for Israel was 'all about the Benjamins,'[166] a fairly clear reference to the notion that groups like AIPAC were using their financial clout to buy off the political class. The notion that Jews would use their money to subvert the political order is a guiding idea in the *Protocols*. The accusation of a Jewish global conspiracy has been embraced in a much cruder form by David Duke, a key figure in the Ku Klux Klan. He released a video on YouTube in 2014

---

[162] Paul Findley, "How to Tame Lobbies Like AIPAC," wrmea.org, accessed 5 March 2022, https://www.wrmea.org/the-israel-lobby-is-it-good-for-the-us-is-it-good-for-israel/how-to-tame-lobbies-like-aipac.html

[163] From a speech Findley gave to the National Press Club, April 10, 2015.

[164] "Helen Thomas: Jews in total control of US," *Ynetnews*, March 19, 2011.

[165] "Rep. Ilhan Omar defends 2012 tweet accusing Israel of 'hypnotizing the world'," *Times of Israel*, January 17, 2019.

[166] Mike De Bonis and Rachel Bade, "Rep. Omar apologizes after House Democratic leadership condemns her comments as 'anti-Semitic tropes'," *The Washington Post*, February 11, 2019.

called 'The Illustrated *Protocols* of Zion' in which he argued that the document was no forgery and that groups like AIPAC revealed the existence of a real Jewish conspiracy. He declared: 'The *Protocols* of Zion could have just as easily been titled 'The *Protocols* of Zionism...The modern elders are leaders of Zionism.'

Many of these demonizing narratives are careful to bury any suggestions of antisemitism by referring to 'Zionist' control of politics. But in a number of cases, the guard slips and critics slide into more transparently racist tropes. Speaking at a pro-Palestinian rally in Lenasia in 2009, South African Deputy Foreign Minister Fatima Hajaig was quoted as saying 'They in fact control [America], no matter which government comes into power, whether Republican or Democratic, whether Barack Obama or George Bush.' To dispel any doubt about who the 'they' referred to, she clarified that the control of America was 'in the hands of Jewish money and if Jewish money controls their country then you cannot expect anything else.' The reference to 'Jewish money' is particularly insidious here. It is meaningless to ascribe some demonic power to money just because it is in the hands of or controlled by someone of the Jewish faith. Moreover, the term suggests that there is some unified and malign agenda when Jews use their money, namely to advance their own interests as a global people at the expense of the countries that they happen to live in.

For some Europeans, this language seems only too seductive. Pertti Salolainen, the vice-chairman of the Finnish Foreign Affairs Committee, stated that America found it 'difficult to take a more neutral stance on the Israel-Palestine issue because they have a large Jewish population who have a significant control of the money and the media' in the country. He described this as a 'sad truth about US policy.'[167] The former Liberal Democrat leader in Europe, Chris Davies, said he would work tirelessly to expose the 'influence of the Jewish lobby,' a lobby which he said had 'far too great a say over the political decision-making process in many countries.'[168] The Spanish journalist and commentator Iñaki Gabilondo slammed the 'powerful Jewish lobby' in the United States, blaming it for forcing the *New York Times* to stop publishing cartoons that had provoked a storm of protest for antisemitic caricaturing. His conspiratorial rant sat easily in a country where conspiratorial antisemitic beliefs found ready acceptance. According to an ADL poll, nearly two thirds of Spanish citizens believed that Jews were more loyal to Israel than to their own country and nearly two fifths believed that Jews controlled the US government.

In Belgium, the new justice minister, Vincent Van Quickenborne, from the Open VLD party, issued a statement in which he claimed that the Jewish lobby was 'working extra hours: After Aalst, now Washington.'[169] The town of Aalst had previously featured a carnival with highly offensive antisemitic floats. Karel

---

[167] Benjamin Weinthal, "Finnish politician: Jews control money, media in US," *The Jerusalem Post*, December 1, 2012.
[168] Hurst, "Email tirade against Israelis.
[169] Tovah Lazaroff, "Belgium's new justice minister has spoken of Jewish lobby," *The Jerusalem Post*, October 1, 2020.

de Gucht, a European commissioner for trade and former Belgian foreign minister, once tried to explain why peace talks in the Middle East were doomed. 'Do not underestimate the Jewish lobby on Capitol Hill. That is the best organised lobby, you shouldn't underestimate the grip it has on American politics - no matter whether its Republicans or Democrats.' He went on to lambast the opinions of 'the average Jew outside Israel,' stating that they cleaved to a belief 'that they are right' and that, as a result, 'it is not easy to have, even with moderate Jews, a rational discussion about what is actually happening in the Middle East.'[170]

Of course, if there is any group of people with whom it is impossible to have a rational discussion about the Middle East (or many other political topics for that matter), it is those who give vent to foul prejudices about Jews. In the case of de Gucht, the objects of his fury were not Israeli politicians or an Israeli 'lobby' somewhere but all Jews, everywhere, regardless of whether they were young or old, secular or religions. To conceptualize an entire people as possessing irrational views and thus to render them worthy of contempt and ridicule is so obviously a form of racist discourse that only a fool or knave would deny it.

In 2010, Gretta Duisenberg, the widow of the first president of the European Central Bank, condemned 'Holland's powerful Jewish lobby' for playing on the country's sense of guilt over the Holocaust. Her words triggered a storm of protest. After commenting in 2005 that she wanted to collect six million signatures for a pro-Palestinian petition, she said that she hoped 'the Jews realize they can't take over the south of Amsterdam the same way they took over the West Bank.' [171] These comments were interpreted as being antisemitic by many in her native country. Nor did it end there. The group *Stop the Occupation*, run by Duisenberg, ran an article in late 2013 called 'The Jewish hand behind Internet, Google, Facebook, Wikipedia, Yahoo!, MySpace, eBay.' [172] For Archbishop Desmond Tutu, one of the principal cheerleaders of the BDS movement, people in the US were scared 'to say wrong is wrong' because 'the Jewish lobby is powerful – very powerful.' He then proceeded to declare that other nefarious movements and causes had also been powerful but had since withered and been defeated, citing among others the apartheid movement, Hitler, Mussolini and Milosevic.[173] None of these individuals would dare to issue such incendiary rhetoric in regard to another ethnic or religious minority. But when it comes to Jews, the rules are different.

False flag attacks: A false flag attack is a hostile act which is designed to look as if it was carried out by another entity other than the one responsible. A classic example was the Mukden Incident from 1931 when Japanese officers

---

[170] Ian Traynor, "Anger at EU chief's Middle East outburst," *The Guardian*, September 3, 2010.

[171] Cnaan Liphshiz, "Controversial celebrity heading Dutch march," *The Jerusalem Post*, March 30, 2012.

[172] "Dutch pro-Palestine Group Defends 'Jews control Internet'," *Haaretz*, February 10, 2014.

[173] Desmond Tutu, "Apartheid in the Holy Land," *The Guardian*, April 29, 2002.

carried out an attack on a section of the South Manchuria Railway. They went on to blame Chinese dissidents for the incident and used it to launch a full-scale invasion of Manchuria. This was a manufactured attack by one party on itself, used as a pretext for an aggressive foreign policy. Today, there is a belief that many of the terrorist attacks launched against Western powers fall into the same category. 9/11 spawned a huge web of conspiracy theories which attempted to explain the atrocity in terms of the sinister machinations of agencies, such as the CIA and the FBI, politicians like George Bush and Dick Cheney or business interests, such as the oil industry. Many turned on Jews, Israel and the Israeli lobby, accusing them of deliberately harming American and western interests to serve their own 'grubby' ones. The Lahore based *Jihad Times* said that 'the 300-member apex Zionist body consisting of peers of the Judaism in the world [sic], decided to avenge the anti-Israel bashing' at the UN Durban Conference of 2001. The conspiracy magazine *Criminal Politics* said that the attacks were carried out by 'brazen criminals in the Secret Societies dominated by Jewish Zionism,' designed to force the American government to intervene in the Middle East. For Amin Hweidi, the ex-chief of the Egyptian Intelligence Service, Israel was 'the only beneficiary of all what [sic] has taken place' while another commentator said that the attacks would 'shift attention from greater Israeli atrocities in the Palestinian territories.' Michael Collins Piper of *The American Free Press* stated that 'these hijackers could well have been Israeli-sponsored fundamentalist Jewish fanatics (posing as 'bin Laden Arabs') hoping to instigate an all-out U.S. war against the Arab world'[174] while Sheikh Muhammad Gemeaha, a former imam with the Islamic Cultural Centre in New York, lamented that Jews 'were behind these ugly acts [of Sept. 11], while we, the Arabs, were innocent.'[175] For some, Mossad, Israel's famed intelligence service, was the prime architect of the attacks as it was the only group with the sophistication, cunning and tools to carry out such a spectacular act. David Duke pointed to Mossad's prowess in infiltrating Arab terror groups as proof that the agency had to be behind 9/11. Thus, by the principle of *cui bono*, Israel was the most likely perpetrator.

Others claimed they had proof that Israel had planned the atrocity, or gained foreknowledge of it, because of the alleged behaviour of Israelis on the day. Almost as soon as the 9/11 attacks had struck New York, a malign rumour was disseminated by Hezbollah's al-Manar channel claiming that 4,000 Israelis did not turn up for work on the morning of the attacks. This was because they had been forewarned by an Israeli government which had carefully planned the atrocity for its own nefarious purposes. This theory was supported by the comments of Iranian President Mahmoud Ahmadinejad who, commenting on a

---

[174] "Unveiling Anti-Semitic 9/11 Conspiracy Theories," *Gorowitz Institute: Anti-Defamation League*, accessed https://www.adl.org / sites / default / files/documents/ assets / pdf / combating-hate /anti-semitic-9-11-conspiracy-theories.pdf, accessed 15 March 2021.
[175] Marina Jiménez, "The radicalization of U.S. Muslims," *National Post*, November 17, 2001.

purported lack of Jewish deaths, said: 'One day earlier they (Jews) were told not go to their workplace.'[176] The malign theory was recited by Amiri Baraka, the African-American former poet laureate of New Jersey, whose poem 'Somebody Blew Up America' contained these lines: 'Who knew the World Trade Centre was gonna get bombed/ Who told 4000 Israeli workers at the Twin Towers/ To stay home that day.'[177] It was no coincidence; he later stated that 'Israel knew, just like Bush knew, and that will obviously come out.' The theory that Israel engineered 9/11 appeared to receive support with a story that the FBI had arrested five Israelis on the day of the attacks who were caught filming the burning New York skyline from the roof of a white van. The men were arrested and detained before being deported back to Israel. Some have speculated that they were Mossad operatives who were spying on local Arabs but there is no evidence that they had any foreknowledge of the events that day with the FBI later clearing them of any involvement.

But for some on the far right, this story was evidence that Israel knew about the attacks and allowed them to happen, proof of the evil designs of Jewish people on America. Thus, David Duke claimed that Israeli spies had penetrated 'American law enforcement and military facilities' and 'conducted intensive surveillance of al-Qaida operatives in the United States' but 'treacherously did not give American officials information that could have easily prevented the attack.'[178] As with practically all conspiracy theories, the demonizing narratives of antisemitism seize on small pieces of factual information which are then either exaggerated in importance or wilfully misinterpreted and distorted to suit a racist agenda.

So unhinged is the belief that Zionists/Jews control global affairs that critics stop at nothing to implicate the Jewish state in some malevolent development. Thus, another staple of such commentary is the belief that Israel has been behind the rise of the murderous Sunni terror group, Islamic State (ISIS). In a press conference in Cairo in 2015, the Egyptian Minister of Islamic Endowment, Mohamed Mokhtar Gomaa, claimed that ISIS served Israeli national interests and, furthermore, that its leader, Abu Bakr Al-Baghdadi, 'was raised by Jews and Israelis.'[179] It was a charge echoed by Iran's Deputy Foreign Minister, Hossein Amir Abdollahian, in 2014, when he said that Israel had created Islamic State in order to tarnish Iran's image.[180] Outside the Middle East, it was one of the themes expressed by left wing activists within the UK Labour party. One such activist claimed that ISIS was 'run by Israel' and that the only reason why the terror group

---

[176] Robin Pomeroy and Ramin Mostafavi, "Iran President: Sept. 11 exaggerated," *Reuters*, August 7, 2010.

[177] Suzy Hansen, "Amiri Baraka stands by his words," *Salon*, October 17, 2002.

[178] "Unveiling Anti-Semitic 9/11 Conspiracy Theories."

[179] "Egyptian Minister Repeats Claim That Jews Created ISIS," adl.org, accessed 2 June 2021, https://www.adl.org/blog/egyptian-minister-repeats-claim-that-jews-created-isis.

[180] "Senior Iran official: Israel's Mossad created ISIS," *Haaretz*, November 4, 2014.

had not attacked Israel was 'because the dog doesn't bite its own tail.'[181] The evidence for this bizarre assertion was that country after country that had recognised 'Palestine' had seen its citizens attacked by ISIS. A Labour Councillor posted a video on Facebook which was titled 'ISIS: Israeli Secret Intelligence Service,' adding: 'I've heard some compelling evidence about ISIS being originated [sic] from Zionists!'[182]

Even if some believe that Islamic State was not created by Israel, they still argue that Israel creates false flag attacks, attributed to ISIS, which further its regional interests. Thus in 2012, Jeremy Corbyn, then a backbench Labour MP, claimed without prompting that an attack which had been carried out by jihadists in Sinai and which killed 16 Egyptian soldiers, betrayed the hand of Israel. He asked 'In whose interests is it to destabilise the new government in Egypt...other than Israel.' In this bizarre rant, Corbyn declared that Israel's apparent motivation was to scupper the growing closeness between Egypt and the Palestinian Authority. He concluded: 'I suspect the hand of Israel in this whole process of destabilization.'[183]

Indeed, for those who demonize Israel, no act of terror, no matter how distant from the theatre of the Middle East conflict, is immune from Israeli involvement. For Norwegian sociologist Johan Galtung, a man often dubbed the 'father of peace studies,' there was a plausible connection between the murderous rampage carried out by Norwegian Anders Breivik and the Israeli state, particularly Mossad. He is said to have commented: 'It will be interesting to read the Norwegian police report on Israel, during the trial.'[184] This was no isolated racist comment. Galtung also claimed that 'six Jewish companies control 96% of the media' and recommended that people read *The Protocols of the Elders of Zion*, adding 'It is impossible to do so today without thinking of Goldman Sachs.'[185] Israeli born Holocaust denier Gilad Atzmon joined Galtung in speculating that Breivik had Israeli connections, calling him a potential 'Sabbath Goy,' a man who kills for the Jewish state and who 'does appear to have treated his fellow countrymen in the same way that the IDF treats Palestinians.' For Atzmon, the Israelis were such a depraved people that they were prepared to slaughter dozens of children simply because they supported an anti-Israel movement. A Palestinian activist from Waltham Forest described the attacks as 'Israeli state sponsored terrorism' and added that 'Christian far-right white supremacists' were working 'hand in hand with Zionist

---

[181] Will Worley, "Labour party member Bob Campbell denies suspension over Israel and Isis comments," *The Independent*, March 28, 2016.

[182] Tom Marshall, "Ex Big-Brother contestant suspended from Labour party over 'anti-Israel' Facebook posts," *Evening Standard*, October 19, 2015.

[183] Juliane Helmhold, "Jeremy Corbyn's top ten outrageous anti-Israel moments this month," *The Jerusalem Post*, August 27, 2018.

[184] Johan Galtung, "Father of Global Peace Studies Hints at Link Between Norway Massacre and Mossad," *Haaretz*, April 30, 2012.

[185] "'Father of peace studies' makes public anti-semitic remarks," *The Times of Israel*, May 1, 2012.

fascists.'[186] A column in *Al Jazeera*, which was written by Wayne Madsen, stated that there was 'a clear link between Breivik and Mossad' because of the former's support for writers such as Pamela Geller and Robert Spencer.[187] Needless to say, Breivik was found guilty of acting alone and very little in his manifesto concerned Israel or Zionism. When a major tower block (Grenfell Tower) in London burst into flames in 2017, a UK pharmacist, Nazim Ali, pointed the finger of blame at 'Zionists.' After claiming that 'some of the biggest supporters of the Conservative Party' were Zionists, he deemed 'Zionist supporters of the Tory party' to be 'responsible for the murder of the people in Grenfell.'[188] So a tragic fire in a building that was caused by poor cladding and inadequate management suddenly became a foul deed carried out by Israel's supporters.

The worst anti-Israel obsessives believe that the entire globe has fallen apart because of scheming, manipulation and deviousness carried out by Israel. According to the communist Greek composer Mikis Theodorakis, 'Everything that happens today in the world has to do with the Zionists,' adding that American Jews were 'behind the world economic crisis that has hit Greece also.'[189] His hysterical diatribe was repeated in slightly different terms by Daniel Bernard, former French ambassador to the UK, who was quoted as saying: 'All the current troubles in the world are because of that shitty little country Israel.'[190] Here, Israel is depicted as a strategic threat to western security, a nation so mired in evil that its behaviour poses risks to humanity. It is but an update of a well-worn trope about Jews threatening humanity with their insidious behaviour.

Israel lobby and international powers: Just as traditional pre-Israeli antisemitism pictured the Jews as the puppet masters behind the actions of modern states and organizations, such as the League of Nations, which they controlled behind the scenes, so too do anti-Israel obsessives argue that Zionists have infiltrated modern states and used them as proxies for their interests. In the Arab and Muslim world, crude and diabolical images conjure up just such a spectre. World powers are routinely depicted as the mouthpiece of an Israeli state with a seemingly insatiable desire to manipulate and control world events. These puppet states automatically do the bidding of the Zionists. On the eve of the Iraq war, the paper *Alhayat Alijadeeda* depicted George Bush as a puppeteer who had in his grasp both the UN and other world powers. However, the master puppeteer was Ariel Sharon, gleefully pulling the strings of the American government. A year later, the Omani paper *Al Watan* produced a cartoon on the Iraq war that featuring an explosion, except that the trigger was being unleashed by a rabbi with a Star of

---

[186] Jessica Elgot, "Oslo massacre opens floodgates to conspiracy madness," *The Jewish Chronicle*, July 28, 2011.

[187] Tzvi Ben Gedalyahu, "Mossad blamed for massacre," *Arutz Sheva*, July 25, 2011.

[188] "Panel clears Al Quds speaker who said 'Zionists' guilty over Grenfell fire," *Jewish News*, November 6, 2020.

[189] "'Zorba the Greek' composer: I'm anti-semitic," *The Jerusalem Post*, February 15, 2011.

[190] Douglas Johnson, "Daniel Bernard," *The Guardian*, May 11, 2004.

David.[191] In the same year, a cartoon from a Jordanian paper showed Secretary of State John Kerry driving through Iraq in a tank that was emblazoned with the Star of David.[192] Other cartoons from that decade have resonated to the same theme. Some feature depictions of a Satanic looking Jew pulling the strings of either the American government, others show a globe which is encased by the Star of David while more than a few show Israeli leaders holding the hands of weak looking western leaders. One cartoon shows American leaders parroting Israeli prejudices as the Jew on the right, dressed in terrifying garb, shouts at his American parrot (the President): 'Repeat after me – I hate the Arabs.'[193]

Rebuttal of Israel lobby: What makes talk of a controlling Israeli lobby so unhinged is the sheer willingness of the media and political class to engage in undiluted criticism of Israel. In the UK, newspapers from *The Guardian* to *The Independent* and from *The Financial Times* to *The Economist* have at times printed critical and hostile commentary on Israeli behaviour. The BBC is the most influential news provider in the country and is often unsparing in its biased coverage of Israel and its relations with the Palestinians. Despite the 'omnipotent' power of the Conservative Friends of Israel, there has been nothing to stop Conservative governments from embracing Palestinian leaders, endorsing a two-state solution, funding UNRWA and criticizing Israeli military actions in Gaza as 'disproportionate.' The UK still does not recognise Jerusalem as Israel's capital city and will not move its embassy there. The UK has also not budged from endorsing the JCPOA nuclear deal with Iran, despite Israel's repeated protestations over many years. Despite friendly relations with Israel under the governments of Tony Blair, Gordon Brown, Theresa May, David Cameron and Boris Johnson, each of these UK administrations has made clear their opposition to Israeli settlements and their belief that this policy constitutes a stumbling block to peace in the region.

The same is true in the US. While AIPAC and other pro-Israel lobbying groups have many friends in Washington, the making of foreign policy is a tug of war between competing interests and groups with different vested interests. There are a multitude of American foreign policy decisions, including the sale of arms to Arab regimes, the decision to recognise the PLO, the nuclear deal with Iran and the condemnation of the Osiraq attack that show the limits of pro-Israel lobbies. A further rebuttal to the idea of US foreign policy being 'dictated' or controlled by a domestic lobby comes from the mouth of Secretary of State George Shultz himself: 'When we make a wrong decision – even one that is recommended by Israel and supported by American Jewish groups – it is our decision, and one for which we alone are responsible. We are not babes in the wood, easily convinced to support Israel's or any other state's agenda. We act in our own interests.'[194]

---

[191] Alkalel, Eason. Cartoon. *Al Watan*, May 18, 2004.

[192] Boukhari, Baha. Cartoon. *Al-Ayyam*, July 25, 2004.

[193] Mahragy, Abdala. Cartoon. *Akhbar Al Khaleej* (Bahrain), June 10, 2002.

[194] Abe Foxman, *The Deadliest Lies: The Israel Lobby and the Myth of Jewish Control* (New York: Palgrave Macmillan, 2009), 17.

In Europe, the failure of pro-Israel groups is even starker. Across the capitals of Western and Northern Europe one finds a host of governments whose attitudes to Israel are frequently cold and often overtly hostile. In those citadels of power, there is a readiness to condemn Israel for its alleged use of disproportionate force, its construction of 'illegal' settlements, its purported failure to move towards a two-state solution and its creeping 'colonialism' in the West Bank. Sweden's media has often hosted commentators whose level of vituperation towards the Jewish state knows no bounds. Thus, Swedish journalist Johannes Wahlstrom published an article in 2005 that was headlined: 'Swedish media is controlled by the Israeli regime.' A number of countries do stand out for their warmer and more understanding treatment of Israel's security concerns, among them Hungary, Poland, Romania, Bulgaria, the Czech Republic, Greece and Cyprus. But with their tiny Jewish populations, this friendship with the Jewish state is more a function of what Israel can offer those countries in terms of enhanced security and intelligence, hi tech and trade. That these factors are not even considered by critics of 'the lobby' is surely revealing.

Criticizing pro-Israel lobby groups, such as Conservative Friends of Israel or AIPAC, can be a legitimate exercise if it is undertaken on the basis of the arguments themselves. One can mount a case that British and American interests are not served by a close relationship with the Jewish state or that the West suffers reputational damage by being aligned to Israel. Such viewpoints, though easily contested, need not involve the application of antisemitic tropes. But age old antisemitic tropes are invoked in the claim that a conspiracy of Jews and Zionists are seeking to control and manipulate western politics and media for their own nefarious purposes.

7. Dual loyalty

Closely related to the accusation of an all-powerful and controlling pro-Israel or Jewish lobby is the charge of dual loyalty, the notion that Jews care more about Israel than their own country. During the 1991 Gulf War, the paleo-conservative Presidential candidate Pat Buchanan condemned the 'only two groups that are beating the drums for war in the Middle East,' namely the 'Israeli Defense Ministry and its amen corner in the United States.' Citing such figures as Charles Krauthammer, Henry Kissinger and Richard Perle, Buchanan completely chose to ignore the non-Jewish voices that were similarly vociferous in the pursuit of Saddam Hussein. Moreover, his suggestion that the Jewish cheerleaders for war were part of Israel's 'amen choir' suggested that these individuals were lobbying for a foreign state in pursuit of its interests rather than those of their own country. That it was the 'indigenous' population of patriotic Americans who would suffer as a result was hinted at in the claim that the fighting in this foreign war would be done by 'kids with names like McAllister, Murphy, Gonzales, and Leroy Brown.'[195] As if to leave people in no doubt about where he stood, Pat Buchanan

---

[195]"Is Pat Buchanan Antisemitic," *Newsweek*, December 22, 1991.

went on to describe Capitol Hill as 'Israeli occupied territory.'[196] He added: 'If you want to know ethnicity and power in the United States Senate, 13 members of the Senate are Jewish folks who are from 2% of the population. That is where real power is at.'[197]

University of Chicago academic Fred M Donner invoked the dual loyalty canard against Richard Perle (and other Jewish conservatives). After noting that he and the others had penned a memorandum (*A Clean Break: A New Strategy for Securing the Realm*) in 1996 for Benjamin Netanyahu, Donner asked 'why is he serving in a high position in an American administration?' In fact, the memorandum was produced by an Israel focused study group, with Perle as its leader, which was part of the Institute for Advanced Strategic and Political Studies. It did not seem to occur to Donner that Perle could both loyally serve his own administration and, at the same time, offer vital strategic advice to a key US ally. At least some commentators admitted that this was the charge they were making. Kathleen and Bill Christison of *The Washington Report* wrote: 'The issue we are dealing with in the Bush administration is dual loyalties – the double allegiance of these myriad officials at high and middle levels who cannot distinguish US interests from Israeli interests, who baldly promote the supposed identity of interests between the United States and Israel.' For Paul Buhle, the presence of leading Jews in the Bush administration made it seem as if 'the antisemitic *Protocols* of Zion, successfully fought for a century, (had) suddenly returned with an industrial sized grain of truth.'[198] Journalist Michael Lind was an early exponent of the Mearsheimer/Walt thesis, writing in 2002 of how Washington's foreign policy had become 'aligned with – if not subordinated to – that of Ariel Sharon's Israel to a degree that nobody could have imagined,' something he argued was entirely contrary to US foreign policy interests.[199] Democratic Congressman James Moran declared to his constituents in northern Virginia that American Jews were ultimately responsible for the unfolding catastrophe in the Middle East. He declared: 'If it were not for the strong support of the Jewish community for this war with Iraq, we would not be doing this.' He added: 'The leaders of the Jewish community are influential enough that they could change the direction of where this is going.'[200] His comments were denounced within his own party and he was forced to issue an apology.

In 2000, Louis Farrakhan, noting the dual citizenship of Senator Joe Liebermann, asked: 'Would he be more faithful to the Constitution of the United

---

[196] Foxman, *The Deadliest Lies*, 36.

[197] "Pat Buchanan's on the Rampage Against Jews," *NBC New York*, May 17, 2010.

[198] Paul Buhle, "The Civil Liberties Crisis and the Threat of 'Too Much Democracy'," *Tikkun*, May 2003.

[199] Michael Lind, "Israel lobby part 3," *Prospect Magazine*, October 20, 2002.

[200] Ted Barrett, "Lawmaker under fire for saying Jews support Iraq war," *cnn.com*, March 12, 2003, https://edition.cnn.com/2003/ALLPOLITICS/03/11/moran.jews/.

States than to the ties that any Jewish person would have to the State of Israel?'[201] In 2019, Democrat Congresswoman Ilhan Omar made a statement slamming AIPAC in 2019. She said: 'I want to talk about the political influence in this country that says it is OK for people to push for allegiance to a foreign country.'[202] While progressing Jews came to her defence, making the obvious point that it was not inherently antisemitic to criticize Israeli policy or the AIPAC lobby, the point they missed was that her attack was on the foreign loyalties of Jewish Americans. The same implicit attack was made in January 2019 by Congresswoman Rashida Tlaib, who tweeted that senators who promoted legislation against boycotts of Israel 'forgot what country they represent.'[203]

Washington remains beset by many interest groups that emerge from within the US population, including the Irish-American lobby, the Chinese-American lobby, Indian Americans and so on. In addition, there is a plethora of voices that campaign for Arab and Palestinian rights. In all these cases, there seems to be no equivalent accusation that such groups undermine American democracy or betray the real patriotic interests of fellow Americans. The fact that the Jewish/Zionist lobby is somehow singled out for vitriolic attack is therefore telling and deserves explanation. As Abraham Foxman has put it:

> No one thinks to demand that Italian Americans or Greek Americans or German Americans or Americans who happen to be members of the Russian Orthodox Church should have to declare their loyalty to this country, much less prove it.[204]

Indeed so. To the non-racist mind, it should be perfectly possible to reconcile a people's degree of concern for the wellbeing of a foreign country with a sense of patriotism at home. There is no reason why an Australian citizen who has moved to the UK cannot both maintain an ancestral tie to his native country and be a good and loyal citizen of his adopted country. Similarly, someone who has lived his entire life in a country but who maintains a familial link with or a deeply felt historical attachment to the people of another country, can scarcely be called unpatriotic on that account alone. Yet when Jews show a deep sense of affection for the people and land of Israel, and argue that it should be supported by the country they live in, that is deemed to be treasonous behaviour.

The political dimension of the dual loyalty canard is also captured by surveys among modern Europeans which ask whether Jews are more loyal to Israel or to their own countries. Turning again to the ADL 100 survey, one finds that in Eastern Europe an astonishing 45% of respondents believed that the statement

---

[201] Adam Entous, "Dems denounce Farrakhan's remarks," *ABC News*, January 6, 2006.

[202] Karen Zraick, "Ilhan Omar's Latest Remarks on Israel Draw Criticism," *New York Times*, March 1, 2019.

[203] Valerie Richardson, "Rashida Tlaib says 'They forgot what country they represent' tweet referred to senators, not Jews," *Washington Times*, January 9, 2019.

[204] Foxman, *The Deadliest Lies*, 22.

'Jews are more loyal to Israel than to the countries they live in' was probably true. Incredibly, one finds the same percentage of respondents agreeing with the statement in western Europe. In Asia, some 37% of people harbour this deeply antisemitic viewpoint, even though Jews form a miniscule fraction of its population and barely exist in most countries. A corollary statement is that 'Jews don't care what happens to anyone but their own kind.' This perspective views Jews as disloyal, untrustworthy and potentially treacherous citizens whose sole concerns are parochial and selfish. It is naturally a view belied by the enriching presence of Jews across a range of civil organizations that are designed to better the societies they live in. While this book focuses on opinion formers and figures of influence across the worlds of academia, religion, politics and journalism, it is clear that those influential figures speak to large audiences of people who imbibe their antisemitic perspective. Allowing for all the usual and expected methodological flaws in the survey data, it is clear that significant percentages of people in dozens of countries are animated by a fantastical view of Jews, either as conspiratorial, deceitful, all powerful or disloyal.

8. Islamic tropes of anti-Israel hatred

As we have seen, the early history of Islam was saturated with negative depictions of the Jews, a dhimmi people regarded as treacherous, deceitful and threatening to Islam. We have seen further that the archetypal Jew of Islamic thinking resonated with Islamist and Salafist ideologues such as Taymiyyah, Qutb, al Banna and Mawdudi and that their writings were laced with venomous antisemitic invective. Such thinkers were influenced by the revolutionary impulses of the age, deriving their belief in authoritarian leadership, ideological purity and utopian redemption from the communist and Nazi movements. But above all, they adopted the eliminationist Jew hatred of the Nazis, believing that Jews were source of all troubles for the Muslim world and that the only Islamic response, indeed the sacred duty, was to slaughter them.

Yet there are many who look upon Israel's Middle Eastern enemies with some sympathy and understanding. They argue that the actors ranged against Israel, both the leaders of countries like Iran and Lebanon and non-state actors (Hamas, Hezbollah, Islamic Jihad), are engaged in a political war with Israel over issues connected to territory, resources and the rectification of historical injustices. For these apologists, this is a confrontation over earthly matters rather than an existential conflict between Jews and Muslims and the mere accident of Israel being a Jewish state is not relevant. They do not hesitate to add that Israel is the stronger party and also the one seemingly committing war crimes against Palestinian civilians.

Yet the truth is nearly completely the opposite. The foundational ideology of the main movements threatening to destroy the Jewish state does not focus on 'opposition to Israel' or rejecting specific policies or governments. The ideological principles that govern Hamas, Hezbollah, Islamic Jihad, al-Qaeda and Iran are deeply antisemitic to their core. All harbour a genocidal hatred of Jews and all depict the war against Jewish civilization as a solemn religious duty incumbent on all Muslims. This antisemitism is a fusion of both archetypal Jew hatred in Islam, though shorn of countervailing positive sentiments, and modern western tropes of conspiratorial power and blood lust. All the groups that demonize Israel plunder (and often twist) scriptural sources to give vent to their modern prejudices.

What underlies the collective thinking of the Islamist and Salafist movements is that the creation of the state of Israel has violated a cardinal principle of Islamic law, namely that for the first time, the Jews no longer have *dhimmi* status and have instead attained sovereignty over other Muslims. Under traditional Islam, Jews were seen as a wretched people whose sins necessitated their continual submission to the Muslim authorities, a reminder of their deception, trickery and corruption. They could live as a *dhimmi* people but always subject to the rule of Sharia. The fact that this people recreated the Jewish state and then proceeded to be victorious over Arab armies in several wars, most notably the 1967 shock, was a deeply wounding affront to Islamic sensibilities, a reversal of the theologically ordained order. In the words of historian Raphael Israeli: 'Their (the Jews) claim to a separate political existence amounts to an insult, as it were, to the holy tradition of Islam.'[205] Islamists see Israel as a potent symbol of the erosion of Muslim power at the hands of the West, and further evidence of the cardinal Jewish 'sins' of 'deceit' and 'treachery.' That such a nation should come into existence and then survive repeated onslaught by the forces of Islam is a grievous blow, pointing to the peculiar crisis that besets modern Islam, a religion once in the ascendant and now surpassed by Western forces. As Robert Wistrich puts it, the Jews are seen as an 'insidious and permanent enemy,' with the struggle against them part of a wider battle to 'throw back the diabolical conspiracy sapping the foundations of the true faith.' In this fight, 'no compromise is possible.'[206] This sub-chapter will examine four actors: Hamas, Palestinian Islamic Jihad, Iran (and its proxy Hezbollah) and al-Qaeda.

Hamas: Hamas is lauded by some as the authentic voice of Palestinian resistance and the organization that Israel must inevitably turn to if there is to be peace with Gaza. But beneath the thin veneer of political dissidence is the booming voice of Islamist hatred and paranoid antisemitism. Hamas is the Palestinian branch of the Muslim Brotherhood and shares that movement's genocidal aims in regard to the Jews. It considers Israel to be a *fey* territory, a permanent part of the *Dar al Islam* where Islamic law must always prevail because the area was once conquered by Islam. For Hamas, Palestine is a *waqf* or religious endowment, a land which the Muslims 'consecrated' at the time of the conquest as an endowment for all generations of Muslims until the day of Resurrection. Much of its hatred of Israel is suffused with the tropes of western conspiracy

---

[205] Raphael Israeli, *War, Peace and Terror in the Middle East*, (London: Frank Cass, 2003), 64.
[206] Wistrich, *Hitler's Apocalypse*, 192.

thinking. The Hamas Charter, the organization's foundational document and one which remains valid to this day, speaks of how the Jews 'took control of the world media, news agencies, the press, publishing houses, broadcasting stations' and, using their money, 'stirred revolutions in various parts of the world with the purpose of achieving their interests and reaping the fruit therein.' Hamas accuses Jews of being 'behind the French Revolution, the Communist revolution and most of the revolutions we heard and hear about, here and there.' It went on: 'There was no war that broke out anywhere without their (Jews') fingerprints on it.' It offered a diatribe against 'limitless' Zionist 'imperialism' and claimed that the Zionists aspired to 'expand from the Nile to the Euphrates.' [207]

But these diatribes are overladen with a theological based hatred of Jews. Hamas sees Israel in apocalyptic terms as a menace to Islamic civilization with the Palestinians merely a minor part of their agenda. In its first leaflet from January 1988, Hamas denounced Jews as 'brothers of the apes, assassins of the prophets, bloodsuckers, warmongers,' and continued: 'Only Islam can break the Jews and destroy their dream.'[208] Hamas' former leader, Khaled Mashal, wrote that 'the Zionist blueprint' constituted 'a danger to the entire (Muslim) nation and not just the people of Palestine.' This menace, he argued, extends to other countries including Iraq, which was occupied 'because of a Zionist agenda.'

The notion that Hamas' anti-Zionism is rooted in a theological rejection of the Jews can also be found in some of the statements made by Hamas representatives. One has stated: 'The Jewish faith does not wish for peace nor stability, since it is a faith that is based on murder...Israel is based only on blood and murder in order to exist, and it will disappear, with Allah's will, through blood and Shahids [martyrs].'[209] Elsewhere we find statements such as these: 'The Jews killed the prophets...slaughtered the innocent...imprisoned our pious...NO PEACE WITH THE MURDERERS.'[210] On Hamas television today, Jews have been routinely referred to as 'the brothers of apes and pigs.' The theological basis of Israeli perfidy comes across in the preamble to the Charter that Israel will only continue to exist 'until Islam will obliterate it.' In which other territorial based dispute is an entire world faith invoked as the means by which that dispute will be (violently) settled? For Hamas, this is not an earth-bound struggle but a metaphysical war against the Jews and their 'evil' scheming. This war cannot be won without extermination, proof of which comes when the Charter invokes the following Hadith: 'The Prophet, Allah bless him and grant him salvation,' has said: 'The Day of Judgment will not come about until Moslems fight the Jews,

[207] "Hamas Covenant 1988 – The Avalon Project," yale.edu, accessed 3 March 2022, https://avalon.law.yale.edu/20th_century/hamas.asp
[208] Matthias Kuntzel, *Jihad and Jew Hatred: Islamism, Nazism and the Roots of 9/11* (New York: Telos Press Publishing, 2007), 108.
[209] Dr. Yussuf Al-Sharafi, Hamas representative, April 12 2007; as reported by Palestinian Media Watch (PMW), April 23, 2007.
[210] Hamas communiqué October 5, 1988, translated and distributed in the U.S. by the Islamic Association for Palestine.

when the Jew will hide behind stones and trees. The stones and trees will say, "O Moslems, O Abdulla, there is a Jew behind me, come and kill him".' It hardly needs stating that this verse was written some fourteen centuries before the State of Israel was founded in 1948 and some thirteen centuries before the faintest stirrings of Zionism had emerged from Europe.

Islamic Republic of Iran: Iran is the epicentre of non-Arab rejection of Israel in the Middle East. But to pretend that this is a purely political position borne of an unrelenting hatred of specific Israeli policies would be a mistake. Iran's opposition to Israel is similarly grounded in a paranoid fear of Jewish power, one that harks back to the ancestral enmity between Muslims and Jews at the founding of the faith. Ayatollah Khomeini thought that Jews posed a threat to Islamic unity and to the integrity of Iran itself. Much of the paranoia in his writings bore the unmistakable echoes of the *Protocols*. Thus, in 1963 he issued a rallying cry to fellow believers by inciting a hatred of Israel. The Jewish state, he declared, 'does not wish the Quran to exist in this country' and 'Israel does not wish the ulama to exist in this country.' He accused both Jews and Israelis of dominating the Iranian economy and pictured the US, a nation purportedly controlled by Jews, as the source of Iran's woes. In 1962 he warned that the independence of Iran and its economy was going to be taken over by Zionists who would drive the country to bankruptcy. Turning to the Islamic region as a whole, he said that Jews had 'appropriated the wealth and the fruits of labor of hundreds of millions of Muslims'[211] and urged his co-religionists not to stay silent in the face of such intimidation. He would later speak of Israel as one of the 'global plunderers' and frequently made references to the 'Great Satan' (USA) as a nation whose actions were co-ordinated by Israel and Zionists.

But Khomeini was careful to depict Jewish enmity as an eternal facet of their character and one which explained the struggles at Islam's birth. In *Islamic Government*, Khomeini wrote that 'since its inception Islam was afflicted with the Jews who distorted the reputation of Islam by assaulting and slandering it, and this has continued to our present day.'[212] He saw the Jews as people 'opposed to the very foundations of Islam' and who wished 'to establish Jewish domination throughout the world.' He warned that unless Muslims were careful, their apathy would 'allow a Jew to rule over us one day.'[213] Making a connection between theological past and political present, Khomeini wrote: 'From the very beginning, the historical movement of Islam has had to contend with the Jews, for it was they who first established anti-Islamic propaganda and engaged in various stratagems, and as you can see, this activity continues down to the present...'[214] The whole point of the Iranian revolution was to create a radical state based on the implementation of the divine law, with a 'government based on divine ordinance' and legislation founded on 'Quran and tradition.' It was the task of such a

---

[211] Patterson, *A Genealogy of Evil*, 185-6.

[212] Schoenfeld, *Return of antisemitism*, 43.

[213] Ayatollah Khomeini, *Islam and Revolution*, (Tehran: Mizan Press, 1981), 127.

[214] ibid. 27

government to fulfil the divine mandate for mankind, the path of which would eventually lead to the creation of a single world government. But the task of spreading jihad throughout the world would be sullied by those who opposed Islam (i.e. Jews, Christians and other unbelievers).

Iran's Islamic jihadists found it easy to identify the key figure in this 'Satanic' conspiracy. Ayatollah Fazlallah Mahalati, in his work *Tariqat va Shariat*, wrote about a world conspiracy against Islam by likening it to a monster with four heads, adding: 'The first and principal head 'and most dangerous' is that of the Jew, the eternal schemer against God...the second head is symbolized by the Cross...The third head of the monster belongs to atheism...The monster's fourth head represents secularism.' [215] The Jewish head was seen as the most dangerous because it was the progenitor of other threats, including secularism in the form of the (Jewish) acceptance of man-made law and democracy. In sum, for Iranian jihadists like their Sunni counterparts, the battle with Israel was intimately connected to the greater need for Islamic purity and spiritual health.

Here we have an essentialist reading from radical Islam which positions the Jews as eternally opposed to Muslim civilization and determined to impose their own power over Islamic states. But as with Hamas, Iranian state antisemitism is a fusion of new and old and the *Protocols* has influenced the thinking of the regime.[216]

PIJ: Iran has influenced or sponsored other terrorist bodies that are ranged against Israel. Palestinian Islamic Jihad, an Islamist party formed by Fathi Shaqaqi, is one such organization, sponsored today by Iran and Syria. It rejects peace with Israel quite openly and calls for a sovereign Islamic state in Palestine ruled by sharia law. This opposition to Israel is not based on a violent disagreement with the country's policies or issues concerning human rights. PIJ does not have a mere 'political' confrontation with Israeli policies but roots its opposition in anti-Jewish theological doctrine. Palestine, according to PIJ, was 'consecrated for Islam' and consequently, Israel was 'an affront to God and Islam.' Moreover, Israel is seen as 'the main enemy of (all) Muslims' and that the entire world needs to be liberated from the 'Jewish cancer' that plagues mankind. This cancer, we are told, 'is embodied in the Zionist presence in Palestine.' [217] The existentialist battle with the Jews is naturally influenced by Nazi doctrines of Judaeophobia, as David Patterson shows in his book *A Genealogy of Evil*, but it is full of references to ancient myth and history. Naturally, PIJ has been opposed to all iterations of the peace process since the 1990s and carried out numerous terror attacks against Israeli civilians.

Hezbollah: It is often claimed that Hezbollah was effectively created by Israel, that is, by Israel's occupation of southern Lebanon in 1982 following the war against the PLO, and that the terror group's confrontation with Israel is purely

---

[215] Patterson, *A Genealogy of Evil*, 197.

[216] Wistrich, *Hitler's apocalypse*, 180.

[217] Yonah Alexander, *Palestinian Religious Terrorism: Hamas and Islamic Jihad* (Leiden: Brill Nijhoff, 2003), 29.

territorial and wordly. In fact, Hezbollah was a creation of Iranian clerics in the 1960s and 1970s who were inspired by Khomeini's calls for an Islamic state. Hezbollah was already entrenched in Lebanon when the Israelis invaded the country in an operation that was designed to eliminate the PLO threat against northern Israel. The ideology of Hezbollah has been spelt out very clearly. Like its Iranian sponsor, it is committed to the destruction of Israel.

Its 1985 manifesto speaks of how its struggle with the 'Zionist entity' will end 'only when this entity is obliterated,' adding: 'We recognize no treaty with it, no ceasefire and no peace agreements, whether separate or consolidated.'[218] For these reasons, Hezbollah's chief, Hassan Nasrallah, has said: 'We are engaged in an existential battle with Israel.'[219] Nor is the battle with Israeli Jews alone. Harking back to Islamic sources, he has said: 'Anyone who reads (the Quran) cannot think of co-existence with them, of peace with them, or about accepting their presence…They are a cancer which is liable to spread again at any moment.'[220] Nasrallah, like all jihadists, believes that the only way to root out this cancer is by extermination, hence his comment that when Jews 'gather from all parts of the world into occupied Palestine… there the final and decisive battle will take place.'[221] Nasrallah has been quoted as saying: 'If we searched the entire world for a person more cowardly, despicable, weak and feeble in psyche, mind, ideology and religion, we would not find anyone like the Jew. Notice, I do not say the Israeli.'[222]

It is not surprising that this metaphysical confrontation with the Jews is reflected in Hezbollah textbooks. In one book, Judaism is described as 'a religion confined to the Jews, the masters of the world and the emperors of the universe, which nobody is entitled to belong to, no matter his station.' Elsewhere, Muslims are advised to learn the lesson of Jewish behaviour, linking the present-day discontent with Israel with archetypal Jewish behaviour: 'For the Zionists are the enemies of humanity in the past, present, and future because of their attributes: deceit, treason, treachery, and breaking pacts.'[223] Nasrallah has elsewhere called Jews the descendants of 'apes and pigs' as well as 'murderers of prophets.'[224] To leave none of his followers in any doubt about the theological underpinning of his venomous hatred, Nasrallah issued this diatribe in 2012, following the burning of a Quran in Afghanistan:

---

[218] Quoted in: Colin Shindler, *A History of Modern Israel* (Cambridge: Cambridge University Press, 2013), 342.

[219] Patterson, *A Genealogy of Evil*, 206.

[220] Quoted in Patterson, *A Genealogy of Evil*, 207.

[221] Yair Rosenberg, "Did Netanyahu Put Anti-Semitic Words in Hezbollah's Mouth,' *Tablet*, March 9, 2015.

[222] Michael Rubin, "Hezbollah Is Neither Reformed nor Moderate," *Commentary Magazine*, January 18, 2015.

[223] "'Lessons in hate': Hezbollah school books teach antisemitism, terror support," *The Times of Israel*, June 18, 2020.

[224] Patterson, *A Genealogy of Hate*, 206.

The Holy Quran told us about this people (the Jews): how they attacked their prophets, and how they killed their prophets, and how they affronted their prophets, and how they affronted Jesus Christ, peace be upon him, and how they affronted Mary, peace be upon her, and how they affronted Allah's great messenger Mohammad...'[225]

For Nasrallah, as for Hezbollah, the perfidious and treacherous nature of Israel is deeply rooted in the character of the Jews, a people for whom he has barely disguised contempt.

Al-Qaeda: Some argue that what underlies the heinous terrorist atrocities committed by Al Qaeda, most notably the 9/11 attacks, is revenge for the war crimes and aggression of Israel and the countries that support it. In his *Letter to America* (2002), Osama Bin Laden listed a set of grievances to explain why his movement was attacking the West. He specifically mentioned the 'military occupation for more than 80 years' of Palestine and 50 years since 1948 that were 'overflowing with oppression, tyranny, crimes, killing, expulsion, destruction and devastation.' He spoke of the 'creation and continuation of Israel' as 'one of the greatest crimes' and added that the 'blood pouring out of Palestine must be equally revenged.' But this was not a harangue of the current Israeli government nor was it purely about anti-Zionist political positioning. In fact, Bin Laden was at pains to scratch out Jewish historical and cultural memory. He said that 'the people of Palestine' were 'pure Arabs and original Semites' and that it was Muslims, not Jews, who were 'the inheritors of Moses.' He added: 'If the followers of Moses have been promised a right to Palestine in the Torah, then the Muslims are the most worthy nation of this.'[226] This is taking religious appropriation to an extraordinary level with its view that the Jews must be denied their most revered prophet. But it is in line with Bin Laden's generalized and deep-seated antisemitism.

Echoing the ideology espoused by Qutb and others, Bin Laden argued that the misfortunes suffered by Muslims for 14 centuries had come about because of 'the Zionist-Crusaders alliance.' Echoing ancient canards of chosenness as well as modern conspiratorial paranoia, Bin Laden said that 'Jews believe as part of their religion that people are their slaves, and whoever denies their religion deserves to be killed.' Elsewhere, in a diatribe from February 2003, Bin Laden, after warnings of the dangers posed to the region by 'Greater Israel,' summed up the attributes of the Jews (which, in turn, explains the danger posed by Israel). These people 'slandered the Creator...killed the prophets and broke their promises.' Jews were 'masters of usury and leaders in treachery.' He concluded: 'They will leave you nothing, either in this world or the next.'[227] The Jews were pictured therefore as an eternal but also universal menace. For Bin Laden, the only

---

[225] Goldhagen, *The Devil that Never Dies*, 26.
[226] Bruce Lawrence (ed.), *Messages to the World: The Statements of Osama Bin Laden* (London: Verso, 2005), 162-3.
[227] ibid. 189-190.

way to deal with such a menace was through unrelenting jihad. Yet it was not a jihad merely against the whole of Israel. As he put it in a statement one month after the 9/11 attacks, 'the strong and brutal battle' was 'between us and the Jews' with Israel merely 'the spearhead.'[228]

Conclusion: Radical Islamists do not oppose Israel because they disagree with its policies towards Arabs and Palestinians or because they are grieving for Muslim victims of the Israeli-Palestinian conflict. They are against Israel not because of anything that it has done but because of what it is – a Jewish state in the heart of what they see as the Muslim *umma*. The central reason why Hamas, Hezbollah, the Iranian Islamic Republic and al-Qaeda reject Israel is because it is an embodiment of the Jews themselves, a people essentialized as treacherous, deceitful, conspiratorial, noxious and evil and one whose nation represents an unconscionable existential threat to Islam and to Muslims everywhere. It would be a mistake to think that antisemitic ways of thinking are confined merely to Israel's external enemies. In the days before signing the Camp David Accords, a moment when one would expect historic hatreds to be diminishing, Anwar Sadat told his foreign minister that he was dealing with 'the lowest and meanest of enemies.'[229] He added: 'They (Jews) even tormented their Prophet Moses, and exasperated their God.' His successor, Hosni Mubarak, once claimed that the Jewish state contained people 'that controls the international press, the world economy, and world finances.'[230] What rankles these Arab leaders, and many others like them, is an awareness of Israel's stunning success as a nation state. In stark comparison to an Arab world marked by economic underdevelopment, poor living standards (except for a rich elite), illiteracy and political despotism, Israel is a shining beacon of success. It is a tiny country with few natural resources that, in less than a century, has transformed itself from an economic basket case to a powerhouse of medical, scientific and technological achievement. This stands as a glaring rebuke to its neighbours and the ruling elites who have allowed the region to sink into social and economic decrepitude. Attacks on Israel are a safe form of political discourse in the Arab world. They are what Bernard Lewis calls 'a licensed grievance,' the only grievance 'that can be freely and safely expressed in those Muslim countries where the media are either wholly owned or strictly overseen by the government.'[231]

Surveying this evidence as a whole, it is clear that a significant number of zealous anti-Israel ideologues have borrowed deeply into the well of antisemitic tropes, motifs and imagery in demonizing the Jewish state. The foul outpouring of hate with its grotesque inversion of truth and unrestrained antipathy is a symbol of political discourse gone awry. It shows the danger of adopting a Manichean

---

[228] ibid p. 126.

[229] Ephraim Karsh, *Islamic Imperialism: A History* (New Haven: Yale University Press, 2006), 183.

[230] Kressel, *Sons of Apes and Pigs*, 9.

[231] Bernard Lewis, *The Crisis of Islam: Holy War and Unholy Terror* (New York: Weidenfeld & Nicolson, 2003), 80.

approach to world affairs where polarized viewpoints and cartoonish representation devoid of nuance have become the norm.

Chapter Five

Double standards in treatment
of Israel and/or Israel supporters

*Over the centuries it has fallen to the lot of my people to be the testing agent of
human decency, the touchstone of civilization, the crucible in which enduring
human values are to be tested.*

Chaim Herzog

The notable Holocaust historian Raoul Hilberg identified three different types
of what we might call 'eliminationist antisemitism.' First, Jews were told by
Christian thinkers that they could not live among Gentiles as Jews; they had to be
converted in order to remove the stain of their Jewish religious identity. When this
was not an adequate solution, they were told they could not live among Gentiles
at all, something that necessitated their ethnic cleansing and expulsion from
society. In the Final Solution, Jews were not permitted to live at all. Translated
into today's anti-Zionism, one can discern a similar pattern of eliminationist
antisemitism. Some anti-Israel ideologues are convinced that Israel must not exist
as a Jewish state, given that such an idea smacks of ethnocentric and racist
exclusivism. Others contend, often in consequence of the first view, that Israel
cannot be part of the family of nations and must be expelled from international
bodies because it has a contaminating and corrupting influence on world affairs.
It is treated as a state 'that is fundamentally negatively distinct from all others,'
and is therefore a pariah among nations.[1] Still other actors, including nation states,
radical activists and terror groups, insist that Israel must not be allowed to exist at
all and regard its destruction as an urgent moral priority. This unholy triumvirate
of anti-Israel positions can be found all too easily among the left-liberal, far right
and Islamist opponents of Israel. For many do call for Israel's destruction, others
believe that its Jewish character is a sign of its irremediably immoral nature and
many more wish to see it expelled from respectable organs of the international
community. This chapter will examine specific ways in which Israel, and its
supporters, have suffered adverse treatment and double standards at the hands of
its opponents. Firstly, it will confront the double standard of calling for the
country's destruction and next, the opposition to Israel as a Zionist state. Then, it
will tackle the BDS movement which has signalled its opposition to Israel's

---

[1] Gerstenfeld, *The War of a Million Cuts*, 35.

normalization among progressive circles. Finally, it will examine the double standards in one of the world's most venerable institutions – the UN.

Opposing Israel's existence, opposing Zionism

One of the consistent themes in the unequal and adverse treatment of the Jews was how they were subjected to purges, murderous rampages, inquisitions and ultimately genocide at the hands of various gentile societies. Such actions constituted an insidious and, at times, existential threat to the lives of Jewish communities in parts of the world. The state of Israel was designed to be a safe haven for a minority group that had just experienced the most barbaric persecution in modern history. Yet none of this stopped Israel's enemies from calling for the country's outright obliteration. From the first day of its existence, Arab countries sought to annihilate the Jewish state, issuing blood curdling threats to its beleaguered Jewish population, some of whom had recently survived the Holocaust.

Today, the insidious demand that Israel be removed from the map continues to be made by rabid anti-Zionists, both in the Middle East and in the West. In the previous chapter, it was shown how the ideology of various jihadi organizations (Hamas, Hezbollah, Al-Qaeda) was geared towards the destruction of Israel, itself a symptom of prior antisemitic hatred and prejudice. At anti-Israeli rallies in the UK and elsewhere, the chant 'From the river to the sea, Palestine will be free' can be heard frequently. Academics who compare Israel to Nazi Germany predicate their senseless hatred on the same eliminationist goals as the terrorist groups: the dissolution of the Jewish state. It is commonplace now to have debates on university campuses about whether Israel has a right to exist.

Israel is not the only country to face an existential threat in the twentieth and twenty first centuries, nor will it be the last. But there is a double standard when it comes to conflict situations. After all, dozens of countries have faced protracted and fractious disputes, ranging from Cyprus and Turkey, Morocco and Western Sahara, Japan and China, India and Pakistan and Iran and Iraq. Yet it is rare to hear protracted calls for the existential eradication of either nation in the conflict, no matter how heated these disputes become. Yet Israel has faced such calls on each and every day of her existence and the voices among misguided western liberals have become ever shriller.

Some will argue that there is nothing inherently antisemitic about calling for Israel's destruction or being rabidly anti-Zionist. This is because there are a number of cases where opposition to Zionism is purportedly neither bigoted nor racist. They include: the historical Jewish anti-Zionist who saw Jewish self-determination in Palestine as detrimental to the status of Jews in the diaspora, the religious Jew who rejects Zionism because it offends against orthodox Judaism, the cosmopolitan Jew who opposes Zionism because it is a species of hated nationalism, and the political activist who rejects Israel because of its real or alleged human rights abuses. Let us deal with each of these in turn.

Historic anti-Zionism: Edwin Montagu was a leading British Jewish politician who served in the wartime cabinets of Herbert Asquith and David Lloyd George. Montagu was deeply opposed to Zionism, calling it 'a mischievous political creed, untenable by any patriotic citizen of the United Kingdom.' He denied that there was a cohesive Jewish nation and argued that Jews from different countries would scarcely be able to communicate with each other. He railed against the idea that Jews were anything other than members of different nations with a separate and distinct religious faith. But his key objection was that Zionism would threaten the settled status and prestige of Jews living around the world. As he wrote to Asquith: 'If you make a statement about Palestine as the national home for Jews, every antisemitic organization and newspaper will ask what right a Jewish Englishman, with the status at best of a naturalized foreigner, has to take a foremost part of the Government of the British Empire.' A country would scramble to 'get rid of its Jewish citizens' and Zionism would therefore be a boon to Antisemites around the world. He added that he would even be tempted to proscribe the Zionist movement as illegal.[2]

These words were issued before there was a Balfour Declaration and decades before the Jewish state was recreated. At this moment, Zionism was a somewhat inchoate idea which revolved around a legally organised ingathering of Jews to Palestine. It was not clear whether that involved a state, an autonomous homeland within a larger state or a mere settlement of Jews. It was not clear how the new political movement would affect Jews in other countries and thus, one might argue that a debate on its merits was entirely legitimate. Those arguments fell away in 1948 when Israel became a concrete reality in the Middle East. What may have been a valid historic debate before the Jewish state came into being was no longer so after independence. After all, when Jews in Israel became citizens, there was no threat to the political status or prosperity of Jews in the diaspora, and that has remained so to this day. Therefore, it is fairer to say that the historic debate about Zionism was legitimate when a Jewish state was merely hypothetical but became illegitimate when the state was an internationally recognised entity. It follows from this that it would be wrong to castigate Montagu as an antisemite when his arguments were not predicated on maligning his fellow Jews. However, those who want Jewish statehood eradicated are prepared to cause real danger and harm to the more than six million Jews who have made Israel their home. To call their political positioning antisemitic is a simple reflection of this fact.

The cosmopolitan: It is true that there are youthful idealists who believe in the disappearance of all flags, anthems, borders, constitutions, armies and all the other tangible and intangible symbols of nationhood that they profess to dislike. In other words, they hark after a pre-modern 'paradise,' shorn of nationality, where people relate to each other without any ostensible political identification. As such, a person will object to the existence of all nations and will naturally

---

[2] Robert Philpot, "How a curious love triangle spurred UK's cabinet to pass the Balfour Declaration," *The Times of Israel*, February 9, 2019.

extend this thinking to the state of Israel too. In theory, such an anti-Zionist is not espousing an antisemitic viewpoint. The problem here is that very few of those who call for Israel's disappearance are doing so because they are enchanted with utopian universalism. Anti-Zionists endorse Palestinian demands and fetishize their claims to sovereignty. They rarely have qualms about the existence of other anti-Zionist states, such as Iran, Syria or Malaysia. Quite to the contrary, they are frequently apologists for those states and their rulers, in line with a deeply anti-western, foreign policy agenda. So, the cosmopolitan anti-Zionist whose opposition to Israel stems from embracing universal values is a practical rarity.

Religious anti-Zionism: Thirdly, there are ultra-orthodox (charedi) Jews who reject the existence of a Jewish state because it was created by secular Jews and not through the intervention of the messiah. Typical are the Neturei Karta (Guardians of the City) who argue that Jews are in exile because of a divine decree and that attempting to build a Jewish homeland and gather in the exiles is tantamount to heresy. As a result, they say that Zionism is evil and that the State of Israel must be brought to an end. How can these people be antisemitic when their anti-Israel views stem from religious conviction?

It is firstly important to remember that Jews can be antisemitic too and the fact that they embrace Jewish rites, traditions and rituals cannot automatically insulate them from the charge of racism. In addition, these sects are a tiny fringe among mainstream Jewish groups, yet their voices are amplified by anti—Zionists because they provide cover for the charge of antisemitism. Secondly, one might usefully remember that *some* of these anti-Zionists have chosen to embrace other antisemites, such as Ahmadinejad of Iran and Palestinian extremists in Gaza and the West Bank. Moreover, they have also adopted the language and narrative of those antisemites, such as the claims that Zionism is to blame for modern antisemitism and strife in the Middle East, that Jews deserved to die in the Holocaust and that Israel constitutes a threat to Jews and the rest of the world. Were these the words of an agitator on the far right or extreme left, few would deny that they were based on prejudice and bigotry. Those words are just as antisemitic when they come from the mouth of a Jew.

Political agitator: The fourth type of anti-Zionist is the political agitator who claims that Israel should not exist because of its real or alleged human rights abuses. Such a person will often cloak themselves in the language of human rights, self-righteously proclaiming that their eliminationist anti-Zionism is for the greater good of humanity. Thus, in his article in *Foreign Policy Journal*, Jeremy Hammond argues that Israel has no right to exist in international law, save a 'right to ethnically cleanse Palestine in order to establish their "Jewish state."'[3] For good measure, he calls Israel 'a fundamentally racist regime that perpetually violates international law and Palestinians' human rights.' In an article in *The Guardian*, journalist Faisal Bodi also states that Israel has no right to exist, arguing that the

---

[3] Jeremy Hammond, "Why Israel has no 'Right to Exist'," *Foreign Policy Journal*, March 15, 2019.

country's founding was illegitimate and that its birth was surrounded by 'a potted history of iniquities.'[4] None of these people need feel any malice towards Jews or Judaism. But there is a crucial litmus test as to whether their words are indeed antisemitic. These individuals may feel malice towards many other states, especially western nations like the USA and the UK that are perceived to be the guardians of the little Zionist Satan. They will likely condemn the Iraq war of 2003 among more recent military interventions as well as their policy towards Muslims, Iran and minorities. Yet they do not call for the destruction of the US or the UK or the ending of their populations' rights to self-determination. The question naturally arises about why they hold Israel to such a unique standard.

The most fundamental reason why anti-Zionism amounts to antisemitism is that it opposes the idea that Jews can have the collective right of self-determination. Zionism is a movement for Jews to 'attain political independence and instigate a national renaissance of the Jewish people.'[5] It is the historic homeland of the Jewish people, the place in which they exercise self-rule and most fully express their culture. Such a right is enshrined in international law. It appears in Article I of the Charter of the United Nations where the 'principle of equal rights and self-determination of peoples' is enshrined. It also appears in the Declaration of Principles of International Law Concerning Friendly Relations and Co-operation among States (1970) which says that the 'principle of equal rights and self-determination of peoples constitutes a significant contribution to contemporary international law,' the Helsinki Final Act adopted by the Conference on Security and Co-operation in Europe (CSCE) in 1975, the Vienna Declaration and Programme of Action of 1993 and the Committee on the Elimination of Racial Discrimination. It is integral to human rights law. In the words of Wolfgang Danspeckgruber, Founding Director of the Liechtenstein Institute on Self-Determination at Princeton: 'No other concept is as powerful, visceral, emotional, unruly, as steep in creating aspirations and hopes as self-determination.'[6] Thus, denying this right to the Jewish people is tantamount to denying them one of the fundamental human rights in international law.

It will do no good to point out that the Palestinians, at least those in the West Bank and Gaza, are being denied political self-determination by Israel. The State of Israel and the pre-state Jewish leadership offered to create a sovereign Arab Palestinian state on at least six occasions (1937, 1947, 2000, 2001, 2008 and 2019). The offer was predicated on the Palestinians accepting the legitimacy and sovereignty of the Jewish state, something that was on each occasion refused by their leadership. In recent years, the principal stumbling block for the PLO/PA has been its refusal to give up a demand for a right of return of some six million Palestinians, the vast majority of whom are erroneously classified as refugees. But

---

[4] Faisal Bodi, "Israel simply has no right to exist," *The Guardian*, January 3, 2001.
[5] Colin Shindler, *What do Zionists believe?* (London: Granta Books, 2007), 4.
[6] "Self Determination," unpo.org, accessed 5th May 2020, https://unpo.org/article/49 57.

if Israel ever acceded to this demand, it would fundamentally alter the population balance in the country to the point where there would no longer be a Jewish majority. Quite simply, a sovereign Jewish state would become an Arab majority one within a generation. Instead of using armies, tanks, aircraft and suicide bombs to bring Israel down, the right of return is a form of sugar-coated genocide, a 'respectable' cover for wiping the Jewish state off the map. There can be no legitimate exercise of self-determination which is predicated on the destruction of another people's right to self-determination and to the removal of their rights under international law. Indeed, the contrast with peaceful movements for national self-determination, such as the Tibetans, makes this point clearly.

Some writers stop short of calling for Israel's destruction, preferring instead to delegitimize the Zionist movement or the Zionist character of Israel. The accusation was made most notoriously at the UN when, in 1975, the General Assembly adopted resolution 3379 which stated that 'Zionism is a form of racism and racial discrimination.' In 2001, the United Nations World Conference against Racism, held in Durban, South Africa, singled out Israel for calumny, condemning its policies as racist and calling the country an apartheid state. Noam Chomsky has argued that in a Jewish state, 'there can be no full recognition of basic human rights... Such limitations are inherent in the concept of a Jewish state that also contains non-Jewish citizens.'[7]

Resolution 3379 inspired a generation of anti-Zionist academics. Ilan Pappe has called for the 'de-Zionization of Israel' as a 'pre-condition for peace'[8] while gender theorist Judith Butler has said that 'an end to political Zionism, understood as the insistence on grounding the State of Israel on principles of Jewish sovereignty' is necessary for peace in the region. The idea of Israel as a Jewish majority state seems alien to these writers because they believe that it contradicts the notion of universal and democratic values. For Butler: 'It would be unjust for any state to insist on one religious and ethnic group maintaining a demographic majority to create differential levels of citizenship for majority and minority populations.'[9] For the philosopher Michael Neumann: 'Advocating the assignment of territory and political power according to ethnicity' is tantamount to 'advocating the political supremacy of an ethnic group.'[10] Neumann's point is echoed by historian Tony Judt when he writes of Israel as a political anachronism, given that it is 'a Jewish state in which one community, Jews, is set above others.'[11]   To drive home the point about the malignity of Zionism, Ken

---

[7] Noam Chomsky, *Peace in the Middle East: Reflections on Justice and Nationhood* (New York: Pantheon, 1974), 17.

[8] Ilan Pappe, "Israeli Jewish myths and the prospect of American War," labournet.net, accessed September 13, 2020, http://www.labournet.net/world/0209/pappe1.html.

[9] Judith Butler, *Parting Ways: Jewishness and the Critique of Zionism*, (New York: Columbia University Press, 2013), 118.

[10] Michael Neumann, *The Case Against Israel* (Petrolia: Counterpunch, 2006), 16-20.

[11] Tony Judt, "'Jewish State' has Become Anachronism," *Los Angeles Times*, October 10, 2003.

Livingstone argued that Zionism was conceived 'at a time when the concept of racial superiority was normal' and when 'belief in race and blood was deep-rooted.'[12] It stands to reason that all these writers assail the law of return, the piece of legislation that enshrines the right of virtually any Jew in the world to become a citizen of Israel, even if they have only one Jewish grandparent. For left wing activist Ben White, the law of return 'shaped an institutionalized regime of ethno-religious discrimination.'[13] For Joel Kovel, it is nothing but racism to have a state where 'one who converts to Judaism or has a Jewish great-grandmother is automatically given full rights to the land' yet those rights are denied to those 'whose families merely happened to have lived there for centuries.'[14] Among non-intellectuals, the term Zionist has been debased in other ways, with multiple reports that Jewish students on university campuses have been attacked as 'Zios.'[15]

These views are based on a set of fundamental misconceptions. It is true that Israeli nationality has been defined by reference to one religion: Judaism. The defining cultural characteristics of the state are Jewish (the flag, the national anthem, official holidays, the majority language) and immigration laws (the law of return) also favour one ethnic group as well. But this does not mean that Jews have exclusive rights on account of their ethnicity or religion or that Jews exercise illegitimate power over non-Jews. Non-Jewish Israelis enjoy the same rights of citizenship as Jews, including the right to vote, the right to receive education, the right to access public facilities, the right to access an independent judiciary and the right to protest. It is therefore both a Jewish and democratic state. It is true that Arab Israelis are not obliged to undergo conscription for security reasons, but many do serve in the Israeli army, in many cases with distinction.

There is a further, far more disturbing inconsistency and double standard. If a 'Jewish state' is inherently racist, why are there not equal reservations about the dozens of countries with similar national characteristics. Countries in Europe such as Finland, Denmark and Hungary have long been established on national lines and define themselves by reference to Christian tradition, heritage or symbolism. Daniel Gordis states in *The Promise of Israel* that several European constitutions 'give a unique place to individual religions,' among which are the constitutions of Norway and Denmark, which make the Evangelical-Lutheran religion the established or official church of those countries. In similar fashion, Muslim countries place Islam at the core of their self-definition though apparently this does not merit any charge of racism or discrimination. Israel is not alone in putting

[12] Ken Livingstone, *You Can't Say That* (London: Faber and Faber, 2012), 512.
[13] Ben White, "Is Israel a democracy or an ethnocracy?" *The New Statesman*, February 5, 2012.
[14] Joel Kovel, "On left antisemitism and the special status of Israel," joelkovel.com, accessed 13 February 2021, http://joelkovel.com/on-left-antisemitism-and-the-special-status-of-israel/.
[15] Sian Griffiths, "Labour students 'jeered Jewish victims in Paris'," *The Times*, March 6, 2016.

religion or ethnicity 'at the core of its self-definition.'[16] The simple question posed by Julia Neuberger is deeply relevant: 'Why is it racist for Jews, but not for Muslims or Christians?'[17]

Some may argue that, in a secular world, it is deeply anachronistic to base a nation state around a religious faith. Indeed, some non-Jews even take it upon themselves to dismiss the idea of the 'Jewish people' as a formal collective entity. Typical is Palestinian writer Susan Abulhawa who, on the 100th anniversary of the Balfour Declaration, rejected the famous letter with this flourish: 'As if citizens of disparate cultures, nationalities, languages and locations constituted a singular race or ethnicity by virtue of their shared religion.'[18] But Jews are not just members of a faith; they are defined as a people in the fully civilizational sense of the term. Jews have a common culture, a set of traditions, a heritage and a sense of togetherness, regardless of their geographic dispersion. They are as much a people as the Armenians, the Uighurs, the Tibetans and the Kurds. To deny them a state is to assail their identity and attack their collective rights as a people.

All those who critique and damn Zionism do so by making the glib assumption that the movement is homogenous. They don't see any difference between a Herzl, an Ahad Ha'am, a Begin or a Kahane. They don't differentiate between Zionists of Peace Now and the hilltop settler youth. They blend together Likud and Labour, secular and religious, left and right, dove and hawk. Zionism is less a symphony of voices than a flat tune with a shrill message. They fail to spot movements within a movement, assess changes over time or differentiate personalities, a failure of both intellect and imagination.

Such flat views of Zionism mean that Israel becomes a bogey man, a pantomime villain in a cartoon conflict where all sense of nuance is missing. If Israelis are seen as uniformly demonic, the same is true of their supporters. The journalist Richard Ingrams once suggested that anyone defending the Israeli government should first declare whether or not he is a Jew. He also said on an earlier occasion that he did not bother to read letters written about Israel if the name of the writer was Jewish.[19] Ingrams was implying that Jews thought in a homogenous way and produced a uniform viewpoint on the Middle East, a view rather absurdly at odds with the visibly disputatious nature of the Jewish community. Moreover, Ingrams suggested that whatever Jews said on this issue was unworthy of engagement or reflection and had to be automatically distrusted. This is because in his eyes, Israel alone was worthy of blame and that all Jews did, uniformly, was try to blind others to Israel's sins. If Jews did declare their ethnicity before speaking on Israel, it would allow the suspicion that the country

---

[16] Daniel Gordis, *The Promise of Israel* (Hoboken: John Wiley & Sons, 2012), 89.

[17] Neuberger, *Antisemitism*, 58.

[18] Susan Abulhawa, "The Balfour Declaration: Enduring colonial criminality," *Middle East Eye*, accessed November 20, 2021, https://www.middleeasteye.net/opinion/balfour-declaration-enduring-colonial-criminality.

[19] Howard Jacobson, "If Richard Ingrams wants us to declare our ethnic identity, I'm very happy to oblige," *The Independent*, August 12, 2006.

had a 'fifth column of politicians, commentators, businessmen, etc, in this country all seeking, at this time, in their different ways, to excuse or explain away Israeli atrocities.' [20]

Not only does this borrow quite manifestly from the vernacular of conspiracy thinking and dual loyalty, it invokes the idea that Jews are a foreign and traitorous presence whose views can only harm those around them. Ingrams is furthermore guilty of what Bernard Harrison calls 'diversity denial,' the refusal to see a defined community as possessing different and complex attitudes to issues and viewing them instead as a 'dummy other.' [21] In other words, it is a conscious refusal to see Jews, like other human beings, as differentiated by social and political identity, substituting instead a unified quality of 'Jewness.' [22] It is also a hallmark of the antisemitic viewpoint to believe that 'people self-identified as Jews are naturally defined by and will support and further Jews' political practices and goals and, most of all, Israel's political practices and goals.' [23] It is the hallmark of a racist to essentialise and construct entire peoples, reducing them to a wholly fictitious chimera.

Boycotting Israel: the case of BDS

An antisemitic double standard haunts the globally orchestrated movement to boycott the Jewish state represented by BDS. The BDS movement originated in a declaration issued at the 2001 Durban conference which called for 'a policy of complete and total isolation of Israel as an apartheid state...the imposition of mandatory and comprehensive sanctions and embargoes, the full cessation of all links (diplomatic, economic, social, aid, military cooperation and training) between all states and Israel.' BDS advocates thus call for boycotts that involve withdrawing support from Israel and from 'complicit' Israeli sporting, cultural and academic institutions across the world. They call for divestment campaigns, urging banks, local councils, churches, pension funds and universities to withdraw investments from the state of Israel. They demand that the international community engages in sanctions against Israel, to end military and trade agreements and suspend Israel's membership in international forums, such as UN bodies and also FIFA. [24] The reason why BDS advocates want to isolate Israel and turn it into a pariah nation is because they see it as the epitome of racist colonialism, the apartheid nation par excellence. Space does not permit a full treatment of why this claim is egregious and historically illiterate. There are excellent studies [25] which show in detail why neither Israeli Arabs nor Palestinians

---

[20] Richard Ingrams, "A short history according to Tony Blair," *The Independent*, August 5, 2006.

[21] Harrison, *The Resurgence of Antisemitism*, 55.

[22] Goldhagen, *The Devil That Never Dies*, 39.

[23] ibid. p. 183

[24] "What is BDS," bdsmovement.net, accessed November 11, 2020, https://bdsmovement.net/what-is-bds.

[25] Alan Johnson, *The Apartheid Smear*, BICOM, 2014.

live under any form of apartheid and why the term is a mendacious, harmful form of demonization. The issue here is how such boycotters are engaging in double standards which single out Israel, Israelis and Jews more generally.

The double standards are indeed glaring. Their apparent concern for human rights is never universalized. There are urgent issues of human rights in dozens of countries around the world yet one only country is ever selected as the target of a boycott - democratic Israel. The boycotters have little to say about tackling the perpetrators of genocide in North Korea and Darfur, the occupation of Tibet, the ongoing slaughter of Syria, the persecution of the Uighurs, the execution of gays in Iran and a host of other crimes. The boycotters would rather target an open liberal democracy with an independent judiciary and mechanisms for addressing human rights abuses than a despotic regime where such abuses proliferate with immunity. Some will argue that, as a democracy, Israel must be held to higher standards of behaviour than a dictatorship. Indeed so but, in this context, it is a specious argument. Quite naturally, we expect higher standards of behaviour in democracies but this gives no licence to ignore the victims of despotic regimes. The selective boycott expresses no generalized concern for human rights or racist policies and is thus a politicized tool for demonizing the Jewish state. Moreover, Israel's record of human rights, while not perfect, compares favourably to other democracies fighting similar wars against terror. There has been no Israeli Abu Ghraib or Guantanamo Bay and no experience similar to the Russians in Chechnya.[26] Israel has achieved a lower ratio of non-combatant to combatant deaths in asymmetric warfare than other democracies. Yet there are few calls to boycott artists, academics and journalists from these or other countries.

BDS leaders respond by saying that they are not required to universalise their concern for human rights. They argue that it is legitimate to highlight Palestinian suffering without simultaneously demanding rights for Copts, Kurds, Uighurs and other groups around the world. Though their positioning suggests a lack of moral seriousness, they are logically right. There are many single-issue campaign groups around the world, each of whom champions a particular cause in isolation from a multitude of others. But in claiming to champion Palestinian rights, they actually open themselves up to a more serious charge of hypocrisy. For they are noticeably silent when Palestinians are the victims of Arab discrimination and unjust treatment. In Lebanon, Palestinians 'have faced institutionalized and non-institutionalized discrimination' and have until very recently been denied working rights by the state. For six decades they could barely obtain work in the country and there are at least 50 professions that are barred to them.[27] Amnesty has said that Lebanese Palestinians suffer 'discrimination and marginalization' which contributes to 'high levels of unemployment, low wages and poor working

---

[26] Anthony Julius and Simon Schama, "John Berger is wrong," *The Guardian*, December 22, 2006.

[27] Josh Wood, "The Palestinians' Long Wait in Lebanon," *New York Times*, March 2, 2011.

conditions.' [28] In Jordan, Palestinians suffer political discrimination, being underrepresented in the Chamber of Deputies and they experience discrimination in private and state sector employment. According to Amnesty, the country's security forces are more likely to torture a detainee if that person is a Palestinian. In 2015, ISIL took control of the Yarmouk refugee camp and carried out atrocities on its inhabitants, with little response from 'pro-Palestinian' groups. [29] The Palestinians have become a mere tool in the war of ideologues against Israel, a pattern that has repeated itself decade after decade.

Why do BDS leaders stay silent when Palestinians suffer at the hands of non-Israeli regimes? The answer strikes at the heart of why BDS, at least in its aims, remains a deeply antisemitic movement. Fundamentally, BDS leaders advocate the racist goal of eliminating Israel. Omar Barghouti says that he opposes a Jewish state in any part of Palestine. [30] Ahmed Moor, another activist, says that BDS 'does mean the end of the Jewish state.' [31] The veteran anti-apartheid campaigner, Ronnie Kasrils, said: 'BDS represents three words that will help bring about the defeat of Zionist Israel and victory for Palestine.' [32] Pro BDS author and scientist John Spritzler has said: 'I think the BDS movement will gain strength from forthrightly explaining why Israel has no right to exist.' [33] As'ad AbuKhalil, a political scientist from California State University, stated: 'Justice and freedom for the Palestinians are incompatible with the existence of the state of Israel.' [34] The goal of removing the world's only Jewish state from the map, of denying self-determination to Jews globally while at the same time advocating the same principle for every other recognised people, is a malicious double standard with antisemitic connotations. Moreover, it has historical overtones that are even more alarming. In the past, the Nazi war waged against the Jews started with a one-day boycott (an economic war). It ended with a war of racial extermination. As Michael Gove observed in 2014:

---

[28] "Lebanon: Exiled and suffering: Palestinian refugees in Lebanon," *Amnesty International*, October 17, 2007, https://www.amnesty.org/en/documents/MDE18/010/2007/en.

[29] Louisa Loveluck, Magdy Samaan and Ruth Sherlock, "Inside the living hell of Yarmouk," *The Daily Telegraph*, April 7, 2015.

[30] D. M Halbfinger, M. Wines and S. Erlanger, "Is B.D.S Antisemitic? A Closer Look at the Boycott Israel Campaign," *New York Times*, July 27, 2019.

[31] Ahmed Moor, "BDS is a long-term project with radically transformative potential," *Mondoweiss*, April 22 2010, https://mondoweiss.net/2010/04/bds-is-a-long-term-project-with-radically-transformative-potential/

[32] "Ronnie Kasrils Speech at Israeli Apartheid Week 2009," *BDS Movement*, accessed 16 October 2020, https:// bdsmovement.net / news / ronnie-kasrils-speech-israeli-apartheid-week-2009.

[33] John Spritzler, "Norman Finkelstein's Criticism of BSD: Wrong, But with a Germ of Truth," *Truthout*, accessed February 1, 2020, https://truthout.org/articles/norman-finkelsteins-criticism-of-bds-wrong-but-with-a-germ-of-truth/.

[34] Nelson, *Israel Denial*, 19.

We need to remind people that what began with a campaign against Jewish goods in the past ended with a campaign against Jewish lives.[35]

But even this is not the main way in which BDS contributes so significantly to global antisemitism.

Anti-Israel attitudes bleed into antisemitism: The crux of why modern anti-Israel attitudes segue into antisemitism is that they help to create a hostile environment for Jews. That is, BDS adopts a poisonous and bigoted attitude towards the Jewish state and believes that it must be ostracized by the international community. It follows that those who support Israel are seen as actively endorsing an apartheid, colonialist and racist state, thus violating the anti-racist principles that define any liberal outlook. As such, those individuals are identified as being outside 'the community of the good' due to their normalizing racism in progressive spaces. It is but a logical step to declare that those Israel supporters must be driven from such circles and actively resisted so as to ensure that their harmful views do not violate the rights of others. There can be no sympathy for such (largely Jewish) Zionists, especially when their charge of suffering antisemitism is seen, under the Livingstone formula, as a charge made in bad faith to protect Israel and censor Palestinian views. At the very least, if Jews are to engage with other progressives, they must be seen to disavow any connection with the hated state of the Jews.

There are myriad examples of how boycotters have encouraged illegal and antisemitic discrimination against Israelis and Jews. In July 2002, Egyptian scholar Mona Baker fired Professor Miriam Shlesinger, an Israeli who taught at Bar Ilan University in Tel Aviv, and Gideon Toury, from the board of two academic journals that she published. Their crime was to be Israeli nationals. She deplored the actions of Israel, claiming: 'Many of us would like to talk about it as some kind of Holocaust, which the world will eventually wake up to, much too late, of course, as they did with the last one.'[36] In the same year, Dr Oren Yiftachel, a left wing academic at Ben Gurion University, had an article[37] (co-authored with a Palestinian academic) rejected for publication by *Political Geography*, with a note stating that it could not consider a submission from Israel. It was later published but only after a protracted battle in which he refused to submit to political censorship. In 2006, Exeter University's Richard Seaford refused to review a book for an Israeli journal, citing as his reason that, as a supporter of the academic boycott of Israel, he opposed its 'brutal and illegal

---

[35] Rowena Mason, "Gove says boycott of Israeli goods is sign of 'resurgent antisemitism'," *The Guardian*, September 9, 2014.

[36] Diana Jean Schemo, "Mideast Strife Loudly Echoed in Academia," *New York Times*, July 11, 2002.

[37] Andy Beckett and Ewen MacAskill, "British academic boycott of Israel gathers pace," *The Guardian*, December 12, 2002.

expansionism' and 'slow-motion ethnic cleansing.'[38] In 2003, an Oxford Professor of Pathology, Andrew Wilkie, was suspended after he refused a request from Israeli student Amit Duvshani to work in his laboratory. In his email, the Professor had written: 'I am sure you are perfectly nice at a personal level, but no way would I take on somebody who had served in the Israeli army.'[39] Another Israeli lecturer, upon applying for a UK based academic post, received a response: 'No, we don't accept any applicants from a Nazi state.'[40] As Gabriel Schoenfeld points out: 'It goes without saying that no academic from any other country around the world, no matter how barbaric its human rights record, has been treated in an equivalent manner.'[41]

Britain is no outlier as something similar has been happening on American campuses for more than a decade. There are innumerable cases of Israeli speakers being harassed and denied the opportunity to speak on campus, simply because they are Israeli. Cary Nelson paints a disturbing picture of the state of American academia:

> The number of disciplines and subdisciplines where...consensual anti-Israel truth reigns is increasing. A political scientist might recognise the need to acknowledge both the Israeli and Palestinian narratives and treat them each as possessing validity. In cultural anthropology, throughout literary studies and ethnic studies, in much of African American studies, Native American studies, and women's studies, and of course throughout Middle Eastern studies, that is no longer the case. In many areas of the academy there is substantial social and professional support for faculty who are devoted to demonizing the Jewish state...They may have no awareness whatsoever that they have turned their classrooms into propaganda machines. That students experience all this as antisemitic is unsurprising.[42]

Moreover, there are clear cases of discrimination against Jewish students, one of the most egregious of which occurred in 2015 at UCLA. A Jewish second year economics student, Rachel Beyda, was applying to the student council's Judicial Board. When she was questioned, she was asked how she could 'maintain an unbiased view' given that she was 'a Jewish student' and 'very active in the Jewish community.' For the best part of the next hour, as minutes and videos clearly record, the council debated intensely about whether a student with her Jewish affiliations could be relied upon to deal with sensitive governance questions in an objective fashion. Such an appalling vilification led to a vote

---

[38] Talya Halkin, "Bar-Ilan warns of 'silent' boycott by UK academics," *The Jerusalem Post*, May 21, 2006.

[39] Kenneth Stern, *The Conflict over the Conflict: The Israel/Palestine Campus Debate* (Toronto: University of Toronto Press, 2020), 90.

[40] Rod Liddle, "Watch Who You Call Nazis," *The Guardian*, July 17, 2002.

[41] Schoenfeld, *Return of antisemitism*, 92.

[42] Nelson, *Israel Denial*, 267.

against her, that is, until it was pointed out that belonging to a Jewish organization was no reason to believe in a conflict of interest. It is scarcely possible to imagine that any such similar debate would be happening on a mainstream western campus if the candidate belonged to any other minority. [43] Stephen Salaita, a former academic at the University of Illinois, has launched a bitter tirade against Zionists, most especially during the 2014 conflict in Gaza, and he has been joined by a large chorus of activists whose sole intent is to prevent Israeli speakers from coming to campus (so-called cancel culture) and to prevent them from being heard when they do speak. In reality, this overwhelmingly targets Jews.

Disloyalty test: Such is the unreconstructed, bigoted nature of the BDS movement that it has all but banished Jews from its meetings, convinced that their pro-Israel views, with associated connotations of racism, white supremacy and colonialism, threaten the 'safe spaces' they control. To ensure that such contamination does not occur, they have introduced a neo-fascist loyalty test to separate the good from the bad Jews, revolving around whether the individual or institution in question is prepared to disavow Israel or Zionism and thus satisfy a test of 'liberal' credentials. It is directly discriminatory and a textbook case of racism.

In Britain, there has been a long history of attempts to ban Jewish student societies for their perceived support for Zionism. Following the 1975 'Zionism is racism' vote at the UN, there was a 'national campaign to ban Jewish and Zionist speakers from campus.'[44] At Salford University, the Jewish society was denied permission to hold an Israel week, which had been planned in response to a 'Palestine week' held weeks earlier, and to set up a bookstall to distribute leaflets about Israel. [45] Similarly, motions proposed at UMIST, York, Lancaster and Salford proposed to restrict the activities of Jewish societies to purely religious matters while elsewhere, there were motions to expel Jewish student societies. While those who were in the forefront of this activity may not have consciously disliked Jews, their proposals amounted to campus antisemitism. The effect of their activity, in ostensibly trying to ban expressions of racism on campus, was to discriminate against Jewish students by banning, or hollowing out the activities of, Jewish societies. The Socialist Workers Party called for funds to be withdrawn from bodies that promoted Zionist speakers or activities but stopped short of calling for their meetings to be banned. In practice, the net effect of such defunding would have been to shut down the societies altogether. In the end, the National Union of Students, following a sponsored trip by a student group to Israel and Lebanon, passed a motion to prevent bans on, or circumscribe the activities of, Jewish (and Palestinian) student societies, while endorsing a two-state solution. Though BDS did not exist at the time, the tactics employed here were a chilling sign of where later supports for boycotts would lead.

---

[43] Adam Nagourney, "In U.C.L.A. Debate Over Jewish Student, Echoes on Campus of Old Biases," *New York Times*, March 5, 2015.
[44] Rich, *The Left's Jewish Problem*, 120.
[45] ibid. 121

BDS Pais Valencia became infamous in 2015 when it successfully pressurized the Spanish Rototom Sunsplash festival to disinvite Matisyahu, a Jewish and non-Israeli singer. His 'crime' was refusing to state whether or not he supported a Palestinian state, the only performer asked such a question. The resulting torrent of anger that this incident unleashed forced the organisers to recant and then re-invite the singer. As a Jew, he was subjected to a blatant double standard when he was asked for his opinion on a Palestinian state. No Chinese performer was asked about Tibet, no Russian about Ukraine, no Australian about the Aborigines, no Turk about the Copts and no American about Guantanamo Bay. Another similar example of loyalty test was imposed on Israeli choreographer Sally Ann Freedland in 2006 when the editor of *Dance Europe* said that she would only publish an article on Freedland if the choreographer first denounced the occupation. When Freedland refused, the article was not published.

These 'progressives' believe that Jews alone must pass a political test to join the community of decent people. Jews must disavow Zionism, endorse Palestinian supremacy and reject the central form of communal Jewish identity today. If they fail to do so, they are considered beyond the pale and treated as pariahs. Moreover, Matisyahu was being asked to criticize Israeli conduct simply because he was a Jew. To hold a Jew responsible for the behaviour of Israel is an egregious form of antisemitism, according to the widely accepted IHRA definition.

Much the same could be said of the decision by Chicago Dyke March to exclude three Jewish participants who were carrying Jewish pride flags (they feature a Star of David on a rainbow background). Having already condemned Zionism as a form of white supremacist ideology and racism, the organisers claimed the flags could be construed as offering support to Israel and asked the women to leave.

Leaving aside the spectacular levels of ignorance behind the assertion that Zionism was a white supremacist ideology, banning a flag which happens to be the universal symbol of the Jewish people is a clear form of racist discrimination. The symbol long predates the state of Israel and has historically adorned the clothing of Jews in centuries past. As one of the Jewish attendees put it: 'I really wanted to just be Jewish and gay in public and celebrate that.'[46] Moreover, holding Jews collectively responsible for the actions of the state of Israel is clearly antisemitic, even more so when the members of other national communities are not interrogated about their views on the countries they claim to support. Moreover, the irony of singling out the one country in the Middle East where gay people live the safest and freest lives should be lost on nobody.[47] Again, when

---

[46] Rachel Cromidas, "Tensions Flare After Chicago Dyke March Demands Star of David Pride Flag Carriers Leave Rally," *chicagoist.com*, accessed November 3, 2021, https://chicagoist.com/2017/06/26/dyke_march_anti-semitism_jewish_flag_chicago. php.

[47] Moreover, Palestinian flags were acceptable, despite the fact that, according to a study conducted by the Arab Barometer Research Network, only 5% of West Bank Palestinians accepted same sex relationships.

there are dozens of countries around the world where gay people are being persecuted and about which nothing is said, it is egregious for the Dyke March to attack the one nation where the protection of gay people is written into law. Journalist Batya Ungar-Sargon best sums up why the actions of these protestors was antisemitic: 'If there's only room in your movement for the 3% of Jews who say they aren't pro-Israel, your movement effectively bans Jews.'[48]

In 2014, the UK Jewish Film Festival (UKJFF) was forced out of the Tricycle Theatre in London where it had showcased its films for 8 years. Indhu Rubasingham, artistic director of the Tricycle, had insisted that the UKJFF refuse funding from the cultural section of the Israeli embassy, offering to fund the shortfall. In her words: 'Given the present situation in Israel/Palestine, and the unforeseen and unhappy escalation that has occurred over the past three weeks including a terrible loss of life, the Tricycle cannot be associated with any activity directly funded or supported by any party to the conflict...' She continued that the UKJFF could show the films provided that it occurred 'without the support or other endorsement from the Israeli government.' Their position was later reversed after many of the theatre's Jewish sponsors expressed outrage with the decision.

Why might the Tricycle's behaviour be considered antisemitic, never mind illegal and discriminatory? The simple answer is summed up best by UK Human Rights Blog: 'There is no similar policy in relation to any other conflict, nor as far as we know has there ever been one.'[49] The Tricycle received funding from the UK government, even as that government was committing troops to a possibly illegal war in Iraq and other controversial conflicts in the Middle East. It hosted the London Asian Film Festival despite it receiving funding from the Indian government, then in a tense standoff with Pakistan. No concerns had previously been raised about whether national governments were funding respective national cinematic festivals. For this reason alone, we end up with politically motivated antisemitic double standards in which a one-sided, myopic view of the Arab-Israeli conflict bleeds into how institutions treat Jewish and non-Israeli institutions. As journalist Nick Cohen points out: 'Racism consists of demanding behaviour from a minority you would never dream of demanding from your friends; forcing them to accept standards or privations because of their race.'[50] In another sense, such loyalty tests feel humiliating to Jews in the sense that they involve, as Steve Cohen says, 'the requirement to grovel.' As he points out correctly, 'Groveling, the humiliation of Jews, is fundamental to all antisemitism.'[51]

---

[48] Weiss, *How to Fight Antisemitism*, 90.
[49] Adam Wagner, "Have the Tricycle Theatre broken the law by refusing to host the Jewish Film Festival," ukhumanrightsblog.com, accessed December 18, 2019, https://ukhumanrightsblog.com/2014/08/07/have-the-tricycle-theatre-broken-the-law-by-refusing-to-host-the-jewish-film-festival/.
[50] Nick Cohen, "Antisemitic double standards: the arts and the Jews," *The Spectator*, August 6, 2014.
[51] David Hirsh, *Contemporary Left Antisemitism*, 105.

What all these cases (and many others besides) have in common is that, under pressure from BDS, Jewish artists, singers, students and filmmakers have been forced to go through a unique test of their 'political' views in order to establish their 'progressive' credentials. In McCarthyite fashion, they are being forced to publicly disown any Zionist association or remain forever outcasts and pariahs. This involves a separation of the world into good and bad Jews, a point that needs some further elaboration.

BDS, like much of the radical left, claims to be against antisemitism. But in characterizing the movement as an antisemitic one (a movement with ultimately antisemitic aims), it is important to realise the distinctness of left-wing antisemitism from its radical right-wing variety. The far right tends to feel a totalizing hatred of international Jewry, seeing Jews as an ethnically homogenous, politically unified threat to the stability and existence of white, western societies. It is not for nothing that the far right believes that Jews are responsible for a policy of white genocide. A blood based, bio-ethnic rejection of Jews as a whole makes it hard for those on the extreme right to conceive of good Jews. By contrast, the nationalist, non-Nazi right does co-opt Zionists and Israelis to their own causes while sharing right wing Jews' contempt for their more socialist, anti-Zionist brethren. For the left as for the nationalist right, the world has good and bad Jews too. Those Jews who eschew capitalism, disdain western political and economic power (especially Israeli and American power) and reject ethnic and religious parochialism are on the good side of humanity. They have rejected the religion of the Jews for the religion of the left with the 'bells and smells' of traditional religion now replaced by the sacred symbols of party loyalty and international solidarity. The Jews that these leftists identify with are the 'progressives' who cannot fathom the concept of Jews having collective rights, especially the right of self-determination. This attack on the Jewish community echoes the chilling words of revolutionary leader Clermont-Tonnerre who said, in the aftermath of the French Revolution, 'We must refuse everything to the Jews as a nation and accord everything to the Jews as individuals…It is repugnant to have in the state an association of non-citizens, and a nation within the nation.' Today's antisemites are followers of Clermont-Tonnerre, believing that when it comes to the Jews, individual rights can be upheld as long as they distance themselves from furthering particularistic Jewish concerns, such as Zionism. As the sociologist Keith Kahn-Harris explains: 'Those Jews who retain a commitment to the Jewish tradition of non-Zionist secular radicalism are, inevitably, the Jews that sections of the left are most comfortable engaging with today.' [52] Whereas once, Jews had to convert to Christianity to escape the contumely of Gentile society, now it is anti-western anti-Zionism that they must embrace. The alternative may not be physical death but it is certainly a form of political or intellectual death.

---

[52] Kahn-Harris, *Strange Hate*, 130.

UN bias against Israel

Nowhere are the egregious double standards against the Jewish state more evident than at the United Nations and all its associated agencies, such as the WHO and UNESCO. For at least half a century, block voting and politicization have tarnished this once hallowed institution, transforming it into a cauldron of unrelenting hatred and discrimination against Israel. By turning against the 'Jew among nations,' it has destroyed its claims to credibility, neutrality and impartiality and compromised its status as a beacon of human rights and international justice. Just as traditional antisemitism was animated by a singular obsession with Jews and with 'the Jewish question,' the UN has pursued its own obsession with the 'Israeli question.' The treatment of Israel and Zionism at the UN suggests that its member states do not see how such a pariah state can fit into the Middle East, or enter the community of nations as a respectable partner. The endless resolutions used to attack Israel are designed to make it an outcast among the nations, much as the endless attacks against Jews in secular Europe were designed to make them *persona non grata* within society.

The frenzy of anti-Israeli hysteria at the UN has been demoniacal in its sheer volume, content and intensity, with a charge sheet of bias, double standards and racism that is truly shocking.

1. Denial of membership

For over half a century, Israel was denied membership in any of the five regional groups (the African Group, Asia-Pacific Group, Eastern European Group, Latin American and Caribbean Group and Western European and Others Group (WEOG)), the only country to be excluded in this way. As such, it could not stand for election to the Security Council or participate in any other UN bodies. This was rectified in 2014 when it became a permanent member of WEOG, after gaining temporary admission in 2000. Nonetheless, for almost its entire history, Israel was treated as a pariah state, subject to a unique policy of debarment that crippled its ability to contribute at the UN.

2. Attack on Jewish self-determination

The UN has singled out Zionism, the foundational movement for Jewish self-determination, for demonization. In 1975, the UN General Assembly passed Resolution 3379, determining that Zionism was 'a form of racism and racial discrimination.' The resolution was part of a concerted effort by the Soviet Union and its Arab and Third World allies to score a victory in its anti-Israel Cold War strategy and its illegitimacy was recognised in 1991 when the resolution was reversed. Nonetheless, no other national liberation movement was traduced in this manner and no other nation so egregiously defamed. Jews were being told by the world's most august international body that the exercise of their collective rights, ones which had been respected by the UN itself on its founding, were inherently racist. It was not the transitory policies of a state that were being criticized or the actions of a temporary government but the very right of a state to exist. The resolution was the first time that the UN had attacked a founding ideology, a philosophical or doctrinal ism, rather than a country's behaviour. As such, it was part of a concerted effort to delegitimize the Jewish state, eject it from the community of nations and dismantle it in its entirety. As Robert Wistrich has masterfully observed: 'The discriminatory principle that traditionally characterised antisemitism had simply been transferred from the realm of individual rights to the domain of collective identity.'[53] To claim therefore that this was being done in the name of anti-racism was palpably absurd, a grotesque inversion of the truth. While it is true that this egregious piece of UN demonization was reversed some three decades ago, the spirit that animated it lives on in the form of a sick obsession with Israel.

3. UN targets Israel with disproportionate criticism

Both in the Security Council and in the General Assembly, Israel has been subjected to ritualistic political condemnation out of all proportion to its real or alleged misdeeds. This is reflected in the pattern of General Assembly resolutions against Israel which single out the Jewish state above any other country. From 2015 to the present, there have been 125 GA anti-Israel resolutions but 28 in total for Iran, North Korea, Syria, Libya, Pakistan, China, Qatar and Cuba. During the same period, there has not been one resolution condemning Hamas. During a period in which the Uighurs have been subject to cultural genocide, millions victimised in communist run North Korean gulags, half a million people killed amid the horrors of the Syrian civil war, religious minorities persecuted in Iran, journalists and human rights activists jailed in Turkey and a population shattered in Yemen, the overwhelming focus of the Assembly has been on the actions of Israel. Emergency special sessions at the General Assembly have also been dominated by anti-Israel activity. The first was held in 1956 and concerned the Suez Crisis and others have been called to discuss the crisis in Congo, the Soviet invasions of Hungary and Afghanistan and the South African occupation of Namibia. Four of these sessions were convened to discuss Israel, the most recent of which has led to more than ten separate meetings.

This pattern of deep seated, structural bias has also become a ubiquitous feature of the UN Human Rights Council based in Geneva. The Council, set up to remedy the grave defects in its predecessor, the UN Commission on Human Rights, has a rotating membership of forty-seven nations and a remit to 'address important thematic human rights' such as 'freedom of assembly, freedom of expression, freedom of belief and religion, LGBT rights, and the rights of racial and ethnic minorities' and in a manner which abides by the principles of 'universality, impartiality, objectivity and non-selectivity.' Yet such hopes were unrealisable from the start when the Council's members were announced. Among the 47 countries elected after three rounds of secret voting were such 'luminaries'

---

[53] Wistrich, *A Lethal Obsession*, 475.

of human rights as Algeria, China, Cuba, Pakistan, Russia, Saudi Arabia and Zambia.

In its first year (2006), the Council managed to condemn just one country, Israel, ignoring restrictions on all the freedoms listed above that took place in every other country on earth. While it later broadened its condemnations, in its first decade, Israel was its number one target. From 2006 until present, this supposedly venerable body has issued over 90 condemnations for Israel, almost as many as for the rest of the world combined. The resolutions are all one sided and automatically pass because of pressure from the Arab/Muslim voting bloc and their allies. None of those resolutions condemn the terrorist forces ranged against the Jewish state, all of whom seek its destruction, and none are balanced by the often laudable work that Israel engages in to improve its relations with the Palestinian Authority and other countries. By contrast, it is the usual practice with resolutions that express concern for other human rights issues to praise the regime that oversees them.

The UN is a resource constrained body and has only a limited amount of time with which to consider issues of concern around the world. As Hillel Neuer writes; 'Because every proposed resolution requires intensive review by various levels and branches of government, a direct result of the anti-Israel texts is a crippling of the UN's ability to take protective action for the world's genuine human rights victims.'[54]

4. Single agenda items focus just on Israel

Allied to this are the single agenda items in UN bodies that single out Israel, quite uniquely, for condemnation. At the UN Human Rights Council, agenda item 7 on 'Human rights situation in Palestine and other occupied Arab territories' is a permanent feature of the Council's agenda with all other human rights issues considered under agenda item 4. Israel is thus the only country with a standalone place on the Council's agenda, a form of systematic bias without parallel in the body. This deeply politicized attack on Israel has been condemned by many western nations who have begun to vote against item 7.

In the WHO's session in 2020, only one country, Israel, was subject to a single agenda item (no. 17). The resolution that was passed condemned Israel for violating the health rights of the Palestinians, despite the fact that the UN's own envoy praised the co-ordination between Israel and the PA during the Coronavirus pandemic. The height of farce was reached when a Syrian delegate condemned Israel for affecting the living conditions for Syrians in the Golan, despite his own regime overseeing the mass murder of its civilians. At annual meetings of the United Nations Commission on the Status of Women (CSW), Israel too has been the only individual country criticized for alleged violations of women's rights. At its meeting in 2016, the International Labour Organization produced a report

---

[54] Hillel Neuer, "The United Nations versus Israel," in Ryvchin (ed.), *The Anti-Israel Agenda*, 22.

called 'The situation of workers of the occupied Arab territories' which slammed Israeli policies for stunting the Palestinian economy. This was the only country specific report at the meeting. There are special agenda items at the United Nations Development Programme and the United Nations Conference on Trade and Development.

Another example of the UN's singular focus on Israel came in 2016 when the UN Human Rights Council passed a resolution requiring the United Nations High Commissioner for Human Rights to produce a database of all business enterprises that 'directly and indirectly, enabled, facilitated and profited from the construction and growth of the settlements.' Leaving aside that there is nothing illegal about companies doing business in settlements in disputed or occupied lands, what concerns us here is the discriminatory nature of this provision. While the UNHRC has claimed that this measure is motivated by human rights and the need for transparency, there is no identical initiative to deal with similar territories. There is no proposed database of businesses operating in other conflict zones or disputed territories, such as Western Sahara occupied by Morocco, Northern Cyprus occupied by Turkey, Nagorno-Karabach occupied by Armenia or the Japan administered Senkaku Islands. It merely shows how these agencies (and others) have become so deeply politicized in recent years, undermining their neutrality, credibility and legitimacy in the process.

What matters in all these cases is not just that the resolutions against Israel are absurdly one sided, lacking in context and devoid of references to Israel's enemies, such as Hamas. It is not just that Israel, a country with an incredible record in promoting the rights of women and employees and furthering the health of Palestinians in Israeli hospitals, is attacked while countries that physically punish women for wearing the 'wrong' clothing (Saudi Arabia) or have no minimum age for consensual sex (Iran) or rape women in war (Syria) are overlooked. It is that these institutions single out the Jewish state for uniquely malign treatment and thus fail to treat it with the equality that any member state deserves. As Hillel Neuer has pointed out: 'If an alien from another planet visited the United Nations and listened to its debates, read its resolutions, and walked its halls, the extraterritorial observer would logically conclude that a principal purpose of the world body is to censure a tiny country called Israel.'[55]

5. The UN has attacked the very basis of Jewish history and heritage at UNESCO.

In the 1970s, UNESCO condemned Israel's archaeological digs as 'crimes against culture,' a form of words which both likened the Jewish state to a fascist regime but also demonized the country for simply trying to unearth its precious heritage. This laid down a marker of ideological inanity which has only increased in more recent years.[56] Part of the Palestinians' diplomatic war against Israel

---

[55] ibid. 19
[56] Alexander, "Stealing the Holocaust," 231.

involves denying that there is any Jewish connection to the land and thus denying that the Jewish state has any foundational legitimacy. Palestinian textbooks routinely twist the facts of history to portray the Jewish inhabitants of Israel as usurpers and colonialists living on stolen land, mere temporary inhabitants akin to the medieval crusaders. In recent years, this pernicious and belligerent perspective has found a new lease of life in UNESCO, an agency which is designed to promote 'cultural heritage and the equal dignity of all cultures.' For one thing, UNESCO has adopted dozens of resolutions critical of Israel, a country in which the freedom of religious minorities to practise their faith is protected by law, while passing barely any on the countries in which religious freedom is actually threatened, such as Iran, North Korea, Saudi Arabia and China. Worse, it has attempted to re-write the Jewish connection to the land. In 2014, UNESCO succumbed to pressure from Arab states when it postponed a planned exhibition on the Jewish presence in the land of Israel. In 2016, UNESCO criticized Israeli policies in the old city of Jerusalem, referring to the Temple Mount complex (the holiest site for Jews in the world) by its Muslim names: al-Aqsa and al-Haram al-Sharif. In 2017, UNESCO declared that the town of Hebron was a 'Palestinian world heritage site.' This completely omitted the Jewish significance of Hebron, the burial place of the Biblical patriarchs and matriarchs and thus a place of central significance to Judaism.[57] President Rivlin rightly slammed the decision, saying that UNESCO was 'determined to keep disseminating anti-Jewish lies'[58] and it led a furious Israeli government to withdraw from the organization altogether. To argue that the holiest places in the Jewish faith have no connection to Judaism, to blot out the connection altogether, is to attack Jewish identity itself. Regardless of the motivation, this sacrilegious appropriation of collective memory is an egregious form of cultural antisemitism.

6. The UN gives unique and unprecedented succour to Israel's enemies

A related accusation is that the UN has provided Israel's enemies with a unique platform to pursue their destructive agenda. This has been manifested by the special treatment accorded to the Palestinian movement and the UN's decades long refusal to condemn terrorism. Just as Israel finds itself singled out for unique condemnation, so too the Palestinians find their cause worthy of a unique level of respect, attention and recognition within the world body.

In 1974, the General Assembly invited a spokesman from the Palestine Liberation Organization to address world leaders. This was an unprecedented event, for as Joshua Moravchik observes: 'No one who was not a representative of a government – except the Pope, and even he was the head of a quasi-state –

---

[57] Peter Beaumont, "UNESCO makes Hebron old city Palestinian world heritage site," *The Guardian*, July 7, 2017.
[58] Barak Ravid, "Israeli Leaders Rage Against 'anti-Semitic' UNESCO Resolution on Hebron," *Haaretz*, July 7, 2017.

had ever before been granted such a privilege...'[59] What made the invitation so chilling was that Arafat was at that moment engaging in a global campaign of international terrorism that had already claimed the lives of Israeli civilians and athletes, foreign nationals and an American ambassador, and which was responsible for numerous attacks on the aviation industry. Yet Arafat was 'greeted like a hero and a statesman, not as a cold-blooded murderer.'[60] Shortly afterwards, the PLO became the first terrorist group to be granted non-state observer status at the UN.

In 1978, the UN inaugurated an International Day of Solidarity with the Palestinian People, which is now held on the anniversary of the 1947 Partition Resolution. The absurdity of this lies in both the fact that the Palestinian leadership turned down the chance for a state on this very day and the fact that the UN, the sponsor of this international day, had been the progenitor of the spurned offer. A special Committee on the Exercise of the Inalienable Rights of the Palestinian People was founded in 1975. Ever since, the CEIRPP has become the sole organ dedicated to a single people and has served as a major global forum for anti-Israel demonization. The recommendations that it makes are adopted by the General Assembly and are, not surprisingly, extremely one sided, placing the burden on Israel to resolve the conflict. Again, what is crucial is that one people, the Palestinians, are accorded a committee to fight for their rights. There are any number of other national groups whose territorial aspirations have yet to be realized, who have never resorted to terrorism and violence in pursuit of their aims and whose leaders have never been offered reasonable solutions to their disputes. Yet these groups have no committee to endorse their claims.

When it comes to terrorism, the UN has indulged the Palestinian cause in a wholly unprecedented way and in a manner that has only encouraged their unrelenting war against Israel. The General Assembly has long held that the Palestinians, like other peoples, have the right of self-determination and independence. General Assembly resolution 2708 affirmed that they could use 'all the necessary means at their disposal' to achieve this, wording that the Palestinians interpreted as sanctioning the use of violence. That the UN really did mean this was confirmed in 1982 with Resolution 37/43 which reaffirmed 'the legitimacy of the struggle of peoples for independence, territorial integrity, national unity and liberation from colonial and foreign domination and foreign occupation by all available means, including armed struggle.'[61] At the time, their armed struggle was directed exclusively at civilian targets. Even after the 9/11 attacks galvanised the UN into providing an international condemnation of terror,

[59] Joshua Muravchik. "The UN and Israel: A History of Discrimination," jewishpolicy center.org, accessed 3 February 2021, https://www.jewishpolicycenter.org/2017/04/03/the-un-and-israel-a-history-of-discrimination/.
[60] Alan Dershowitz, *Why Terrorism Works* (New Haven: Yale University Press, 2002), 49.
[61] The UN has since gone on to condemn terrorism, most especially in light of the 9/11 attacks. One example is UN Security Council Resolution 1566.

the OIC wanted anti-Israeli terrorists to be exempted. As of 2022, the UN still cannot bring itself to condemn the actions of Hamas, a deeply antisemitic Islamist organization whose aim is the destruction of Israel.

This obsessive deification of the Palestinian cause has ensured an endless drumbeat of anti-Israeli resolutions, all of which are one-sided in nature. Israel's real or alleged misdeeds are excoriated in the most savage terms while there is no condemnation for Palestinian terror, incitement and rejectionism. That is also reflected in the one-sided mandate of the Special Rapporteur for Israel/Palestine, namely to investigate Israeli excesses, not those of its enemies. Israeli victims of terrorism are seen through the lens of Israeli occupation and 'apartheid' policies, to such an extent that they are seen as perpetrators of the very violence they experience. As Robert Wistrich has observed, 'Human rights violations by Palestinians *against* Jews cannot, indeed, be addressed at all in the UN framework.'[62] It is therefore no wonder that reports, such as that produced by Judge Richard Goldstone following Israel's war with Hamas in 2008-9, are so heavily biased against the Jewish state and so replete with mendacious charges.

UNRWA (the UN Relief and Works Agency for Palestine Refugees in the Near East) has provided a unique form of succour to Israel's enemies. The failings of this agency offer a textbook example, not just of the UN's unhealthy fetish for the Palestinian cause, but also its double standard when dealing with Israel. Firstly, UNRWA has jettisoned the internationally accepted definition of a refugee provided by the 1951 Convention Relating to the Status of Refugees. This states that a refugee is 'Any person who: (2) owing to well-founded fear of being persecuted for reasons of race, religion, nationality, membership of a particular social group or political opinion, is outside the country of his nationality and is unable or, owing to such fear, is unwilling to avail himself of the protection of that country; or who, not having a nationality and being outside the country.' By contrast, UNRWA has defined Palestinian refugees as 'Persons whose normal place of residence was Palestine between June 1946 and May 1948, who both lost their homes and means of livelihood as a result of the 1948 Arab-Israeli conflict.' In 1965, a third-generation descendant of an original refugee was classed as a refugee, and in 1982, all descendants of Palestine refugee males, including legally adopted children, regardless of whether they had been granted citizenship elsewhere, were classed as Palestinian refugees. This unprecedented and unwarranted change in definition led to an expansion in the number of purported Palestinian Arab refugees. Whereas only (at most) 750,000 Palestinians voluntarily or forcibly left the area of mandate Palestine during the 1947-9 war, with only a small fraction alive today, there are 5.43 million refugees in Jordan, Lebanon, Syria, and the West Bank and Gaza Strip as of 2019. In the unique case of UNRWA, a second, third, fourth or fifth generation descendant can live a life completely disconnected from an ancestor and still have derivative status as a refugee.

---

[62] Wistrich, *Lethal Obsession*, 488.

Whereas UNHCR exempts from the status of refugee anyone who has a newly acquired nationality, this is not so with UNRWA. Thus, UNRWA still considers Palestinians living in Jordan (some 2 million people) with full Jordanian citizenship to be refugees. This is despite the fact that the majority will have been born in Jordan, lived their whole lives in Jordan and, in some cases, made wealthy careers in Jordan. This is at odds with Article I (c) (3) of the 1951 U.N. Convention and Protocol Relating to the Status of Refugees, which states explicitly that a person is no longer a refugee if he or she has acquired a new nationality, and enjoys the protection of the country of his new nationality.

UNRWA has also proposed a unique solution to their refugee problem. Whereas the UNHCR puts forward a range of options for resolving refugee crises, from resettlement and repatriation to financial compensation, UNRWA advocates just one, namely the right of return for all refugees. Moreover, this is a right conferred not on those who were made refugees in the 1948 war but on all their descendants, in perpetuity. There is no precedent for such a solution in international law. It is a blatant case of having one rule for Israel's political opponents and one rule for every other country. It need hardly be stated that the right of return is a formula for the destruction of Israel wrapped up in the language of human rights. In other words, a UN agency encourages its client population to believe in a radical solution to the conflict that would effectively destroy another UN member state. It is an absurdity of Alice in Wonderland proportions.

7. The UN has shown tolerance for antisemitism

The UN was founded in the aftermath of the systematic mass murder of six million Jews in the Holocaust. One might have expected the organization to show a special form of sensitivity to this form of racism. Yet there are many times when the UN has become a forum for antisemitic views and become a cesspool of anti-Jewish prejudice. At the 1980 World Conference of the United Nations Decade for Women in Copenhagen, there were reports of comments including 'The only good Jew is a dead Jew' and 'The only way to rid the world of Zionism is to kill all the Jews.'[63] Jewish feminists were hounded and intimidated, leading one, Phyllis Chesler, to describe the conference as 'a pogrom of nonstop words and ideas, an exercise in total intimidation.'[64] Saudi Arabia's permanent representative to the UN, Jamil Baroody, called Zionists 'an alien people in our midst' and claimed that 'exclusivity and exclusiveness' would be 'the bane of the Zionists.'[65] The blood libel has been a mainstay of a number of diplomats. One Saudi representative told a UN seminar in 1984 that Jews who did not drink

[63] Wistrich, *Lethal Obsession*, 471.
[64] Phyllis Chesler, *The New Antisemitism: The Current Crisis and What We Must Do About It*, (San Francisco: Jossey-Bass, 2003), 53.
[65] Paul Hofmann, "Why and How Anti-Zionism Move Won," *New York Times*, November 12, 1975.

Gentile blood would be eternally damned[66] while Kuwait's representative to the General Assembly accused Zionists of having an 'unquenchable thirst for Arab blood.'[67] Other senior diplomats have invoked the myth of world Jewish conspiracy and the notion that Jews controlled the media and the financial system. A Syrian delegate accused Zionists of wanting to 'establish a racist empire starting in Palestine and extending to other parts of the world' while his colleagues labelled Zionists 'enemies of mankind.'[68] Still others sought to explain Israel's apparently limitless deception by reference to the allegedly perfidious nature of the Jewish faith, leading to endless attacks on religious practices in Israel. In 1997, the Palestinian representative claimed that Israel had injected 300 Palestinian children with the HIV virus, a claim that remains unchallenged on the UN record. And in recent years during Israel's wars with Hamas in Gaza, the Jewish state has been compared to Nazi Germany.

As previously observed, the 2001 Durban Conference against racism turned into an egregious hate fest against Jews filled with incendiary language and antisemitic tropes. Copies of *The Protocols of the Elders of Zion* were being sold and participants tried to revive the notion that Zionism was racism. The proposal to label Holocaust denial as a form of antisemitism was defeated, silencing the Jewish victims of antisemitism. At an NGO discussion on Palestinian issues, one Jewish official (Anne Bayefsky) was asked to leave due to her alleged bias on the issue. Mary Robinson, then the UN High Commissioner for Human Rights, admitted that 'horrible antisemitism' had marked the event and added: 'A number of people said they'd never been so hurt or so harassed or been so blatantly faced with antisemitism.'[69]

Antisemitism has become *de rigueur* among UN officials, with one example that is especially noteworthy. In 2011, Richard Falk published a blog about the International Criminal Court's indictment of Colonel Gaddafi which included a highly offensive cartoon. It showed a dog, which was wearing a kippah (Jewish head covering) and a sweater emblazoned with 'USA,' urinating on a symbol of justice while feasting on the bones of a skeleton. This suggested that 'Jewish controlled' America was violating the norms of justice in attacking Libya, invoking the myth of Jewish and Israeli control of global affairs.[70] A year later, he explained why he was drawn to the Palestinian struggle with the following words: 'I formed a well-evidenced belief that the U.S. Government and the organized Jewish community were responsible for the massive and enduring

---

[66] The comment was made by Marief Dawalibi, Saudi representative to the UN Seminar on Religious Intolerance in Geneva in 1984.
[67] Tel Aviv University, *Israeli yearbook on Human Rights vol. 17* (Boston: Martinus Nijhoff Publishers, 1987), 64.
[68] Wistrich, *Lethal Obsession*, 478-9.
[69] Peter Wertheim, "The Role of Governments in the Assault on Israel's Legitimacy Part 1 – Israel Among the Nations," in Ryvchin (ed.), *The Anti-Israel Agenda*, 86.
[70] Jeremy Sharon, "UN's Richard Falk under fire for 'antisemitic' cartoon," *The Jerusalem Post*, July 8, 2011.

confiscation of Palestinian land and rights.'[71] Following the Boston Marathon bombing, Falk released a statement which claimed that the attack was blowback for past American foreign policy in the Middle East, particularly two 'illegal' wars in Iraq and Afghanistan that had failed to enhance American security. He then added that 'as long as Tel Aviv has the compliant ear of the American political establishment, those who wish for peace and justice in the world should not rest easy.'[72] Not only is this a denial of the role played by jihadi ideologues in propagating terror attacks against the West, it is a deliberate attempt to suggest that American foreign policy is dictated by Israel, itself a core antisemitic trope. Falk has also compared Israel with Nazi Germany on a number of occasions and referenced the Holocaust in his vicious assessments of Israeli behaviour. He has also endorsed the book *The Wandering Who?*, written by the notorious, self-confessed Jew hater and Holocaust denier Gilad Atzmon.[73] Such a person was never fit to stand in judgment on Israel and should never have been tolerated. That he was not expelled tells one a great deal about how seriously antisemitism is taken at the UN. It is hard to imagine that any other form of racism would ever be tolerated in this way.

It is true that the UN did have a conference in 2015 to condemn antisemitism, Islamophobia and hate-crimes. The UN also has an annual day of commemorating the Holocaust and the theme in 2020 was '75 years after Auschwitz - Holocaust Education and Remembrance for Global Justice.' With some courage and conviction, Tijjani Muhammad Bande, the President of the 74th Session of the UN General Assembly, acknowledged that it was 'difficult to grasp the level of hatred that killed six million Jews' and spoke of the 'wave of antisemitism plaguing countries around the world.'[74] UNESCO's Holocaust Remembrance Day on 27 January 'reaffirms its unwavering commitment to counter antisemitism, racism, and other forms of intolerance that may lead to group-targeted violence.'[75] These are worthy events which encourage participant nations to reflect on the horrific consequences of undiluted Jew hatred and racism. But so long as the UN maintains its unhealthy obsession with demonizing the one Jewish nation, it will remain Janus-faced on this most pressing problem.

Some UN Secretary Generals acknowledge the long history of crippling anti-Israel bias in their institution. In 2013, Ban Ki Moon declared: 'Unfortunately,

[71] Richard Falk, "For What?" richardfalk.org, accessed February 20, 2021, https://richardfalk.org/2012/07/20/for-what.
[72] Aaron Kalman, "UN official says US had Boston attack coming," *Times of Israel*, April 23, 2013.
[73] Daniel Sugarman, "Arkush urges Jewish students to 'shun LSE and study elsewhere'," *The Jewish Chronicle*, March 21, 2017.
[74] "75 years after Auschwitz – Holocaust Education and Remembrance for Global Justice," un.org, accessed December 1, 2021, https://www.un.org/pga/74/2020/01/27/75-years-after-auschwitz-holocaust-education-and-remembrance-for-global-justice/.
[75] "International Holocaust Remembrance Day, 27 January" unesco.org, accessed 3 March 2020, www.en.unesco.org/commemorations/holocaustremembranceday.

because of the [Israeli-Palestinian] conflict, Israel's been weighed down by criticism and suffered from bias — and sometimes even discrimination.'[76] It was a correct statement of the problem but a false explanation. The bias and discrimination has not happened 'because of the conflict' itself, but has occurred because key diplomatic players in that conflict have chosen to launch a diplomatic offensive against Israel in international forums. The current Secretary General, Antonio Guterres, also understands the gravity of the problem. In 2017, he told the World Jewish Congress: 'As secretary general of the United Nations I consider that the State of Israel needs to be treated as any other state.'[77]

None of this is to suggest that Israel should get a free pass at the UN. Countering the obsessively disproportionate focus on the Jewish state should never mean immunity from criticism. If Israel fails to live up to its own high ideals and standards of human rights, it must be held to account in an appropriate and proportionate way. The key point is that Israel deserves equality of treatment in international forums, just as Jews need equality before the law as citizens of their countries. It should receive criticism proportionate to the gravity and urgency of the conflict in which it is engaged, tempered by an understanding that many regional actors are contributing to the lack of peace.

In the last 70 years, one can see that this has not been the case. Judged by death toll, the Arab-Israeli conflict has claimed over 116,000 lives over a 70-year period,[78] an average of around 1,657 deaths per year. While this is a relatively high number, it is vastly dwarfed by nearly every other major conflict on earth since 1950, including the Korean War, the Algerian war against France, the Vietnam conflict, the civil wars in Nigeria, Uganda, Burundi and Ethiopia, the Bangladesh Liberation War, the war in Afghanistan from 1978 onwards, the Iran-Iraq war, the First and Second Congo wars, the Syrian Civil War and the genocides that have taken place in Darfur, East Timor and Rwanda. Not only is the death toll higher in those conflicts, but they are compressed into a smaller timespan, making the urgency of intervention all the greater. When Israel is targeted unfairly by UN resolutions, the real losers (apart from Israel) are the victims of these other wars and genocides whose suffering is prolonged by inattention. This fundamentally contradicts the entire point of the UN which was set up to maintain international peace and security and promote respect for human rights. According to the Borgen Project report in 2015, the most 'societally repressive' countries on earth were Burma, Equatorial Guinea, Eritrea, Libya,

---

[76] Michael Shmulovich, "Israel faces bias at UN, Ban acknowledges," *The Jerusalem Post*, August 17, 2013.
[77] "UN chief vows to stand up against anti-Israel bias, anti-Semitism," *Times of Israel*, April 24, 2017.
[78] "Vital statistics: Total casualties, Arab-Israeli conflict," jewishvirtuallibrary.org, accessed 4 march 2022, https://www.jewishvirtuallibrary.org/total-casualties-arab-israeli-conflict

North Korea and Sudan. [79] Yet it is these countries that get a free pass in international bodies, precisely because they so often chair their committees. Thus, we see how the UN's propaganda war against Israel disfigures victims of other conflicts and undermines the status of the UN itself, simply because unending attacks on one state undermine the cherished principle of the sovereign equality of all nations.

Finally, it is worth recalling a comment made in Chapter 1. One does not have to believe that the diplomats who attend UN conferences and vote in resolutions are motivated by any antisemitic prejudice. Not one of them needs to intend any harm to the Jewish community or believe that Jews should be subjected to a double standard. Intent has never been a necessary condition for this or any other form of prejudice. Antisemitism can be judged by outcome too. It is clear from the examples outlined that Israel, together with its supporters, has been held to a unique double standard by its most determined opponents as well as by the international institutions that legitimise them. What results is a textbook case of political antisemitism that is as glaring as it is ignoble.

---

[79] "Top Three Countries with the Worst Human Rights Violations," borgenproject.org, accessed 19 February 2022, https://borgenproject.org/human-rights-violations/

Conclusion

If we accept and acquiesce in the face of discrimination, we accept the responsibility ourselves and allow those responsible to salve their conscience by believing that they have our acceptance and concurrence.

Mary McLeod Bethune

It is an oft cited argument that anti-Israel discourse belongs in a separate category from traditional antisemitism. It is viewed as a form of political criticism which, because it is part and parcel of legitimate debate, should be automatically insulated from charges of racism. Strong critics of Israel advocate a firewall between antisemitism, understood as negative attitudes and actions towards Jews as Jews, and anything which is Israel related. Thus, the notion that hostility to Israel or its (largely Jewish) supporters, in any of its manifestations, could be construed as antisemitic is treated with disdain. The mere accusation of antisemitism is scorned as an act of hostility by the powerful rather than a cry of despair from its victims. It is treated as a weaponization of debate by the unscrupulous, rather than a vicious onslaught by bigots. It is regarded as a shabby and dishonest trick rather than an honest reckoning with genuine prejudice. When Jews claim to be victims of antisemitism, they are treated as a hostile entity rather than as people wronged by hateful acts and rhetoric.

The preceding discussion has hopefully put paid to this notion. The anti-Israel movement has become saturated with prejudice and weighed down by bigotry, reproducing the most virulent features of Jew hatred from centuries past. Tropes connected to the blood libel, bestiality, avarice, deicide, chosenness, global control and dual loyalty, an iconography so familiar to Jewish populations from centuries past, has been re-ignited and given a new lease of life in representations of Israel. Those tropes form part of the visual culture of the Middle East. They have become part of a deeply hostile vocabulary among hard leftists, hard rightists and Islamists. They have become the 'go to' terms of reference among *de rigueur* anti-Israel scholars. It is true that not all those who use such ideas, images and conceptual understandings do so because they hate Jews. They may be unaware of the resonance of their language and blind to the historical connotations of their outlook. But antisemitism has never required racist intent because what matters is the content and outcome of what a person says or writes.

For those who doubt whether political narratives can ever be racist, imagine an alternative scenario involving criticism of a black community leader. Let us imagine that doubts surfaced about the leader's background with insinuations of criminality, corruption and public malfeasance. When journalists are assigned to investigate, they manage to produce some damning evidence against the individual concerned. Now if those journalists provided a balanced, evidence-based critique, it would be absurd and insulting to suggest that it was tinged with racism. Indeed, it would be equivalent to the criticism one might offer of a leader from any racial or national background. But now imagine that a cartoon appeared which depicted that black leader with absurd and exaggerated physical features, animalistic growls or other images directly borrowed from nineteenth century imperial caricature. Would anyone seriously question that such an appalling image was racist? Furthermore, if black people complained bitterly about such vile iconography, would it not be morally perverse to deny the validity of their complaint, with the additional claim that they were merely 'weaponizing' anti-black racism to further their own agenda? Such an obnoxious view, involving accusations of deception and manipulation, would undoubtedly be seen as part of the experience of racism faced by black people. The same must surely go for the reproduction of antisemitic images and tropes in the anti-Israel movement.

The same applies to the issue of double standards affecting Israel, which have been a textbook example of singling out the 'Jew among nations' for special, and highly adverse, treatment. The eliminationist mentality that sought to convert, expel or kill the Jews has been hideously transformed into an unrelenting campaign to de-Zionise, delegitimize and destroy the Jewish state. The relentless, knee jerk criticism of Israel within the UN is tantamount to a disfiguring, cult like obsession within the world body, and it is being pursued with a near pathological intensity which is out of all proportion to the country's real misdeeds. In the past, western civilization was beset by the Jewish question, an issue of how to deal with the Jewish people who lived in the midst of gentile populations. Today, the Jewish question has become the Israel question. But just as the Jews were not primarily responsible for solving this question, given that the only rational solution was for gentile societies to adopt a set of liberal values by which they could welcome Jews as equal citizens, so too the Jewish state is not responsible for solving the Israel question. Again, the only solution is for Israel's neighbours, as well as world bodies, to accept the legitimacy and sovereignty of a Jewish state, and to subject it to equal treatment in every global forum. Of course, it is also true that hostility towards Israel, influenced as it is often is by antisemitism, then feeds into further hostility towards Jews, whether or not they support Israel. Thus, we see how supporters of the campaign to boycott and divest from Israel launch attacks on Jews whom they perceive to be Zionists, even claiming that they have a progressive rationale for doing so.

Now that this has all been demonstrated, there are no grounds for the anti-Israel critic to deny the strong presence of antisemitic tropes, discourses and symbols in the demonization of the Jewish state. But that critic might still demand to know what a non-antisemitic criticism of Israel looks like.

So, what might a non-antisemitic critique of Israel look like?

Let us imagine that a severe critic of Israel understood the full force and power of antisemitic tropes, canards, ideologies and perspectives due to a thorough immersion in its long history, including up until the present. Now let us suppose that the person still wanted to express a strong disdain for the policies and behaviour of an Israeli government but in a way that avoided the potent stench of antisemitism. What might such a critique look like? Here, there are many things that critics might want to say, all of which will be challenged in the next section.

They might say any of the following: that Israel's behaviour in the West Bank has been harsh or counterproductive; that the measures that Israel was taking to defend itself, such as the security barrier and the checkpoints, have imposed too high a cost on Palestinian civilians and incentivised support for Hamas or other terror groups; that Israel's settlement policy is illegal, a barrier to peace or a provocation to the Palestinian population; that the far right in Israel have introduced a toxic atmosphere of racism and extremism affecting minorities; that there is social discrimination against the Arab population; that the presence of ultra-orthodox parties in Israel's unstable system of proportional representation ensures that parties with narrow agendas hold the balance of power in the Israeli political system and that this translates into support for politically unsustainable policies; that Israel's counter terrorist strategies or its behaviour in war were disproportionate and harsh towards the Palestinian population, and that Israel's leaders have not gone the extra mile for peace or given sufficient incentives to their opponents.

These criticisms focus on public policy and are an attempt to engage with the record of governments, past and present, in terms of commonly understood areas of concern. They do not denigrate the entire country or its population, nor do they demonize Israel's founding ideology (Zionism). They are also the kind of criticisms that one might read in some of Israel's own newspapers. They have attempted to criticize Israel in the same terms as they would any other country, a point crucial to the IHRA definition of antisemitism.

Of course, this narrative, which is familiar to many in the West, can still be challenged. For starters, Israel has made bids for peace, not just before the state was created, but on many occasions since 1948. This has resulted in a series of agreements with Arab neighbours, including the historic accords with Egypt (1979) and Jordan (1994), both of which involved political normalization and the return of territory and, more recently, with the UAE, Bahrain and South Sudan. Israel also signed the Oslo accords in 1993, part of an attempt to reach a long-term settlement of the conflict with the Palestinians. Yet despite offering concessions on settlements, borders, refugees and territory, Israel has been met with an iron wall of rejectionism and hatred from the Palestinian leadership.

The current stalemate in the West Bank is, once again, regrettable. It is in Israel's long-term interests to reach an agreement which separates Israel from the Palestinians and which allows the latter to rule over themselves with dignity and prosperity. Only the most blinkered would deny that there are also rights and wrongs on both sides of the conflict, or that settlements add a layer of complication to any long-term peace agreement. That said, the principal stumbling block to a resolution of the Arab-Israeli conflict remains the long-term Palestinian acceptance of a sovereign Jewish state in their midst. This is why PLO/PA leaders insist on a bogus right of return in any peace settlement, knowing that it would spell the end of their dream of a greater Palestine.

It is true that there is a level of racism and inequality that affects Israel's Arab population and this creates gaps between the Jewish and Arab community in terms of educational performance, employment and economic prosperity. Israel must continue to plug these gaps and iron out discrimination in whichever sector it is manifested. Yet, despite this, the Arab population in Israel has far more rights in the Jewish state than in any neighbouring Arab country and most still value Israeli citizenship when asked. Israeli Arabs can vote, stand for office, form political parties, demonstrate in public, go on strike and attend a place of worship while benefiting from the various rights laid down in Israeli legislation which apply to all its citizens.

In addition, Israel has taken strides in recent years to equalize the treatment of Jews and non-Jewish communities It is undeniable that the security infrastructure in the West Bank does have a negative effect on some Palestinian civilians and this is a regrettable outcome of the conflict. At the same time, it is necessary to recognise that the barrier is in place purely to thwart the terrorist attacks that are planned by a variety of Palestinian groups in the West Bank and Gaza. Finally, while Israel's responses to terror have killed more Palestinians than Israelis, this is a morally meaningless argument to make. One does not tot up the number of dead among the two sides to a conflict and assign blame or virtue depending on which side has suffered the greatest losses. One differentiates between the actions of a terror group which intends to cause mass casualties through indiscriminate warfare and those of a nation state which has an absolute entitlement under international law to defend its citizens from attack.

Thus, Israel can counter the arguments of its strongest critics. But that is not the point of these responses. What matters is that the strong anti-Israel critic in this exchange has managed to avoid describing Israel in an antisemitic manner.

A last word: antisemitism is a huge problem for the Jews but also a big problem for wider society. In part, this is because antisemites are so often ill disposed towards other minorities, posing a threat to human rights on multiple levels. In addition, antisemitism is an irrational conspiracy theory which reflects dangerous habits of mind and patterns of thought. It is inimical to facts, evidence and logic and usurps the role of knowledge and rationality in deciding issues of public policy. It is based on a conspiratorial way of thinking, the substitution of lies for truth and fantasy for reality. It toxifies and demoralises the culture from which it arises, causing direct harm to the foundations of a democratic order and contradicting the liberal values on which such a society is based. The suggestion that Jews or the Jewish state are part of a malign conspiracy to harm humanity only encourages the type of radical politics which harms all of society. Extreme political movements thrive on extreme ideas and the more widely those ideas are spread and supported, the more such movements receive oxygen. Antisemitism is therefore a profound threat to liberal democracies which value education, pluralism, tolerance and free expression. That is at least one of the reasons why the world must take notice and call out antisemitism, wherever it arises. It is time for people of decency and goodwill everywhere to raise their voices against the expression of this odious and most persistent prejudice.

Works Cited

Alexander, Yonah. *Palestinian Religious Terrorism: Hamas and Islamic Jihad.* Leiden: Brill Nijhoff, 2003.

Applebaum, Barbara. *Being White, Being Good: White Complicity, White Moral Responsibility, and Social Justice Pedagogy.* Minneapolis: Lexington Books, 2010.

Baddiel, David. *Jews don't count.* London: TLS Books, 2021.

Bard, Mitchell. *The Arab Lobby: The Invisible Alliance That Undermines America's Interests in the Middle East.* Northampton: Broadside Books, 2011.

Benjamin, Daniel and Simon, Steven. *The Age of Sacred Terror.* New York: Random House, 2002.

Bey, Major Osman. *The Conquest of the World by the Jews: An Historical and Ethnical Essay.* European Freedom Foundation, 2019.

Bin Laden, Osama. *Messages to the World: The Statements of Osama Bin Laden,* New York: Verso Books, 2005.

Bostom, Andrew. *The Legacy of Islamic Antisemitism: From Sacred Texts to Solemn History.* Amherst, N.Y.: Prometheus, 2008.

Brent, Jonathan and Naumov, Vladimir. *Stalin's Last Crime: The Doctor's Plot.* London: John Murray, 2003.

Brown, Michael. *Christian Antisemitism: Confronting the Lies in Today's Church.* Florida: Charisma House, 2021.

Bruckner, Pascal. *The Tyranny of Guilt: An Essay on Western Masochism.* Princeton: Princeton University Press, 2012.

Brustein, William. *Roots of Hate: Antisemitism in Europe Before the Holocaust.* Cambridge: Cambridge University Press, 2003.

Butler, Judith. *Parting Ways: Jewishness and the Critique of Zionism.* New York: Columbia University Press, 2013.

Butz, Arthur. *Hoax of the Twentieth Century: The Case Against the Presumed Extermination of European Jewry.* Uckfield: Historical Review Press, 1975.

Bryan Cheyette. *Constructions of 'the Jew' in English Literature and Society: Racial Representations, 1875–1945.* Cambridge: Cambridge University Press, 1993.

Jeremy Cohen. *Christ Killers: The Jews and the Passion from the Bible to the Big Screen.* Oxford: Oxford University Press, 2007.

Norman Cohn. *Warrant for Genocide.* Middlesex: Pelican, 1970.

Dan Cohn-Sherbok. *Antisemitism.* Cheltenham: The History Press, 2011.

Curtis, Michael (ed.). *Antisemitism in the Contemporary World*. London: Routledge, 1986.

Darwish, Nonie. *Cruel and Usual Punishment*. Nashville: Thomas Nelson, 2008.

Darwish, Nonie. *Now They Call Me Infidel: Why I Renounced Jihad for America, Israel, and the War on Terror*. New York: Sentinel, 2006.

Dershowitz, Alan. *Why Terrorism works*. New Haven: Yale University Press, 2002.

Fatah, Tareq. *The Jew is not my enemy: Unveiling the Myths that Fuel Muslim Antisemitism*. Toronto: McClelland and Stewart, 2011.

Foxman, Abe. *The Deadliest Lies: The Israel Lobby and the Myth of Jewish Control*. New York: Palgrave Macmillan, 2009.

Garfinkle, Adam. *Jewcentricity: Why the Jews are Praised, Blamed, and Used to Explain Just About Everything*. New Jersey: John Wiley & Sons, 2009.

Gerstenfeld, Manfred. *Demonizing Israel and the Jews*. New York: RVP Press, 2013.

Gerstenfeld, Manfred. *The War of a Million Cuts: The Struggle Against the Delegitimization of Israel and the Jews, and the Growth of New Antisemitism*. New York: RVP Press, 2015.

Gold, Dore. *Hatred's Kingdom: How Saudi Arabia Supports the New Global Terrorism*. Washington: Regnery Publishing, 2004.

Goldhagen, Daniel. *The Devil that Never Dies*. New York: Little, Brown and Company, 2013.

Gordis, Daniel. *The Promise of Israel*. John Wiley & Sons, 2012.

Griech-Polelle, Beth. *Antisemitism and the Holocaust: Language, Rhetoric and the Traditions of Hatred*. London: Bloomsbury Academic, 2017.

Hanebrink, Paul. *A Specter Haunting Europe: The Myth of Judeo-Bolshevism*. Cambridge: Belknap Press, 2020.

Harrison, Paul. *The Resurgence of Antisemitism: Jews, Israel and Liberal Opinion*. Lanham: Rowman & Littlefield, 2006.

Hertzberg, Arthur, *The French Enlightenment and the Jews*. New York: Columbia University Press, 1968.

Hirsh, David. *Contemporary left antisemitism*. London: Routledge, 2018.

Hitler, Adolf. *Mein Kampf*, trans. Ralph Manheim. Boston, 1943.

Holmes, Colin. *Antisemitism in British Society, 1876-1939*. New York: Holmes & Meier, 1979.

Israeli, Raphael. *War, Peace and Terror in the Middle East*. London: Frank Cass, 2003.

Johnson, Alan. *The Apartheid Smear*, BICOM

Julius, Anthony. *Trials of the Diaspora*. Oxford: Oxford University Press, 2010.

Kahn-Harris, Keith. *Strange Hate: Antisemitism, Racism and the Limits of Diversity*. London: Repeater Books, 2019.

Katz, Jacob. *From Prejudice to Destruction: Antisemitism, 1700-1933*. Cambridge: Harvard University Press, 1980.

Khomeini, Ruhollah. *Islam and Revolution*. Tehran: Mizan Press, 1981.

Kotek, Joel. *Cartoons and Extremism*: *Israel and the Jews in Arab and Western Media*. London: Vallentine Mitchell, 2008.

Kuntzel, Matthias. *Jihad and Jew Hatred: Islamism, Nazism and the Roots of 9/11*. New York: Telos Press Publishing, 2007.

Lacquer, Walter. *The Changing Face of Antisemitism: From Ancient Times to the Present Day*. Oxford: Oxford University Press, 2006.

Lavin, Talia. *Culture Warlords: My Journey into the Dark Web of White Supremacy*. New York: Hachette Books, 2020.

Lewis, Bernard. *Semites and Anti-Semites*. London: Phoenix Giant, 1997.

Lewis, Bernard. *The Crisis of Islam: Holy War and Unholy Terror*. New York: Weidenfeld & Nicolson, 2003.

Lindsay, James and Pluckrose, Helen. *Cynical Theories: How Activist Scholarship Made Everything About Race, Gender, and Identity - and Why This Harms Everybody*. London: Swift Press, 2020.

Lipstadt, Deborah. *Antisemitism Here and Now*. London: Scribe, 2019.

Litvinoff, Barnet. *The Burning Bush* (London: Collins, 1988)

Livingstone, Ken. *You Can't Say That*. London: Faber and Faber, 2012.

Manji, Irshad. *The Trouble with Islam*. Edinburgh and London: Mainstream Publishing, 2004.

Marcus, Kenneth. *The definition of Antisemitism*. Oxford: Oxford University Press, 2015.

The Nation of Islam, *The Secret Relationship Between Blacks and Jews*. Chicago: The Final Call, 1991.

Negrin, Howard and Perry, Martin (eds.). *The Theory and Practice of Islamic Terrorism: An Anthology*. New York: Palgrave Macmillan, 2008.

Nelson, Carey. *Israel Denial: Anti-Zionism, Antisemitism, and the Faculty Campaign Against the Jewish State*. Indiana: Indiana University Press, 2019.

Netter, Ronald. *Past Trials and Present Tribulations: A Muslim Fundamentalist's View of the Jews*. Oxford: Pergamon Press, 1987.

Neuberger, Julia. *Antisemitism: What It Is. What It Isn't. Why It Matters*. London: Weidenfeld & Nicolson, 2019.

Patterson, David. *A Genealogy of Evil: Antisemitism from Nazism to Islamic Jihad*. New York: Cambridge University Press, 2011.

Perry, Marvin and Schweitzer, Frederick. *Antisemitism: Myth and Hate from Antiquity to The Present*. New York: Palgrave, 2002.

Poliakov, Leon. *The History of Antisemitism I: From the Time of Christ to the Court Jews*. Philadelphia: The University of Pennsylvania Press, 2003.

Poliakov, Leon. *The History of Antisemitism II: From Voltaire to Wagner*. Philadelphia: The University of Pennsylvania Press, 2003.

Poliakov, Leon. *The History of Antisemitism III: From Voltaire to Wagner*. Philadelphia: The University of Pennsylvania Press, 2003.

Pranaitis, Justinias. *The Secret Rabbinical Teaching Concerning Christians*. Facsimiled Publisher, Delhi.

Qutb, Sayyid. *In the shade of the Quran*, vol. 1. Leicester: The Islamic Foundation, 1999.

Rich, Dave. *The Left's Jewish Problem: Jeremy Corbyn, Israel and Antisemitism*. Hull: Biteback Press, 2016.

Roth, John and Rubinstein, Richard. *Approaches to Auschwitz*. Louisville: Westminster John Knox Press, 2003.

Rubin, Barry & Schwanitz, Wolfgang. *Nazis, Islamists, and the Making of the Modern Middle East*. New Haven: Yale University Press, 2014.

Ryvchin, Alex (ed.). *The Anti-Israel Agenda: Inside the Political War on the Jewish State*. Jerusalem: Gefen Publishing House, 2017.

Safieh, Afif. *The peace process: From Breakthrough to Breakdown*. London: Saqi Books, 2010.

Schoenfeld, Gabriel. *Return of Antisemitism*. San Francisco, Encounter Books, 2004.

Shepherd, Robin. *A State Beyond the Pale: Europe's Problem with Israel*. London: Weidenfeld & Nicolson, 2009.

Shindler, Colin. *What do Zionists believe*? London: Granta Books, 2007.

Tatum, Beverley. *Why Are All the Black Kids Sitting Together in the Cafeteria? and Other Conversations About Race*. Basic Books, 2003.

Trachtenberg, Joshua. *The Devil and the Jews: The Medieval Conception of the Jew and Its Relation to Modern Antisemitism*. Philadelphia: The Jewish Publication Society, 1995.

Weiss, Bari. *How to Fight Antisemitism*. London: Allen Lane, 2020.

Wisse, Ruth. *Jews and Power*. New York: Schocken Books, 2020.

Wistrich, Robert. *Hitler's apocalypse: Jews and the Nazi legacy*. London: Weidenfeld & Nicolson, 1985.

Wistrich, Robert. *Hitler and the Holocaust*. London: Weidenfeld & Nicolson, 2001.

Wistrich, Robert. *A Lethal Obsession: Antisemitism from Antiquity to the Global Jihad*. New York: Random House, 2010.

Scholarly Articles

Amir, Menachem. "Criminality among Jews: An Overview." *Issues in Criminology*, 6, no. 2, 1971: 1–39.

Ashley, W. J. "Booth's East London." *Political Science Quarterly* vol. 5, no. 3 (1890): 507–19. https://doi.org/10.2307/2139261.

Auerbach, Jerold S. "From Rags to Robes: The Legal Profession, Social Mobility and the American Jewish Experience." *American Jewish Historical Quarterly* 66, no. 2 (1976): 249–284.

Bachrach, Bernard. "Reassessment of Visigothic Jewish Policy, 589-711." *The American Historical Review* 78, no. 1 (1973): 11–34.

Bayefsky, Anne. "The UN World Conference against racism: a racist antiracism conference." *Proceedings of the Annual Meeting (American Society of International Law* 96, (2002): 65–74.

Bertman, Stephen. "The Antisemitic Origin of Michelangelo's Horned Moses." *Shofar* 27, no. 4 (2009): 95–106.

Brinks, J. "Political Anti-Fascism in the German Democratic Republic." *Journal of Contemporary History* 32, no. 2 (1997): 207-217.

Coope, Jessica A. "Religious and Cultural Conversion to Islam in Ninth-Century Umayyad Córdoba." *Journal of World History* 4, no. 1 (1993): 47–68.

Cooper, John. "Jews who helped make the health service." *The British journal of general practice: the journal of the Royal College of General Practitioners* 69, 678 (2019): 32-33.

Ehrman, Albert. "The Origins of the Ritual Murder accusation and blood libel," *Tradition: A Journal of Orthodox Jewish Thought* 15, no. 4 (1976): 83–90.

Flores-Borjabad, Salud Adelaida. "Political Cartoons in the Middle East: a New Form of Communication and Resistance." *US-China Foreign Language* 16, no 6 (June 2018): 320-329.

Friedman, Jerome. "Jewish Conversion, the Spanish Pure Blood Laws and Reformation: A Revisionist View of Racial and Religious Antisemitism." *The Sixteenth Century Journal* 18, no. 1 (1987): 3–30.

Halperin, Edward. "Why did the United States Medical School Admissions Quota for Jews end?" *The American Journal of the Medical Sciences* 358, no. 5 (2019): 317-325.

Hirshfield, Claire. "The Anglo-Boer War and the Issue of Jewish Culpability." *Journal of Contemporary History* 15, no. 4 (1980): 619–631.

Israeli, Raphael. "Poison: The Use of Blood Libel in the War Against Israel." *Jerusalem Centre for Public Affairs*, April 15, 2002.

Langmuir, Gavin I. "The Knight's Tale of Young Hugh of Lincoln." *Speculum* 47, no. 3 (1972): 459–82. https://doi.org/10.2307/2856155.

Muravchik, Joshua. "THE UN AND ISRAEL: A History of Discrimination." *World Affairs* 176, no. 4 (2013): 35–46.

Stacey, Robert C. "From Ritual Crucifixion to Host Desecration: Jews and the Body of Christ." *Jewish History* 12, no. 1 (1998): 11–28.

Straus, Raphael. "The 'Jewish Hat' as an Aspect of Social History." *Jewish Social Studies* 4, no. 1 (1942): 59–72.

Waldman, Lois. "Employment Discrimination against Jews in the United States - 1955." *Jewish Social Studies* 18, no. 3 (1956): 208–216.

Index

www.ingramcontent.com/pod-product-compliance
Lightning Source LLC
Chambersburg PA
CBHW060416100426

42812CB00037B/3488/J

*9 7 8 1 6 8 0 5 3 7 8 0 2 *